# THE RISE OF THE
# *NOUVEAUX RICHES*

# THE RISE OF THE
# *NOUVEAUX RICHES*

*Style and Status
in Victorian and Edwardian
Architecture*

## J. Mordaunt Crook

JOHN MURRAY
*Albemarle Street, London*

© J. Mordaunt Crook 1999

First published in 1999
Reprinted 1999

Reissued in paperback in 2000
by John Murray (Publishers) Ltd
50 Albemarle Street, London W1X 4BD

The moral right of the author has been asserted

A catalogue record for this book is available from the British Library

ISBN 0-7195-6040-3 (*hardback*)
ISBN 0-7195-6050-0 (*paperback*)

Typeset in 12½ on 14pt Garamond, by Wearset, Boldon, Tyne and Wear

Printed and bound in Great Britain by The University Press, Cambridge

# CONTENTS

# ILLUSTRATIONS

engineering contractor. Demolished 1967. RCHME (1948)

5. Hillingdon Court, Middlesex (1860s). Extended for Charles Mills, 1st Baron Hillingdon, banker. RCHME

6. Whitbourne Hall, Herefordshire (1860–2). Designed by Edmund Elmslie for Edward Bickerton Evans, vinegar manufacturer. J. Gibson *Country Life* (1975)

7. Belleview, Halifax (1856–7): Remodelled by G.H. Stokes for Frank Crossley, carpet manufacturer and future baronet. A. Starkey *Country Life* (1970)

8 and 9. Fonthill Pavilion, Wiltshire (1776–84; 1839–44; 1846–8). The surviving wing of Alderman Beckford's Fonthill Splendens, refurbished by J.B. Papworth and enlarged by David Brandon for James Morrison, a millionaire haberdasher. RCHME (1885)

10. Gatton Park, Surrey, portico (1888; 1891). Designed by Sextus Dyball for Jeremiah Colman, the mustard magnate. RCHME

11. Theobolds Park, Hertfordshire, Temple Bar (1670–2). Transported from the Strand, London in 1888, to dignify the estate of Sir Henry Meux, 3rd Bt, heir to a brewing fortune. RCHME

12. Cowley Manor, Gloucestershire (1855; 1890). Extended by R.A. ('Bungalow') Briggs for Sir James Horlick, 1st Bt, malted-milk magnate. *Country Life* (1906)

13. Bearwood, Berkshire (1865–70). Built to designs by Robert Kerr for John Walter, proprietor of *The Times*. A. Starkey *Country Life* (1968)

14 and 15. Basildon Park, Berkshire, lodges and entrance front (1776; 1839–44). A house by Carr of York bought by James Morrison and enlarged by J.B. Papworth. RCHME (1965)

16 and 17. Basildon Park, Berkshire, octagon room and drawing room (1839–44). Refurbished for James Morrison, to designs by J.B. Papworth. RCHME (1964)

18. Cragside, Northumberland (1869–85). Designed by Richard Norman Shaw for Lord Armstrong, the millionaire armaments manufacturer. J. Gibson *Country Life* (1969)

19. Kinmel, Denbighshire (1870–4). Remodelled by W.E. Nesfield for Hugh Hughes, a Welsh copper magnate. *Country Life* (1969)

20. Ellel Grange, Lancashire (1856–60). Built by William Preston, a Liverpool wines and spirits importer. *Country Life* (1979)

21. Underley Hall, Westmorland (1825; 1870s). A Regency house much extended for the Earl of Bective, who married the heiress daughter of William Thompson, ironmaster and shipowner. RCHME

22. Brantwood, Lancashire (*c.* 1835; 1872; 1878 etc.). Extended for John Ruskin, son of a London sherry merchant. Mark Fiennes *Country Life* (1984)

23. Broadleys, nr Cartmel Fell, Lancashire (1898–9). A villa on Lake Windermere, designed by C.F.A. Voysey for a coal-owner, Arthur Currer Briggs. RCHME (1985)

24. Jardine Hall, Dumfriesshire (1814; 1892–7). A Regency mansion, altered and enlarged for the Jardine family, China traders, by E.J. May. Demolished 1964. RCHMS (1964)

LONDON HOUSES

*(pages 188–212)*

81. Dorchester House, Park Lane, the great hall (1846–63). Built to designs by Lewis Vulliamy for R.S. Holford, who inherited a fortune derived from law and bullion speculation. Demolished 1929. *Country Life* (1928)

82. 12 Kensington Palace Gardens (1846; 1866). Designed by R.R. Banks for Samuel Morton Peto, contractor; extended for Alexander Collier, a City financier. J. Gibson *Country Life* (1971)

83. The Hill, Hampstead (1895; 1904–25). Terraces and pergolas designed by T.H. Mawson for William Lever, 1st Viscount Leverhulme, the millionaire soap magnate. *Country Life* (1918)

84. 46 Grosvenor Street (1910–11). A Franco-Florentine palazzo designed by Detmar Blow and Fernand Billerey for Sir Edgar Speyer, banker. RCHME

85. Grosvenor Square, north side: These eighteenth-century houses were increasingly occupied by New Money from the 1880s onwards. RCHME (1927)

86. 34 Grosvenor Square, drawing room (1890). 'A gilded pantechnicon': the Mayfair home of Barney Barnato's nephew, Jack Barnato Joel. RCHME (1890)

87 and 88. 45 Grosvenor Square, dining room (1897). Refurbished by Charles Mellier & Co of Paris and London, for Sir James Miller, 2nd Bt, heir to a Scottish trading fortune. RCHME (1897)

89 and 90. Chesterfield House, South Audley Street, drawing room and music room (1890s). Rococo interiors of the 1740s by Isaac Ware, refurbished for Michael Bass, 1st Baron Burton, the millionaire brewer. RCHME (1894)

91 and 92. 17 Grosvenor Place, staircase hall and ballroom (c. 1890). Refurbished by Joel Joseph Duveen for Sir Arthur Wilson, a shipowner from Hull and friend of the Prince of Wales. RCHME (1890)

93. 12 Hyde Park Gardens, bedroom (c. 1907). Furnished for Anton Dunkels (né Dunkelsbuhler), a Jewish diamond dealer from South Africa. RCHME (1907)

94. 5 Hamilton Place, bathroom (c. 1880). Fitted up by W.R. Rogers (né Rodriguez) for Leopold de Rothschild, banker. RCHME (1889)

95. 27 Berkeley Square, drawing room (c. 1900). Decorated for Sir Robert Mond, of the chemical and metallurgical dynasty. RCHME (1906)

96. Bath House, 82 Piccadilly, drawing room (1821; 1900). Rebuilt for Lord Ashburton; refurbished for Baron de Hirsch; remodelled for Sir Julius Wernher. Demolished 1960. RCHME (1911)

97. 139 Piccadilly, study (1891). Designed by R.S. Wornum for Algernon Borthwick, 1st Baron Glenesk, proprietor of the *Morning Post* and *Daily Telegraph*. RCHME

98. 145 Piccadilly, drawing room. London home of Hamar Bass, of the Burton brewing dynasty. RCHME (1927)

99. 11 Hill Street, library (c. 1903). Designed by J. Leonard Williams for George Coats, 1st Baron Glentanar, heir to a Paisley cotton fortune. RCHME (1903)

# INTRODUCTION

'Nineteenth Century History is like a kipper with all the guts
cleaned out . . . we get all the Gladstones and Lincolns and
Ramsay MacDonalds and such, and nothing about the gold
rushes and the booms and slumps and Krupps and Zaharoffs
and suchlike realities.'

H.G. Wells, 1932

In 1845 Benjamin Disraeli looked out in imagination over the landscape of England and saw what he wanted to see: the English country
house. All those mansions of nobility and gentry, each with its atten-
dant village and parish church, struck him chiefly as products of accumulated capital; but capital tamed, capital civilised by the continuities
of history.

In a commercial country like England, every half century develops some
new vast source of public wealth, which brings into national notice a new
and powerful class. A couple of centuries ago, a Turkey merchant was the
great creator of wealth; the West India Planter followed him. In the
middle of the last century appeared the Nabob. These characters in their
zenith in turn merged into the land, and became English aristocrats; while,
the Levant decaying, the West Indies exhausted, and Hindoostan plun-
dered, the breeds died away, and now exist only in our English comedies
. . . The expenditure of the revolutionary war [against France] produced
the Loanmonger, who succeeded the Nabob; and the application of
science to industry developed the Manufacturer, who in turn aspires to be
'large acred', and always will, as long as we have a territorial constitution; a

I

better security for the preponderance of the landed interest than any corn-law, fixed or fluctuating.[1]

During Disraeli's lifetime, thanks partly to his own instinct for franchise reform, that territorial constitution – basically a land-owning electorate – began to be translated, tentatively and imperfectly, into a wider property-owning democracy. The earlier stages of that process – the transition from gentry to bourgeoisie; from aristocracy to plutocracy – form the background to the subject of this book.

Architectural history is a fairly new discipline; the social history of architecture is newer still. Here an attempt has been made to combine both approaches: to explain the houses of the Victorian and Edwardian *nouveaux riches* in a context of accelerating social change. Without the publications of a shoal of economic historians – notably Professor J.V. Beckett, Professor David Cannadine, Professor S.D. Chapman, Professor Martin Daunton, Sir John Habakkuk, Dr David Kynaston, Professor W.D. Rubinstein, Professor Lawrence Stone and Professor F.M.L. Thompson – this book could never have been written. Together – or rather, between them, for they often disagree – they have opened up an extraordinarily fruitful field of study: the emergence in nineteenth- and twentieth-century Britain of a new aristocracy of money, in effect the democratization of wealth.

This evolving aristocracy of riches was based on a fusion of old and new money; its appearance marked the birth of the modern upper class. In 1895 one master at Rugby School could be heard asking another about the social origins of their new headmaster, the Revd H.A. James: 'Tell me, is James a gentleman? Understand me, I don't mean, Does he speak the Queen's English? But – had he a grandfather?'[2] By that date such a static, hierarchical view – 'it takes three generations to make a gentleman' – was already at odds with the facts of British society. As the traditional criteria of class – heredity, land, title – became less binding, so a new social order based frankly on money began to emerge. By 1843 *Punch* had already spotted the way in which money was first corroding, then dissolving, the chains of hierarchy. The Spangle Lacquers, a *nouveau-riche* family, are caricatured as socially rootless: they had made their money from 'soap, gin, tallow, rags, or something equally interesting, by a process of alchemy which leaves all the old philosophers far behind'; and their friends were of the same ilk: 'you can assign [them] no fixed position in society [since they are generally met with] in places where distinction was acquired by paying for it'.³ Clearly purchase was already beginning to be confused with acceptance. And by the mid Victorian period it seemed possible to buy gentility more easily than ever before. Even so, full acceptance was slow. Trollope's Mr Longestaff spoke for the old order.

> He was immensely proud of his position in life, thinking himself to be immensely superior to all those who earned their bread. There were, no doubt, gentlemen of different degrees, but the English gentleman of gentlemen was he who had land, and family title-deeds and an old family place, and family portraits, ... and family absence of any usual employment.⁴

Not until the 1880s did new money make dramatic inroads into this traditional county ethos. After that the process of change accelerated. By the end of the First World War, in London and the shires, the ascendancy of money was indisputable. A new type of élite had been established. This book will focus on that emerging élite, exploring its social geography, dissecting its architectural patronage. It will also explain the operation of a slow-motion conjuring trick: the reinvention of the British aristocracy as a self-renewing plutocracy.

The subject of wealth is unarguably intriguing. As long ago as 1872, when *The Spectator* published a list of recent millionaires it noted that the article aroused intense interest. 'People who rarely read anything else spelled over that long, closely-packed column of names and figures ... with a sort of smacking of the intellectual lips.'⁵ Perhaps also, we might think, with one or two qualms of conscience. In 1905 Sir Leo Chiozza Money – quite a name for an Edwardian analyst of wealth – put it like this:

> More than one third of the entire income of the United Kingdom is enjoyed by one thirtieth of its people ... In an average year eight millionaires die leaving between them three times as much wealth as is left by 644,000 poor persons who die in one year ... the wealth left by a few rich

people who die approaches in amount the aggregate property possessed by the whole of the living poor.[6]

Yes, there is a problem about money, and a magnetism too. And when it is linked to architecture the topic becomes irresistible. What I have tried to do here is to humanise some of the statistics; to make a serious subject palatable to both scholars and non-specialists. I began by identifying the houses of the richest *nouveaux riches,* then set out to unravel the social context in which they were created. Like the poor, the *nouveaux riches* are always with us; but there is more than enough evidence to suggest that the Victorian and Edwardian period was the age, *par excellence,* of the *arriviste.* And yet historically speaking, as individuals, the rich often remain invisible. More than thirty years ago, Lawrence Stone complained: 'the map of English social history is full of huge blank spaces, more often than not labelled "here be the rich".'[7] Well, who were they? Where did their money come from? What did they do with it? Above all, where and how did they live? This book supplies a number of answers, at least as regards one particular breed, the newly rich.

So much of British architectural history has been written through the eyes of aristocracy and gentry. This book concentrates on the parvenu. Even so, its focus is necessarily indistinct. All old money was new money once. The traditional time-span of assimilation may well have been three generations; but such nostrums will always be imprecise. This is not a book for statisticians. Its method is impressionistic rather than statistical, and for one very good reason: the statistics will always be incomplete. Even when all probate records have been definitively scanned, we will only know how much money was saved, not how much money was spent or given away. Still, the evidence available at present is considerable. In this book it is given an architectural perspective. And that perspective illuminates a major social revolution: the re-making of the British ruling class.

So much of nineteenth- and early twentieth-century architectural history has also been written from the point of view of the avant-garde. The path of stylistic progression, from Pugin, through Morris, to the Arts and Crafts and Modern Movements, is only too well worn.

4

This book reverses that progressive teleology by concentrating on mainstream styles: Neo-Classical, Italianate and Beaux Arts. For these – except in Scotland – turn out to be the chosen styles of the richest *nouveaux riches*. Such symbols are perennially intriguing: as class distinctions grow hazier, their trappings re-emerge as style.

No attempt is made here to deal with the *nouveaux riches* as collectors. That would require quite a different approach. 'Our millionaires', noted *The Spectator* in 1872, 'are maniacs for collecting things.'[8] Often enough it was through the medium of collecting that the *arriviste* revealed his cultural identity. New money – though not necessarily millionaire money – tended to buy contemporary paintings; old money inherited houses stocked with old masters.[9] But patterns of collecting made little stylistic difference to the architecture of houses. That is why this book is about the house as a social phenomenon, not the house as a receptacle of art. It is also concerned as much with the perception of architecture as with architecture itself: hence the frequency of quotation from contemporary memoirs and novels.

Each chapter shakes the kaleidoscope in a slightly different way. The first traces the assimilation of new money into the ruling Establishment; the second examines the style of millionaires in building and rebuilding country houses; the third chapter narrows the focus a little and surveys the proliferation of villas for the very rich in one particular area: the Lake District; the fourth deals with that quintessential parvenu: the Edwardian metropolitan plutocrat; and the fifth chapter spotlights key groups of the newly rich in a sequence of vignettes or snapshots. All five chapters – essays in the social history of architecture – contribute to a composite theme: the taste and style – what Henry James called the 'Gilded Bondage' – of the Victorian and Edwardian *nouveau riche*. The story is not without humour, and not without warning: hence the number of anecdotes. The illustrations have been chosen to illuminate a way of living which already seems curiously remote: hence the number of antique photographs by Bedford Lemere and *Country Life*. The canvas is crowded, and necessarily so: I have tried to individualise a whole class through the medium of its domestic architecture. No doubt there are many errors, despite the sharp eyes of several friends. But the attempt to hammer a theme out of a heap of fragments was surely an attempt worth making. If the result is Social history rather than social history, so be it. In H.A.L. Fisher's phrase, the wheels of history are seldom moved by the poor. This is not just a book about the rich; it is a book about the very rich.

# I
# CROSSING THE LINE
## *The Titled and Untitled Aristocracy*

'As we were going out [of Buscot Park, Berkshire], a scholarly
man, whom I'd seen carefully studying the catalogue, pauses
by the desk.
  "Could you tell me", he asks of the lady on duty, "how the
first Lord Faringdon made his money?"
  She gives him a vinegary look as if the question was in very
bad taste: "I've no idea."'

Alan Bennett, 1996

Lord Faringdon was a *nouveau riche*, very much so; in fact he was a
millionaire. But what is a millionaire? A man – they tend to be men –
who leaves a million, or a man who spends a million? A man who lives
like a millionaire, or a man who dies like one? And anyway, which
million? Inflationary pressures and currency revolutions have made
the term a pretty nebulous label. To arrive at even a rough approxima-
tion of modern value we must multiply early Victorian fortunes by
forty, and Edwardian bank balances by nearly fifty. Nobody in
eighteenth-century England would have been called a millionaire. The
very word did not exist before the early nineteenth century. French in
origin, it was soon most commonly applied to the new rich of industrial England and America. Similarly *nouveau riche*: the label
seems to have been imported from France during the Napoleonic
period; by 1813 it was being used by Maria Edgeworth to describe the
commercial magnates of Liverpool and Manchester.[1] Of course not
every *nouveau riche* was a millionaire; but almost every millionaire was
newly rich. In any case, such definitions are less important than the
image of sudden riches in popular perception. By 1826 the young

Disraeli certainly knew a millionaire – and a millionaire's wife – when he saw one.

> Mrs Million entered . . . All fell back. Gartered peers and starred ambassadors, and baronets with blood older than the creation, and squires, to the antiquity of whose veins chaos was a novelty, all retreated . . . Even Sir Plantagenet Pure, whose family had refused a peerage regularly every century . . . 'Ah! there is nothing like old families!' remarked Mrs Million, with all the awkward feelings of a parvenue.[2]

Mrs Million, of course, was a *nouvelle riche*.

This tension between the old world and the new – and ultimately the resolution of that tension through the fusion of capital and land – has led at least one recent historian to christen the mid nineteenth century 'the Age of Equipoise'.[3] In the early nineteenth century land was still king. 'An observer entering a room full of Britain's top 200 wealthiest men in 1825', notes Professor Rubinstein, 'might be forgiven for thinking that the Industrial Revolution had not occurred.'[4] Thereafter the balance begins to shift. Between 1850 and 1880 the British economy was at its most dynamic, with a doubling of GNP, a 25 per cent increase in population, rising wages, low inflation, low taxation, booming markets domestic and foreign, an improving infrastructure of transportation and services, and a largely unregulated market with burgeoning financial networks abroad and undeveloped trade unions at home. Between 1809 and 1858 only twelve men died worth more than one million pounds in cash, shares and bonds; most big fortunes were still based on land. After mid century, however, that situation began to change. Looking back in 1920, W.H. Mallock reckoned that at the time of the Battle of Waterloo fewer than five hundred people – outside the landed class – had incomes of more than £5,000 a year; sixty years later there were eight times as many.[5] The boom years of the 1850s and 1860s – and the declining fortunes of land in the last quarter of the century – tilted the balance decisively towards commerce and industry. Between 1895 and 1914 no fewer than thirty men left over two million pounds. Of these no more than three came from landed families. And lower down, among the half- and quarter-million pound fortune holders – all multi-millionaires in the money of today – the balance of power was equally clear. As landed capital dwindled, trading capital multiplied. And as the phasing of capitalism in Britain shifted from primary to secondary – from industrial production to financial services – so the speed of capital accumulation accelerated, and with it the changing focus of social prestige.

In the mid and late Victorian period the absorption of trade by land and land by trade – what sociologists call the homogenising of a new élite – has led some historians to pose an unquantifiable question: was this the *embourgeoisement* of the aristocracy or the feudalising of the bourgeoisie? Just who was hegemonising whom?[6] Karl Marx himself admitted to some confusion: 'The ultimate aim of this most bourgeois of lands would seem to be the establishment of a bourgeois aristocracy and a bourgeois proletariat, side by side with the bourgeoisie.'[7] At least one contemporary explained the situation in terms of continuous mobility. In 1860 the first edition of a new 'Dictionary of the Upper Ten Thousand' – Edward Walford's *County Families: Titled and Untitled Aristocracy* – noted a 'constant addition of fresh families' swelling the roll-call of county gentry. 'Mainly owing to the influence of trade and commerce', Walford observed, 'individuals and families are continually crossing and re-crossing the narrow line which severs the aristocracy from the commonalty.'[8] By 1879, 73 of the 250 Cheshire families in his list had made their money in manufacturing or trade; by 1900, so had nearly half the families listed in south Staffordshire.[9] And in Lancashire the process was similar: by the mid 1870s nearly half the 118 owners of estates of more than 3,000 acres had bought their way into the landowning élite during the previous hundred years.[10] These newcomers were in turn absorbed into the rituals of county society and local government.[11] At the same time, more and more landed families were being drawn into commerce. So who was hegemonising whom? The answer must be that the process was reciprocal.

Crossing the line and assuming at least the trappings of gentility was most certainly achievable within a single lifetime. Carl Meyer, a Jewish banker and diamond magnate, was born in Hamburg in 1851 and prospered in South Africa; he died in 1922 a multi-millionaire in money of today, a Tory baronet with a penchant for shooting, owner of a London mansion off Berkeley Square and a country house in Essex. His son, the second baronet, was christened at St George's, Hanover Square and went to Eton and New College, Oxford before becoming a Conservative MP. In August 1909 Charles Addis, a London banker with business in Hong Kong, visited the future Sir Carl at Shortgrove, his seventeenth-century seat:

> A motor was waiting at Audley End station and drove me through the beautiful wrought iron gates of Shortgrove, across the quaint old bridge with three spans under which the Cam glides deeply below, with a vignette on one side of a curious classic temple on the bank and on the other a covey of wild duck. The drive winds up hill, through the finest timber I have ever seen anywhere, to Shortgrove itself, an old Queen Anne mansion four storeys high and 13 windows wide. Two centre halls with galleries on which the bedrooms open. In the dining room a superb portrait of Mrs Meyer by Sargent [see front cover] ... Everywhere, curious furniture, old pictures, superb carpets and tapestries. Fine library but not up to the rest of the house in my idea. For many of the fine books I noticed were uncut and oh! horreur, in one corner stood a pianola ...
>
> We walked through the house and emerged on the glorious lawn backed by the most astonishing variety of trees, among them an old oak said to be 1000 years old. The space is wonderful. Two cricket pitches, a private golf course, croquet lawn, several tennis nets and a swimming bath, not to mention the rifle range.
>
> We watched for a while the cricket match that was going on between the local cricketers and a London eleven.
>
> Tea was served in a Japanese house on the lawn ... Mrs M. took me through such lovely old gardens ... Against the south wall was about 100 yards of tall sweet peas of wonderful variety looking like so many butter-flies ...
>
> We went over the stables next, old and extensive like the house, saw the model cottages and the home farm and the pedigree herd of Jersey cows, and so to dress for dinner ... Excellent dinner, lobster, grouse etc ... Coffee and cigars on verandah in open air.
>
> Bedroom very fine with Empire furniture. Old prints and oil paintings. Superb views across the Cam. And there I lay, amidst all that luxury could do to lull me pleasantly to sleep, and counted the hours as they tolled from the stable tower until as dawn broke I fell into a short and troubled sleep.[12]

As he tossed and turned, did Mr Addis think perhaps of the contrast between the diamond mines of Kimberley and the pastoral paradise in which he lay? Which was reality and which the dream? Any such partnership between old and new can never have been easy. Still, these marriages of convenience between the ethics of the boardroom and the ethos of the hunting field turned out to be full of creative tension. As new money fructified in the pockets of the gentry, so the mores of landed society did battle with the shibboleths of trade. Maybe there was a 'social distancing of land from money' in the early Victorian era. *Punch* certainly thought so:

> A sister of Mrs [Spangle] Lacquer's married a gentleman of property, and resides in the country. Her name is Mrs Champignon Stiffback ... In company with their London relatives [they] ... partake largely of the nature of mushrooms, in as much as they have not only sprung up with great rapidity ..., but have also risen from a mould of questionable delicacy ... [Indeed] their position is ... uncomfortably poised between the real county aristocracy and the petty agricultural gentilities, belonging to neither, and occasionally looked shy at by both. [As a result] they are in perpetual fear of losing *caste*.[13]

In the end, however, new money talked. When H.G. Wells's fictional uncle, Edward Ponderevo, exchanged his chemist's shop for the lordship of Lady Grove, he found the local vicar a useful bridge into county society.

> The vicar ... was an Oxford man ... with ... a general air of accommodation to the new order of things. These Oxford men are the Greeks of our plutocratic empire. He was a Tory in spirit, and what one may call an adapted Tory by stress of circumstances, that is to say he was no longer a legitimist, he was prepared for the substitution of new lords for old. We were pill vendors, he knew, and no doubt horribly vulgar in soul; but then it might have been some polygamous Indian rajah ... or some Jew with an inherited expression of contempt. Anyhow, we were English and neither Dissenters nor Socialists, and he was cheerfully prepared to do what he could to make gentlemen of ... us ... So he ... gossiped informingly about our neighbours on the countryside, Tux the banker, Lord Boom the magazine and newspaper proprietor, Lord Carnaby, that great sportsman, and old Lady Osprey.[14]

Meanwhile the traditional landed gentry were themselves becoming increasingly drawn into the world of commerce and finance. As Marx had prophesied, they were turning into 'a bourgeois aristocracy'. By 1896 there were 167 peers with company directorships: a quarter of the entire nobility. When Foreman, the Socialist spokesman in W.H. Mallock's *The Old Order Changes* (1886), attacks the falsity of the gentry's position, he has plenty of evidence to hand:

> You, the gentlemen of the country, the old landed families, ... you no longer stand on your own proper foundations. You are reduced financially to mere hangers-on of the *bourgeoisie*. Your material splendour, which once had a real meaning, is still, no doubt, maintained. But how? ... The yellow stucco of ninety years ago has given place to the towers of a Gothic castle ... [but only because] his Grace ... has five million dollars' worth of railway stock in America ... You could no longer live like seigneurs if you were not half tradesmen.[15]

By the late Victorian period the results of mutual assimilation were clear for all to see: in Mayfair as much as in the City, at Newmarket or Cowes, in Brighton, in Melton Mowbray, in the Highlands, new money was calling the shots, even if the language used was the patois of the shires. By 1880, noted William Morris, London had become 'the richest city, of the richest country, of the richest age of the world'.[16] And in that metropolis of wealth, the shift from aristocracy to plutocracy was most famously manifest. 'Nowadays', observed the Countess of Cardigan in 1911, 'money shouts and birth and breeding whisper!'[17]

The process of assimilation – a marriage of land and capital, gentry and *haute bourgeoisie* – is certainly visible, for example, in the saga of the Fielden dynasty. Joshua Fielden, founder of the Todmorden cotton spinning empire, died a Tory Quaker in 1811. His five sons – most famously John Fielden, MP, author of the Factory Act – became, or at least began as, Radical Unitarians. Two left personal fortunes approaching a quarter of a million; another, Thomas, and a grandson, 'Black Sam' Fielden, died in 1869 and 1889 worth £1,300,000 and £1,170,000 respectively. But this first generation of millionaires stayed close to their roots, living initially cheek by jowl with their work-force.

Mr Thornton lived close to the mill ... The lodge-door was like a common garden-door; on one side of it were great closed gates for the ingress and egress of lorries and wagons. The lodge-keeper admitted them into a great oblong yard, on one side of which were offices for the transaction of business; on the opposite, an immense many-windowed mill, whence proceeded the continual clank of machinery, and the long groaning roar of the steam-engine, enough to deafen those who lived within the enclosure. Opposite to the wall, along which the street ran, on one of the narrow sides of the oblong, was a handsome stone-coped house – blackened, to be sure, by the smoke, but with paint, windows and steps kept scrupulously clean ... Margaret only wondered why people who could afford to live in so good a house ... did not prefer the country.[18]

Within a generation, Mrs Gaskell's heroine was proved right. After John Fielden's death in 1849 the Fielden family as a whole began to take on the protective clothing of the gentry. They started to invest heavily in land: first Greenbank at Caton Green, described by Thomas Fielden as 'the prettiest place in Lancashire'; then Crowborough Warren, Sussex, a Georgian seat near Ashdown Forest, which cost the family £22,000 in 1849; then Beachamwell Hall, near Swaffham, Norfolk, a 4,000-acre Breckland estate which cost £35,000 in 1851.[19] In 1872 Grimston Park, Tadcaster[20] – a mansion by Decimus Burton, with 2,875 acres in the Vale of York – was bought from Lord Londesborough for the exorbitant sum of £265,000 (the Fieldens outbidding the Fosters of Black Dyke Mill, Bradford). In the 1880s Stockeld Park, near Wetherby, a striking Neo-Classical house by James Paine, was rented for the shooting. And then came the purchase and rebuilding of Nutfield Priory, Redhill, Surrey, a Tudor Gothic seat designed by John Gibson in 1870–74 – Pevsner calls it 'an elephantine pile' – decorated with stained glass illustrating the triumphs of the Fielden dynasty.[21]

When a family memorialises itself in stained glass – another spinning dynasty, the Bazleys of Lancashire, did the same thing at Hatherop Park, Gloucestershire – its glory days are over. The third generation of Fieldens – mostly Anglican and Conservative by now – set themselves up as country gentry, becoming *rentiers* and financiers, gradually severing their links with the industrial source of their wealth. One of John Fielden's granddaughters triumphantly married the son of an earl, and at St George's, Hanover Square too. Their son in turn succeeded as the 9th Earl Fitzwilliam of Wentworth Wood-house. By the fourth generation the industrial links had become all but invisible. Todmorden, J.A. Fielden complained in the 1880s, is 'damp, dirty and dull; it has no society; it is a humdrum place which deadens the spirits.' He much preferred Cambridge, and in 1890 pur-chased Lawrence Court, Huntingdon, not far away. In 1902 he bought Holmewood near Peterborough, a solid red brick Tudoresque house of 1874, and retired there for the rest of his life. Meanwhile, in 1896 Condover Hall with 4,000 acres – 'the grandest Elizabethan house in Shropshire' – had been bought from the Cholmondeleys by Edward Fielden for £120,000: old money selling out to new. And in 1912 Joshua Fielden acquired Kineton House, Warwickshire, which was conveniently situated for the kennels of the Warwickshire Hunt.[22] Almost forgotten in Todmorden, the Fieldens had become a family of *rentiers* devoted to field sports and country living.

Assimilation upwards was not always easy. In fact, it was fraught with social hazard. When John Stewart Parnell went up to Magdalene College, Cambridge in 1865 he found that 'the sons of moneyed par-venus from the North of England tried to liken themselves to country gentlemen and succeeded in looking like stable boys.'[23] Among the undergraduates at that very same college was young Joshua Fielden – the future squire of Kineton – who arrived at Magdalene, fresh from Eton (the first of his family to go there), in 1867. In the mid Victorian period the Fieldens had been numbered among the entrepreneurial giants of the north. Their rewards had been huge. In 1872, for example, 'the king of Todmorden' – genial John Fielden II of Dobroyd Castle – had an income of £20,000. The girls who worked his machines – and from among whom he chose his wife – earned two shillings per day.[24] By 1890 the family as a whole had accumulated something in the region of £4 million: equivalent perhaps to £200 million today. Tod-morden had acquired a Classical town hall, a Gothic castle and a Gothic Unitarian Church, all designed by John Gibson and all paid for by the Fielden family.[25] But by that date the cotton industry was in decline. The Fieldens had become part of England's ruling élite, rural or metropolitan but above all post-industrial.

The Crawshays of Cyfarthfa were less easily absorbed. From their blast furnaces at Merthyr Tydfil came the cannon balls which defeated Napoleon, the girders which upheld the railway boom. Through four generations they remained cantankerous and tyrannical, largely resisting the blandishments of gentrification. The first two generations, operating both ends of the business – production and distribution – oscillated between a villa at Stoke Newington and Cyfarthfa House, a small property near the ironworks. It was the third Iron King, William Crawshay II, who built Cyfarthfa Castle to designs by Robert Lugar in 1824–25 – spending £30,000 in the teeth of his father's opposition – and purchased a country estate for the first time, in 1848, at Caversham Park, Berkshire. For a while he even owned a third seat, Hensol Castle, Glamorgan.[26] One of his brothers reinforced this change of image by acquiring three estates in succession: Rowfant, Sussex; Honingham Hall, Norfolk; and Ottershaw Park, Surrey. Even so, iron remained their business; none of this third generation could be said to have joined the gentry – still less the aristocracy – either by marriage or by education. The first Iron King, Richard Crawshay – perhaps the first new-money millionaire – refused a peerage from the Tories. The third Iron King – who left over £2,000,000 – refused a peerage from the Liberals. 'The possession of [Cyfarthfa]', he wrote, 'is the height of my ambition.' From its battlements he could look over a sea of smoke and flame redolent of industrial apocalypse. Here was capitalism at its wildest. When Nelson visited the ironworks in 1802 Richard Crawshay cried out above the din: 'Here's Nelson, boys; shout, you beggars!'[27]

By 1830 the Crawshays employed 5,000 on an annual payroll of £300,000. Then came the Merthyr riots, followed by cycles of boom and recession. For the fourth generation the lure of a country estate – Bradbourne Hall, Kent; Oaklands Park, Gloucestershire – became more attractive.[28] When the fourth Iron King, Robert Crawshay, died in 1879 – worth over a million but tortured by illness and by years of struggle with trade unions – he had clearly lost faith in industry. He directed that three words be carved upon his tombstone: 'God Forgive Me'. His wife had long felt the impossibility of their position. 'The time is fast passing', she wrote, 'when one sort of people could say to another . . . "You shall do all the work, and we shall do all the play".'[29]

That did less than justice to the ruthless energies of a family which – literally and metaphorically – had forged the industrial economy of England. Their profits were indeed huge: six personal fortunes of over half a million between 1810 and 1915. But only in the fifth generation did the Crawshays retire from the front line of the industrial revolution. By then iron had given way to steel, and the family's entrepreneurial energies had dwindled. Of the fourth Iron King's sons, *rentiers* all, one retreated to a house in Rome; another is remembered only as one of the twelve best pheasant shots in Edwardian Britain.

Such gradual assimilation – the slow magic of gentrification – could be paralleled in the progress of many parvenu dynasties: the Brasseys (railways), the Rothschilds (banking), the Peels (cotton), the Morrisons (haberdashery), the Goldsmids (finance), the Loders (foreign trade). Sometimes the process was not even slow: the Fosters of Bradford, for example.[30] John Foster I was the founder of Black Dyke Mill, famous for worsted, alpaca and mohair – to say nothing of its celebrated brass band. By the time of his death in 1879, worth a quarter of a million and still talking broad Yorkshire, all four of his sons were owners of major estates: Hornby Castle, Lancashire (£205,000); Egton Manor, Yorkshire (£155,000); Canwell Hall, Staffordshire (£191,000); and Moor Park, Shropshire (£128,000). His eldest son, William Foster I of Hornby Castle, married three daughters into the gentry and two sons into the peerage; he left over a million and a quarter in 1884. By that date the third generation of Fosters had already crossed the line; they were undoubtedly gentry – in Lancashire, Yorkshire, Shropshire, Herefordshire, Leicestershire and Oxfordshire. One of John Foster's granddaughters married the 15th Baron of Inchiquin, another married the 3rd Marquess of Normanby. Five of his grandsons were Etonians. The road to gentility – from Bradford to Boodle's – had taken less than a quarter of a century. And the Fosters were by no means unusual. It has been estimated that 90 per cent of millionaires – and 50 per cent of half-millionaires – dying before 1880 bought land, and 80 per cent succeeded in founding county families.[31]

> Mr Temple had the most profound respect for property ... Even personal
> property was not without its charm; but a large landed estate, and a large

landed estate in the county of York, and that large landed estate flanked by a good round sum of Three per Cent Consols duly recorded in the Rotunda of Threadneedle Street, it was a combination of wealth, power, consideration, and convenience which exactly hit the ideal . . .[32]

Land, as Disraeli knew well, was a key ingredient in the formation of the *nouveau-riche* identity. But there was at least one other factor as well.

Of the three props which supported the ruling élite – money, land and title – it was the third of these, the possession of an hereditary peerage or baronetage, which was the clearest determinant of class and thus the most obvious focus of ambition.[33] Apart from bankers – Smith (1797), Baring (1835), Bateman (1837), Loyd (1850) – the English peerage remained closed to trade and commerce until the arrival of one exceptional cotton-spinner, Edward Strutt, 1st Baron Belper, in 1856. The grandson of Arkwright's partner, Jedediah Strutt, Belper lived long enough to become a landed proprietor in his own right; his son married a daughter of the 2nd Earl of Leicester; his great-granddaughter married the 16th Duke of Norfolk. Even so, in the mid Victorian period, apart from a further cohort of banking families – Baring (1866 and 1885), Glynn (1869), Marjoribanks (1881), Rothschild (1885), Mills and Denison (1886) – the House of Lords remained a difficult hurdle for new money. Not until the 1880s did both Liberal and Tory governments surrender their patronage to the market. Hardy (iron), Guest (steel), Eaton (silk), Armstrong (engineering), Brassey (railways), Guinness, Allsopp and Bass (beer): the pendulum was beginning to swing. By 1890 the proportion of business and commercial families achieving peerages was 25 per cent, and rising. Thereafter the barriers were down. Smith (newsagency), Cubitt (building), Cunliffe-Lister (velvet), Mulholland (flax), White (chemicals), Vivian (copper), Stephen (railways); besides further peerages for Barings and Guinnesses: all these followed between 1891 and 1893 alone. Between 1886 and 1914 about two hundred new peers were created, at least half from non-landed backgrounds; of those about one-third compensated for their origins by buying big estates. Thirty-five years after Strutt's elevation, business capital had clearly achieved some sort of parity with land. Samuel Cunliffe-Lister, 1st Baron Masham – spinner – bought up over 34,500 acres. Samuel Loyd, 1st Baron Overstone – banker – accumulated 30,849 acres. Ivor Guest, 1st Baron Wimborne – ironmaster – amassed 83,600. The Guinnesses between them must have had even more, not to mention the Rothschilds and the Barings. These men were clearly giants of new money. But something of the same sense of land-hunger is apparent among nearly all the ennobled late Victorian super-rich. Of those becoming peers between the 1850s and the 1890s, hardly any were content with a country house in less than 2,000 acres. It is no coincidence that an estate of roughly that size was the customary criterion of landed-gentry status.

The advance of new money can be measured even more clearly in the dramatic expansion of the Edwardian baronetage. When Queen Victoria's creations are compared with those of Edward VII it can be seen that the annual number of new baronets quintupled within a generation. And it was not only the number which was novel. There had of course been Victorian baronets whose origins lay in trade: Sir Thomas Bazley, a Bolton cotton-spinner; Sir Lowthian Bell, a Hartlepool ironmaster; Sir Thomas Borthwick and Sir Charles Cameron, newspaper proprietors; Sir Francis Crossley, Sir Samuel Cunard, Sir Walter Gilbey, Sir Gilbert Greenall – carpets, shipping, wine and beer: clearly the image of a baronet was not quite what it had been. But the Edwardian baronetage was overwhelmingly *nouveau-riche*. In 1905 alone, for example, the Tories nominated eight millionaires: Birkin (lace), Holcroft (coal), Coats (cotton), Royden and Ellerman (shipping), Stern (banking), Cooper (American property) and Wernher (South African gold). Not all of these set themselves up as country gentlemen. Ellerman, the richest by far, was content with a Mayfair house and a seaside villa. But long before 1914 a pattern of aspiration had been established: new money, new land, new title. And in one industry, at least, this social progression has been subjected to quantitative scrutiny. The proportion of peers, baronets and knights among steel manufacturers rose from one in seven in 1865 to one in five in 1895 and one in three among men holding top executive posts between 1905 and 1947.[34] Few of these, however, were rich enough to establish major landed dynasties.

Tying up capital – and committing income – to maintain the apparatus of gentility was a long-term option only for the very rich. Lady Dorothy Nevill recalled that running a town house and country house – dancing in the summer, shooting in the autumn, hunting in the winter – cost at least £10,000 a year in the 1860s, perhaps £500,000 in today's money.[35] And the expenditure grew. Towards the end of the nineteenth century, even traditional landowners like the 3rd Marquess of Salisbury were having to float their country estates on the back of incomes derived from urban property. After all, between 1875 and 1897 the value of agricultural land had fallen from £54 to £19 per acre. Financially and socially, out of instinct and out of necessity, the old and new élites were beginning to converge. But the culture in common – the focus of convergence – was still the house in the country. When in 1908 Beatrice and Sidney Webb spent upwards of a month in a lodge on the Luton Hoo estate [plate 56] as guests of Sir Julius Wernher, they were struck by the wasteful symbolism of it all:

> From the extreme corner of the millionaire's park, we surveyed a machine for the futile expenditure of wealth ... No doubt to please his 'society'-loving wife [Wernher has bought a great estate]. The family spend some Sundays at Luton Hoo and a few months in the autumn, but all the rest of the 365 days the big machine goes grinding on, with its 54 gardeners, 10 electricians, 20 or 30 house servants and endless labourers for no one's benefit ... The great mansion stood, closed and silent, in the closed and silent park – no one coming or going except the retinue of servants, the only noises the perpetual whirring and calling of the thousands of pheasants, ducks and other game that were fattening ready for the autumn slaughter. At the gates of the park, a bare half-mile distant, lay the crowded town of Luton – drunken, sensual, disorderly – crowded in mean streets, with a terrific infant mortality. The contrast was oppressingly unpleasant, and haunted our thoughts as we sat under the glorious trees and roamed through wood and garden, used their carriages, enjoyed the fruit, flowers and vegetables, and lived for a brief interval in close contact with an expenditure of £30,000 a year on a country house alone.[36]

Luton Hoo was a sizeable estate, but land alone could never pay such a bill. The Wernhers' game park was subsidised by the gold fields of the Transvaal. Like the Fieldens, like the Rothschilds, and even in the end like the Crawshays, the Wernhers had become mesmerised by an aspirational ideal: the image of the English country gentleman.

Of course, such a progression – from entrepreneur and manufacturer to *rentier* and landowner – was never universal. Plenty of alternative instances could be cited. Joseph Ruston – Mayor, MP and Sheriff, the man who made Victorian Lincoln world-famous for agricultural machinery – died in 1897 worth upwards of a million pounds, with scarcely an acre to his name.[37] Many a magnate – especially those without immediate heirs – preferred to stay in town. Many an industrialist – John Rylands of Manchester, for example – preferred caution to symbolism. And many a new-rich landowner remained entrepreneurially active. Even so, the numbers involved in the process of gentrification were clearly significant.[38] It has been estimated – albeit on an arbitrary basis – that between 1835 and 1889 about five hundred major country houses were either newly built or substantially rebuilt; of these, up to half involved 'new' or non-gentry families. In the 1830s hereditary landowners may have been building three times as many houses as the *nouveaux riches*; by the 1880s, only half as many; by the 1890s, fewer than a fifth. Figures for land purchase suggest a similar picture. During much the same period one third of those leaving half a million pounds – one half, if we include their immediate heirs – acquired landed property of 2,000 acres or more. By the 1880s, one in ten of the greatest landed estates had been purchased during the previous hundred years. Between 1809 and 1880 the annual number of probated fortunes reaching £100,000 or more rose almost tenfold, ending with a total of nearly 3,500 for that seventy-year period. Of these perhaps two-thirds were businessmen, more it seems in commerce than in manufacturing. And of those, between one-third and one-half appear to have set themselves up in the country. Between 1890 and 1914, these included – not surprisingly – a clear majority of London bankers, most of whom in any case married into landed families. And of course many more – particularly towards the end of the century – were content to rent: the image of landownership was more important than the technicality of possession.

H.G. Wells, with his childhood experience of the servants' hall at Uppark, could read the signs only too well.

> The great houses stand in the parks still ... the English countryside ... persists obstinately in looking what it was ... [But] the hand of change rests on it all ... Bladesover House is now let furnished to Sir Reuben Lichtenstein, and has been since old Lady Drew died ... To borrow an image from my mineralogical days, these Jews were not so much a new British gentry as 'pseudomorphous' after the gentry ... Hawksnest, over beyond, I noted, had its pseudomorph too; a newspaper proprietor ... had bought the place outright; Redgrove was in the hands of brewers.[39]

Setting aside the anti-Semitic tone – he thought Jewish new money had erupted saprophytically over the gentry's body politic – Wells was stating no more than a statistical truth. The richest *nouveaux riches* at the end of the nineteenth century were not content to stay within their own caste: they set out to ape the established gentry. And when they did so they found the old landed order resilient but not impermeable. During the Victorian period as a whole as many as eight out of ten millionaire or half-millionaire families acquired landed estates within two generations; between 1858 and 1879 the proportion is as high as 26 out of 30. At the top or magnate level – an Arkwright, a Peel, a Brassey or a Guinness; an Armstrong, a Baring, a Guest or a Rothschild [plate XI] – this involved, besides a London house, the acquisition of a country seat and 10,000 acres; in all, perhaps a half-million-pound investment. Lower down, for those aiming at gentry status only – Marshall, Pease, Bölckow [plate IV] or Lowthian Bell – 1,000 or 2,000 acres might suffice. Lower still – Kenrick or Cadbury, Chamberlain or Attwood – it was a villa rather than a seat; but a villa with the appurtenances of rurality.

The cost of building a country house could be formidable. A minimum of £10,000 – say, half a million today – was needed for a substantial property without an estate, the sort of house usually staffed by fifteen servants: Didsbury Towers, Manchester, for instance, a

Loire Gothic château built in 1865 to designs by Thomas Worthington for John Taylor, proprietor and editor of the *Manchester Guardian*.[40] But even without contents a great house could cost very much more than that. Pickenham Hall, Norfolk, a Neo-Georgian seat remodelled in 1903–4 by Robert Weir Schultz for G.W. Taylor, a banker who inherited a button-making fortune, cost over £20,000; Buchan Hill, near Crawley, Sussex, a Dutch Renaissance house designed in 1880–83 by George and Peto for P. Saillard, an ostrich-feather merchant, cost £45,000.[41] And after construction, there was always the cost of servicing: by the 1890s a country house with an estate of even middling size could require as many as 170 male staff; that meant an annual wages bill of about £8,000.[42] Such a house, after all, was a very obvious symbol of conspicuous consumption. Avery Hill, near Eltham, Kent, a lavish Italianate retreat designed in 1889–91 by Thomas Cutler for Colonel North, the nitrate king, cost with contents more than £100,000. So did Bearwood, Berkshire (1865–70) [plate 13], a massive mixed-Classic mansion designed by Robert Kerr for John Walter, proprietor of *The Times*. And the seats of the super-rich made even those figures seem small. Westonbirt – R.S. Holford's Jacobethan pile in Gloucestershire, designed by Lewis Vulliamy – may well have cost £200,000. And as for Eaton Hall, Cheshire – Waterhouse's Gothic palace for the Duke of Westminster – that is said to have topped £600,000. No wonder one visitor protested that staying at Eaton was like breakfasting in a cathedral.[43] All but the last of these houses had been built by new money. House-building on this scale was clearly the sport of parvenus; but it was a game which only the richest *nouveaux riches* could play.

Building at such a level was in any case something of a gamble. Sir George Philips, MP, 1st Bt, a Manchester cotton-spinner, the richest Mancunian of his day, was worth £20,000 a year in the 1820s. The son of a Methodist hat-maker – of very minor gentry family – he set out to conquer the citadel of landed society. By the time he died in 1844 – an Anglican by now, even a defender of the Corn Laws, with £70,000 in the bank – he had spent upwards of £420,000 on a 6,000-acre estate at Weston Park, Warwickshire, with Tudor Gothic seat to match. Using Blore as his architect, he spent £150,000 in

1826–31, simply rebuilding and refitting this house. His son was appalled at such extravagance: 'You have erected a house quite inconsistent with our status,' he told his father, 'which I fear you will repent of.' Repent he did not. With settlements on his children amounting to another £280,000, Philips cannot have spent much less than three-quarters of a million on establishing his family among the county gentry. Socially speaking, the investment paid off. His son – for all his reservations, an Eton and Cambridge man – married a daughter of the 2nd Baron Waterpark. His nephew, Mark Philips, MP, followed suit by building an equally massive house in the same county: Welcombe, near Stratford-on-Avon, designed by Henry Clutton in 1867. And the first baronet's three granddaughters all succeeded in marrying noblemen: the 2nd Earl of Camperdown, the 2nd Baron Carew and – a symbolic prize – the 14th Earl of Caithness. As if to mark this last, expensively-won status, the second baronet then spent £16,000 on a shooting lodge at Brabstoar in that same remote county. When he died in 1883 he was worth £260,000, with almost the same amount in land. Meanwhile, reinforced with third-generation cotton money, lucky Lord Camperdown was moving at ease between his eponymous seat – Neo-Classical Camperdown House, near Dundee, designed by William Burn in 1824–6 – and his secondary properties at Weston and Gleneagles, Perthshire. In London, the family had by now advanced from the Reform Club to Brooks's, and from Hill Street to Charles Street, Mayfair. But the first Sir George Philips was soon forgotten; his baronetcy died out, and his house was demolished in 1933.[44]

To at least one visiting American, Adam Badeau in 1886, the explanation of all this manoeuvering was crystal clear: 'The wealthiest tradesmen, bankers, brewers, merchants, find their consequence incomplete until they can purchase estates and rank with the county families.'[45] This was in fact an age-old pattern, but a pattern already multiplying as the eighteenth century became the nineteenth: Arkwrights in Derbyshire, Peels in Staffordshire, Barclays in Norfolk, Whitbreads in Bedfordshire, Hanburys in Hertfordshire and Essex. The Fosters of Stourbridge – the biggest ironfounders in the Black Country – are a nice case in point. In 1853 William Orme Foster inherited more than half a million from his bachelor uncle, the real founder of the firm, James Foster,

MP. Within fifteen years he had expanded the business, bought a 20,000-acre estate, Apley Park, Shropshire, and turned its chapel into a dining room as a base for appropriate entertaining. He even bought additional land in Ireland, at Camolin Park, Co. Wexford. Foster was gentry now – JP, DL, MP, and High Sheriff twice over – with a son at Eton and Christ Church and a house in Belgrave Square. He died in 1899, a member of Brooks's and the Athenaeum, worth £3,150,000. But the key to his social advancement had been the purchase of the Apley estate in 1868 for £550,000.[46]

Another family of ironmasters, the Hardys of Bradford, followed a similar social trajectory. Starting from a slightly higher base – John Hardy I, founder of the Low Moor ironworks in 1788, was at least an attorney – the Hardys had by the third generation notched up a baronetcy, a viscountcy and an earldom. By the mid Victorian period their mines and foundries, their heaps of waste and slag, were legendary: 'The accumulation of cinders and calcined shale', noted Murray's *Handbook for Yorkshire*, 'overspreads the country, and exceeds in cubic bulk the mass of the pyramids.' The family were also landowners on a formidable scale. John Hardy II, MP for Bradford, bought Dunstall Hall, Staffordshire plus 2,000 acres in 1851; he left more than half a million in 1855. His three sons did even better. John Hardy III, also an MP, became a baronet in 1876 and left over £1 million in 1888; Charles Hardy left a mere half-million in 1867, but died the owner of a 3,000-acre estate at Chilham Castle, Kent; Gathorne Gathorne-Hardy (he doubled his surname in 1878) was the first of his family to go to Oxford: he did well in law, then took up serious Tory politics, becoming Viscount Cranbrook (1878), then Earl of Cranbrook (1892), after paying £124,000 for a 5,000-acre estate at Hemstead, Kent, on which he rebuilt Hemstead House to designs by David Brandon in 1859. No fewer than seven sons of the next generation – grandsons of John Hardy II – were Etonians. But the turning-point in the Hardys' social ascension had been the purchase of the Dunstall estate in 1851. Ironically, the reverse was also true: the family lost much of its status when in 1918 Charles Hardy II, by now a member of White's, sold delectable Chilham to – symbolically – a dealer in South African metals, Sir Edmund Davis [plate II].[47] Acquiring 'a place', as *The Spectator* decided in 1872, had always been new money's top priority, unless of course its owner was 'abnormally un-English'. And that process of purchase and re-purchase was a guarantee of continuous mobility. Whatever the exceptions, the overall pattern is clear. As late as the 1880s the established peerage still owned about 5.7 million acres, and many a great estate was still held by pre-Reformation gentry; but as many as a million or a million and a half acres were already in the hands of new money.[48]

In a sense, therefore, the skirmishes of economic historians – serving and volleying quantifications of mobility – are beside the point. The key question is not how many *nouveaux riches* failed to buy landed property, but how many magnates who could afford to secure a great estate for themselves or their families actually failed to do so. When the question is posed in that way, the answer becomes pretty obvious. The majority of landed properties inevitably remained in traditional hands, and the businessman willing and able to buy a large estate remained a rarity. But the balance was shifting as the nineteenth century gave way to the twentieth.

What matters is the pattern of aspiration. Some of these new men were bourgeois in origin, some were proletarian; but, on the whole, their focus of mobility was the same: the aspirational image of the English country house. The number of medium-rich magnates – quarter-millionaires, for example – who did not buy land is not so important. It was the richest who bought most land. Maybe only one-tenth of great landowners in 1883 were new men; but, within the ranks of the *nouveaux riches*, they were on the whole the richest tenth.[49] And that is the clinching argument. It was the wealthiest *nouveaux riches* who were drawn into landed society, and they supplied an incentive for those below. Up and down the social pyramid, woven into the links of the social chain, land retained its status – even if that status diminished after the 1880s – as the principal yardstick of gentility. The hierarchy of country house values – 'the 18th century system', as H.G. Wells called it – remained a 'social datum'.[50] Well into the Edwardian period the gentry continued to act out their immemorial role as models for the *nouveaux riches*.

For so it had always been. 'Gentility', observed Sir Thomas Holles in the reign of Elizabeth I, 'is nothing but ancient riches.' As if to prove it, his descendants became Dukes of Newcastle. 'Trade in England makes gentlemen,' noted Daniel Defoe in 1726; 'for after a generation or two, the tradesmen's children, or at least their grand-children, come to be as good gentlemen, statesmen [i.e., yeoman free-holders], parliament men, privy councillors, judges, bishops and noblemen as those of the highest birth and most ancient families.' That was the English tradition, even after the industrial revolution had multiplied alternative possibilities for investment. As the nine-teenth century progressed this assimilative process accelerated, at least as measured by a three-generational yardstick. James Morrison the haberdasher set up several sons as landed gentlemen; so did John Mar-shall the flax-spinner; so did Thomas Brassey the railway builder. And they were only the most conspicuous examples. 'See', exclaimed Cobbett in 1831, 'how every successful trader buys an estate and tries to perpetuate his name in connection with "that ilk" by creating an eldest son.'[51] All three sons of George Brettle, spinner, for example, acquired country houses with land: Edward at Henley Park, Surrey; George Henry at Mongewell House, Oxfordshire; Alfred at Combe Hay House, Somerset. All three were *nouveaux riches*, and Alfred, in particular, took the *nouveau-riche* way of life to extremes: he died young in 1856, falling out of his carriage in the Champs-Élysées after drinking too much champagne at the Chantilly races.[52] That was the predictable sequence: first the money, then the land, then the cham-pagne. Almost 'the first step for a wealthy *parvenu*', it was pointed out in 1879, 'is to buy up land right and left'.[53] Not necessarily a major estate; not even enough to absorb the greater part of a business fortune; but just sufficient to give additional standing. Rubinstein calls it the respect paid by wealth to status.[54] Throughout the Vic-torian and Edwardian periods, houses built on land – seat, mansion, villa, shooting box – gained something, however vestigial, from the aura of territorial dominion. And architecture, as always, turns out to be the barometer of class, the index and reflex of social change.

But is architecture also a barometer of taste? 'Taste', unfortunately, is a slippery term. It can be specific or generic; descriptive or judge-mental; value-free or else loaded with cultural luggage. One of the purposes of this book is to untangle at least one aspect of this semantic conundrum: the relationship between taste and money. There is plenty of evidence to evaluate: all those houses of the richest *nouveaux riches*. But how much can be construed as individual taste? How much is merely status-seeking in three dimensions? When the great Andrew Carnegie set out to explain the economic supremacy of late Victorian Britain, he gave much of the credit to individual millionaires, 'The Cunards, Ismays, Allens, Elders, Bessemers, Rothschilds, Barings, Clarks, Coatses, Crossleys; the Browns, Siemens, Cammels, Gillotts, Whitworths; the Armstrongs, Listers, the Salts, Bairds, Samuelsons, Howards, Bells and others'.[55] The achievements of such men seemed to him to create a new economic and even cultural hegemony. But what of its architectural expression? Carnegie's own home – Skibo Castle, Sutherland (1899–1902) [plate 43] – was, as we shall see, aesthetically parasitic: an inflated version of a traditional Caledonian icon. In that respect he was a typical millionaire. He put his social ambition into house-building; his genius was reserved for business.

On the whole, nineteenth-century millionaires made their money in the town and spent it in the country. The progress of the Wilson family, shipowners from Hull – collectively multi-millionaires – could be described as paradigmatic. In four generations between the mid eighteenth century and the First World War, they went through every phase of *nouveau-riche* existence: entrepreneur, capitalist, landowner, socialite and *rentier*. The first generation were coastal lightermen, the second founded the shipping line; the third generation became minor politicians, lords of the East Riding, and courtiers to the Prince of Wales; the fourth sold out, and retired to Wimbledon and the French Riviera.

What did they leave behind? In less than seventy years the Wilsons transformed the economy of Hull. At its peak the Wilson Line – the largest private shipping line in the world – employed 10,000 workers, and produced annual six-figure incomes for both Arthur Wilson and Charles Wilson, 1st Baron Nunburnholme. Both brothers moved out from the centre of Hull during the 1870s and bought their way into county society: Arthur at Tranby Croft, designed by C.H. Chorley in 1874–6; Charles – who had married the Duke of Wellington's niece – at Warter Priory, formerly a seat of the 5th Baron Muncaster, which he extended in 1880. Both houses were Classical in style, Franco-Palladian and crude Italianate. Neither was in any way architecturally memorable. Arthur's retreat at Cap Ferrat – the Villa Maryland, designed by H.A. Peto in 1904 – suggested rather more taste. But the scale of expenditure was formidable: Warter Priory, set in eighteen square miles of agricultural land, had 21,000 square feet of glasshouses devoted to the production of fruit and flowers. It was all rather vulgar, and appropriately it was the Tranby Croft affair which gave the family their niche in history.[56] At Arthur Wilson's house party for the Doncaster Races of 1890, with the Prince of Wales as guest of honour, Lieutenant-Colonel Sir William Gordon Cumming was accused of cheating at cards. What made the subsequent libel action sensational was the appearance of the Prince in the witness box. What gives the story continuing interest for historians, however, is the tension between old and new money. On one side an officer and a gentleman (though Princess Alexandra called Gordon Cumming 'a vile snob', and his fellow officers at the baccarat table failed to back him up); on the other side, a clutch of *arrivistes*: Jack Wilson, son of a shipowner; Edward Lycett Green, son of an ironmaster; and Reuben Sassoon, the Prince's unofficial turf accountant. At the trial the Prince came down firmly on the side of his parvenu friends: it was rumoured that he had fallen out with Gordon Cumming over the favours of Lady Warwick. The jury found against the Colonel. But Gordon Cumming had one last card to play. Before he retired to his Scottish estate at Gordonstoun, indeed on the very day he was cashiered from the Scots Guards, he married an heiress from New York worth £20,000 a year. New money had the last laugh.

In so many instances throughout the Victorian and Edwardian periods, despite all the exceptions and anomalies, this key factor emerges repeatedly: the transfer of accumulated capital from city to country, from trade to land. 'Men who have made their fortunes in trade', observed The Hon. George Brodrick in 1881, 'are . . . covetous

of land which for them is the one sure passport to social consideration.'[57] Hence that 'twentieth century fusion' noted by T.H.S. Escott
in 1903, 'between ... old acres and ... new wealth.'[58] Goldsmids in
Gloucestershire, Rothschilds in Buckinghamshire, Sassoons in Sussex
and Kent: City money found a natural outlet in the countryside. Out
of more than two hundred men who died worth a million pounds or
more between 1809 and 1914, fewer than two dozen denied their
families the luxury of a country house and estate. The country house
was not always a seat; often it might more properly be described as a
house in the country, its estate a plantation rather than a park. Still, it
was the imagery that counted. Those who did resist the lure were
mostly metropolitan money-men like the Sterns or the Raphaels; or
metropolitan misers like Duncan Dunbar, Samuel Lewis and Henry
Silver.[59] On the whole, for the very rich at least, the social imagery of
the country house would seem to have been irresistible.

> There is nothing on earth [noted *The Spectator* in 1876] – we doubt if in
> the history of the world there ever has been anything like – the position of
> an Englishman who owns 20,000 acres and can extract from them even a
> pound an acre. Rich, secure, and treated with a deference that nothing but
> crime can distort, civilisation may in one sense be said to exist for them.
> They can live lives of political strife, or intellectual excitement, or supreme
> personal luxury, at discretion, can know all men, collect all things; and
> greatest boon of all, live absolutely their own lives, without reproach or
> fear of society, or dread of coming change ... The English territorialist is
> as safe in his home as a king in his capital.[60]

This extraordinary privilege, the product of primogeniture and entail
– 710 individuals owning one-quarter of England and Wales, a situation paralleled only in Hungary or Bohemia – made land the
inevitable apex of ambition. *The Economist* – probably Walter Bagehot
– was stating no more than a truism when it commented in July 1870:
'It would [better] pay a millionaire to sink half his fortune in buying
10,000 acres of land to return a shilling per cent than [to] live upon
the whole without land: he would be a greater person in the eyes of
more people.'[61]

When Sir William Harcourt visited 'Radical Joe' Chamberlain at
Highbury, King's Heath – a house designed by J.H. Chamberlain

in 1878–80 in the heart of suburban Birmingham – he was struck by the anomalous continuity of what he saw. 'Upon my word, Chamberlain,' he remarked, 'you are perpetuating in this pretty place the worst vices of the country gentleman.'[62] Harcourt spoke as Gladstone's Chancellor of the Exchequer, worried no doubt by such unproductive investment. Beatrice Webb's reaction to the Chamberlain style – at least in his previous house – was rather more acerbic: 'there was a good deal of taste', she noted, 'and all of it bad'. Chamberlain, though never quite a millionaire, seems to have had no doubts at all: a new man himself, he believed in the hegemony of new money. So too, in their Quaker way, did Chamberlain's neighbours, the Cadburys: Richard Cadbury of Uffculme, King's Heath, and George Cadbury of The Manor, Northfield. So too did at least one wise outsider: Montalembert. Visiting England in 1855, he saw the best omen for the social and political future of the country in the supremacy of the *marchand enrichi*. And half a century later Escott seized upon the same phenomenon as evidence of social cohesion. Writing in 1906, he noted approvingly that the new plutocracy – the Whitbreads of Southill, the Jameses of West Dean, the Rothschilds of Gunnersbury, Mentmore, Waddesdon [plate 66] and Tring [plates 67–8] – had achieved a level of social standing comparable almost to the territorial magnates of old. 'The correlative,' he observed, 'as it is also most frequently the cause, of the country house [today] . . . is the office in the city . . . There has been a change of scene, but not of spirit or method. Nowhere are the old traditions preserved more faithfully than beneath the new roofs.'[63]

That had been Brodrick's conclusion exactly in 1881:

> The law of Primogeniture and the custom of Entail has erected great landowners into a privileged caste, admission to which is the highest aspiration of the English plutocracy . . . They hold in their gift that social promotion which is the most seductive of bribes to English minds . . . [But as a result the] 'landed aristocracy' of England is no longer an exclusive noblesse of ancient lineage, but rather a territorial plutocracy, largely recruited from the wealthiest class of traders . . . Bankers, stockholders, and brewers, millowners, shipowners, Manchester warehousemen [i.e., wholesalers], and merchants of every degree are already naturalised within the magic circle of county society and even admitted freely to matrimonial

alliances ... The fact that such parvenus fall so easily into the duties of their new position [as JP, MP, Sheriff, Deputy-Lieutenant, etc.] is surely encouraging, for it shows that blood and breeding are not the only qualities that make a county gentleman.[64]

New wine in old bottles. Of Sir Gilbert Parker, a notorious *arriviste*, it used to be said that 'in the dead silence of the night you [can] hear a distant but monotonous sound – Sir Gilbert Parker, climbing, climbing, climbing'.[65] Parker never achieved landed status, but he did rise fast within the ranks of Tory society: from Carlton Club to Beefsteak, from knighthood to baronetcy, from Member of Parliament to Privy Councillor. And this endless process – the gravitational thrust of social change – operated most clearly in the relationship between town and country, city and land.

Two curious vignettes – one in Kent, one in Buckinghamshire – may stand as symbols of several of these interlocking themes. In the garden at Owletts,[66] home of the architect Sir Herbert Baker, stands a conspicuous garden ornament. Baker was no millionaire, though he did consort with diamond magnates. But it was he who reconstructed – or rather, destroyed – the old Bank of England building, Soane's masterpiece in the City. As a trophy of that enterprise, *c.* 1926, he placed a Classical capital from the Bank in his own garden: English land, colonised and adorned by a capital symbol of mercantile wealth. About the same time, Baker's colleague Lutyens was doing exactly the same thing at Tyringham, Buckinghamshire.[67] Soane had designed this house in 1792–7 for a banker, William Praed, MP. In 1907 it was bought by another banker, F.A. König, a Silesian Theosophist Jew with business in New York and London. He employed E.E. Van Ihne to transmogrify the house in 1907–9, and Lutyens to transform the garden in 1924–8. There, amid the terraces and pergolas, we find three more capitals from the old Bank of England: symbols again of that endlessly productive love–hate relationship between English land and international finance.

What then of the 1st Baron Faringdon, with whom we began this chapter? Alexander Henderson (1850–1934),[68] financier, politician and country squire, was one of the 'Fathers' of the Stock Exchange; a City tycoon, specialising in South American railways, who became first a Liberal Unionist MP, then a baronet, then a baron, then a Companion of Honour and a member of Brooks's. By 1889 his fortune had been made. He bought a Georgian seat, Buscot Park in Berkshire, from the trustees of an Australian railway magnate, and proceeded to decorate it with mesmeric paintings by Burne-Jones. In 1904 he commissioned H.A. Peto to design a water garden worthy of the Mughal gardens of Kashmir.[69] And in the same year he added the obligatory Scottish estate – at Glenalmond in Perthshire – to his seat in Berkshire and his mansion in Arlington Street, Piccadilly, just behind the Ritz. He died – the son of a printer's reader – worth £1,117,408, master of 3,500 acres. His fortune descended to his grandson, a Socialist, anti-imperialist exquisite who hated all his grandfather stood for.[70] But in one respect their tastes coincided. The grandson was devoted to Buscot; he filled it with elegant furniture by Thomas Hope and decorated its walls with inelegant paintings of the Labour Party. Today Buscot Park – 'as perfect as a house can be'[71] – is the property of the National Trust. The riches of the 1st Baron Faringdon have added not a little to the stock of England's heritage.

I. Sir Ernest Cassel (1852–1921):
'The Napoleon of Finance'

II. Sir Edmund Davis (1862–1939):
'The Premier Magnate of
the Jungle Mines'

III. Solly Barnato Joel (1865–1931):
'The Ace of Diamonds'

IV. Henry William Bölckow
(1806–78): 'Founder of Teesside'

V. Sir Joseph Robinson, 1st Bt
(1840–1929): diamonds and gold

VI. Sir Julius Wernher, 1st Bt
(1850–1912): gold and diamonds

VII. Leopold Albu [né Blau]
(1860–1938): diamonds

VIII. Sir Friedrich Eckstein, 1st Bt
(1857–1930): gold

IX. Michael Thomas Bass
(1799–1884): beer

X. W.H. Smith (1825–91):
newspapers

XI. Nathan Meyer, 1st Baron
Rothschild (1840–1915): banking

XII. Lady Orr-Ewing [née Hon.
Mabel Addington]: dyeing

XIII. Mrs Henri Bischoffsheim [née Clarissa Biederman]: banking

XIV. Mrs Charles Wertheimer: fine art

XV. Mrs Frank Hills: chemicals

XVI. Mrs Ronald Greville [née Margaret McEwen]: beer

# 2
# THE STYLE OF MILLIONAIRES
## *Country Houses, 1810–1914*

'Rich men's houses are seldom beautiful, rarely comfortable, and never original.'

Margot Asquith, 1922

Economic historians deal in money. Art historians deal in taste. But architectural historians have to understand both. Was capital accumulated in the industrial revolution frittered away on the status symbols of country houses and landed estates? Was industry sacrificed to a romantic dream? And if it was, what form – stylistically speaking – did it take? Statistical evidence supplied by economists makes intriguing material for historians of style.

The starting point for analysis has to be the table prepared by Professor Rubinstein in 1974.[1] This lists every Victorian and Edwardian millionaire; that is, every man who left a million pounds, according to the records of the probate registry. It is a table which should be used with a number of caveats. It lists only those men – and they are nearly all men – who died as millionaires, not those who lived at least part of their lives in that blessed state of wealth. Even so, it does supply a rudimentary canon of riches. An analysis based on the first section of that table, 1810–1914, has also the merit of manageability. Here are the names of more than two hundred millionaires who died between the Napoleonic wars and the start of the First World War – the classic period of British capital accumulation.

First of all, the caveats. Rubinstein's list contains only those millionaires whose bequests – excluding until 1898 all non-freehold land and, until 1926, all entailed or settled land – topped the magic million. If the value of entailed land – say, a traditional estate like Belton, Lincolnshire or Bowood, Wiltshire,[2] or several of the great Scottish fiefs – were included, the list would probably be nearly twice as long. We are dealing here with investments and cash, not real estate. So the figures are skewed towards industrial wealth and – still more – in favour of City fortunes. Rubinstein's table is predominantly a table of new money. And much of it is Jewish.[3] Of course it also includes aristocrats whose land turned out to be rich in minerals – like the St Oswalds of Nostell Priory, Yorkshire,[4] or the Vanes of Raby Castle, Co. Durham;[5] or aristocrats whose urban property was profitably redeveloped, like that of the Grosvenor family in London. But on the whole it is new money in new hands, and that gives us just the evidence we need to evaluate the taste of the *nouveaux riches*. For the nineteenth and early twentieth centuries the accuracy of these figures can be accepted; but as death duties begin to loom larger the sums involved clearly become less reliable. Nuneham Park, Oxfordshire stands half-empty today as a memorial to its one-time owner, the inventor of estate duties (1894), Sir William Harcourt.[6] One final caveat: since 1914, inflation has eroded the value of sterling to a ferocious degree. To achieve anything like comparability, we must multiply pre-First World War figures by more than forty. Charles Morrison's £11 million of 1909 – cash, shares and bonds, not land – would be worth £500 million today. And income tax was eight pence in the pound. Rubinstein's table is therefore a list of men with huge amounts of ready money. We are talking – in modern terms, given the vastly different scale of capital distribution – of cash billionaires.[7] What did they spend it on? And what conclusions – positive or negative – can we draw on the subject of *nouveau-riche* taste?

But first, another caveat. Some millionaires are not on the list because they spent much of their capital on building before they died: the great ironmaster Sir Josiah Guest, for example. After rebuilding Canford Manor, Dorset in Tudor Gothic to designs by Sir Charles Barry in 1847–51, he left only half a million.[8] So did John Fielden II, the cotton-spinning king of Todmorden, who built Dobroyd Castle on the hills overlooking his own factories.[9] And so did Thomas Holloway, patent medicine magnate and patron of the château-style Royal Holloway College, Egham, designed by W.H. Crossland in 1879–87. He actually advertised for ways to dispose of his fortune before his death.[10] Robert Stayner Holford needed no suggestions: Dorchester House, Park Lane [plate 81] and Westonbirt, Gloucestershire – art collection and arboretum – reduced even his formidable fortune below the million-pound level.[11] Others built houses worthy of millionaires, but died some way short of the magic number: Sir Henry Peek of Peek Frean biscuits, for instance, lord of Rousdon, Devon (1874–83), designed by Sir Ernest George in Franco-Flemish Gothic;[12] or William Gibbs – Butterfield's patron at Keble College, Oxford – whose fortune, based originally on guano, was significantly dented by the Gothic skyline of Tyntesfield, Somerset [plate 48], built to designs by John Norton in 1863–6.[13] Julius Drewe falls into the same category. A millionaire grocer dreaming of his thirteenth-century ancestor Drogo de Teigne, Drewe spent much of his fortune on Castle Drogo, Devon, an Edwardian fortress begun to designs by Sir Edwin Lutyens just before the First World War.[14] Or again – one final example in this group of big spenders – Lord Tollemache of Peckforton Castle, Cheshire, a baronial fantasy built to designs by Anthony Salvin in 1844–50. Tollemache spent £68,000 on his castle and £280,000 on estate improvements and farmhouses; as a result he left rather less than one million.[15]

Conversely, some millionaires appear in the list because they preferred to spend as little as possible on building; that is why they stayed so rich. Henry Cavendish, grandson of the 2nd Duke of Devonshire, for example, scientist and recluse, of Cavendish House, Clapham Common and 11 Bedford Square. He was the first man to leave a million pounds – in 1810 – and the first to calculate the weight of the world. Incidentally, his money was not just Cavendish money: he inherited, at least in part, from Henry Grey, Duke of Kent (d. 1740), reputed to be 'moderate in everything, except wealth and odour'.[16] And of course some millionaires spent not on houses but on rather more basic pleasures. 'Old Q', the 4th Duke of Queensberry, spent a

39

good deal on horses and girls, but still left the statutory million. In his case there was little point in rebuilding Drumlanrig; it was already an ultimate symbol of wealth.[17] At the other end of the felicific calculus, Joseph Fry, the Quaker cocoa magnate, devoted his fortune to philanthropy. He seems to have been quite uninterested in building; indeed, he conducted his business from the same room in which he had been born, in Union Street, Bristol.[18] George Salting, 'the greatest collector of his age', who inherited a fortune based on Australian sheep and sugar, contrived to operate from a small flat in St James's Street, above the Thatched House Club.[19] And Hubert, 2nd Marquess of Clanricarde – a millionaire miser and absentee Irish landlord – was quite content with a plain set of chambers in Albany.[20]

So much for the exceptions. Now for the principal players. One myth can be scotched right away: the idea that the Gothic Revival was somehow based on new money dressed up in the trappings of antiquity. The roll-call of those leaving more than £1,000,000 reveals very few parvenu Goths. William Crawshay II of Cyfarthfa, ironmaster; Sir Richard Arkwright of Willersley Castle, Derbyshire,[21] cotton-spinner; W.H. Forman, ironmaster, once of Doncaster, later of Pippbrook House, Surrey;[22] William Foster I, of Hornby Castle, Lancashire, worsted manufacturer; and William Orme Foster of Apley Park, Shropshire, ironmaster – all these were millionaire Goths, and new men.[23] As indeed was Herbert Stern, of the banking family – later 1st Baron Michelham – who chose to live for a while in the very mecca of Gothic, Strawberry Hill, Middlesex.[24] But there are hardly any others, even if we include J.J. Bibby, the Merseyside shipowner, who in 1868 bought Hardwicke Grange, Shropshire,[25] a mildly Gothic seat designed in 1820 by a Neo-Classicist, Thomas Harrison of Chester.

The greatest Goths among Victorian millionaires turn out to be representatives of old families. Christopher Talbot of Margam Abbey, Glamorgan, designed by Thomas Hopper in 1830–5;[26] the 4th Duke of Cleveland of Battle Abbey, Sussex (purchased 1858 and extended by Henry Clutton);[27] the 3rd Marquess of Bute of Cardiff Castle and Castell Coch (both by William Burges, 1866 onwards; 1872 onwards);[28] and the 1st Duke of Westminster of Eaton Hall, Cheshire, designed by Alfred Waterhouse in 1870–83[29] – all these, thanks to mineral and property development, might be described as newly rich. But they were scarcely parvenu. The taste of the *merely* super-rich in the nineteenth century was rarely medieval.

What about Tudor or Jacobean? Here a more plausible case can be deployed. Quite a number of nineteenth-century millionaires chose to build their homes in this style. 'The Spinning Jenny', Prime Minister Robert Peel, built Drayton Manor, Staffordshire to designs by Sir Robert Smirke in 1831–5,[30] with the million he inherited from his father 'Cotton Peel'. Francis Wright, owner of the Butterley ironworks, built Osmaston Manor, Derbyshire (1846–9);[31] and John Hodgson, sugar refiner, built Gilston Park, Hertfordshire, to designs by P.C. Hardwick in 1852.[32] All these were vaguely Tudor in style. Sir Gilbert Greenall, brewer, rebuilt Tilstone Hall (*c.*1875) and Walton Hall (1836–8; 1870), both in Cheshire;[33] William Sturdy, stockbroker, re-built Pax Hill Park, Lindfield, Sussex (1865);[34] Sir Cuthbert Quilter, another stockbroker, did the same for Bawdsey Manor, Woodbridge, Suffolk (1886);[35] and the brewing brothers Michael and Hamar Bass built Rangemore Hall (1879 onwards) and Byrkley Lodge (1887–91) – both by R.W. Edis – on adjacent estates in Staffordshire.[36] All these are Tudor or Jacobethan. But such houses are a minor percentage of the total list of houses owned by millionaires, even if we include Sir Julian Goldsmid, Bt, a financier who divided his time between a vast Jacobean mansion – Somerhill, near Tonbridge, Kent (enlarged still further in 1884)[37] – and his seaside retreats at Brighton and Cannes. More tellingly, it was the 7th Duke of Devonshire, not exactly *arriviste*, who built Holker Hall, Lancashire to designs by Paley and Austin from 1871 onwards, one of the most striking examples of this genre.[38] Neither Tudor nor Jacobean therefore can be described as a specifically parvenu style. Iwerne Minster in Dorset might well be labelled Tudor Gothic; but, designed by Waterhouse in 1877–82 for the banker George Grenfell Glynn, 2nd Baron Wolverton – grandson of Pascoe Grenfell – it was in any case only marginally *nouveau-riche*.[39]

It was in fact not the new men but the old families who favoured the styles of 'olden time', patrons like Disraeli's Eustace Lyle, lord of St Genevieve,

... a pile of modern building in the style of Christian architecture ... Built of white and glittering stone, it sparkled with its pinnacles in the sunshine as it rose in strong relief against its verdant background ... a [veritable] gathering ... of galleries, halls, and chapels, mullioned windows, portals of clustered columns and groups of airy pinnacles and fretwork spires ...

'I always fancy a siege must be so interesting,' said Lady Everingham ...[40]

Disraeli's evocation – modelled no doubt on Pugin's work at Alton – could be echoed in the houses of many an old family, newly rich. Witness two rich but non-millionaire landowners in Warwickshire: the Shirleys of Ettington Park (J. Prichard; 1858–63),[41] and the Mordaunts of Walton Hall (G.G. Scott; 1858–62).[42] Both built Gothic. Both would have been horrified by the label 'New Money'. In neither Gothic nor Jacobethan do we see the essential mark of the millionaire.

What then was the millionaire style? The great majority of Victorian and Edwardian millionaire houses – in England at least; Scotland, as we shall see, is a different matter – turn out to be Classical.

It was a house of pillars, porticoes, and statues, designed ambitiously in what was meant to be a classical style; and though its splendours might not be all perhaps in the best taste, nor even of the most strictly Roman pattern, there was yet an air about its meretricious stateliness by which the days of the Empire were at once suggested.

W.H. Mallock's imaginary country house of 1876 was indeed 'a type of its builder', the identikit *nouveau-riche* retreat. And so was Bulwer-Lytton's archetype of 1828: 'the white and modern mansion of a *nouveau riche*'.[43]

Millionaires either bought or built, or bought and rebuilt, in some form of Classicism. Several explanations come to mind. Classicism had urban connotations, and new money was money made in town. Classicism was a European language, emblematic perhaps of international finance. By contrast, Jacobethan may have seemed too stridently nationalist; and Gothic – thanks to the Ecclesiologists – too specifically Anglican. More importantly, Renaissance or Neo-Classical, or what the Victorians called Italianate, remained the Establishment style in England – sometimes even in Scotland – despite the

Romantic eclecticism of the nineteenth century. By the 1840s, for bourgeois patrons, Italianate had become almost a badge of upward mobility. At a higher level, hereditary millionaire magnates inherited Classical seats, which they simply embellished: Chatsworth (Duke of Devonshire),[44] Wentworth Woodhouse (Earl Fitzwilliam),[45] Althorp (Earl Spencer),[46] Petworth (Lord Leconfield),[47] Welbeck (Duke of Portland)[48] or Bowhill (Duke of Buccleuch).[49] In each of these cases, increasing wealth merely augmented old taste.

> Gatherum Castle ... was a new building of white stone, lately erected at enormous cost by one of the finest architects of the day ... [It] would probably be called Italian in its style of architecture, although it may ... be doubted whether any such edifice, or anything like it, was ever seen in any part of Italy. It was a vast edifice ... having long wings on each side ... and a portico so large as to make the house behind it look like another building of a greater altitude. This portico was supported by Ionic columns, and was ... approached by a flight of steps, very broad and very grand ... Opening from the porch was the grand hall, which extended up to the top of the house. It was magnificent, indeed: being decorated with many-coloured marbles, and hung round with various trophies of the house of Omnium.[50]

Whatever its inconvenience, the Whig ideal had by Trollope's time become iconic: Trollope's Gatherum Castle was loaded with symbolic resonance for the rising parvenu.

Disraeli's portrait of the successful industrialist Oswald Millbank translates this traditional imagery, of hierarchy and order, into the new world of industry.

> [The factory of Mr Millbank – perhaps Henry Ashworth of Bolton – was] a vast deep red brick pile, which though formal and monotonous in its general character, [was] not without a certain beauty of proportion and an artist-like finish in its occasional masonry. The front, which [was] of great extent, and covered with many tiers of small windows [was] flanked by two projecting wings in the same style, which formed a large court, completed by a dwarf wall crowned with a light and rather elegant railing; in the centre, the principal entrance [incorporated] a lofty portal of bold and beautiful design, surmounted by a statue of Commerce ... The building had been fitted up by a capitalist as anxious to raise a monument of

the skill and power of his order, as to obtain a return for the great investment.

'It is the glory of Lancashire!' exclaimed the enthusiastic Mr Benson . . .

[Nearby] appeared a village of . . . picturesque character . . . On a sunny knoll in the background was a church, in the best style of Christian architecture, and near it was a clerical residence and school-house of similar design. The village, too, could boast . . . an Institute where there was a library and a lecture-room; and a reading-hall . . . On the other side . . . about half-a-mile up the valley, surrounded by beautiful meadows, and built on an agreeable and well-wooded elevation, was the mansion of the mill-owner . . . built in what is called a villa style . . . [with] a capacious and classic hall, and at the end a staircase in the Italian fashion . . .

'Your situation', said Coningsby, looking up the green and silent valley, 'is absolutely poetic'.

'I try sometimes to fancy', said Mr Millbank, with a rather fierce smile, 'that I am in the New World . . . Saxon industry competing successfully with Norman manners . . .'[51]

The new world of Mr Millbank – secular, utilitarian, Classical – is thus balanced against the old world: religious, communitarian, Gothic. But Disraeli's fusion of old and new – in effect, Carlyle's new feudalism – was never a realistic proposition. Millbank himself might move on to Hellingsley, a Jacobean mansion whose congruent elements – 'Grecian, Gothic and Italian' – summed up the Disraelian synthesis. But the new industrial order turned its back on both the ethics and the aesthetics of Romanticism. Not for nothing is that modern status symbol, the Rolls-Royce radiator, Classical not Gothic.

And what if Doric columns proved too plain, too understated, too bland for the palate of the parvenu? In that case there was always the ultimate model of mixed-classic ostentation: the French château. The Classicism of the French Court – in architecture, in furniture, in decoration – did not disappear with the Revolution; it survived to supply both the Second Empire and its rivals with suitable symbols of hierarchy. The *haute bourgeoisie* of mid nineteenth-century Europe draped itself in the trappings of the *ancien régime*. Nor was the Channel any barrier. Between the 1880s and 1914, French Classicism reconquered England as the style of the *Entente Cordiale*. The Graeco-Roman tradition thus turned out to be extraordinarily persistent. Classicism, in all its chameleon forms, has generally been the vernacular of the ruling classes.

One instant way to acquire the status that only Classicism could bring was to buy a major Georgian seat.

> Hainault House had been raised by a British peer in the days when nobles were fond of building Palladian palaces. It was a chief work of Sir William Chambers, and in its style, its beauty, and almost its dimensions, was a rival of Stowe or Wanstead. It stood in a deer park, and was surrounded by a royal forest. The family that had raised it wore out in the earlier part of [the nineteenth] century. It was supposed that the place must be destroyed and dismantled. It was too vast for a citizen . . . In this dilemma Neuchatel stepped in and purchased the whole affair – palace and park, and deer, and pictures, and halls, and galleries of statue and bust, and furniture, and even wines, and all the farms that remained, and all the seigneurial rights in the royal forest . . . The stables . . . had been modelled on those at Chantilly, and were almost as splendid a pile as the mansion itself . . . The conservatories and forcing houses looked, in the distance, like a city of glass . . . [52]

Disraeli's fiction turns out, often enough, to be fact. Neuchatel may or may not have been Rothschild, Hainault may or may not have been a mixture of Gunnersbury and Tring [plates 67–8], but there were plenty of other examples too. Vyall Walker, brewer, the only Victorian millionaire to play cricket for England, bought Arnos Grove, Southgate, Middlesex (*c.* 1875).[53] This was not a great estate (after all, he was a bachelor), but it was a famous Classical house, designed in part by Sir Robert Taylor. Francis Wise, distiller, 'the wealthiest man in Ireland', bought up the great seventeenth-century house of Anngrove, Co. Cork.[54] Thomas Brassey, the railway king, bought Heythrop, Oxfordshire (Thomas Archer, *c.* 1706), a much grander house than the family's Bulkley Hall, Cheshire; then called in Waterhouse in 1870 to remodel it for his son as a wedding present.[55] John Fielden – Fieldens of Todmorden again – bought Grimston Park,

Yorkshire – a Greek Revival house of 1840–50 by Decimus Burton – from the family of its builder, the 2nd Baron Howden, diplomat and soldier. Edward Brook, a sewing-thread manufacturer from Huddersfield, purchased – among several other seats – Kinmount, Dumfriesshire (1812),[56] built to designs by Sir Robert Smirke a generation before for the heir to the estate of 'Old Q'. Smirke's austere Neo-Classicism presumably struck just the right note of dignity and restraint. A parallel example would be Basildon Park, Berkshire (Carr of York, 1776; J.B. Papworth, 1839–44) [plates 14–17], bought by James Morrison, the multi-millionaire draper, who made his first fortune out of black funeral crêpe and his second out of imported silk. Born the son of a Hampshire innkeeper, this 'Napoleon of Shopkeepers' had amassed by his death in 1857 more than 100,000 acres in six counties.[57] Also by Carr of York was Gledhow Hall, near Leeds (1766–7), built originally for the clothier Jeremiah Dixon and then symbolically purchased by James Kitson, later 1st Baron Airedale, locomotive manufacturer: first new money, then newer money still.[58] The status of Classicism, at least in the eyes of the *nouveaux riches*, appears almost to have been magnetic. When the merchant banker Samuel Montagu, later 1st Baron Swaythling – son of a Liverpudlian watchmaker – bought South Stoneham House in Hampshire he was not only entering the landed aristocracy, he was identifying himself with what by then had become one of its archetypal images: a Classical seat worthy even of the Barings.

> I suppose this place of [Thomas] Baring's [wrote the American Henry Adams on a visit to Norman Court, Hampshire (H. Harrison; 1818–20)] is as near the true idea of aristocratic perfection as is permitted to imperfect mortality. Some people say that one's ear is offended by the rustle of banknotes. It is a calumny, if said invidiously, for there could not be more luxury with less show.[59]

Much the same image of bankers' country-house Classicism was no doubt in the mind of Samuel G. Smith when he leased Sacombe Park, near Ware, Hertfordshire, a Neo-Classical house dating from 1802–8.[60] Another banker, David Barclay Chapman – shadier this time: he was known as 'Gurney's Liar' – set himself up at Downshire House, Roehampton, designed by Brettingham in the 1770s.[61] Railway kings could play the same card: Edward Mackenzie bought Fawley Court, Buckinghamshire – partly by Wyatt – in 1853; George Wythes bought Copped Hall, Essex – wholly by Wyatt – in 1869.[62] And so could diamond magnates: Friedrich Eckstein's mansion, Ottershaw Park in Surrey (*c.* 1761; 1910), Alfred Beit's retreat at Tewin Water, Hertfordshire (*c.* 1810; *c.* 1900) and Julius Wernher's seat, Luton Hoo, Bedfordshire (1766; 1815; 1903) [plate 56] all began as Neo-Classical and ended up generically Beaux-Arts.[63]

The lure of Classicism never had much to do with comfort or convenience. Ever since Alexander Pope, the Palladian mansion had been a byword for haughty discomfort:

> Is this a dinner? This a genial room?
> No, 'tis a temple, and a hecatomb.

Its attraction was rooted in the imagery of power. And this preference runs right through the nineteenth century and even into the twentieth. When Frederick Cawley retired from Manchester to Herefordshire, with a fortune made in bleaching, dyeing and calico – and a barony from Lloyd George to boot – it was to Berrington Hall (1778–81) that he went, an exquisite Neo-Classical seat by Henry Holland.[64] And when millionaires happened also to be amateur architects, the private houses they designed for themselves proved to be Classical too. Alexander Peckover of Wisbech, banker, made Sibbald's Holme House Italianate; Edmund Beckett, later 1st Baron Grimthorpe, another banker, made Batchwood Hall, St Albans (1874–76) utilitarian outside but Classical within.[65] And if bankers' Classicism occasionally accommodated a little associational Gothic, it remained Classical none the less: Milton Abbey, Dorset, designed by Sir William Chambers in 1769–75 and bought with 8,000 acres for £240,000 by Baron Hambro in 1852, was essentially a Classical house with an exterior tricked out to match its noble medieval church. A Polish artist, Elizabeth Baumann, sent her husband a pointed description of life in this particular banker's palazzo:

> Last night I dined with the Hambros. These are my impressions of the unnatural life of the rich. At 8.30 p.m. the dinner was served. Earls and

47

barons inside, and the most beautiful [Capability Brown] landscape outside behind drawn curtains! Everything imaginable *ad nauseam* in the way of delicacies was offered: melons, strawberries, grapes, figs etc., and then the inevitable champagne. And against this a background of thousands of poor starving children lacking the barest necessities. I had place-of-honour at the table, but I would much rather have eaten porridge and cod with you and the children in our country cottage.[66]

Another way of joining the Classical set was to buy a minor Georgian house and then turn it into a major one.

The villa of Mr Vigo was on the Thames and had once belonged to a noble customer. The Palladian mansion contained a suite of chambers of majestic dimensions – lofty ceilings, rich cornices, and vast windows of plate glass [ – ]the gardens were rich with the products of conservatories which Mr Vigo had raised with every modern improvement, and a group of stately cedars supported the dignity of the scene and gave to it a name. Beyond, a winding walk encircled a large field which Mr Vigo called the park, and which sparkled with gold and silver pheasants, and the keeper lived in a newly-raised habitation at the extreme end, which took the form of a Swiss cottage ... Mr Vigo was a London tradesman, [and] though a [newly elected] member of Parliament ... he understood all about rolling stock and permanent ways, and sleepers and branch lines ... cabbalistic terms to the general ... the engagements for one session [of Parliament] alone amounted to one hundred and thirty million sterling ... Social invitations ... fell like a continuous snow-storm on [Mr Vigo's] favoured roof ... The fine ladies were eager in their homage ... [Mr Vigo] was seen between rival countesses ... 'When this excitement is over', said Mr Bertie Tremaine, 'I hope to induce him to take India' ... [67]

The career of Sir William Abdy, seventh and last baronet of the third creation and London property tycoon, was never so dramatic. But he did buy eighteenth-century Chobham Place, near Chertsey, Surrey, and in the 1850s turned it into a full-blown Italianate mansion.[68] Similarly, Sir James Horlick, 1st Bt, the malted milk magnate – half-way to being a millionaire at his death – bought Cowley Manor, Gloucestershire [plate 12] – designed by G. Somers Clarke in 1855 – and in

1890 transformed it into an Italianate extravaganza by R.A. 'Bungalow' Briggs.[69] The ostentation in that instance was worthy of Surtees' Scattercash family. Less lavishly, Albert Worthington, brewer, added wings to his late Georgian house, Maple Hayes, near Lichfield (*c.* 1885–90); so did John Williams, copper-smelter – the richest man in Cornwall – at Pengreep, near Gwenap (*c.* 1840).[70] G.F. Muntz, a Birmingham metal-roller, was rather more expansive: he bought Umberslade Hall, Warwickshire (*c.* 1695) and employed a local architect, G.F. Bidlake, to enlarge it considerably.[71] Sometimes the property in question was a villa rather than a seat. Georgian Doughty House, on Richmond Hill, was much expanded in the 1850s by Sir Francis Cook, merchant draper, to display his superb collection of pictures;[72] and St John's Lodge, a villa in Regent's Park, was turned into a veritable country house under the direction of Sir Charles Barry – architect to the Grand Whiggery – working this time for Sir Isaac Lyon Goldsmid, a bullion broker who ended his days as Baron Palmyra in the peerage of Portugal.[73] But it was the country house proper which remained the ideal. Colston Bassett Hall, Nottinghamshire, for example: an overscaled villa, stuccoed and Italianate, enlarged in the 1870s for a Lancashire millionaire coal-owner, Robert Millington Knowles.[74] Further south, Buckland House in Berkshire was re-conceived on an even grander scale. A massive mid Georgian seat by Wood of Bath, Buckland was hugely extended in 1910 by Romaine-Walker for the daughter of a millionaire banker, H.L. Bischoffsheim.[75] When Bischoffsheim died in 1908, his daughter – who had married the 20th Knight of Kerry – turned Buckland into a formidable symbol of *nouveau-riche* aggrandisement. If Classical was good, aggrandised Classical was even better. Such a process was carried to extremes by that idlest of brewers, Sir Henry Meux, 3rd Bt. To please his greedy, parvenue wife – 'ever seen Lady Meux wolf potatoes?' – he not only installed a roller-skating rink at Theobalds Park, Hertfordshire; in 1888 he even transported Temple Bar from the Strand to dignify the entrance to his estate [plate 11].[76] Dickens would surely have been amused:

'I don't know why it should be such a crack thing to be a brewer; but it is indisputable that while you cannot possibly be genteel and bake, you may be as genteel as never was and brew. You see it every day.'

'Yet a gentleman may not keep a public house; may he?' said I.

'Not on any account,' returned Herbert; 'but a public house may keep a gentleman . . .'77

A more sober example of progression by purchase and improvement – from factory to country seat, and eventually from north to south: Classical all the way – is provided by the Allhusen family, chemical manufacturers. Beginning close to the source of their wealth in Gateshead, they proceeded south from the grimy elegance of Elswick Hall, Newcastle (William Stokoe, 1803) to Stoke Court, Buckinghamshire (1745–73; purchased 1872) [plate 58], a comfortable retreat with Adamesque interiors, close to the churchyard where Thomas Gray composed his celebrated *Elegy*. From his birthplace in Schleswig-Holstein to the boardrooms of the City – via workshops foul with the smell of alkali – Christian Allhusen clawed his way up from immigrant to millionaire. He was not exactly a philanthropist. The most that his biographer could bring himself to say was that 'spreading all his sail to catch the favouring winds of commercial progress and financial development, he reached the haven of opulence and commanding social status.'78 Indeed he did. That leap-frogging manoeuvre, from Gateshead to Stoke Poges, tells us a good deal about the aspirations of the mega-rich in Victorian Britain. Even William Crawshay II – the third Iron King of Cyfarthfa – escaped eventually to softer pastures at Caversham Park, near Reading. There, on a spectacular site, he added Ionic wings, designed by J.T. Crew in 1850–2, to an already Classic house.79 Gilliat Hatfield, snuff and tobacco manufacturer, took an easier route; he simply developed his snuff mills in a Georgian park, Morden Hall, Surrey.80

Usually, it was just a case of buying Georgian and then 'improving'. James Morrison could hardly resist Fonthill Pavilion, a surviving wing of Fonthill Splendens, the Wiltshire palace of Alderman Beckford: it needed only refurbishment by J.B. Papworth in the 1830s and a little enlargement by David Brandon in 1846–8 [plates 8–9]. Mrs Morrison was less confident: 'I always dread', she wrote, 'Mr Papworth's love of gold and [fondness for] loading decoration.' But the prince of haberdashers was delighted. And when he saw Basildon Park, Berkshire [plates 14–17], he realised its potential at once. Despite its price tag – perhaps £140,000 in all – here was an estate, and a 'Palladian palace', worthy of any plutocrat. 'Such a house,' he wrote to his architect, 'and such a situation! What a casket to enclose pictorial gems!' Papworth obliged with extensions and improvements in appropriately gilded style.[81] Childwickbury, Hertfordshire (*c.* 1680; 1854; 1900), a Georgian house with delicious chinoiserie interiors, was similarly bought and then – as they say in the trade – 'earlied up' by Sir Blundell Maple.[82] It was Maple, 'the first upholsterer to be converted by royal favour into a Baronet', who turned interior decoration into a popular language of status. Would that his eye for detail had been placed at the service of the Assheton-Smith family. When that newly rich dynasty decided to move away from the fount of their fortune – slate quarries in Wales – they built themselves an elegant Classical house, Tidworth Park, Hampshire, and then wilfully aggrandised it. In doing so, they demonstrated how Victorian millionaire taste usually chose Classical and then, often enough, over-egged the pudding: Neo-Classical purity (1828–30) is obscured by heavy Italianate trimmings (*c.* 1860). When the new Duke of Omnium discovered similar 'improvements' in progress at Gatherum Castle, he was appalled at such parvenu flummery:

> There was an assumed and preposterous grandeur [about it all, redolent] . . . of some rich swindler or of some prosperous haberdasher . . . [Besides, it had] a look of raw newness about it which was very distasteful to him . . .
>   'There is a – a – a – I was almost going to say vulgarity about it which distresses me.'
>   'Vulgarity!' . . . exclaimed [the Duchess], jumping up from her sofa . . .[83]

Trollope's Duchess was sensitive in such matters; ironically, her son will marry the daughter of an American capitalist. But not every *nouveau riche* tumbled into the same trap. In 1907 Ludwig Mond, the swashbuckling chemical magnate, employed Walter Cave to make extensions at Combe Bank, near Sundridge, Kent, involving Adamesque decorations of unusual subtlety.[84] He had already taken up residence in the Wyatts' Winnington Hall, Cheshire (*c.* 1775; 1782–5) between sojourns at the Palazzo Zuccari in Rome.[85] Clearly Mond had a Classical eye. Less successful were the interior alterations made to Grantley Hall, near Ripon, Yorkshire (? Carr of York; 1760), by Christopher, 1st Baron Furness, a self-made shipowner, ironmaster and engine builder. His additions spoiled rather than improved the original.[86] The same is true of the Adam-style interiors added to Neo-Classical Wilton Park, near Beaconsfield, Buckinghamshire (1790; 1803–5) [plate 4] by Sir John Aird, a self-made engineering contractor.[87] And the additions inflicted in 1894–8 on Stapleford Park, Leicestershire by a formidable brewer, John, 1st Baron Gretton, did little to improve that exquisite sixteenth- and seventeenth-century house.[88] Gretton's architect, curiously, was a sensitive Goth, J.T. Micklethwaite; his alterations culminated in a grandiloquent Wrenaissance stable block for meetings of the Cottesmore Hunt.

What then of Classical country houses, newly built by new, or newish, millionaire money? They turn out, predictably, to be legion. They begin with Keswick Hall, Norfolk (1817–19; 1837), designed by the Greek Revivalist William Wilkins for Hudson Gurney, banker and brewer.[89] A richer example is Gunnersbury Park, Middlesex (*c.* 1834), rebuilt by Sydney Smirke for Nathan Meyer Rothschild. Graeco-Roman with touches of Renaissance, this banker's palazzo manages to translate the imagery of Pall Mall into the context of suburban Ealing.

> [Lavender Hill was] a mansion situated in unusually ample grounds for a villa residence and approached through lodges and by roads ingeniously winding ... [Hartmann Brothers] were bankers to more than one European potentate, and whenever any member of the Royal or Imperial families paid a visit to England they spared one day to be entertained at Lavender Hill with much magnificence; banquets and balls in colossal tents, and all the bowers and groves of Lavender resonant with musicians and illuminated with many lamps of many colours ... [But today] was a Bank holiday and Mr Hartmann was absorbed in a new work of a friend of Schopenhauer which had just arrived.[90]

Not every magnate could match Disraeli's Maecenas, but at Sundridge Park, Kent (Nash and Repton, 1799 onwards), the banking family of Scott first built and then extended an intriguing Neo-Classical house.[91] A little later Longford Hall, Stretford, Manchester (1857) was cautiously built in an Italianate style by John Rylands the cotton magnate.[92] 'Vaguely Italianate' too were Abbeylands, Co. Antrim, built by the stockbroker Hugh McCalmont; Craigavon, Co. Down, built by the distiller James Craig; and Ballywalter, Co. Down, built by the Belfast flax-spinner Andrew Mulholland to designs by Sir Charles Lanyon in 1846.[93] Ballywalter, in particular, sums up the symbolism of the palazzo style in a provincial setting. When he bought the estate for £23,500 Mulholland was already Mayor of Belfast; by rebuilding the house he turned himself into an Irish country gentleman. His son, a Tory MP and celebrated yachtsman, predictably became a nobleman – 1st Baron Dunleath – in 1892.

Irish new money was clearly attracted by Classical symbols. But it was English millionaires who showed greatest loyalty to the style. Grossly Italianate, for instance, was Oaklands Park, Gloucestershire: another Pall Mall palazzo, built in the 1840s by Henry Crawshay, second son of the third Iron King, but marooned this time on the banks of the Severn. Equally large, though in this case eccentrically Italianate, was a very strange mansion, Grittleton House, Wiltshire (J. Thomson; 1842 onwards), built by Joseph Neeld to contain his collection of Neo-Classical marbles. Neeld had inherited some £900,000 in 1827 from his great-uncle, Philip Rundell of Rundell and Bridge, goldsmiths to the Crown.[94] That money, so cunningly accumulated from French royalist refugees, was quickly spent – and spent with a particular purpose. Like so many millionaires before and since, the Neelds seized the opportunity of being absorbed into the landed class. So too did the Evanses of Worcester. Edward Bickerton Evans was never quite a millionaire, but he did own the biggest vinegar factory in the world. That was enough to trigger county ambitions; and recruited – or self-recruited – into the county set he certainly was. Successively High Sheriff of Herefordshire and of Worcestershire, he symbolised his rising status by building the last Greek Revival country house in England: Whitbourne Hall, Herefordshire, designed by Edmund

Elmslie in 1860–62[95] [plate 6]. Now, Evans's tastes were not exclusively Neo-Classical: his vinegar warehouse in Gracechurch Street, London was famously Gothic. But a country seat was different: its status cried out for Classicism.

This fondness of the very rich for Classicism of all kinds continued throughout the nineteenth century. Its format remained integral to the imagery of authority: 'White and modern,' concluded Bulwer-Lytton in 1862, '[here is] the handwriting of our race, in this practical nineteenth century, on its square plain masonry and Doric shafts.'[96] One example at least has an arch poignancy. When in 1906 John Lancaster III – not a millionaire, but a substantial magnate, owner of the Rugby Gas Company – decided to build himself a house, he was only too conscious of the symbolism involved. His father, John Lancaster II, Chairman of the Lancashire Main Railway, had been elected Liberal MP for Wigan in the reformed Parliament of 1868. Two years before that he had purchased Bilton Grange in Warwickshire from the brother-in-law of Pugin's patron, the 16th Earl of Shrewsbury; and there, in manorial splendour, he had installed a glass case containing a single pair of clogs: to remind his family of its origins. That was perhaps mock modesty; but his son's house nearby – Dunchurch Lodge, near Rugby, designed by Gilbert Frazer and T.H. Morrison in the year of the Liberal avalanche – made a subtler but equally symbolic statement: its cherry red brickwork was unmistakably Wrenaissance.[97]

The imagery of the Classical tradition survived even the vernacular instincts of the Arts and Crafts movement. In 1897 Sir Weetman Pearson, 1st Bt, later 1st Viscount Cowdray – contractor extraordinary – called in Aston Webb to add a sumptuous Baroque dining room to Paddockhurst, Sussex. This was a house previously designed by Salvin for George Smith, another contractor, who in turn sold it to Robert Whitehead, inventor of Whitehead's torpedo. Pearson's achievements – from digging the Blackwall Tunnel to damming the Blue Nile – clearly called for something special. Walter Crane supplied a frieze which allegorised the history of locomotion, culminating with an image of Lady Pearson riding a silver bicycle from Tiffany's.[98] In the same year appeared another symbolic house, but built this time in very sober vein: Red Court, Haslemere, Surrey [plates 74–5], designed by Ernest Newton for John Stefanovitch Schillizzi, a millionaire twice over from foreign trade. Red Court's Classicism is so restrained, so terrified of overstatement, as to be almost invisible. But Classical it is, none the less. Such houses – another is Moundsmere, Hampshire [plate 72], designed in 1908–9 by Reginald Blomfield for an Anglo-American trader, William Buckley – marked the final stage of the Classical tradition in English domestic architecture. In the hands of Newton and Blomfield, Classical had now become Neo-Georgian, sterile or suave according to taste.[99]

All these are instances of Classical mansions newly commissioned by millionaires or near-millionaires. But the ideal example is perhaps Manderston, Berwickshire [plate 26], rebuilt to designs by John Kinross in 1894–1905 for the Russia merchant Sir James Miller, 2nd Bt. His father, Sir William Miller, 1st Bt, had made a fortune out of Baltic hemp and herrings; the second baronet married Lord Curzon's sister. Sir William had made his house French Renaissance; Sir James re-made it Neo-Classical. Regenerating Robert Adam – without Adam's sense of scale – Manderston perfectly represents the Classicising (or socialising) of new money. When the architect tentatively enquired about the prospective cost, he received the perfect reply: 'It doesn't really matter.' There was of course a marble bathroom; but there was also a silver-plated bath. The ballroom curtains provided by the Parisian decorator Charles Mellier were woven with gold and silver thread. The stair-rails were made of crystal. There were so many echoes of Kedleston that Curzon himself felt quite at home. Today it survives complete, with its formal gardens, and with all its auxiliary buildings – lodges, stables, steadings – in appropriately lower-case vernacular: an epitome of the hierarchy of established taste, Classical at the top, vernacular at the bottom.[100]

So new money played safe – witness one prototypical instance: Joseph Love of Durham. Starting work as a boy at the coal-face, he became an itinerant trader and then married the daughter of a Jarrow timber-merchant. Spotting the advantages of low-grade coal for coking, he bought up – and ruthlessly exploited – large sections of the Durham coalfield. His relentless drive for wealth – at his death he had over

£1 million in the bank – brought him eventually to Mount Beaulah, Durham (1858), an overblown villa in richest Italianate.[101] There – stylistically speaking – he could look established landowners in the eye. No doubt another self-made magnate from a little further north, the railway contractor Sir Walter Scott, 1st Bt, of Beauclere, Riding Mill, Northumberland, felt much the same.[102] And one object of emulation lay just the other side of the Tyne: Bywell Hall, seat of Wentworth Beaumont, 1st Baron Allendale, a Classical mansion by Paine and Dobson (1766; 1817), already the focus of an old estate, but an old estate newly enriched by mineral wealth.[103]

Millionaires – at least those who died millionaires – turn out on the whole, then, to have been stylistically conservative: like John Remington Mills, silk manufacturer and merchant. At Tolmers Park, Newgate Street, near Hertford – and at his shooting box, Clermont, near Thetford in Norfolk – he seated himself behind the most conventional of porticoes, Ionic and Doric respectively.[104] Similarly the future 1st Earl of Iveagh, king of Guinness, at Farmleigh (1881; 1900) in Phoenix Park, Dublin.[105] There his house, though luxurious inside, was conventionally, discreetly Georgian: a big house trying to look (fairly) small, and at the same time absorbing the Classical manners of the Ascendancy. At Elveden Hall, Suffolk [plate 57], enlarged in 1899–1904 for Iveagh by William Young, there was at least no worry about size; but its style had to be sober enough not to frighten the pheasants. The result, in a kind of Anglo-French Baroque, was municipal rather than patrician. Inside Iveagh did indulge himself with a vast, centrally-heated marble hall in Indo-Islamic style: the apotheosis of Edwardian eclecticism. The details seem to echo the Taj Mahal; but the room's spatial dynamics are curiously Baroque. And even here precedent ruled: the Guinnesses were merely keeping up with the décor of the previous owner, the Maharaja Duleep Singh. Duleep's drawing room had been designed in 1869 to evoke the glitter and sparkle of the legendary Shish Mahal, or Glass Palace, in India. Iveagh decided to follow suit: his Durbar Hall was supposedly based on 'the best examples of Mughal architecture'. But one suspects that comfort was the overriding consideration. 'Chips' Channon certainly loved the house's 'calm . . . luxurious Edwardian atmosphere'; Elveden, Augustus Hare had already agreed, was 'almost appallingly luxurious, such masses of orchids, electric lights everywhere etc . . . [and] an electric piano which goes on pounding away by itself with a pertinacity which is perfectly distracting'.[106]

The taste of Sir Henry Tate, inventor of the sugar cube, was certainly Classical. Besides commissioning a whole series of Baroque galleries and libraries by S.R.J. Smith, he chose as his own residence Park Hill on Streatham Common, a Classical house by J.B. Papworth (1830–41). This he duly extended in 1880.[107] Classical too was the style chosen by an even greater figure in the history of art patronage, Sir Richard Wallace. His was not exactly new money: he inherited as the illegitimate son of the 4th Marquess of Hertford. Wallace was one of those Victorian millionaires who spent a good deal of time abroad, like John Bowes of the Bowes Museum – another illegitimate son who lived many years in Paris – and Sir Francis Cook, who employed J.T. Knowles Snr to redesign Montserrat Palace at Cintra, Portugal (1858–65).[108] In Wallace's case the chosen retreat was Bagatelle in the Bois de Boulogne. He did buy a Georgian house, Sudbourne Hall, Suffolk – later the childhood home of Lord Clark of *Civilisation* – and inevitably he enlarged it. And he did build himself an Italianate mansion in Ireland, Castle House, Lisburn, designed by Thomas Ambler in 1880. But his chief concern was that extraordinary art collection at Hertford House, London.[109] Salting and Tate, Iveagh, Morrison and Cook – to say nothing of Mond in his buccaneering way – were all collectors of distinction; the Rothschild treasures were hardly negligible; but the Wallace collection – thanks largely to the acquisitions of the 4th Marquess of Hertford – was a formidable accumulation. Wallace was a committed Francophile, and the whole ethos of his collection was French. When Hertford House was reconstructed – again by Ambler – in 1872–5, its principal feature was an architectural trophy salvaged from the French capital: the staircase of the Hôtel de Nevers, better known as the Bibliothèque du Roi. This preference for Gallic grandeur brings us to a recurrent theme in the taste of the richest Victorian and Edwardian *nouveaux riches*: a fondness, sometimes a passion, for a more exotic form of Classicism, the French château style.

Classicism pure and simple could be perhaps too safe, too discreet; depriving the millionaire of his full measure of self-expression. The answer, in that case, was to choose a form of Classicism which was almost limitlessly rich: an eclectic Renaissance which synthesised Italian, French and English.

We can watch the synthesis developing in Preston Hall, Aylesford, Kent (1844–50) [plates 50, 52–3], indigestibly designed by John Thomas for one railway baron, E.L. Betts, and then redecorated for another – and even richer – man, H.A. Brassey, co-heir to the fortune of Thomas Brassey. At this stage the ornament – in Pevsner's words, 'repellent in the extreme' – is still English Renaissance in origin. So too is the over-ripe decoration of Somerleyton Hall, Suffolk (J. Thomas; 1844–51) [plate 51], begun for Samuel Morton Peto and completed for Sir Francis Crossley.[110] Then comes Overstone Park, Northamptonshire (1859–65) [plate 49], rebuilt to designs by W.M. Teulon in a mongrel François Premier mode for the banking millionaire Samuel Loyd, 1st Baron Overstone. This unlovely mansion seems to have been foisted on the unwilling magnate by his wife's 'extraordinary enthusiasm for building'. Perhaps she did indeed choose the architect; but only the younger Teulon could have chosen the style: Franco-Jacobethan-Renaissance. 'The New House', Overstone complained angrily, 'is the source of unmitigated disappointment and vexation. It is an utter failure ... The House though very large and full of pretension, has neither taste, comfort nor convenience. I am utterly ashamed of it ... I grieve to think that I shall hand such an abortion to my successors ... [We might as well] have undertaken to whitewash a black-a-moor.'[111] Pevsner just calls it 'asymmetricalissime'. The house was certainly as grandiloquent as Overstone's portfolio of landed estates, accumulated over the years in no fewer than six counties.[112] In only slightly lower key, Rendcomb House, near Cirencester, Gloucestershire, was redesigned in 1863 by P.C. Hardwick for Sir Francis Goldsmid, bullion broker, in a loud Italian manner with touches of French detail in the stables.[113] The style here is still best described as eclectic Renaissance, but the vocabulary is changing: by the mid 1860s, the French accent was becoming stronger than the Italian. By 1867, at Normanhurst, near Battle, Sussex, Thomas Brassey – another of the three sons of the railway king – was able to go wholeheartedly French. The Brasseys liked to think that they had Norman blood, and the house was built as near as possible to the site of the Battle of Hastings. 'The outlay', commented *The Builder* tartly, 'has, of course, been large.'[114]

No doubt Lord Leverhulme spoke for most British plutocrats when he set out the following stylistic menu: 'I prefer Georgian dining rooms as the rooms in which to give large dinners. For small dining rooms I prefer Tudor. For drawing rooms I prefer what is called the Adam style; for entrance halls the Georgian.' Appropriately, at Thornton Manor, Cheshire (1888–1914) – Tudor outside; mixed Classical within – he employed half a dozen architects, and almost as many variations of style.[115] Such miscellanies seldom made for good design. Port Sunlight has an honourable place in the history of social housing; but when it came to his own houses, Leverhulme – always collecting, always building – was really in too much of a hurry to think about stylistic consequences. In 1928 the 27th Earl of Crawford and 10th Earl of Balcarres visited one of Leverhulme's conflations, The Bungalow, Rivington, near Bolton. His comments – very much *de haut en bas* – were scathing:

> What a place! The late Leverhulme bought it years ago, kept extending it – only a year or two before his death [in 1925] he added a huge ballroom – and now this preposterous accumulation of rooms and verandahs is perched in the middle of Rivington Moor; large gardens [by Mawson] surround the house itself, and the week after he died a hundred gardeners were sacked. What a queer old fellow he was. He was uncontrolled and one sees the odd potpourri of rubbish and good things he collected – a few really nice bits of tapestry hung between monstrous forgeries, and a number of wretched canvases by RAs of the eighties and nineties.[116]

Perhaps Leverhulme felt that Rivington Moor cried out for a touch of Picturesque rusticity: the park includes a full-scale replica of Liverpool Castle in ruins. If so, few shared his taste. Roynton Cottage, as The Bungalow was eventually called, was first burned by suffragettes and then demolished by Liverpool Corporation.

In London, at least, and in his eponymous art gallery at Port Sunlight, Leverhulme chose Classicism. And, given a free hand, it seems likely that Victorian and Edwardian millionaires would surely have agreed, even if they preferred their Classicism French: *tutti Louis*, as the decorators say, especially for interiors. That had been Thomas Holloway's preference when he insisted on the château style for Royal Holloway College; John Bowes's too, when he endowed the Bowes Museum at Barnard Castle (J. Pellechet, 1869).[117] Its advantage was a combination of ostentation and flexibility. Chronologically, the style ranged all the way from Renaissance to Beaux-Arts; from François Premier to Second Empire. It was a style which appealed most powerfully to the imagination of the next, American and South African, generation of plutocrats. When Isaac Singer, the sewing-machine king, retreated to The Wigwam, Paignton, Devon, in 1873 he specified French Renaissance as the style of his house. This choice was more than maintained by his son, Paris Singer, who remodelled the interior *à la Versailles*.[118] But by that date the French château style can have caused no real surprise. Henry Clutton had supplied it – complete with a skyline worthy of Blois – as early as 1858–62 for Raikes Currie, banker, at Minley Manor, Hampshire; at much the same time Sir Benjamin Guinness, 1st Bt, transformed a Georgian shooting box into a French château at Ashford, Co. Galway (1855 onwards; later much extended); Samuel Barbour, the Belfast linen magnate, built himself a Franco-Italian mansion at Danesfort, Co. Antrim (W.J. Barre, 1864); and at Bedgebury Park, Kent (Carpenter and Slater, 1854–9) even an ecclesiologist like Beresford Hope reverted to his banking roots by opting for Louis Quatorze.[119] By the late 1860s the vague eclecticism of 'Old French' had clearly become a recognised symbol of ostentation.

It was around this time, at the end of the 1860s, that W.E. Nesfield embarked on the reconstruction of Kinmel, Denbighshire [plate 19] for Hugh Hughes, the Welsh copper magnate.[120] The Hughes family were not particularly new – they could claim descent from Prince Cadwaladr – but they were most definitely newly rich. From the copper mines of the Parys Mountains came profits sufficient to create not one but two major country houses. The first was a sprawling Greek Revival mansion by Samuel Wyatt and Thomas Hopper. The second, as remodelled by Nesfield in 1870–4, proved to be a stylistic conjuring trick. By combining Wren's bricky façades at Hampton Court with touches of Dutch, Jacobean and even Japanese, Nesfield set out the agenda of the Queen Anne Revival. In a sense he had Anglicised 'Old French' for the British domestic market.

Even so, a display of French *boiserie* remained socially *outré*, very much a *nouveau-riche* characteristic. When from 1893 onwards William Waldorf Astor fitted out his dining room at Cliveden with Rococo trimmings from the Château d'Asnières, near Paris, he surely surprised nobody. But when Henry Isaac Butterfield – a Yorkshire manufacturer with Parisian connections – crammed Cliffe Castle, Yorkshire (G. Smith; 1875–8; 1883) with draperies *à la français*, he must certainly have astonished the burgesses of Keighley. Butterfield, however, had access to two *nouveau riche* trump cards: French taste and American money. Mrs Butterfield – a niece of Judge Roosevelt of New York – had once been a favourite of the Empress Eugénie. With the fall of the Second Empire, she no doubt hankered after a little courtly opulence. There were gilded capitals of Caen stone, and ceilings painted by Leroux. There were five interconnecting drawing rooms draped with silk and hung with figured satin. There were French carpets, and French chandeliers: some had actually been owned by Lord Byron, others by the great Napoleon himself. There was a French chimney-piece of malachite mounted with ormolu, and French furniture said to come from the residence of the duc de Mornay. There were even French volumes in the library. And gazing down on all this, glowing in stained glass, were 'all the present and past members of the Butterfield family', not to mention 'the steward of the estate . . . [and] the late Emperor of the French . . . [and] the Empress Eugénie [and even] . . . the Madonna and Child . . . All figures, except of course the Madonna and Child, [rejoicing] in Elizabethan dress'.[121] Clearly *tutti Louis* would have been too precise a term for so much Anglo-French *bric-à-brac*.

Ever since Benjamin Wyatt launched the Rococo revival at Crockford's Club (1827; 1850s) it had been a style which carried overtones of the casino. In the words of the Regency decorator George Smith, it was a style 'in no ways answerable to the dwellings of persons of small fortune'. J.D. Jagger, the original 'man who broke the bank at Monte

Carlo', scooped £80,000 at the roulette tables in 1886 before dying of boredom in 1892 worth only £2,000. Had he managed to build himself a house in his native Bradford, it would surely have been decorated in the 'Old French' style. For by that date no newly-minted millionaire would have settled for anything else. 'Arriviste', 'millionaire', 'nouveau riche', 'parvenu': the very words themselves were French. And French Classicism had all the overtones of opulence. It was the style of the *belle époque*. By 1903, when the Wernhers came to remodel Luton Hoo, it must have seemed quite natural for them to choose as their architects Messrs Mewes and Davis of the Ritz Hotel. Their decorators – George Hoentschal of Maison Leys, Paris – were in turn more specific: they made it Louis XV. Fabergé in the dining room, *boiserie* in the drawing room, Luton Hoo is quintessentially plutocratic. Indeed, the staircase hall [plate 56] of this much-altered house – gilded, marbled and bronzed, in all its Beaux-Arts elegance – sums up the highest aspirations of millionaires' country-house taste.[122]

It was the Rothschild family who took this French fashion to its extreme. In 1885 T.H.S. Escott, editor of the *Fortnightly Review* and a perceptive if waspish commentator, noted that 'English society, once ruled by an aristocracy, is now dominated by plutocracy. And this plutocracy is to a large extent Hebraic in composition.' No doubt he had in mind the Rothschild purchase in the 1850s and 1870s of large swathes of Buckinghamshire, chiefly from the families of the Dukes of Buckingham and Marlborough. In 1907 he recorded the advance of so much new money in a splendidly orotund passage:

> The rural dominion of the Rothschilds begins with suburban Gunnersbury; it stretches to the Chilterns. Their country houses within this area have brought fertilising capital into impoverished neighbourhoods, have studded them with model farms and with improved dwellings for a long neglected peasantry ... Smart indeed, or rather magnificent, all their dwellings are, but today, whether it be from Lord Rothschild's Tring, Mr Alfred Rothschild's Halton, his brother's Ascott, or his cousin's Waddesdon; the Israelitish annexation of Buckinghamshire and its modish hospi-

talities have given the toiling masses of the country no reason to regret the replacement of old landlords by new.[123]

Surtees, less generously, rechristened the Vale of Aylesbury 'Jewdaea'.[124]

When Lionel Nathan de Rothschild purchased Tring Park, Hertfordshire in 1873 he was content with a Classical house by no less an architect than Sir Christopher Wren. It was the 1st Baron ('Natty') Rothschild – probably with the help of George Devey – who turned that house into a version of a French château [plates 67–8]. When he stayed there as a young man Lord Crawford was so appalled – 'overpowering ostentation and vulgarity' – that he vowed 'never again [to] stay in one of the big Jewish houses'. When he returned in 1939, to organise its conversion for purposes of biological research, he was equally aghast:

> I was horrified by the whole *mise-en-scène*. Though many of the pictures have been removed and furniture has been collected in various rooms according to categories, one has a very good idea of what the house was like. In one room was a group of thirty clocks, table clocks which were all modern and would cost up to £50 apiece. Horrors. Another room seemed to have 20–30 sideboards ornamented with modern Sèvres plaques. Awful inlaid chairs and tables were classified, huge costly fitments, vast China vases of the worst period, sophisticated tapestries, mantlepieces which ruined the whole room – I passed from one monstrous apartment to another with ever growing consternation.[125]

Enthusiasm for all things French – *le goût Rothschild* – could clearly run out of control.

Waddesdon Manor, Buckinghamshire (1877–83; 1889) [plate 66] was actually designed by a Frenchman, H.A.G.W. Destailleur, and it epitomises this recurrent strand of millionaire taste; the ideal, at this point, of Baron Ferdinand de Rothschild. His house was as richly eclectic – 'Blois, Chambord, Anet, Maintenon' – as his world-famous collection of works of art. There were emus and mountain goats in the park, and in the dairy a collection of Dresden porcelain animals. Outside there were echoes of the Loire; inside, trophies from Versailles and several Parisian hotels. The Green Boudoir has been traced to the rue de Richelieu, the Marble Dining Room to the rue de Grenelle, the

Grey Drawing Room to the rue de Varenne. These rooms, in fact, were encrusted with *boiserie* from half a dozen French mansions. Gladstone's daughter Mary was not at all pleased: 'felt much oppressed', she noted in her diary, 'with the extreme gorgeousness and luxury'. 'The pictures in [Baron Ferdinand's] sitting room are too beautiful, but there is not a book in the house save some twenty improper French novels.'[126] Lord Crawford – at least in 1898 – was more sympathetic: 'the ostentation was as marked as at Tring, but being a bachelor establishment there was less nonsense and perfumery'.

> Waddesdon is a marvellous creation; a real creation – not an old mansion taken over with its gardens, park and stabling – but a vast château built by its present owner, surrounded by endless gardens planted by him, and towering over a big park reclaimed from agricultural meadows by our host . . . [However] I failed to gather that his priceless treasures gave him true pleasure. His clock for which he gave £25,000, his escritoire for which £30,000 was paid, his statuary, his china, and his superb collection of jewels, enamels and so forth ('gimcracks' he calls them) – all these things give him meagre satisfaction.

Some guests, at least, revelled in the luxury of it all: R.B. Haldane, for instance. 'I love luxury,' he admitted . . . 'Yes – I do love all seemly luxury. When lying abed in the morning it gives me satisfaction when a lacquey softly enters the room and asks whether I will take tea, coffee, chocolate or cocoa. This privilege is accorded to me in the houses of all my distinguished friends: but it is only at Waddesdon that on saying I prefer tea, the valet further enquires whether I fancy Ceylon, Souchong, or Assam.'[127] Henry James was more caustic. After visiting Waddesdon in 1885, he noted drily: 'the gilded bondage of that gorgeous place will last me for a long time'.[128]

Aston Clinton, Buckinghamshire, rebuilt in the Italianate style by Sir Anthony de Rothschild in the 1850s to designs by G.H. Stokes, can never have been so exciting; but Halton House [plate 71], in the same county, designed in 1881–84 by W.R. Rogers (né Rodriguez) for Baron Alfred de Rothschild, is – in Henry James's phrase – characteristically 'Rothschildish'. Like Tring and Waddesdon – and like Alice de Rothschild's Eythrope Pavilion, designed by George Devey in 1876–9 – its style eludes all labels except the generic 'French'. Sir Algernon West, Gladstone's closest confidant, was appalled. He had to admit that the Rothschilds knew how to play the *grand seigneur*: 'In the cold bitterness of winter mornings,' he noted in 1895, Baron Alfred 'sent a cart round every morning with hot coffee and bread and butter to every labourer on his estate.' But Halton itself – for all its 'lovely pictures' – was 'an exaggerated nightmare of gorgeousness and senseless and ill-applied magnificence'.[129] Everything was done to excess. Looking back on those heady days at the turn of the century, one of the junior gardeners recalled a veritable riot of bedding plants:

> I once heard it said that rich people used to show their wealth by the size of their bedding-plant list: 10,000 plants for a squire; 20,000 for a baronet; 30,000 for an earl and 50,000 for a duke. Mr Rothschild aimed pretty high, because my list for 1903, with no fewer than 40,418 plants, put him well above an earldom.

In the winter-garden – kept consistently at 63 °F – the proud proprietor liked to conduct a Hungarian band; he even surveyed his park from a dogcart drawn by two zebras. Lady Frances Balfour, daughter of a duke and sister-in-law of a prime minister, was brutally scornful:

> I have seldom seen anything more memorably vulgar [than Halton House]. Outside it is a combination of a French Château, and a gambling house. Inside it is badly planned ... and gaudily decorated ... oh! but the hideousness of everything, the showiness! the sense of lavish wealth thrust up your nose! the coarse mouldings; the heavy gilding always in the wrong place, the colour of the silk hangings! Eye hath not seen nor pen can write the ghastly coarseness of the sight![130]

Impney Hall, Worcestershire – later known as Château Impney [plate 70] – is not a Rothschild house, nor was it designed for a full-blown millionaire. It was conceived in 1869–75 by Auguste Tronquois for a rich salt manufacturer, John Corbett. But its style is very much an echo of the Rothschild dream;[131] the style of grand hotels and great extravagance; an image to which, as we shall see, lesser and shadier magnates – Jabez Balfour, for instance, or the ill-starred Baron Grant – were also dangerously susceptible. Brewers like Charles Combe (of

Watney, Combe and Reid), who chose E.M. Barry to rebuild
Cobham Park, Surrey (1870–3) in 'very ugly French Renaissance';[132]
merchant bankers like George (later Viscount) Goschen, who –
following Beresford Hope – chose Carpenter and Slater to design
Seacox Heath, Hawkhurst, Sussex (1867–72) in the form of a Renaissance Gothic château:[133] these were the sort of men – certainly rich,
often millionaires – whose dream of perfection was the Louvre of
Napoleon III or the high-flown turrets of the Loire. Thomas Cundy
designed one such house (Park Place, Henley-on-Thames, 1868–70)
for John Noble, a paint manufacturer.[134] E.M. Barry designed another
in the north of England (Stancliffe Hall, Derbyshire, 1879) for Sir
Joseph Whitworth, armaments manufacturer, and two more in the
south, both for new money from London: Shabden, near Chipstead,
Surrey (1871–5) for John Cattley, a Baltic merchant; and – grandest of
them all – Wykehurst, near Bolney, Sussex (1871–4), a mansion commissioned by the bibliophile banking heir Henry Huth. Huth's
father had been the epitome of caution: he 'always disapproved of
excessive luxury, considering it wrong that bankers should blossom
out as landed gentry'.[135] His sons soon put paid to that idea. Wykehurst combined the silhouette of a Loire château with the opulence
of a metropolitan hotel.

By mixing Jacobean, Italian and French Renaissance, this *nouveau-
riche* style managed to look above all *expensive*. When in 1875 a copper
magnate, Francis Tress Barry, employed C.H. Howell to remodel St
Leonard's Hill, near Windsor [plate 69],[136] he managed to make it
look very expensive indeed. The house gazed out over a glorious view
of Windsor Castle. The roof-line bulged with protruding pyramidal
mansards. The octagonal staircase was lined with huge slabs of
Mexican onyx.

> 'We got to have Style [said Mr Ponderevo]. See! Style! Just all right and
> one better. That's what I call Style ... [Anyway] it's a very useful lan-
> guage, [French] ... puts a point on things ... It's a Bluff. It's all a Bluff.
> Life's a Bluff ... That's why it's so important ... for us to attend to
> Style.'[137]

Of course, not every millionaire went French. Neither Sir John

Schröder nor his nephew Baron Bruno, for example, followed that stylistic route. At The Dell (1864–70) and again at Dell Park (1912–14), Englefield Green, Surrey – not far from St Leonard's Hill – they both enjoyed a life of comfortable, gabled obscurity. But when a millionaire consciously set out to make a stylistic statement, it usually ended up as some form of French Classicism. By the end of the century this very *nouveau-riche* mode had emerged as a style fit for courtiers and cosmopolites, from the d'Abernons at Esher Place to the Marlboroughs at Blenheim; for anyone indeed who aspired to the magic circle of the Prince of Wales. When May Goelet, American wife of the 8th Duke of Roxburghe, came to redecorate Floors Castle, she made sure that even the electric light switches were Louis XVI. 'Few decorative styles', enthused *The Lady* in 1899, 'have ever been devised which possess the fascination of the Louis Seize.'[138]

Interiors in the *nouveau-riche* style are abundant. At Witley Court, Worcestershire from 1855 onwards, the future 1st Earl of Dudley – hugely rich from coal royalties – greatly expanded a Neo-Classical house by John Nash, including in his operations an impressive music gallery, *à la* Louis Quinze [plates 1–2, 62].[139] His family had been prosperous since the seventeenth century; now they were excessively rich. He was rumoured to have spent no less than £250,000 on improvements. Nesfield's elaborate gardens astonished visitors; Forsyth's gargantuan fountain became a visible symbol of wealth, quite 'barbarous in its magnificence' [see back cover]. But it was that Rococo gallery which epitomised the taste of the richest of the rich. It was a style which could survive almost any amount of dilution. At King's Walden Bury, Hertfordshire (1893) [plates 54–60], for example, T.F. Harrison, a Liverpool shipping millionaire, smothered his dining room with second-hand French ornament. And at Redleaf House, near Penshurst, Kent, 1870 onwards, the chemical magnate Frank Hills festooned his drawing room with what can only be described as Louis Chintz décor [plate 61]. 'There was a . . . grand piano with a painted lid and a metrostyle pianola, and an extraordinary quantity of artistic litter and *bric-à-brac* scattered about. There was the trail of the Bond Street showroom over it all.'[140] These Anglo-French interiors – so loathed by H.G. Wells – must always have seemed exotic in an English country-house setting. It was basically a metropolitan style, the style of the new plutocracy. Mrs Humphry Ward called it 'Monte Cristoish'.

Mentmore Towers, Buckinghamshire, designed by Paxton and Stokes in 1850–4 for Baron Meyer Amschel de Rothschild, is mixed Renaissance of a staider kind on the outside; it was modelled in fact on Wollaton, Nottinghamshire. But inside it was famously crammed with French furniture. 'It was like a fairyland,' remembered Lady Eastlake, 'filled with gorgeous masses of flowers and every sumptuous object that wealth can command ... the house is a museum of everything ... I do not believe the Medici were so housed at the height of their glory.'[141] Disraeli visited this extraordinary place soon after its construction and hastened to write a breathless description to Lady Londonderry. Mentmore, he explained is 'a hunting palace'; to the Vale of Aylesbury 'what Belvoir is to the vale of that name'.

> For more than fifteen years Rothschild has had agents in every part of Europe, regardless of cost, collecting its contents, but the taste of their distribution is as remarkable as their curiosity and costliness. The hall [is a] ... masterpiece of modern art and decoration, glowing with colour, lit by gorgeous Venetian lamps of golden filigree that once were at the head of Bucentaurs. Such chairs – Titian alone could paint them, such clocks of lapis lazuli, such cabinets of all forms and colours, such marble busts of turbaned Moors, such a staircase of polished marble from this vast central salon for such it really is, glittering with its precious contents, and yet the most comfortable and liveable-in apartment in the world ... [142]

Here was a paradigm of plutocratic luxury, complete with hot-water heating and artificial ventilation. Nearly one hundred years later – with less benefit from central heating – Chips Channon stayed at Mentmore and felt again the grandeur and absurdity of the place.

> It must be twenty years since I stayed here and I had forgotten what glorious meubles and pictures they have. There are twelve Fragonards in my bedroom, small ones, but Fragonards, and all over the large cold, icy palace are French pictures of the very finest quality; more and better, too, than the ones at Boughton [Northamptonshire]. A pair of cupboards, not yet removed, they have just sold for £15,000. There is a pathetic Sèvres model of 'Papillon', Marie Antoinette's favourite dog ... several Rembrandts, and two pictures of Madame de Pompadour. I have never seen

such richesse, not even at Lançut [in Poland] ... I am, I fear, sick with envy.

Perhaps Channon was also feeling a little guilty. On his previous visit, having over-indulged the night before, he 'somehow smashed ... Napoleon's [chamber] pot ... a very grand affair covered with 'N's and Bees'.[143] Henry James was more reverential. The collection, he surmised, had been 'written in great syllables of colour and form, the tongues of other countries and the hands of rare artists. It was all France and Italy with their ages composed to rest. For England you looked out of old windows.'[144]

Today Mentmore is a collection no more. This supreme example of millionaire's taste – at best gorgeously miscellaneous, at worst a pile of 'geegaws and hideous rarities' – was dispersed in the sale of 1977. But many of the choicest treasures found their way to Dalmeny, the Rosebery seat in West Lothian: a prime example of City money ensnared by the landed embrace, and now appropriately guarded by a Derby winner cast in bronze.

One striking fact does emerge from a study of the country houses of Victorian and Edwardian millionaires: very few were designed by architects of the first rank, and even fewer have proved to be, art-historically speaking, of the first importance. Quite a few now seem just impossibly ugly. But the setting of many of these houses was, and often still is, spectacular. Crawshay's Caversham was magnificently placed. Loder at Leonardslee, Faringdon at Buscot, Sassoon at Trent Park [plates 76–7] and Port Lympne [plate 80]: all these created superb gardens. At Witley Court [plates 1–2] and Somerleyton [plate 51] W.A. Nesfield's formal parterres were perhaps the most elaborate in England; and at Waddesdon [plate 66], Baron Ferdinand de Rothschild managed to conjure up a forest of transplanted trees, appropriately rich and instantly venerable. The formal gardens at Waddesdon – designed by yet another Frenchman, Elie Lainé – remain a triumph of complexity and colour. But however glorious the setting, the buildings themselves often disappoint. The composition of Waddesdon, for instance, is considerably less than the sum of its parts. When in 1939 Chips Channon called on Mrs Ronnie Greville at Polesden Lacey [plate 65] – a minor Georgian house aggrandised twice over with banker's and brewer's money – he could not disguise his disappointment. White Allom and Mewes and Davis had done their best: there were *boiseries* in the tea room and a Wren reredos in the hall; the drawing room was filled with panelling in the style of Louis Quatorze, especially imported from Italy. But Channon found the whole effect stultifying.

> I drove in the rain to Polesden Lacey, where I had not been for fifteen years, a long time. The gardens are glorious, the grounds magnificently green and well kept. Everywhere there is the silence, and graciousness that come from long-established wealth. But the house, while Edwardian to a degree and comfortable and full of rare china and expensive treasures, is really a monster.[145]

Some architects specialised in catering for the super-rich: J.T. Wimperis, Romaine-Walker, Philip Tilden, A.N. Prentice, for example. They were certainly not untalented, but – perhaps as a consequence of limitless budgets – they did tend to gild every possible lily. Tilden's unexecuted castle for Gordon Selfridge on Hengistbury Head, Hampshire (1919) – to take an extreme example – would surely have been more a nightmare than a dream.[146] When *The Spectator* produced its survey of millionaires in 1872 it suggested that their houses were often architecturally 'shocking' because as patrons they tended to dominate their architects.[147] There may be something in that: Westonbirt and Overstone [plate 49], for example, both suffered from overbearing clients. Art dealers, of necessity, tend to be professionally accommodating. But top-flight architects expect to call the aesthetic tune. A self-made magnate, used to getting his own way, might well prefer a pliant, pedestrian designer to some celebrated prima donna. After all, the client does hold all the best cards. Sometimes that client may be inhibitingly austere: Leverhulme slept in a bare bedroom, open to the four winds; he even exercised with Indian clubs at dawn. More often a monied patron simply had too many business distractions. When

David Davies – 'Dai Davies yr Ocean' – king of the Ocean Coal Company, built himself a house (Broneirion, Llandinam, Montgomeryshire; designed by D. Walker in 1864) he chose an unimaginative architect and an unimaginative style: Italianate.[148] No doubt he was too busy to bother. And there may be another factor, too. Perhaps an element of caution – or, to put it bluntly, downright miserliness – comes into the equation. Had the sample in this chapter been drawn not from men who left a million but from men who spent, say, half a million – actually an impossible category to quantify – then the result might well have been very different. No architect enjoys working for a miserly patron. Thomas and Samuel Fielden, for instance, were both famously tight-fisted, to say nothing of Joseph Love and Christian Allhusen. James Morrison, who was said to be worth £4 million – say £200,000,000 today – lived in terror of ending his days in a workhouse.

Still, whatever the cause, hardly any country houses built by newmoney millionaires are cited as key buildings in textbooks of architectural history (leaving aside Nesfield's mould-breaking performance at Kinmel) [plate 19]. Such a brief list would certainly include Cragside, Northumberland (1869–75) [plate 18], built for Lord Armstrong the armaments king, to designs by Richard Norman Shaw.[149]

> And on yon brown and rocky hill
> See princely Cragside lies
> Where boundless wealth and perfect taste
> Have made a paradise.

Cragside's romantic site, perched on a rocky ledge high up above the River Coquet, made any form of exterior Classicism impossible. Instead it forms one of a group of perhaps three or four houses of this period which fall into the category of *avant-garde* or trend-setting designs – in this case Old English in style – produced for millionaire patrons. The others would include Beauvale House, Greasley, Nottinghamshire, designed in 1872 for Earl Cowper by E.W. Godwin;[150] and Dawpool, Cheshire (1882–84), also designed by Shaw, for the shipping magnate Thomas Henry Ismay;[151] as well as another stylistically very advanced mansion, the now demolished Cloverley, Shropshire, designed in 1864 by Nesfield for the Liverpool banker J.P.

Heywood.[152] Houses such as these were not typical of the richest *nouveau-riche* taste; if anything they anticipate in magnified form the cosy preferences of the suburban bourgeoisie. Millionaires tended to prefer something more traditionally assertive: columns and pediments; plenty of crystal; and, above all, oodles of ormolu. Even Cragside could not entirely resist the Renaissance: Shaw's drawing room inglenook is a riot of multi-coloured marble putti.

Two millionaire patrons, W.R. Sutton and William Whiteley, can claim responsibility for buildings of unusual interest. A millionaire twice over from bulk transportation, and self-made to boot, Sutton founded the Sutton Housing Trust (Sutton Dwellings, a housing programme not unlike Peabody Buildings). He chose as architect of his own home – Sunnydene, on Sydenham Hill (1868–70), as well as its next-door neighbour, Ellerslee – no less a figure than young J.F. Bentley, the future architect of Westminster Cathedral. The result was an intriguing brick essay in eclectic Queen Anne.[153] Whiteley – the self-made Universal Provider of Whiteley's Store, Bayswater – was a patron on a rather grander scale. When he was murdered in 1907, shot by a deranged youth who claimed to be an illegitimate son, his will turned out to be a surprise: he left £1,000,000 for the creation of an ideal retreat for thrifty old people. Today Whiteley Village, near Cobham, Surrey (1911–21) – a symmetrical Hampstead Garden Suburb in miniature – boasts housing by some of the star practitioners of Edwardian Classicism: Frank Atkinson, Ernest Newton, Mervyn Macartney and Aston Webb.[154]

But Sutton and Whiteley were exceptions. The general run of country houses commissioned by millionaires does add up to a rather soporific list. Of course there are a number of outright winners: the gardens at Waddesdon [plate 66], the entrance hall at Whitbourne [plate 6], the music gallery at Witley [plate 62], the dining room at Paddockhurst, the staircase at Luton Hoo [plate 56], the *porte-cochère* at Bearwood [plate 13], even the Durbar Hall at Elveden [plate 57]. All these have an appropriately plutocratic swagger. But too many millionaire houses are simply monuments to bland extravagance. At the very least there is too often a curious mismatch – for example, between the quality of paintings collected and the quality of their country-house settings. In the end new money proves to have been just as predictable as old money in the conservatism of its architectural instincts, and rather less capable of creative patronage.

One curious footnote as regards the consistency of millionaire taste is to be found in the fact that millionaires tended not only to go for the same style, and similar locations, but even for the same house. No doubt top-calibre estates came on to the market comparatively rarely. Still, the limited repertoire of names may tell us something about the predictability of millionaires' taste. Denbies, near Dorking, Surrey, was the house first of W.J. Denison, banker; then – rebuilt in 1850 in very 'swagger Italianate' – of Thomas Cubitt, builder.[155] Combe Bank, near Sundridge, Kent, was home first to the Mannings (sugar), then to the Gurneys (banking), and then to the Monds (chemicals). Dauntsey Park, Wiltshire was in turn home to the families of Miles (sugar), Meux (beer) and Brassey (railways). The Fosters of Stourbridge bought Apley Park, Shropshire from another family of ironfounders, the Whitmores of Coalbrookdale. Ottershaw Park passed from the Crawshays (iron) to the Ecksteins (gold); and Nutfield Priory, Surrey went from the Gurneys (banking) to the Fieldens (cotton). Buscot Park, Berkshire passed in quick succession through the hands of three millionaires: Bacon Williams, Robert Campbell, and the 1st Baron Faringdon.[156] Lord Wolverton, banker and railway financier, lived at Stanmore Hall, Middlesex, where the family of William Hollond, nabob, had lived a generation before. A generation later the same house was famously redecorated by William Morris for another millionaire, the gold and oil magnate W. Knox D'Arcy.[157] Rangemore Hall, Staffordshire (R.W. Edis; 1879, etc.) was owned by two linked brewing families in succession: first Bass, then Ratcliffe.[158] Sir Andrew Walker, brewer, bought Osmaston Manor, Derbyshire from the Wrights.[159] Jack Barnato Joel bought Childwickbury from Maple. The Sassoons bought Trent Park, Hertfordshire [plates 76–7] from an older banking family, the Bevans. And at Dunstall, Staffordshire, Arkwright was followed in 1851 by the millionaire ironmaster Sir John Hardy.

Clearly these preferences were dictated as much by location as by price or style. Towards the end of the century, between Henley-on-Thames and Medmenham – conveniently close to the metropolis, but secluded in bosky Buckinghamshire – there lived a whole clutch of late Victorian millionaires: Robert Hudson the soap baron at Danesfield (W.H. Romaine-Walker; 1889–1901);[160] Edward Mackenzie the railway contractor at Fawley Court (1684; 1721);[161] Hudson Kearley, Viscount Devonport, lord of International Stores, at Whittington (Sir Reginald Blomfield; 1897–1904; 1909);[162] and W.H. Smith, greatest of newsagents, at Greenlands, near Hambledon (1853; enlarged by W.J. Green 1872). Greenlands, moreover, had previously been the home of Edward Marjoribanks, banker.[163] Close by, looking out in majesty across the Thames Valley, stood the ducal seat of Cliveden, sold in 1893 to William Waldorf Astor, 'the inevitable money-king from the United States'. 'In Mr Astor's hands,' noted Escott in 1904, 'Cliveden has become the riverside social centre for the fashion and intelligence of the Anglo-Saxon world.'[164] Needless to say, all these houses, except Tudor Gothic Danesfield, were Classical. The redecoration of Cliveden by J.D. Crace was, predictably, François Premier. And Greenlands – briefly immortalised in *Three Men in a Boat* – is a prototype rich man's retreat: its gleaming stucco bays are a generation out of date.

In the centre of London this homing – or herd – instinct concentrated as we shall see in Piccadilly, in Park Lane, in Grosvenor Square, in Kensington Palace Gardens and in St James's Square, where – not quite simultaneously – we find the Duke of Cleveland, Hudson Gurney, Earl Cowper, the Earl of Derby and the Earl of Iveagh all resident. A significant number of men who left more than £1,000,000 lived – as again we shall see – comparatively inconspicuous lives in conventional Classical houses in London. Others, of course, did not: the *nouveau-riche* interior proved to be a perfect vehicle for metropolitan ostentation. But, at least until the 1880s, neither old money nor new money made London the focus of its social ambition. And even after the decline in the value of land, the country house retained its mystique as a symbol of status and power. When Russell Sturgis, an American, became a partner at Barings in 1849 he soon began looking for a country retreat. His senior colleague, Joshua Bates, also an American, did not approve:

74

> Took a holiday [he noted in August 1856] it being Saturday and drove to Mount Felix at Walton on Thames to see the house Mr Sturgis thinks of buying. It was built by Barry, and is a palace beautifully situated on the Thames with 35 acres of land … No one should live in such a house that has not a fixed income of £10,000 a year independent of business … It would be a delightful house for a large family, the Gentleman out of business, but too far from the City for a junior partner in a commercial House. Mr S. evidently wants to have it and would agree to pay £15,000 for it, if he gets the smallest encouragement from his Partners. That would take out all his capital. Who ever heard of a man laying out all his capital on a country House?[165]

Well, Sturgis bought his house. Canny Mr Bates remained closer to London, and left £600,000. Sturgis's instinct for status overcame his business sense, and in that respect he was more typical than his critical colleague.

So the verdict leaves little room for doubt. Of the two hundred men who left more than a million pounds between the 1820s and the 1920s, the great majority – particularly those with very new money – proved extraordinarily obtuse in their choice of country house architect. Lord Leverhulme's architects, for example, may have been numerous but they were curiously undistinguished: Lutyens may have been his guest at Stornoway, but he was never employed at Lews Castle or Borve Lodge, still less at Thornton Manor, or The Bungalow, or The Hill. The Rothschild team, spread over a dozen houses in the home counties, were even more numerous and only slightly less obscure. C.S. Thelusson, having waited a lifetime for his inheritance, chose a totally obscure architect, Philip Wilkinson, for Brodsworth Hall, Yorkshire (1861–70), with an Italian sculptor – Casentini of Lucca – as an equally obscure ghost. The result, on that occasion, was surprisingly impressive. 'The 1860s', notes Mark Girouard, 'have been miraculously preserved in the amber richness of [those] rooms.'[166] But what made Francis Wright, lord of the Butterley Ironworks, choose H.J. Stevens for Osmaston Manor? And how did Lord and Lady

Overstone, with millions to play with, come to place themselves at the mercy of W.M. Teulon? One longs to know why. How was it that William Crawshay II, with all the profession to choose from, selected J.T. Crew for Caversham Park? And why did the greatest of the Guinnesses pick William Young for Elveden? It is all rather puzzling. What made Sir Henry Tate, a formidable businessman and an influential patron of the arts, retain such persistent confidence in the genius of S.R.J. Smith? How did John Thomas, a sculptor and not a very good one, come to design not one but two mansions – both of them incompetently planned – for not two but three railway magnates?[167] Just who was W.J. Green, and why did W.H. Smith select him to design his lavish Thames-side retreat? Odder still, why did H.D. Pochin – richest of china clay magnates – also choose him as architect of Bodnant, Denbighshire (1881)? Whatever the reason, the result on that occasion was one of the ugliest houses in Britain. And, finally, why on earth did Sir James Horlick, the malted milk mogul, consider 'Bungalow' Briggs just the man to turn Cowley Manor into a palazzo? No doubt answers could be found to all of these questions; but they might have to be couched in terms of psychology rather than aesthetics.

There are some big names on the list: Wilkins, Hardwick, Smirke, Blomfield; Scott, Waterhouse and Devey; Godwin, Bentley, Ernest George, Norman Shaw and Nesfield; even Burges – though he is always a special case. But their best work is not here; and the bulk of millionaires' country-house architects – even when they can be identified – form an unexciting crew. Edis, Gibson, Daukes and Vulliamy; Young, Bidlake, Knowles, Cave: all sound, second-eleven figures. C.H. Chorley and J.T. Crew would have had trouble making the junior team. Did the more interesting architectural practices gravitate naturally to a different sort of client? Lutyens's patrons were all rich men, but none of them left a million pounds before the First World War. He did of course design important Classical houses for Edwardian *nouveaux riches*: Ednaston (1912–13) for W.G. Player, Chairman of Imperial Tobacco; Great Maytham (1907–9) [plate 79] for H.J. Tennant, heir to a chemical fortune; Heathcote (1905–7) [plate 78] for J.T. Hemingway, a Bradford wool broker who married a mill girl. These are all vintage performances by England's master Classicist.[168]

But they were not designed for millionaires. So there is a problem here. Did Arts and Crafts architects, for example, prefer to work for the rich rather than the super-rich? Were many of the ablest practitioners – Butterfield, Street, Bodley, Sedding – just too preoccupied with churches to bother with country houses for some of the richest men on earth? When able Goths did find their way to the country houses of the mega-rich – J.L. Pearson at Cliveden, J.T. Micklethwaite at Stapleford – their talent seems to have sunk beneath the enormity of their budgets.

So was it the fault of the patrons themselves? Vast sums were spent on country-house building, but to what end? All those lions of the free market economy – did they suffer a collective failure of nerve when faced with the agonies of aesthetic choice? Was the range of stylistic choice available at the end of the nineteenth century simply too great? Were in fact these men less interested in taste than in comfort? Or was it just a matter of class: the parvenu flummoxed by the imagery of status? That certainly brings us closer to the key question. Did most of these *nouveaux riches* just prefer to play safe, buying up Georgian mansions – or replicating French châteaux – as symbols of social success? On the whole, that seems the likeliest explanation: a familiar style, an acceptable image, a biddable architect.

Cecil Rhodes may have been an extreme case: he had little time for aesthetics. But his treatment of the architect C.E. Mallows strikes the right millionaire note:

'Here are the plans [of Dalham Hall; 1704–5]', announced Rhodes; 'and on this side I wish to arrange a business room for myself, with a secretary's room adjoining, and then a writing room and a separate entrance, and somewhere you must arrange for a bath and cloak-room. Over the rooms I wish you to add a complete suite of apartments for my secretary, for whom you must provide a separate staircase.'

Mallows, with generous enthusiasm, remarked: 'Mr Rhodes, that is splendid; but you have said nothing about the corresponding wing to the south.'

'There will be no corresponding wing on the south side.'

'But, Mr Rhodes, you will destroy the balance of parts, which Dalham calls for.'

'I don't care a fig about balance of parts; all I care for at the moment is to find an architect willing to carry out my instructions. I hope, Mr Mallows, you understand this.'[169]

Perhaps Margot Asquith was right after all, at least as regards the country houses of the richest *nouveaux riches*: 'Rich men's houses are seldom beautiful, rarely comfortable, and never original. It is a constant source of surprise to people of moderate means to observe how little a big fortune contributes to Beauty ... Money has never yet bought imagination.'[170]

# 3
# PRIVILEGE AND THE PICTURESQUE
## *New Money in the Lake District, 1774–1914*

'We arrived [at Tent Lodge, Coniston] last night. Mr [J.G.]
Marshall's park looked as lovely as the Garden of Eden . . .
We have a very beautiful view from our dining room
windows, crag, mountain, woods and lake . . . We found the
seat of a Marshall on almost every lake we came to, for it
seems there are several brothers who have all either bought or
been left estates in this country; and they are all, report says,
as wealthy as Croesus.'

Alfred Tennyson, 1850

Now for an excursion to the Lakes: new money in search of an ideal
retreat, a retreat in the form of a villa. But first, what is a villa? Since
its origins in ancient Rome, and its revival in the Renaissance, the
word 'villa' has carried a plethora of meanings. In terms of size, it
must be bigger than a cottage, and smaller than a mansion. In terms
of ownership, it can be anything from the retreat of a City magnate to
the haven of Mr Pooter. Ruskin came as near as anybody to a more
precise definition. And in creating his own villa retreat by the shore of
Coniston Water, he came himself to epitomise one particular strand
of late nineteenth-century patronage: new money in the Lakes.

The cottage, Ruskin tells us in *The Poetry of Architecture* (1837–8), is
the 'rural dwelling of the peasant'; the villa is 'the ruralised domicile of
the gentleman'.[1] So a villa is not a seat, i.e. the focus of a great estate.
Even so, it is 'a dwelling of wealth and power'; it needs 'a domain to
itself, at once conspicuous, beautiful and calm'.[2] And therein lies a

difficulty: 'the cottage enhances the wildness of the surrounding scene, by sympathising with it; the villa must do the same thing by contrasting with it.'[3] A farmhouse, however elegant, is not a villa; nor is a rectory, however charming. For the villa is not linked to its context – as those are – by ties of occupation and social function. The villa, in fact, differs from all of these in its self-conscious pursuit of art: it is architecture rather than building. The link between such a structure and its context is therefore correspondingly tenuous. There is a far closer connection between the villa and the personality of its inhabitant.[4] And that inhabitant, by education, by travel, by occupation, has become culturally autonomous: his house is a cultural capsule implanted in an alien land. Thus the architecture of the villa forsakes the real for the ideal. And that way danger lies.

Because those who can afford to build villas do not build them in the fashion of the neighbourhood; they build them in their own image: 'the polished courtier brings his refinement and duplicity with him to ape the Arcadian rustic of Devonshire ... and the rich stock-jobber calculates his percentages among the dingles and woody shores of Westmoreland.'[5] And so, 'we have staring, square-windowed, flat-roofed gentlemen's seats of the lath-and-plaster, much-magnified, Regent's Park description, rising out of the woody promontories of Derwentwater'.[6] It was a problem inherent in the nature of the villa, but a problem exacerbated by the peculiarities of England. 'The only criterion capable of forming a national style', Ruskin explains, 'is the idea of correspondence with situation.'[7] But since Britain is composed of a multiplicity of scenic contexts, 'we can have no national style'; there will be 'as many forms of edifice as there are peculiarities of situation'.[8] This heterogeneity is diversified still further by 'the peculiar independence of the Englishman's disposition'; for 'there [is] much obstinate originality in his mind'. This 'hedgehog independence' of the Englishman makes him unpredictable, exhibitionist and unsociable. So while 'wealth is worshipped in France as the means of purchasing pleasure [, and] in Italy [is] an instrument of power [,] in England [it is a] means of "showing off" ... it is [the Englishman's ambition] to hear everyone exclaiming, "What a pretty place! whose can it be?" '[9]

Italy, Ruskin has to admit, is 'the native country of the villa'.[10] Greece had long been insufficiently peaceful for villa building; Austria too despotic – a place for 'palaces not villas'; and Switzerland too democratic: 'power is so split among the multitude that nobody can build himself anything'. Historically, France and Germany had been too feudal, so 'the villa was lost in the château and the fortress'. But Italy – the Villa Serbelloni at Bellagio on Lake Como, for example – that is the villa's natural home.[11] In England such a building would be 'utterly and absolutely absurd, ugly in outline, worse than useless in application, unmeaning in design, and incongruous in association'.[12] The climate must be Italian; 'the inhabitant must be Italian'; such 'a villa inhabited by an Englishman ... will always be preposterous'.[13] Why? Because England lacks a coherent tradition of villa building. Here the nobility live in mansions, the merchants in town houses; only gentry build villas, and they lack the taste to do it properly. 'For we do not understand by the term "villa" ', he notes, 'a cubic erection with one window on either side of a verdant door, and three on the second and uppermost storey, such as the word suggests to the fertile imagination of ruralising cheesemongers.'[14]

How has all this come about? 'Taste', Ruskin explains, 'is the slave of memory; and beauty is tested, not by any final standard, but by all the chances of association.'[15] Hence the root cause of bad architecture in the nineteenth century: 'the principle of imitation ... [that is] endeavouring to combine old materials in a novel manner ... at once the most baneful and the most unintellectual, and yet perhaps the most natural [principle] that the human mind can ... act upon'.[16] Our architects will never learn good English, he implies, by speaking bad Greek; and borrowing the vocabulary of Merrie England will never make them write like Shakespeare. Exact copying has at least the merit of archaeology. 'But imitation, the endeavour to be Gothic, or Tyrolese, or Venetian, without the slightest grain of Gothic or Venetian feeling; the futile effort to splash a building into age, or daub it into dignity, to zigzag it into sanctity, or slit it into ferocity, when its shell is neither ancient nor dignified, and its spirit neither priestly nor baronial – this is the degrading vice of the age.' 'All imitation has its origin in vanity, and vanity is the bane of architecture.'[17]

In architecture, as in all arts, Ruskin concludes, we cannot seem what we cannot be.[18] Whatever the style, whatever the disguise, the grubby fingerprints of the nineteenth century will somehow show through.

So, what hope for the villa? For suburban villas there is no hope: even as early as 1837, Ruskin knew they were doomed to be Franken-stein monsters. What of his adopted home, the Lake District? 'Nine-tenths of all mountain scenery', he admits, is 'totally unfit for villa residence.'[19] The Scottish Highlands, North Wales, the Alps, the Apennines: all these are impossible. The only portions of this hill ter-ritory – or Brown country, as he calls it – which escape 'the sweeping range of this veto' are firstly 'quiet' valleys, and secondly 'the shores of the Cumberland lakes'.[20] Here, the ideal villa is 'the cottage villa' or 'mountain villa', nestling beneath the shadow of some native crag. Unfortunately, this 'affords the greatest scope for practical absurdity'.[21] To avoid it, the building must be essentially 'unclassical; . . . not a vestige of column or capital must appear in any part of the edifice – all should be English; and . . . much of [it should be] utilitarian'.[22] Little or no ornament is necessary; the colour should be white, not cream – or better still, 'a warm rich grey' – and the roof should be composed of local coarse slates, 'the more lichenous the better'.[23] 'He who prefers neatness to beauty, and who would have sharp angles and clean sur-faces in preference to curved outlines and lichenous colour, has no business to live among hills.'[24]

In that respect, Windermere was a warning. Perhaps the classic Regency Lakeland villa was Storrs Hall, rebuilt in 1808–11 to designs by Joseph Gandy for Sir John Bolton, a Liverpool merchant and slave trader.[25] Bolton's estate ran to 1,000 acres; but his villa – at least in Ruskin's eyes – set the landscape at defiance. There was even a Temple of the Heroes, designed by Gandy in 1804, commemorating Admirals Howe, St Vincent, Duncan and Nelson. Why place such chauvinistic symbols amid the peace and solitude of Lakeland? The paradox of the Picturesque – classicism in a romantic setting – was by the 1830s beginning to break down. To Ruskin the austere Neo-Classicism of Storrs had come to seem somehow at odds with its woodland context. And at the other end of the lake he saw even less to please him.

Beginning at the head of Windermere, and running down its border for about six miles, there are six important gentlemen's seats, villas they may be called; the first of which [Brathay Hall, 1788;[26] built for George Law, a West India planter, but occupied in Ruskin's time by Giles Redmayne, a Bond Street haberdasher][27] is a square white mass, decorated with pilasters of no order, set in a green avenue, sloping down to the water; the second [Croft Lodge, Clappersgate, 1827;[28] home of James Brancker, a Liverpudlian sugar merchant][29] is an imitation, we suppose, of something possessing theoretical existence in Switzerland ... set on a little dumpy mound, with a slate wall running all round it, glittering with iron pyrites; the third [Calgarth Park, 1789;[30] built for Dr Richard Watson, absentee Bishop of Llandaff][31] is a blue dark-looking box, squeezed up into a group of straggly larches, with a bog in front of it; the fourth [Highfield Hall] is a cream coloured domicile, in a large park, rather quiet and unaffected, the best of the four, though that is not saying much; the fifth [Rayrigg Hall, sixteenth-century, remodelled 1702 and *c.* 1790][32] is an old-fashioned thing, formal and narrow-windowed, yet grey in its tone, and quiet, and not to be maligned; and the sixth [Belle Isle, 1774, 1781;[33] designed by John Plaw for Thomas English 'who had travelled in Italy'][34] is a nondescript, circular, putty-coloured habitation, with a leaden dome on top of it.[35]

Further down the lake, on the other side, Ruskin notices Wray Castle, designed by H.P. Horner in 1840–47:[36] an extraordinary 'affectation'; 'a castellated mansion with round towers, and a Swiss cottage for a stable', 'whose proprietor ... has ... [actually] painted the rocks at the back of his house pink, that they may look clean'.[37] The proud owner – James Dawson, a Liverpool surgeon with shipping interests – was rumoured to have spent £60,000.[38]

There must, Ruskin believed, be better models than these. In the cultivated landscapes of the South and East – 'Simple Blue' country, he calls it – brick is perfectly acceptable, suitable indeed for 'the business part of the nation'.[39] Rougher landscapes – 'Picturesque Blue' – require something different. In 'the cultivated parts of the North and East Ridings of Yorkshire ... [in] Shropshire ... North Lancashire, and Cumberland beyond Caldbeck Fells, [best of all in] the country [round] Stirling', the architect should take as his model the Italian [Tuscan] villa: 'the forms should be square and massy', irregular in plan and horizontal in profile; and the style should be vaguely Greek or Roman, never Gothic or Elizabethan, still less castellated. Only in heavily wooded – or Green – scenery does the Tudor style come into its own; never the Baronial. 'Nothing can be more absurd than [for] . . . peaceable old gentlemen, who never smelt powder in their lives, to eat their morning muffins in a savage looking round tower, [or to] admit quiet old ladies to a tea-party under the range of twenty-six cannon . . . pointed into the drawing room windows.'[40]

The temptation to turn lakeside villas into miniature castles goes back at least to Lyulph's Tower on Ullswater. Lyulph's Tower[41] – constructed in 1780 to his own designs by the Earl of Surrey, the future 11th Duke of Norfolk – seems to have been only the second lakeside retreat to be built entirely for the view. The first, of course, was Belle Isle. Neither made much concession to context; both were designed as memories in three dimensions: one medieval, the other antique. Lyulph's Tower was a semi-hexagonal eyecatcher designed to snare the angled views of Ullswater. Its planning involved a revolution in sensibility. A century before, and not far away, Glencoyne farmhouse had been built in the vernacular fashion, turning its back on the water to shelter from the wind. By the third quarter of the eighteenth century, taste had shifted one hundred and eighty degrees. When the Revd William Braithwaite built a castellated summer-house at Ferry Point, Windermere, he made it octagonal. Belle Isle was the logical conclusion of this optical process: a circular villa encompassing the whole panorama of Windermere. Neither Lyulph's Tower nor Belle Isle, however, begins to grapple with the problem of scenic context; in fact, both set out to create a conceptual context of their own.

One anecdote illustrates the artificiality of this phase rather well. In 1818 to 1820 John Glover, landscape painter, owned a house at Patterdale. He sold it for £1,000, which he used to buy a painting by Claude. Our 'English Claude', as Constable sarcastically christened him, clearly preferred image to actuality.[42] In any case, the imagery itself was wholly unreal. Thomas Gray's impressions of Grasmere will stand for many:

> One of the sweetest landscapes that art ever attempted to imitate. Not a single red tile, nor flaring gent's house, nor garden wall breaks in upon the

repose of this unsuspected paradise, but all is peace, security and happy poverty.[43]

Illusions like that were better expressed in follies than in houses. However, as Lakeland retreats become more numerous, more bourgeois even, their affectation becomes less obtrusive. More and more the Lakeland villa shrinks back into its setting. First sited for the view, it becomes – reciprocally – part of that view.

Three examples of assimilation will do for the moment. Hammershead Villa (*c.* 1830), built for the Revd B. McHugh, itself partakes of its own rocky setting. Esthwaite Lodge, Hawkshead, probably designed by George Webster in 1821, and built for Thomas Alcock-Beck, makes Arcady itself more Arcadian still.[44] And not far away the lacy verandas of Highfield Cottage, Blawith (*c.* 1830) succeed in making the prospect as much a part of the villa as the villa is part of the prospect.[45] Such lakeside conjuring tricks were all part of an evolving Picturesque tradition. During the Victorian period they also became a vehicle for the leisure pursuits of a newly affluent bourgeoisie. For, in the end, it happened just as Ruskin had prophesied: the industrial revolution turned industrialists themselves into romantic escapees, fleeing the source of their wealth, as often as not by railway.

The mill owners of England were never quite as rich as legend suggests. Apart from the founding names of the textile industry – Peel, Arkwright, Fielden and Strutt – only three 'cottontots' left over a million pounds: Edward Langworthy of Salford, J.P. Thomasson of Bolton and John Rylands of Manchester. Most left about one-tenth of that sum. Even so, it has been calculated that 39 Lancashire cotton lords achieved minor gentry status, with estates of 1,000 acres or more.[46] By 1875 some 23 of these cotton families had been accepted into the magic circle of Burke's *Landed Gentry*. When Sir George Philips, 1st Bt, spinner, was driven from Sedgeley by the smoke of Manchester, he found – as we saw in chapter 1 – ample refuge in

Weston Park, near Chipping Norton, a substantial mansion set in 6,000 acres.[47] Most cotton men were less ambitious: Langworthy lived in a villa surrounded by villas, in Victoria Park, Manchester. When they did buy land it involved, often enough, a villa on the fringes of town rather than a genuine country estate. J.P. Thomasson, for instance, built Woodside (1877–80) at Heaton on the edge of Bolton. And on Eccles Old Road – Salford rather than Manchester – there gathered a whole cluster of Mancunian *nouveaux riches*. Thomas Agnew, art dealer (Fair Hope, *c.* 1850); Edward Tootal, spinner (The Weaste, *c.* 1865); Sir Benjamin Heywood, banker (Claremont, *c.* 1860) – he died in 1865 worth £400,000 – and Elkanah Armitage (Hope Hall, *c.* 1850): he began life as a handloom weaver and died in 1870, a knighted Mayor of Manchester, worth a quarter of a million pounds.[48]

These were villas of substance. And it is worth noting, at this point, that by the 1870s a sizeable villa on the fringe of an industrial town could cost as much as eight or nine thousand pounds – not far short of the building costs of a bona fide country house, minus of course the price of the land. And the largest villas – or 'Vulgarian Country Houses', as they were sometimes called – could cost nearly twice as much. 'There are a good many vulgar people in Old England', noted *The Architect* in 1874, and they certainly knew the value of architectural imagery. Still, such houses were essentially suburban. 'A gun room', as *The British Architect* pointed out, also in 1874, 'is seldom required by the Manchester merchant.'[49] Equally, their equivalents in Liverpool, the mansions built at Allerton by Morris (coal), Leather (cotton), Tate (sugar) or Bibby and Brocklebank (shipping), were all suburban in scale and location.[50] But a house in Manchester or Liverpool did not preclude a retreat in the Lake District: F.W. Grafton, for example, an Accrington calico-printer, eventually owned Hope Hall, Salford as well as Heysham Hall, near Morecambe. There were many fortunes in the North West besides fortunes based on cotton, and many of them found their way into the Lakes. In 1884 Jimmy Williamson, the tyrannical linoleum millionaire, bought a considerable estate: 1,500 acres at Ashton Hall, a Jacobean castle on the banks of the river Lune, once owned by the Dukes of Hamilton.[51] That set a high standard indeed. Other incoming magnates were less expansive.

When Thomas Wrigley, Manchester paper magnate and millionaire insurance broker, began to look for a retreat his choice fell on Windermere; and there, on the eastern shore, he built Wansfell House, a Tudor Gothic villa conveniently accessible by road and rail.[52] In any case, Lancastrians had no monopoly. Over in Yorkshire, a similar process was taking place. When James Morrison bought Malham Tarn from Lord Ribblesdale in 1852, it was not just the 10,400 acres of shooting he was after – it was the location: from his newly built Italianate tower he could gaze out across miles of water and moorland towards the distant valley of the Ribble.[53] Such tempting prospects were perhaps more frequently found on the western side of the Pennines. And so, in this way, the greatest Lakeland incomers of all turned out to be a tribe of Yorkshire linen-yarn makers, the Marshall family of Leeds.

When John Marshall – the acknowledged king of flax-spinners – married at the age of thirty in 1795, he spent his honeymoon in the Lake District. Thus began a relationship between the Marshall dynasty and the Lakes which eventually turned large tracts of fell and pasture into a family fiefdom spanning thousands of acres. John Marshall's rise to fortune had been prodigious: from small beginnings he had, by 1805, accumulated some £70,000. By 1815 he was already worth nearly half a million, and his iron-framed mills at Leeds and Shrewsbury were world-famous. By 1840 speculative investments had brought in at least another million. At his death in 1845 estimates of his wealth varied between £1.5 million and £2.5 million. Perhaps £1 million would be nearer the mark. But by any standard he was enormously rich. To put his fortune in perspective, we must not only multiply those figures by 40 or 50: we must remember that Marshall's mill girls – the hands who worked the machinery – received about six shillings per week.[54]

How then was it spent? Looking back in 1828 on the boom years after 1815, Marshall noted with satisfaction a gradual widening of his own horizons: he began to take pleasure in spending.

A taste for paintings has been productive of considerable pleasure to me, though it has been somewhat displaced by other pursuits. [In particular] a taste for natural scenery and for laying out ornamental grounds, has been a source of high enjoyment ... The novelty of a change of dwelling is a source of pleasurable feeling, and I have experienced this more particularly, because I have made frequent changes for the better ... [55]

Indeed he had. He spent perhaps £1,000,000 between 1815 and 1845 on property and paintings, and on political and household expenses.

First came New Grange, a substantial estate on the outskirts of Leeds; then Headingly House (extended 1819) not so far away. Both were Neo-Classical houses comparable, for example, to Armley Park, Leeds, designed by Robert Smirke *c.* 1818 for one of Marshall's rivals, the wool-spinner Benjamin Gott.[56] Both Gott and Marshall had profited handsomely from the Napoleonic trade embargoes, and both invested in property. But there the comparison ends: the Gotts remained within the orbit of Leeds; the Marshalls emerged as lords of Lakeland.

Marshall's earliest objective had been a villa on the Ambleside shore of Windermere. Then he discovered Ullswater, probably through the influence of Dorothy Wordsworth who was a close friend of his wife. Summer holidays at Watermillock led in 1812 to a key decision: he purchased the estate of Hallsteads, a woodland promontory sublimely situated on Ullswater's margin. There, from 1819 onwards, he built a Neo-Classical retreat. The estate cost him £11,800; running costs were £3,000 a year. But the money was not important. From his Doric portico he could now survey perhaps the finest view in England, and therefore – as Ruskin would say – in the world:[57] on one side, the majestic fells of Martindale; on the other, Wordsworth's favourite prospect from Gowbarrow Park. Here, by moonlight, he could row towards another portion of his estate, a farmhouse on the site of a ruined medieval church: this he rebuilt as Old Church House, a veritable retreat within a retreat, set in pasture and lapped by water. No wonder Dorothy Wordsworth complimented Marshall on his 'beautiful home among the mountains'. Hallsteads, he had to agree, had 'as beautiful a situation as any upon the Lakes'.[58] It was a world and more away from the industrial reality of Leeds.

By 1826 Marshall had bought properties worth £90,000 in Lakeland, mostly at Loweswater, Buttermere and Ullswater.[59] It was ideal territory for a romantic parvenu: glorious scenery, and few ancient families for social competition. Since 1821 he had been High Sheriff of Cumberland. Within a few years he was a Member of Parliament, with a *pied-à-terre* in Mayfair: first 4 Grosvenor Square, then 34 Hill Street, Berkeley Square. Marshall of Leeds might be an industrialist; he might be a Dissenter; he might be a Utilitarian, a founder indeed of University College, London. But at heart he was a romantic, dreaming of moonlight on the rippling surface of Ullswater. And it could be so inexpensive. In 1806 the *Gentleman's Magazine* noted that 'a small family occupying a comfortable house [on Windermere] and an estate of ten acres of land, with an adequate establishment of servants, a horse and a cow, may live upon the finest mutton, the best-fed poultry etc., upon an income of £200 p.a.', all in 'uninterrupted seclusion'.[60]

In 1824, as a twenty-eighth birthday present, Marshall presented his eldest son William with Patterdale Hall, an estate on the southern tip of Ullswater worth £13,000.[61] The Marshall family were now kings of Patterdale; and to confirm their status they employed Salvin in 1840–45 to design a grandiose extension to Patterdale Hall in Italianate Tuscan style.[62] In 1832 another son, John Marshall II, was presented – on the birth of a son and heir – with the Castlerigg estate near Keswick. On this occasion the cost was £49,800. Castlerigg had once been the property of the attainted Earls of Derwentwater. Again Salvin, or perhaps a local man, was called in: the result was a curious mixture of French Renaissance and Gothic (1832; 1883).[63] Wordsworth seems to have acted as adviser. This, he told the great magnate, was a site with 'picturesque beauty above all praise'; 'Mr Southey will be pleased to hear that you are the Purchaser, as will all men of taste.'[64] Ruskin would surely have agreed. For here, at Friar's Crag, aged only five, he had first felt the intoxication of Lakeland scenery. Finally, in 1838 and 1843, two more sons – Henry and James Marshall – purchased additional Lakeland retreats. Henry Marshall, by then Mayor of Leeds and ensconced at Westwood Hall to the north of that city, bought an island in the northern reaches of Derwentwater. Its name was Pocklington's Island (previously Vicar's Island), taking its name from an eccentric Newark copper merchant – Wordsworth's 'alien improver' – who had built a villa there in 1778. In 1850, under the name of Derwent Isle, Henry Marshall extended it in the Italianate Tuscan style, once more to designs by Salvin. From his study window the new owner could now gaze out over the incomparable 'jaws of Borrowdale'. That privilege cost him £5,000 annually in running costs.[65] James Marshall had by then bought Monk Coniston Hall, a faintly Gothic villa of *c*. 1800.[66] This had been built by an ironmaster named William Ford and was originally known as Coniston Waterhead, from its idyllic position on the northern extremity of the lake. And here the financial and aesthetic elements in our story converge. From the mullioned windows of Monk Coniston the Marshall family would eventually look out across the water towards another property, home of a sherry-merchant's son named John Ruskin.

By 1840 – on Ullswater, on Coniston, on Derwentwater – the second generation of Marshalls were in place. One daughter married Baron Monteagle; another married the Master of Trinity College, Cambridge. One son married the daughter of a Whig Chancellor of the Exchequer. By the late Victorian period, it was calculated, as many as one hundred and eleven Marshalls were living in the Lake District – and they were only the male members of the family.[67] The Marshalls were now Cumbrian gentry whose financial status seemed likely to be for ever buttressed by their ownership of the most extraordinary factory building in the world. That mill was so remarkable that it merits a brief digression: without it we cannot understand the huge disparity built into the family's way of life. On one hand they were landlords of an expanding swathe of mountain scenery; on the other, they were employers on a huge scale and proprietors of a technological marvel.

Flax-spinning was legendarily the invention of the ancient Egyptians, and Egyptian cotton was famous for its excellence. So when Marshall and Co. rebuilt their Leeds headquarters in 1838–42, Egyptian seemed the logical style to choose. But Egyptian forms supplied only the imagery. The firm's previous factories had incorporated the first iron-framed construction in the world. Temple Mill went one step further, combining archaeology and technology in an unprecedented way: John Marshall, after all, was a romantic Utilitarian. Designed by an Egyptologist, Joseph Bonomi Jnr, from evidence collected by David Roberts, and constructed by a local specialist in factory design, James Combe, at a cost of £50,000, the mill consisted of a vast two-acre workroom, raised on vaults and covered by a brick-groined roof lit by sixty-six conical glass skylights – for all the world, as Whewell put it, 'like cucumber frames in a garden'.[68] In the vaulted catacombs below, engines strong as a hundred horses supplied endless momentum for the machines. Above, the roof itself was covered with 'a layer of earth, sown with grass, [which] flourishes so well that sheep are occasionally sent to feed upon it'.[69] There was even a boiler-house whose chimney silhouette recalled the lineaments of Cleopatra's Needle. Here indeed was the symbolic headquarters of new international wealth. Far away on Ullswater an aged spinning millionaire knew that he had created one of the wonders of the industrial world.

> Trafford ... became very opulent, and ... built a factory, which was now one of the marvels of the district; one might almost say, of the country: a single room, spreading over nearly two acres, and holding more than two thousand workpeople. The roof of groined arches, lighted by ventilating domes at the height of eighteen feet, was supported by hollow cast-iron columns, through which the drainage of the roof was effected ... By an ingenious process, not unlike that which is practised in the House of Commons, the ventilation was ... carried on from below, so that the whole building was kept at a steady temperature ... One of [Mr Trafford's] first efforts had been to build a village where every family might be well lodged ... behind the factory were the public baths [and schools] ... In the midst of this village ... was the house of Trafford himself, who comprehended his position too well to withdraw himself with vulgar exclusiveness from his real dependants, but recognised the baronial principle, reviving in a new form ... [70]

Disraeli was a little too sanguine. *Sybil* was published in the very year of John Marshall's death, 1845. His children and grandchildren were rather less attached to Leeds. Even as Temple Mill was being built, the Marshall empire was beginning to crumble. Changing market conditions, foreign competition, rising costs, falling sales – to say nothing of the soft seduction of the Lakes – gradually did their work. By the early 1880s, Marshall and Co. were in terminal decline. The end came in 1886. 'In the last analysis', concludes the historian of the firm, 'managerial fatalism and paralysis sealed the fate of Marshall and Co.'[71] Perhaps; but such directorial somnolence cannot have been unrelated to the charms of Derwent Isle and Patterdale. From entre- preneur to *rentier* in three generations: the Marshalls in the end pre- ferred Ullswater to Headingley. And – not surprisingly – so did their workers. Within a generation, they had followed them there, by train.

'The Lake District', noted Murray's *Handbook* in 1889, 'is encircled with railways and partly penetrated by them.'[72] Windermere had received its railway more than forty years before, in 1847. Liverpool and Manchester had been brought within two hours' journey; 100,000 passengers per year passed through Windermere station alone. By 1887 the *Oxford Magazine* was protesting against yet another railway which would 'villa-fy the shores of Rydal'.[73] But by then the pass had already been sold. Ruskin might fulminate, but he was himself a prime example of growing social and geographical mobility: new money in the Lakes. He was not the only wine importer's son: there was Elliot of Eden Bank, Cumberland (1834)[74] and Preston – later Sandeman, too – of Ellel Grange, Lancashire (1856–60) [plate 20].[75] But most of the new money came from sources much closer to home. Banking in Manchester and Liverpool, for example: J.P. Heywood of Norris Green, West Derby (*c.* 1850);[76] or A.H. Heywood of Elleray (1808–27; 1869), a delectable villa on the shores of Winder- mere.[77] And there were other sources of wealth as well, and not too far away. Engineering at Barrow, for instance, and spinning at Bradford. H.W. Schneider, one of the creators of Barrow-in-Furness, chose Bels- field, a stuccoed villa perched high above Windermere (1845; 1870, etc.).[78] John and William Foster – millionaire masters of Black Dyke Mills – chose Hornby Castle, Lancashire (1849–52; *c.* 1889).[79] Here was status built into an ideal retreat: from battlements bristling high above the Lune, its new owners could look out over a landscape worlds away from the smoke and grime of Bradford. And others could play the same game. From Liverpool came shipowners like the Bibbys, the Bowrings and the Brocklebanks, the Boltons, the Rathbones, the Leylands, the MacIvers. From Manchester came engineers like Crossley, fustian finishers like Howarth, rope-makers like Heginbottom, brewers like Holt. There were cotton-spinning dynasties: the Dixons, the Fergusons, the Horrockses, the Tippings and the Kays. There were railway contractors like Brogden and Dawson. There was Alderman Thompson, ironmaster and financier, Cropper the paper-maker, Robinson the gunpowder king, Forwood and Clayton, cotton brokers, Daulby and Riley the brewers, Bridson the bleacher, Carr the Quaker biscuit baron, Borwick the monarch of baking powder, and of course Ashton the emperor of linoleum. Besides the flax-spinning Marshalls, there were the worsted-spinning Ecroyds and the lace-making Moores; there were coal merchants like Harris, Morris, Mercer and Briggs; insurance magnates like Wrigley and Scott; ironmasters like Lindow, Ley, Ford and Ramsden, Ainsworth, Torbock and Cammel.[80]

These were the new men noted by the *Morning Post* in 1865: 'cotton-spinners, cotton-brokers, brewers, ironmasters and engineers overflowing with ready cash'.[81] Some of their houses were by no means negligible: they were mansions rather than villas. When the Welch family – Liverpool merchants who had done well out of the slave trade – rebuilt Leck Hall, Lancashire, in 1801 and again in the 1830s, they were creating a seat rather than a retreat. When Sir James Kay-Shuttleworth – yet another spinner – built Barbon Manor, near Kirkby Lonsdale (E.M. Barry: 1863), it was not so much a seat as a 'miniature schloss'. Flass, near Penrith (G.J. Mair; 1851–4), designed by a pupil of Decimus Burton for Lancelot Dent – a tea-trader turned opium-smuggler – is certainly a seat rather than a villa: it combines an exterior Italianately Picturesque with an interior worthy of a Pall Mall club house. Underscar House, near Keswick (1858), built by a Liverpool merchant named William Oxley, is smaller, but quite superbly placed: the view over Derwentwater and Borrowdale must be one of the most spectacular in England. Some of the new men clearly had an eye. Others, equally clearly, did not. Sir William Crossley, 1st Bt, a Manchester engineering contractor, retreated regularly to the Lake District from Altrincham in the 1880s. Unfortunately he eventually transferred his own architect there, too, with instructions to re-create a little bit of Cheshire on the banks of Lake Windermere. Pull Woods, near Hawkshead (G. Faulkner Armitage, 1890–91) – 'large, illiterate, gabled, Black and White timbered and red brick' – was the result.[82] There was no mistaking these *nouveaux riches*. By 1886 it was reported that 'a new class of competitors for the ownership of the soil has arisen in the merchant princes of the manufacturing districts who eagerly buy up any nook where they may escape from their own smoke, and enjoy pure air and bracing breezes, with shooting and fishing'.[83] These were the offcomers, or 'new comers', to the Lakes, so neatly described by Tennyson:

> . . . new-comers in an ancient hold,
> New-comers from the Mersey, millionaires
> . . . [in] cotton-spinning chorus.[84]

By 1905 three-quarters of the members of the Royal Windermere Yacht Club had addresses in the industrial north.[85] All these newcomers were rich men, some of them very rich indeed. Bibby,[86] Heywood and Wrigley, Foster, Holt and Carr all died worth more than a million; Thompson was only a few pounds short of that magic figure, and that as early as 1854. Ashton, Leyland and Moore would certainly have left the statutory million if they had not spent or given away so much money during their lifetimes.

Despite this influx, however, the old hierarchies were maintained. There were Howards at Naworth, and Lonsdales still at Lowther; there were Howards at Greystoke and Stricklands at Sizergh; the Lawsons remained at Isel; the Machells stayed on at Crackenthorpe; there were Grahams and Musgraves, and Curwens, and there would be for generations to come. The bulk of landed property remained in traditional hands. When William Wordsworth attended church at Grasmere, he sat in the front row; but his landlords, the le Flemings of Rydal Hall, sat in their own box, fitted with its own chimney-piece. Even so, the social landscape of Lakeland was changing. William Thompson, the millionaire ironmaster and shipowner, is a prime example of mobility. Inheriting his first fortune from a partner of Richard Crawshay, then moving south from Kendal to London, he made a second fortune in shipping, railways and insurance. By 1828 he was Lord Mayor of London; by the 1830s he was a Director of the Bank of England and Chairman of Lloyds. By 1841 he had succeeded no less a family than the Lowthers as MP for Westmorland, and that involved a major change of county status. Buying up land extensively – he acquired the Benacre estate from the Duke of Hamilton for £98,000 – Thompson set himself up with 20,000 acres at Underley Hall, near Kirkby Lonsdale [plate 21]. In 1842 his only daughter married the Earl of Bective, later 3rd Marquess of Headfort. By the 1880s the family holdings in England and Ireland amounted to 40,000 acres; they were even kinsmen to the Duke of Devonshire.[87]

Such transitions take time. However, a few paces behind, others were following in Alderman Thompson's footsteps. From Liverpool and Manchester, from Bolton and Bradford, new money had permeated Cumberland, Westmorland and North Lancashire. The quasi-gentry, living in the country but in villas rather than seats, had arrived. Men like William Carver (d. 1875), a Manchester cotton broker; or Henry Pearson Banks (d. 1891), the son of a Keswick draper who made a fortune selling factory-made clothes to Australia. Carver built the conspicuous Gothic Priory (1869) which still stands in a prime position on Lake Windermere.[88] Banks constructed a monstrous mixed-Classical campanile (1887) at Highmore House, near Wigton: its mighty bell could be heard tolling the hours of the day from a distance of at least twelve miles.[89] Such sights eventually became tourist attractions. When trippers came by train to Windermere, they could even indulge in a little celebrity-spotting at Ambleside: Dr Arnold at Fox How,[90] W.E. Forster at Fox Gill,[91] Harriet Martineau at The Knoll (1845–6),[92] Mrs Hemans at Dove Nest.[93]

Sometimes the newcomers were in fact returning natives: George Moore, for example. Son of a Cumberland farmer, Moore built up a mighty fortune in London and Nottingham through drapery and lace-making. At the age of fifty-two he was able to buy the Whitehall Estate near Wigton for £40,000. Here was a mansion – 'Whiteladies' in Scott's *Redgauntlet* – 'at which he used to gaze with almost wor-shipping eyes as a rude country lad. Now he entered as its proud owner. The first person to greet him as he entered its portals was the old dame who acted as lodge keeper ... for years they [had] sat upon the same bench at the village school.' When eventually, in 1876, he was knocked down by a horse in the streets of Carlisle, he was worth nearly half a million.[94]

Such stories – and that was one of Samuel Smiles's favourites – cannot have been wholly representative. Most of the newcomers were refugees from the environmental impact of their own success. They were not returning to their roots but escaping from them. This collective escape – the retreat of the bourgeoisie – from Manchester and Liverpool, from Bolton and Leeds, forms part of a continuous process: the polarising of capital and labour. The older families were slower to move – the Lindsays of Haigh Hall, near Wigan, for example – but the new-rich industrialists tended to drift away from their roots in the second and third generation. T.H. Mawson, a land-scape architect whose carefully textured settings are integral to the Lakeland idyll, admired the patronage of these new men – W.W. Gal-loway, for instance, a partner in Horrockses of Preston, who created a famous garden at Ashton-on-Ribble: 'a typical example of the art-loving Manchester manufacturer ... These men really are genuine lovers of the beautiful, and not merely rich plutocrats with a pose.' But in 1916 he also spotted the danger signals. Writing of the town-planning potential of Bolton, he noted:

I am afraid that Bolton as a desirable place of residence, comparable ... with ... Windermere and Cheltenham and Bristol may sound a little absurd ... I wish we could count up how many people have left the Bolton district because they preferred to live elsewhere during the last fifty years. It is a common sneer against Englishmen that, as soon as they obtain a little money they leave the place in which they have made it to sink or swim as best it can and spend it elsewhere without any thought for what becomes of their neighbours.[95]

That is a little hard, but only a little. The family of T.R. Bridson (d. 1863), first Mayor of Bolton, follows exactly this pattern. A successful bleacher by trade, he had two sons. One moved to Torquay. The other took up residence at Belle Isle on Windermere before building himself a Jacobean house, Bryerswood (R. Knill Freeman, 1886), on the western shore of the same lake; his son married the heiress to a delectable estate, Water Park on the fringe of Lake Coniston, and changed his name to Brydson.[96]

So many of these themes coalesce in the building of Brantwood [plate 22].[97] Ruskin bought Brantwood in 1871, sight unseen, from W.J. Linton – Chartist and wood-engraver – for £1,500.[98] He found it a 'mountain cottage', 'old, damp, decayed, smokey-chimneyed and rat-riddled'. He left it a 'mountain villa'.[99] He knew Coniston already, of course: in 1838 he called it 'that Arcadia of Western meres'.[100] So too did his friends: Tennyson had spent his honeymoon there, at Tent Lodge (*c.* 1830), in 1850. Visitors on that occasion included Matthew Arnold, Carlyle, Coventry Patmore and Edward Lear. Turner's first exhibited painting at the Royal Academy was *Morning Among the Coniston Fells*. But the views from Brantwood itself – 'the finest views in Cumberland or Lancashire', as Ruskin called them – came as a revelation. During the next twenty-five years or so, Ruskin doubled the size of the house. It had been extended before, in the 1830s; now it was extended again. First, in 1872, came the hexagonal bedroom with views to three points of the compass: north, south and west. Then came the lodge and coach house. Then, in 1878, came the dining room, with its seven-mullioned window looking south: a prospect of paradise multiplied seven-fold. In the 1890s a studio at the back, plus a second storey with school-room, nursery and extra bedroom, were added for the use of his relatives, the Severn family. After Ruskin's death came balconied and terraced additions to the drawing room in 1905. Meanwhile the estate had grown dramatically, from sixteen acres to five hundred, including a mile of shoreline and a boathouse for Ruskin's gondola, *Jumping Jenny*. But there was no architect. There was a builder, of course – a local man called George Usher – and local artisans, but no fashionable practitioner up from London to stamp it with an alien image. That had been part of Ruskin's dream: to rescue architecture from the architects, and return it to the artisans. Looking at it today, the result is by no means happy: what Brantwood gained in spontaneity, it lost in compositional coherence. In this Ruskin was following exactly his dicta of 1838: 'the house must NOT be a noun substantive, it must not stand by itself, it must be part and parcel of a proportional whole: it must not even be seen all at once, and he who sees one end should feel that, from the given data, he can arrive at no conclusion respecting the other [end].'[101] Quite. This is a house to be looked from, not a house to be looked at. It is a machine for seeing in. Organic, maybe; agglomerative, certainly; but cohesive, never. Brantwood is the *reductio ad absurdum* of Ruskin's ideal villa.

Within a few years of Ruskin's death, the pursuit of the villa ideal came rather closer to perfection exactly where the Lakeland quest for the ideal retreat had begun one hundred years before: Lake Windermere. C.F.A. Voysey – an Arts and Crafts architect with a Cumbrian background – turned out to be the magician who solved the riddle. It could not have happened on Ullswater. For there, until the end of the nineteenth century, the Dukes of Norfolk and Portland still retained land right down to the water's edge; there were few houses, and they were already in the hands of the gentry. Men like Arthur Marshall of Hallsteads and Henry Hargreaves Bolton of Leeming House, second-generation *rentiers*; Andrew Wilson of Bank House, traveller, orientalist and man of letters; and a trio of retired gentleman-soldiers: James Salmond of Waterfoot, H.H. Askew of Glenridding House and Paxton Parkin of Sharrow Bay. Each of these men inherited property on the loveliest lake in England; none was particularly rich; and none showed any inclination either to move or to rebuild. So the villas of late Victorian Ullswater – none of them architecturally distinguished – remained essentially Georgian in conception. In 1905 a parvenu did appear: T.H. Roberts, a shipping magnate from the North East. He built himself a vaguely Arts and Crafts retreat, Hawk House, near

Glenridding. But the experiment was not repeated. New money preferred the accessibility of Windermere.

Voysey's villas on Windermere fit neatly into the social pattern set during the previous century. All four – two built, two unbuilt – were designed as Lakeland retreats for northern businessmen. But by this time the lessons of Ruskin's teaching – and practice – have been learned. There is indeed an architect; each villa has its own coherence; and each design takes its stylistic cue from the landscape setting. The four clients were all very much of a type: Sir George Toulmin, a Preston newspaper proprietor and Liberal MP for Bury;[102] J.W. Buckley, a mill-owner from Altrincham; H. Rickards, heir to a Manchester paper-making fortune;[103] and Arthur Currer Briggs, scion of a family of Yorkshire coal-mine owners.[104] Nothing came of the plans for Toulmin and Rickards: they seem to have had trouble finding a site. But for Buckley Voysey designed Moor Crag (1898–1900), the archetypal Voysey villa in a garden setting by Thomas Mawson; low-slung and sweeping, its silhouette is integral to the Lakeland landscape.[105] And for Briggs he produced Broadleys (1898–9) [plate 23], a house which must stand as the paradigm Lakeside retreat:[106] local limestone and local slate; shallow bow windows which scan the margins of the water; and a low-slung roof designed almost to echo the sweeping contours of the hills. Ruskin would surely have approved of these, and equally of four related Edwardian villas, each built in similar vein: Cragwood, Windermere; Birket Houses, Cartmel Fell; White Craggs, Clappergate; and Dawstone, Windermere – all shaped to designs by Mawson's partner Dan Gibson. Each of these manages to respond creatively to the genius of the place. Still more so do two further Arts and Crafts houses on the margin of Windermere: Kelwith (1910), designed by H.L. North for Alex Rea, a Liverpool steamship magnate with an American wife;[107] and Blackwall (1898–1900), designed by Baillie Scott for a brewing millionaire who was twice Lord Mayor of Manchester, Sir Edward Holt.[108]

These Arts and Crafts houses sum up the ideal of the *nouveau-riche* villa as it developed in the Victorian and Edwardian periods: a combination of convenience and status, prominence and isolation, compressed within the radius of an easy train ride from Liverpool or

Manchester. In the 1780s and 1790s Lakeland retreats had been something of an eccentricity for the gentry: William Gell on Grasmere (Silver Howe, *c.*1798); the Earl of Surrey on Ullswater (Lyulph's Tower, 1780); Lord William Gordon on Derwentwater (Water End, 1784).[109] A century later there was still an Earl of Lonsdale on Windermere (Holbeck Ghyll, 1888). But his neighbours were more likely to be prosperous tradesmen, men like Sir James Scott (né Schott), 1st Bt, of Yews near Windermere, a cotton-spinner turned insurance broker – once of Frankfurt, later of Bolton – who lived to found one of the new county families of Lakeland.[110] When H.W. Schneider set out each morning from Windermere to Barrow-in-Furness – from Arcadia, he must sometimes have thought, to the very heart of Babylon – he could travel swiftly and luxuriously by steam-yacht and steam-train. When Arthur Currer Briggs returned each weekend from Whitwood Colliery to Windermere – backwards, this time, from Babylon to Arcady – there was already a motor car at his disposal. Not far away, at Loughrigg Brow, Ambleside, designed by Ewan Christian in 1863,[111] Isaac Storey was able to manage his Lancaster cotton mill by radio. The villa, moving down-market for the best part of two centuries, had finally been democratised; it had in fact become irredeemably middle class. No longer the prerogative of the territorial aristocracy, it was now a status symbol of the parvenu.

1. Witley Court, Worcestershire (1805; 1855 onwards): A house by John Nash, remodelled by Samuel Daukes for the 1st Earl of Dudley, coal owner. Gutted 1937

2. Witley Court, Worcestershire (1855 onwards): Sculpture Hall with Galleries, designed by Samuel Daukes

3. Brodsworth Hall, Yorkshire (1861–70): Built to designs by Philip Wilkinson and Casentini of Lucca for C.S. Thelusson, heir to an Anglo-Swiss banking fortune

4. Wilton Park, Buckinghamshire (1790; 1803–5): Remodelled for
Sir John Aird, engineering contractor. Demolished 1967

5. Hillingdon Court, Middlesex (1860s): Extended for Charles Mills, 1st Baron
Hillingdon, banker

6. Whitbourne Hall, Herefordshire (1860–2): Designed by Edmund Elmslie for Edward Bickerton Evans, vinegar manufacturer

7. Belleview, Halifax (1856–7): Remodelled by G.H. Stokes for Frank Crossley,
carpet manufacturer and future baronet

8 and 9.   Fonthill Pavilion, Wiltshire (1776–84; 1839–44; 1846–8):
The surviving wing of Alderman Beckford's Fonthill Splendens, refurbished by
J.B. Papworth and enlarged by David Brandon in the 1840s for James
Morrison, a millionaire haberdasher

10. Gatton Park, Surrey, portico (1888; 1891): Designed by Sextus Dyball for Jeremiah Colman, the mustard magnate

11. Theobolds Park, Hertfordshire, Temple Bar (1670–2): Transported from the Strand, London in 1888, to dignify the estate of Sir Henry Meux, 3rd Bt, heir to a brewing fortune

12. Cowley Manor, Gloucestershire (1855; 1890):
Extended by R.A. ('Bungalow') Briggs for Sir James Horlick, 1st Bt, malted-milk
magnate

13. Bearwood, Berkshire (1865–70): Built to designs by Robert Kerr
for John Walter, proprietor of *The Times*

14 and 15. Basildon Park, Berkshire, lodges and entrance front (1776; 1839–44): A house by Carr of York bought by James Morrison and enlarged by J.B. Papworth

16 and 17. Basildon Park, Berkshire, drawing room and
octagon room (1839–44): Refurbished for James Morrison, to designs
by J.B. Papworth

18. Cragside, Northumberland (1869–85): Designed by Richard Norman Shaw for Lord Armstrong, the millionaire armaments manufacturer

19. Kinmel, Denbighshire (1870–4): Remodelled by W.E. Nesfield for
Hugh Hughes, a Welsh copper magnate

20. Ellel Grange, Lancashire (1856–60): Built by William Preston,
a Liverpool wines and spirits importer

21. Underley Hall, Westmorland (1825; 1870s): A Regency house much
extended for the Earl of Bective, who married the heiress daughter
of William Thompson, ironmaster and shipowner

22. Brantwood, Lancashire (*c.* 1835; 1872; 1878 etc.): Extended for John Ruskin, son of a London sherry merchant

23. Broadleys, nr Cartmel Fell, Lancashire (1898–9): A villa on Lake Windermere, designed by C.F.A. Voysey for a coal-owner, Arthur Currer Briggs

24. Jardine Hall, Dumfriesshire (1814; 1892–7): A Regency mansion, altered and enlarged for the Jardine family, China traders, by E.J. May. Demolished 1964

25. Craigtoun Park, Fife (1904): Rebuilt by Paul Waterhouse for James Younger, a brewer from Alloa

26. Manderston, Berwickshire (1894–1905): Rebuilt to designs by John Kinross
for Sir James Miller, 2nd Bt, Russia merchant

27. Glen, Peeblesshire (1858; 1874; 1906): Built to designs by David Bryce, and partly rebuilt by Sir Robert Lorimer, for Sir Charles Tennant, the Glasgow chemical magnate

28. Ballikinrain Castle, Stirlingshire (1862–4): Built to designs by David Bryce for Sir Archibald Orr-Ewing, the millionaire Glasgow dyer

29. Rosehaugh, Ross-shire (1872; 1898–1908): Remodelled by William Flockhart for J.D. Fletcher, heir to a Liverpool fortune made from Peruvian alpaca

30 and 31. Glen Tanar, Aberdeenshire (1869 onwards):
Extended to designs by George Truefitt for Sir William Cunliffe Brooks,
a Manchester banker

32. Auchendennan Castle, Dumbartonshire (1885): Built to designs by A.N. Patterson
for George Martin, an East India merchant from Glasgow

33. Meggernie Castle, Perthshire (fifteenth century; much rebuilt): Extended for John Bullough, inventor of the ring-spindle

34. Wyvis Lodge, Evanton, Ross-shire (1886): A shooting box on the edge of Loch Glass, built for Walter Shoolbred, a furniture manufacturer

35. Ardkinglas, Argyllshire (1905–6): Built to designs by Sir Robert Lorimer for Sir Andrew Noble, chairman of Armstrong, Whitworth & Co., armaments manufacturers

36. Lews Castle, Stornoway (1848–60): Rebuilt to designs by Charles Wilson for Sir James Matheson, opium trader

37. Kilmaron Castle, Fife (*c.* 1820; 1860): A castle designed by Gillespie Graham, extended for Sir David Baxter, the Dundee jute spinner. Demolished 1984

38. Castlemilk, Dumfriesshire (1864–70): Rebuilt to designs by
David Bryce for Sir Robert Jardine from a fortune made in the China trade

39. Arden House, Dumbartonshire (1866–8): Designed by John Burnet for
Sir John Lumsden, a successful stationer and publisher

40. Overtoun House, Dumbartonshire (1859–62): Built to designs by William Smith for James White, a Glasgow chemical magnate

41 and 42. Ardross Castle, Ross-shire (1880–1): Rebuilt to designs by Alexander Ross
for Sir Alexander Matheson, China trader

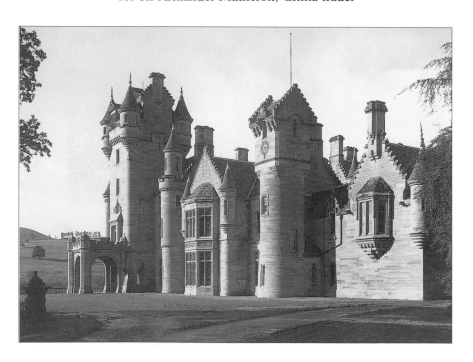

43. Skibo Castle, Sutherland (1899–1903): Rebuilt to designs by Alexander Ross and R.J. Macbeth for Andrew Carnegie, the Scottish-American steel magnate

44. West Shandon House, Dumbartonshire (1850): Built to designs by J.T. Rochead for Robert Napier, 'the father of steam shipbuilding'

45. Kinloch Castle, Isle of Rum (1897–1901; 1906): Designed by the Halifax firm of Leeming and Leeming for George Bullough, of the Accrington engineering family

46. Islay House, Argyllshire (1841–5 onwards): Bought by James Morrison in 1849, and subsequently much extended

47. Keiss Castle, Caithness (1859–62): Reconstructed by David Bryce for the 5th Duke of Portland; later owned by Francis Tress Barry, a dealer in Portuguese copper

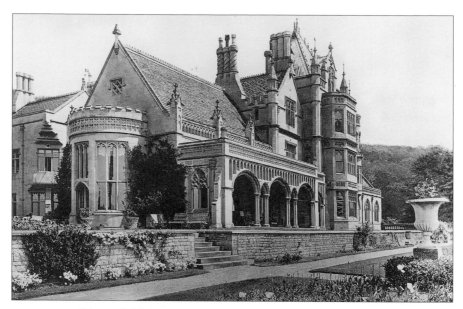

48. Tyntesfield House, Somerset (1863–6): Built to designs by
John Norton for William Gibbs, banker and High Churchman,
whose fortune derived from guano

49. Overstone Park, Northamptonshire (1859–65): Rebuilt
to designs by W.M. Teulon for a millionaire banker, Samuel Loyd,
1st Baron Overstone

50. Preston Hall, Aylesford, Kent (1844–50): Begun to designs by John Thomas for one railway magnate, E.L. Betts; then redecorated for another, H.A. Brassey

51. Somerleyton Hall, Suffolk (1844–51): Begun to designs by John Thomas for the building contractor Samuel Morton Peto; completed for Sir Francis Crossley, the carpet king

52 and 53. Preston Hall, Kent, entrance front and summer-house (*c.* 1850):
The family of H.A. Brassey, co-heir to the fortune of a millionaire
railway builder, Thomas Brassey

54. King's Walden Bury, Hertfordshire (1894): The family of T.F. Harrison,
a millionaire Liverpool shipowner. House demolished 1971

55. Palace House, Newmarket, garden front (1668–71 and later):
Bought and extended by Leopold de Rothschild, banker, a
member of the Prince of Wales's racing set

56. Luton Hoo, Bedfordshire, staircase hall (1903): Designed by Mewes and Davis for Sir Julius Wernher, the South African gold millionaire

57. Elveden Hall, Suffolk, the Durbar Hall (1899–1904): Designed by William Young and C.P. Clarke for the 1st Earl of Iveagh, the Guinness millionaire

58. Stoke Court, Buckinghamshire (1745–73; 1872 onwards):
A Georgian house refurbished for Christian Allhusen, a millionaire
chemical manufacturer from Schleswig-Holstein

59. Addington Park, nr Maidstone, Kent: Extended and refurbished for
Charles Sofer Whitburn, a millionaire bill broker

60. King's Walden Bury, Hertfordshire, drawing room (1894):
Designed by Beeston and Burmester for T.F. Harrison,
shipowner. Demolished 1971

61. Redleaf House, nr Penshurst, Kent, drawing room (1870 onwards):
The home of William Wells, shipbuilder and collector; remodelled
for the chemical magnate Frank Hills. Demolished

62. Witley Court, Worcestershire, music room (1850s): Remodelled by Samuel Daukes for the 1st Earl of Dudley, a millionaire coal-owner

63. Hursley Park, Hampshire, drawing room (1902): Remodelled to designs by A. Marshall Mackenzie for Sir George Cooper, who married the niece of 'Chicago' Smith

64. West Dean Park, Sussex, library (1891–3): Designed by Ernest George and Harold Peto for the American railway magnate, William Dodge James, with interiors by Charles Mellier & Co

65. Polesden Lacey, Surrey, drawing room (1910): A Georgian house remodelled for Mrs Ronnie Greville, daughter of the Scottish brewer John McEwen, by White Allom and Mewes and Davis

66. Waddesdon Manor, Buckinghamshire (1877–83; 1889):
Designed by H.A.G.W. Destailleur for Baron Ferdinand
de Rothschild, banker and collector

67 and 68. Tring Park, Hertfordshire (1873 onwards): Remodelled, probably by
George Devey, for the 1st Baron ('Natty') Rothschild, banker

68.

69. St Leonard's Hill, near Windsor, Berkshire (1875): Remodelled by C.H. Howell for Francis Tress Barry, copper magnate

70. Château Impney, Worcestershire (1869–75): Designed by Auguste Tronquois and R. Phené Spiers for John Corbett, a local salt manufacturer

71. Halton House, Buckinghamshire (1881–4): Designed by W.R. Rogers for Baron Alfred de Rothschild, banker and collector

72. Moundsmere, Hampshire (1908–9): Designed by Sir Reginald Blomfield for William Buckley, an Anglo-American trader

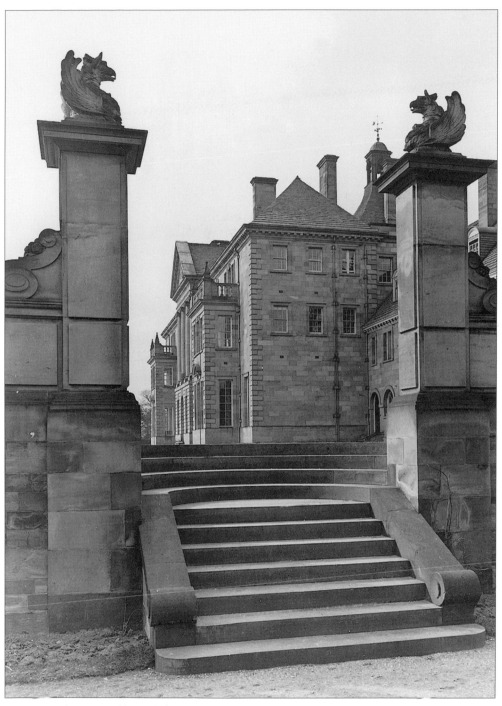

73. Crathorne Hall, Yorkshire (1903–9): Designed by Sir Ernest George and Alfred
Yeates for J.L. Dugdale, son of a cotton printer

74 and 75. Red Court, Haslemere, Surrey (1897): Designed by Ernest
Newton for J.S. Schillizzi, a millionaire trader from Greece

76 and 77. Trent Park, Hertfordshire (1926 onwards): A Georgian mansion remodelled for Sir Philip Sassoon, heir to a banking and trading fortune

78. Heathcote, Ilkley, Yorkshire (1905–7): Designed by Sir Edwin Lutyens for J.T. Hemingway, wool broker

79. Great Maytham, Rolvenden, Kent (1907–9): Designed by Sir Edwin Lutyens for H.J. Tennant, heir to a Glasgow chemical fortune

80. Port Lympne, Kent, the *scala regia* (1912; 1918–21): House and garden, overlooking Romney Marsh, designed by Sir Herbert Baker and Philip Tilden for Sir Philip Sassoon

# 4

# THE NEW PLUTOCRACY

## *London Houses, 1870–1939*

'The company was not such as we exclusives think quite the
thing. There was a little too much St Mary Axe about it
–Jewesses by dozens and Jews by scores . . . the sound of
fiddles was in mine ears, and gaudy dresses and black hair,
and Jewish roses were fluctuating up and down before mine
eyes.'

Thomas Babington Macaulay, 1831

Now for the quintessential *nouveau riche*, the metropolitan plutocrat.
Between the 1870s and the 1920s – between the diamond strikes at
Kimberley and the Great Crash on Wall Street – the architecture of
the rich, the very rich, went through a period of dazzling excess, a veritable Age of Ostentation. Their world, as analysed by Thorstein Veblen
in 1899, was indeed a society of 'Conspicuous Consumption' and 'Ostentatious Waste'.[1] Sir Osbert Sitwell remembered it as a time of
'unparalleled materialism'.[2] 'There has probably never been a period
in the history of the world', wrote Lecky in 1901, 'when the conditions
of industry, assisted by the great gold discoveries in several parts of the
world, were so favourable to the foundation of fortunes . . . and when
the race of millionaires was so large.'[3] Rockefeller, Guggenheim,
Gould, Harriman, Ford, Mellon, Vanderbilt, Astor, Carnegie, Morgan, Frick, Huntington – these were American fortunes, but their ten-
tacles were transatlantic. And as the nodal point in a network of
international capital, London was the chosen base of Hirsch and
Cassel, of Neumann and Speyer, of Beit, Robinson, Wernher and
Barnato – to say nothing of half the Rothschilds and quite a few of the

Sassoons. London, the Imperial City, was 'the banker of the world', the financial lifeline between New York, Johannesburg, Frankfurt and Paris. In its heyday, say 1890 to 1914, the City controlled almost half the international flow of capital. As early as 1879 the Rothschilds alone were said to control capital of £100,000,000. 'Neither Rockefeller, nor Carnegie, nor Astor, nor any other transatlantic prince of finance', it was claimed in 1913, 'has capital to equal that of the Rothschilds.'[4]

Of course England and Scotland had had millionaires before the 1870s – and we have already encountered quite a few of them – in banking, in spinning, in railways, in mining, in shipping, in chemicals, in provisions. But the means of accumulating wealth had now accelerated. As capitalism moved from its primary to its secondary phase, from production to finance, so the playing field was internationalised. It was this internationalisation of capital which gave London's Age of Ostentation its cosmopolitan flavour. From America came Astor, Morgan, Burns, Drexel and Emmet. Hirsch came from Munich, Robinson from Cape Colony, Schiff from Trieste, Neumann from Bavaria, Wernher from Darmstadt, Albu from Berlin, Bischoffsheim from Amsterdam; Cassel came from Cologne; the Rothschilds came from Frankfurt; Beit, Schröder, Ellerman and Meyer all came from Hamburg; Davis came from Australia via Paris; the Sassoons came from Baghdad via Bombay and Shanghai. Most of these immigrant Londoners also bought country estates. Lionel Phillips – the Randlord son of an Aldgate pawnbroker – took the trouble to rebuild Tylney Hall, Hampshire in 1897–1916; J.B. Robinson, the Kimberley Buccaneer, built himself a house at Lewins, Kent, to designs by J.M. Brydon in 1876; and Alfred Beit chose to end his days not in Germany or South Africa but at Tewin Water, Hertfordshire, a Regency house dating from *c.* 1810. But none of these figures could possibly be described as a countryman. London was their chosen home; their London houses became yardsticks of their identity.

This metropolitan emphasis reflects a shift in economic fortunes and thus in social priorities. After 1879 agricultural profits dwindled and land prices declined. Many great estates were broken up in the first decades of the twentieth century. 'Land as a hobby', suggested *Country Life* in 1911, 'has lost many of its attractions for capitalists.'

'Although the fascination of the ownership of land – land hunger – is still a dominant characteristic of the British race,' noted A.C. Fox-Davies in 1912, 'it cannot be said to possess its ancient importance . . . The growth of the new landless plutocracy has shifted the importance of things.'⁵ Indeed it had. Instant fortunes were more instantly translated into status symbols in the metropolis than in the countryside. And symbols there were in plenty. When Sir Edgar Speyer – surely the sinister villain in Buchan's *Thirty-Nine Steps* – built himself a Franco-Florentine palazzo at 46 Grosvenor Street [plate 84] to designs by Blow and Billerey in 1910–11, he thought it worth spending £150,000. There were rooms in a whole gamut of styles: Florentine, Venetian, Queen Anne, Louis XVI; he even installed a silver bath.⁶ But Speyer was also installing himself in a setting which he hoped – in vain, as it happened – would make him socially invulnerable. When J.P. Morgan II moved into 12 Grosvenor Square (*c.* 1727) he was similarly taking to himself the mores of an older, more prestigious world. William Waldorf Astor had laid down the international rule: 'America is no place for a gentleman.' On the contrary, sneered American newspapers, Astor had merely flown 'to the land of lust and baccarat'. And London, no doubt, had a plentiful supply of both. 'London', Escott concluded in the 1880s, 'is not the most beautiful, the most splendid, or even the most convenient city; but it is pre-eminently the smart metropolis of Europe. And the Americans have found it out. Formerly good Americans were said to go to Paris after they died; depend upon it their souls now migrate to London.'⁷

By the same token, London was no longer the place for native English gentry. It had become the capital of capital; a social summit open to talent, accessible to worldwide ambition. 'Social control' of London, noted Escott in 1903, is now divided between 'the Semite and the Yankee'. This 'Judaising of the West End' had its advantages: 'such humanising elements as leaven London today', he observed, 'largely come from the Jewish element . . . Say what you will, the Jews are the salt of smart Society'; without their patronage, 'English art and music could scarcely live in the English capital . . . To talk of Jew influence materialising Society in London is silly *blague*. The Israelite might rather claim to be a spiritualising force . . . [At the very least he supplies] a whetstone for the wits of his adopted countrymen.'[8] Maybe so; but the visibility of this social segment, with all its manifest success, was sure to attract hostility, not least from the older aristocracy. One afternoon in June 1900 Lord Balcarres, later 27th Earl of Crawford – a patrician to his fingertips – attended a reception in Mayfair and was taken aback by what he saw:

> In the afternoon Connie and I went to Hertford House, where a large party invited by Alfred Rothschild and Rosebery assembled to meet the Prince of Wales. The number of Jews in this palace was past belief. I have studied the anti-semite question with some attention, always hoping to stem an ignoble movement; but when confronted by the herd of Ickleheimers and Puppenbergs, Raphaels, Sassoons, and the rest of the breed, my emotions gain the better of logic and justice, while I feel some sympathy for Lüger and Drumont – John Burns, by the way, says the Jew is the tapeworm of civilisation.

Two years later, with Edward VII now on the throne, Balcarres noted that these 'ignoble' feelings were widespread: 'at Aldershot they called out "King of the Jews" ... there is much dormant anti-semitism, specially against [royal patronage] in Park Lane and Grosvenor Square'.[9] And there was substance in this popular suspicion. It has been estimated that just before 1914 over one-fifth of all non-landed millionaires were Jews, although the Jewish population of London was no more than 3 per cent of the total, and the Jewish proportion of the British population as a whole was only 0.3 per cent.[10] As aristocracy moved inescapably towards plutocracy, London's leading Jews emerged as lords paramount of smart Society.

> 'George' ... cried [my aunt] ... 'Do I stink of money?'
> 'Lunching?' I asked
> She nodded.
> 'Plutocratic ladies?'
> 'Yes.'
> 'Oriental type?'
> 'Oh! Like a burst hareem!'[11]

And H.G. Wells was not alone in his prejudice. 'What with the Ecksteins, Sassoons and Mosenthals,' complained Lord Northcliffe in

1912, 'we shall soon have to set the [Society] column in Yiddish.' Hilaire Belloc even protested that the House of Lords had been turned into 'a committee for the protection of the Anglo-Judaic plutocracy'. 'These over-civilised European Orientals', sniffed *The Spectator* in 1897, probably 'go to bed in satin and live upon ices and water biscuits.'[12]

The new financiers came here for profit, and they stayed here for prestige: men with names – in Masterman's phrase – like a cellar-full of 'Rhenish wines'.[13] London was the financial centre of the world, home to the greatest international banking dynasties: Rothschild, Bischoffscheim, d'Erlanger, Lazard, Seligman, Speyer and Stern. The crises of 1846, 1857 and 1866 were now history. The Stock Exchange expanded hugely:[14] a splendid new marble structure, designed by J.J. Cole and known irreverently as Gorgonzola Hall, opened in 1885. Backed by firm adherence to the gold standard, the pound sterling became the international currency; and the purchasing power of the pound reached a peak in 1896. At the same time, Britain had the most permissive commercial regulations in Europe. Here was a financial climate which attracted speculators from all over the globe. 'Capital', noted one commentator in 1906, 'knows no patriotism. Like water it spreads itself over the earth's surface, only instead of seeking the lowest level it finds the highest.'[15] Hence the fluctuations of capital export. Hence the successive waves of company promotion in 1889, 1898, 1910 and 1929. Hence too the astonishing – and often criminal – careers of Baron Grant and Whitaker Wright; of Jabez Balfour, Moreton Frewen, Jimmy White and Clarence Hatry – to say nothing of Terah Hooley and Colonel North, the nitrate king.

This was capitalism's unacceptable face. But the buildings such men left behind them – sometimes in London, sometimes in the country - were often appropriately spectacular: the French château built by Baron Grant (né Gottheimer), for example, Kensington House, Kensington Gore, designed by J.T. Knowles Jnr in 1872. This glittering pile – the largest private house in the capital – was the talk of Society; but it was never finished. By 1876 the whole £200,000 extravaganza – a monument to high risk stock flotation – was up for sale: the marble staircase ended in Madame Tussaud's, the entrance gates in Richmond Park.[16] Whitaker Wright's legacy was only a little more permanent. He made his first million in America, his second in Australia, but swallowed prussic acid at the Law Courts in 1904, minutes after his conviction for fraud. At Witley Park, Surrey – designed by H. Paxton Watson in 1890 – he spent £400,000 on a luxurious house complete with observatory, theatre and under water billiards room.[17] That surreal image – Whitaker Wright playing billiards under water in a manorial mansion – has an appropriately *fin-de-siècle* flavour. Jabez Balfour – another London operator with countrywide ambitions – was scarcely less flamboyant. A fast-talking building society fraudster and property developer, he was reputedly the model for Mr Ponderevo in H.G. Wells's *Tono-Bungay* (1909). In 1869 he moved into Wellesley House, Croydon, and became Croydon's first mayor; in 1886 he bought Burcot, Oxfordshire from the Earl of Abingdon; ten years later he was in Parkhurst Prison. But by the time he fled to Argentina in 1892 – with debts of £8,000,000 – he had at least left his mark on the skyline of London: the luxury apartments of Whitehall Court and the Hyde Park Hotel (both by Archer and Green, 1886–90) – to say nothing of the Hotel Cecil (1900–6) – sum up all the extravagance and excess of those years.[18] By comparison Moreton Frewen – known to his victims as 'Mortal Ruin' – led a comparatively quiet life: he was a gentleman speculator, a London clubman who married Clara Jerome of New York and lived comfortably at Brede Place, Sussex.[19] Comparative quiet was not at all the aim of Jimmy White. A property speculator who quit Lancashire for London, White was reputedly the original of Arnold Bennet's *The Card* (1911). Repeatedly bankrupt, he eventually committed suicide at his racing stable, Foxhill, Wanborough, near Swindon.[20] And Clarence Hatry played for even higher stakes. When his speculations collapsed in 1929 – 'the most appalling frauds that have ever disfigured the commercial reputation of this country' – his debts were put at £14,000,000.[21] Hatry in fact built little, but Terah Hooley enjoyed life in the grand manner. By origin a Nottinghamshire lace-maker —neither Irish nor Jewish – Hooley successfully floated Dunlop, Singer, Bovril, Humber and Schweppes. London was his theatre of operations, but he bought land in six counties: he lived ostentatiously at Risley Hall, Derbyshire and Papworth Hall, Cambridgeshire – done up by 'my old friend Maple'. And of course it was all too good to last: his extravagance finally brought him to bankruptcy and prison. Eleven thousand pounds had secured him admission to the Carlton Club; fifty thousand failed to buy him a baronetcy in 1897.[22] As for J.T. North – a nitrate speculator notorious from Holbech to Peru – he lived lavishly at Avery Hill, Eltham, Kent, designed in 1889-91 by T.W. Cutler. The apogee of his career was reached with a fancy-dress ball at London's Hotel Metropole in 1889. Dressed as Henry VIII, this egregious colonel greeted eight hundred guests including thirteen peers and two Rothschilds.[23]

Such ostentation had its occasional public benefits, in the metropolis as elsewhere. In 1888 North presented the ruins of Kirkstall Abbey to the people of Leeds. In 1875 Baron Grant presented Leicester Square to the citizens of London. A grandiose gesture, indeed; but Lord Derby was not deceived. Grant had inveigled at least one Tory Minister, Lord Henry Gordon-Lennox, into joining his conspiracies; but he was a conspirator none the less.

> In a disreputable speculator, who has more than once narrowly escaped prosecution for fraud, [this generosity] is an ingenious device for putting himself right with the world. And in that point of view it will be a very good investment ... He has done too many dirty acts to be whitewashed: and too many that are useful to be neglected. Probably some day he will ask for a baronetcy.[24]

How then shall we characterise the plutocrat? Du Maurier's cartoon figure Sir Georgius Midas, the 'successful *sausage maker*' of Midas Towers, Surrey, is a home-grown millionaire. 'He has married his sons and daughters to [the old nobility, noted Du Maurier], and spoiled the lovely curve of those noble noses.'[25] But Anthony Trollope has left us a rather more cosmopolitan image: Augustus Melmotte in *The Way We Live Now* (1875).

> Mr Melmotte [of Grosvenor Square and Pickering Park, Sussex: that is, Albert Gottheimer, Baron Grant] had made his wealth in France ... It was said he had made a railway across Russia, that he provisioned the

159

Southern army in the American civil war, that he had supplied Austria with arms, and had at one time bought up all the iron in England. He could make or mar any company by buying or selling stock, and could make money dear or cheap as he pleased ... it was also said that he was regarded in Paris as the most gigantic swindler that had ever lived ... that he had endeavoured to establish himself in Vienna, but had been warned away by the police; and that he had at length found that British freedom would alone allow him to enjoy, without persecution, the fruits of his industry.[26]

Such were the richest of the *nouveaux riches*. Their dealings were international, but London was their focus of ambition. And that ambition, often enough, was expressed through the medium of architecture. The *nouveau-riche* style – a type of Anglo-American Beaux-Arts – emerged in its most dazzling form in Edwardian London. These men were cosmopolitan; so was their taste; so too was the figure at the very summit of their social ambition – the Prince of Wales. 'Behold', announced the French press in 1881, 'the first cosmopolitan Prince of Wales.' When that Prince became King the plutocrats came into their own. Their friendship with the new monarch confirmed 'the social sovereignty of wealth'. After all, complained Lady Paget, he shared 'the same luxurious taste as the Semites, the same love of pleasure and comfort'.[27] In 1895, a few years before the start of the new reign, William Waldorf Astor found himself dining at Sandringham; around the table were J.B. Robinson the Kimberley Buccaneer, Colonel North the nitrate king – and the heir to the throne of England.[28] That same year Sir Algernon West was invited to Christmas dinner at Baron Alfred de Rothschild's:

> Eight nationalities were represented at dinner, made up, I think, by Prince Duleep Singh, Indian; Baron Alphonse [de Rothschild], French; the Brazilian and Belgian Ministers; Mrs Sassoon, Austrian; M       , a German; M. De Soveral, Portuguese; and ourselves [English]. After dinner we saw some wonderful billiard tricksters, one American and one English ... The next day we played golf, very unsatisfactory in the snow.[29]

Four years later the Prince of Wales spent Goodwood week at West Dean Park [plate 64]: he clearly preferred the company of Mrs William Dodge James to the hospitality of the Duke of Richmond.

In such ways were the seals of social approval redistributed. By 1903 the King was dining regularly with Leopold de Rothschild at Palace House, Newmarket [plate 55], and weekending at Brighton in the company of the Levitas, the Van Raaltes or the Sassoons. Far from 'dropping the Semites' at his accession, noted Escott, the monarch's continuing patronage reinforced the social resonance of 'the great Jews'. And this process of assimilation, wave upon wave of wealth, began to seem almost endless. Even the Rothschilds were in danger of being upstaged by newer money still. 'Park Lane', Escott announced, 'has been annexed by the South African millionaires, each new-comer more aggressively wealthy than his predecessor. The Beits, the Robinsons and the Wernhers, in the popular eye, do but degrade the principle of wealth.'

And there was more to come. The money in Carlton House Terrace was newer even than the money in Park Lane. Between the 1860s and the First World War, the number of old aristocratic families occupying those grand houses fronting St James's Park – Cavendish, Ridley, Lyttelton, Bruce, Lowther, Churchill, Fitzroy – falls away sharply. In their place come the scions of new money: Guinness (stout), Horlick (malted milk), Stern (finance), Waterlow (printing), Morrison (haberdashery), Crossley (carpets), Astor (property), Cunard (shipping), Pearson (contracting), and Stephen (railways). 'The trans-Atlantic Midases – peltry or pork kings – have established themselves on the site once consecrated by Carlton House. Their rivals from the Antipodes are coming over,' Escott concluded, '[and even our] native nobility are successfully returning to the commerce . . . on which their family fortunes were [once] founded.'[30]

Whether this 'influx of the rich foreign element' really brought about 'a new conception of life altogether . . . [with] wealth as the ultimate end of existence' must remain doubtful. Lady Dorothy Nevill – inveighing against 'the insensate avarice of the age' – clearly enjoyed the role of social Cassandra. Others just talked of 'that frisky futility which is known as smartness'.[31] But there was a change of tone, a coarsening of attitudes. Soon titles were being bought in return for political finance, and titles were being sold in return for guinea-pig directorships in dubious companies. This is the process – a peerage doubly debased – scrutinised by Professor Cannadine. City peerages had once been rare: Smith (Baron Carrington); Loyd (Baron Overstone); Glyn (Baron Wolverton). Now, in 1885, simultaneous titles for the City houses of Rothschild and Baring showed the direction from which a new wind was blowing. Between 1890 and 1914 more than two hundred peerages were created, more than a third from commerce or industry. Between 1901 and 1910, twenty-four out of seventy new peers came from business. Brewers like Guinness, Allsopp and Bass emerged as Iveagh, Hindlip and Burton. Shipping magnates came to rejoice in titles like Inverclyde, Nunburnholme and Inchcape. Press barons like Northcliffe, armaments manufacturers like Armstrong, newsagents like W.H. Smith: the infiltration of aristocracy by plutocracy accelerated mightily towards the end of Victoria's reign. Between 1885 and 1914 the number of baronets doubled, and the number of knights bachelor trebled.[32] Between 1892 and 1896, 35 per cent of new peers came from non-landed backgrounds; between 1897 and 1911, it was 43 per cent. And the number of City men involved was strikingly high: a dozen peerages and a score of baronetcies were awarded to merchant bankers. Inevitably, it was suspected that money played an increasing part in this process.

Rosebery's resignation honours list of 1895 marked something of a watershed. Peerages for one Jewish financier (Stern) and one Lancastrian linoleum manufacturer (Williamson) were bad enough. Both were denounced as political corruption in Tory and Liberal newspapers. But a baronetcy at the same time for a turncoat back-bencher (Naylor-Leyland) was the last straw. In the pages of *Truth*, Henry Labouchère was withering:

> 'It does not smell', said Vespasian of the money that he had acquired from a tax on the latrines of Rome. But the money brought in by this trafficking in hereditary legislatorships reeks of corruption. It stinks!'[33]

From then on it was a straight and downhill path to the era of Lloyd George. 'I am distressed at being obliged to lay so large a list of honours before Her Majesty,' wrote Lord Salisbury in 1895; 'if she comments on it, pray remind her that this is a Coalition Government.'[34] In 1908 the Rosebery Committee revealed that the roll-call of the House of Lords had increased by 20 per cent in twenty-five years. Bagehot had prophesied the danger in this process as early as 1867. 'The rule of wealth, the religion of gold . . . the worship of money'; all this, he predicted, would soon overwhelm the aristocratic '*style* of society . . . The rise of industrial wealth . . . has brought in a competitor [to the old landed and hereditary system] . . . Every day our companies, our railways, our debentures, and our shares, tend more and more to multiply these *surroundings* of the aristocracy, and in time they will hide it.'[35]

> 'When we make peers of our tradesmen . . .' said [Lord] Framlingham with a chuckle . . . 'we know what we are about; we are soldering our own leaking pot . . . [the] *novi homines* [have] kept the English aristocracy vigorous and popular.'
> [Katherine Massarene] gave a scornful gesture of denial.
> 'It is the *novi homines* who have degraded the English aristocracy . . . Mr Mallock . . . has forgotten to satirise its most shameful infirmity, its moral scrofula – its incessant and unblushing prostration of itself before wealth *qua* wealth. It likes hot-house pines and can no longer afford to keep them for its own eating. It can only grow them for sale and eat them at the tables of those who buy them.'
> 'That is very severe!' [replied Lord Framlingham.][36]

Outside politics, similar processes were at work. In the last twenty years of the century the number of presentations at Court doubled; by 1891, more than half involved the daughters of non-landed families. 'The social sieve', comments Professor Thompson, 'became decidedly coarser from the 1890s onwards.'[37] How else can we explain the tolerant reception given to Charles Tyson Yerkes, the Chicago tramcar king who arrived in London at the turn of the century, hoping to develop the capital's underground railway? He even installed his current mistress – the 'Kentucky Beauty' – in a villa in Maidenhead and a house off Berkeley Square.[38] American influence was becoming pervasive. By 1899 the *Peerage* included fifty American ladies; by 1914, 17 per cent of the peerage and 12 per cent of the baronetcy had an American connection, frequently through marriage to an heiress.[39] 'Failing the dowries of Israel and the plums of the United States,' noted Escott, 'the British peerage would go to pieces tomorrow.' At the turn of the century it was estimated that New World heiresses had enriched Old World husbands to the tune of £40,000,000.[40] The ducal families of Newcastle, Roxburghe, Manchester, and Marlborough were all rejuvenated by New World money. So were the marquessates of Anglesey, Hertford and Ormonde. And so were a whole catalogue of earldoms: Camperdown, Craven, Donoughmore, Granard, Strafford, Suffolk, Essex, Howe, Orford and Tankerville. The nobility of Britain was being simultaneously plutocratised by business and Americanised by marriage. Of course, only a minority of transatlantic marriages were simple cash-for-title transactions: neither Sir Sydney Waterlow nor Sir Francis Cook, still less the 1st and 3rd Barons Cheylesmore or Lord Berkeley of Berkeley Square, had any need of New World wealth when they selected American brides. Still, the mutual attraction of new money and old title seems often to have been irresistable. Even a Tory diehard like Sir Almeric Paget married two Americans in succession, the first being a considerable heiress, daughter of William C. Whitney of Fifth Avenue, New York. In 1902 May Goelet, also of New York and co-heir to a $25,000,000 fortune, noted that Captain George Holford had hopes of marrying her: 'Dorchester House, of course, would be delightful and I believe he has two charming places [Westonbirt and Lasborough, Gloucestershire]. Unfortunately, the dear man has no title ...'[41] She settled for the Duke of Roxburghe.

Money from commercial sources closer to home had for some time been performing the same function a little lower down the scale. Society was indeed expanding. In the 1870s that magic circle was reckoned to number about five hundred families; by the eve of the First World War an estimate of four thousand would have been nearer the mark. Marriages between City and Land multiplied. The future Lord Northcote married an adopted daughter of the future Lord Mount Stephen, the Canadian financier and railway tycoon. Lord Bathurst married the daughter of the proprietor of the *Morning Post*. Nor were they alone. Through marriage, as through occupation, old money and new money were becoming interchangeable.[42] As plummeting land values pulled the territorial aristocracy downwards, so exploding international finance pulled the plutocracy upwards. And the expansion of the peerage became an index of all these social changes. In six years, 1916 to 1922, Lloyd George created 90 peers. In eighteen profligate months in 1921 and 1922 he created 26 peerages, 74 baronetcies and 294 knighthoods. Between 1905 and 1934, 649 baronetcies were gazetted; between 1916 and 1922 more than 1,500 knighthoods were granted; between 1921 and 1925 alone there were no fewer than 1,026. 'The rule of the rich', noted one observer as early as 1880, 'has simply been substituted for the rule of the noble'.[43]

It was certainly a time of extraordinary mobility, geographical and social. Anton Dunkelsbuhler, a Jewish diamond dealer born in Belgium, made his million in South Africa before transferring to London, adopting English nationality, sending his sons to Harrow and dying in Hyde Park Gardens [plate 93] under the name Anton Dunkels.[44] Samuel Lewis, a Jewish moneylender, became eventually a resident of Grosvenor Square, and lived to stable his horses in North Audley Street.[45] And the career of Sir Edmund Davis was more remarkable still. A company promoter and mining financier who spent his early life between Australia and Paris, Davis made a fortune out of base metal in southern Africa, and ended as 'one of the most influential capitalists in the City of London', director of forty companies, 'a veritable Napoleon of finance'. Feared and distrusted as a dealer, he earned grudging respect as a collector and patron of the arts. His houses – the Palazzo Desdemona in Venice, Lansdowne House in Holland Park and Chilham Castle in Kent – were famous for their cuisine and filled with works of art by Rodin, Conder and Brangwyn. Herbert Baker was his architect at Chilham. William Flockhart designed him adjoining studios for Charles Ricketts and Charles Shannon close to his own home in Lansdowne Road. But he must have been one of the most distrusted men in London, 'a Jew who would cheat his blind grandmother at cards'. His photographic portrait is sinister, almost a caricature of the Edwardian money-man: 'the Premier magnate of the Jungle Mines' [plate 11].[46]

Sometimes the nobility managed to float with the tide. When Jenny Jerome married Lord Randolph Churchill in 1874 she brought with her $250,000. When the 5th Earl of Carnarvon married the illegitimate daughter of Alfred de Rothschild in 1895, he found himself half a million pounds richer. Lord Curzon – with the prospect of Kedleston to keep up – married the daughter of a millionaire shop-keeper from Chicago. The 5th Baron Decies married the daughter of a legendary financier, Jay Gould of New York. The 4th Earl of Strafford married the widow of Colgate's soap. The hostesses of New York seem to have been particularly fond of English lords. One New York heiress successively married the 2nd Marquess of Dufferin and Ava and the 4th Earl Howe. Another – as we have seen – dared even to wed Sir William Gordon Cumming, 4th Bt, the card-sharper of Tranby Croft. The 4th Baron Ribblesdale – so memorably portrayed by Sargent – married money on both sides of the Atlantic: first the daughter of Sir Charles Tennant and then the widow of J.J. Astor. But then, as the *Annual Register* pointed out, he did look rather like an Old Master.[47] The prizes were there, for those with the nerve to take them. But first the old, insular hierarchy of birth, land and title had to come to terms with the new international hierarchy of wealth. The signals of read-justment were certainly visible in the 1880s; and all these processes of change were accelerated by the First World War. While the nobility and gentry were dying in the fields of Flanders, noted Lord Henry Bentinck in 1918, England was being turned into a paradise for profi-teers.[48] These were the hard-faced men remembered by Philip Tilden playing poker with Gordon Selfridge: 'The conversation', he recalled, 'turned mostly on thousands of pounds, hundreds of thousands of pounds, and millions of pounds ... Sir Thomas Lipton, Sir Ernest Cassel, Mr James Beck of America. It was an Indian summer for many of them.'[49] Indian summer indeed: by the 1920s Selfridge was enter-taining the Dolly Sisters at Lansdowne House.

So, at the end of the nineteenth century, what was the London mil-lionaire style, the architectural image of these metropolitan plutocrats? How did they build, or rebuild, or decorate?

First of all, the exceptions. Robert Hudson, a soap baron from Birkenhead, built himself a fanciful late Gothic mansion, Stanhope House, at 47 Park Lane [plate 108], designed by W.H. Romaine-

Walker in 1899–1901.[50] William Waldorf Astor, later 1st Viscount Astor, with means enough for any form of building, retreated each evening to his 'strongbox', the Astor Estate Office, a Tudorbethan extravaganza on the Embankment designed by J.L. and F.L. Pearson in 1893–5.[51] But these are both atypical. As with country houses, Gothic was never the style for London millionaires.

The London houses of the old nobility had been traditionally Classical, and the new men followed suit. Old money – the Stanleys, the Leveson-Gowers – had been at home in Derby House (1773) or Stafford House (1825–43);[52] new money would one day boast Home House, Portman Square, designed by James Wyatt and Robert Adam in 1773–6 and eventually the adopted residence of the greatest of spinner–collectors, Sam Courtauld.[53] Where Adam built and Courtauld span, who was then the gentleman? New money simply took on old money's stylistic mantle. Dorchester House [plate 81] in all its splendour – Lewis Vulliamy's palazzo of 1846–63 for R.S. Holford – outdid even Stafford House in the parallactic drama of its staircase hall.[54] Holford, of course, came from gentry stock, but gentry grown suddenly plutocratic: few *nouveaux riches* could match that sort of display. When northern millionaires moved south, they mostly slipped into standard Classical houses: John Rylands, the Manchester cotton king, at 67 Queen's Gate; or Duncan Dunbar, a dour Scottish shipowner, in Porchester Terrace;[55] Sir John Hardy, the Staffordshire ironmaster, at 22 South Street, Mayfair; William McEwen, the great Scottish brewer, at 16 Charles Street, Berkeley Square; or John Gretton of Burton-on-Trent, co-partner in the largest brewery in the world, at 66 Ennismore Gardens.[56] Ennismore Gardens was similarly home to Charles Sofer Whitburn, a formidable bill-discounter, and Sir John Brunner, 1st Bt, a mighty chemist from Liverpool.[57] All these self-made men took on the protective clothing of inherited taste. Even Sir John Ellerman, 1st Bt, richest of them all – the 'Silent Ford', the 'Invisible Rockefeller' – preferred to hide his riches in an anonymous house in South Audley Street.[58] Stucco Classicism on the fringes of Hyde Park – Queen's Gate, Lancaster Gate, Connaught Place, Hyde Park Place, Westbourne Terrace – attracted a whole cluster of *arrivistes*: Charles Butler, insurance broker;[59] Sir Donald Currie, shipowner;[60] John Nixon, colliery proprietor;[61] Maurice Beddington [né Moses], wholesale clothier;[62] and – not exactly parvenu – Sir Joseph Sebag-Montefiore, merchant banker.[63] Likewise, a veritable clutch of City-based Sterns and Raphaels.[64] All these men left a million and more in money of that day; but their town houses were inconspicuously Classical. The stylistic running in London was not made by men like these. It was made by men who were not just rich: a plutocrat was conspicuously rich.

The truly plutocratic style did not in fact sit easily on the shoulders of home-grown millionaires. Some, of course, never left the provinces: Sir William Brown, 1st Bt (linen and banking), stayed in Liverpool; Sir Frederick Mappin, 1st Bt (cutlery and steel), remained in Sheffield.[65] Others, when they did move south, were already beginning to prefer suburbia. James Eno, of Eno's Fruit Salts, lived healthily in Dulwich to the ripe age of ninety-five.[66] Sir Joseph Beecham, of Beecham's Pills, selected a hilltop home in Hampstead, where he could play the organ in peace.[67] Francis Reckitt, starch manufacturer, chose Highgate; Seth Taylor, miller, chose Putney; Charles Beasley, brewer, chose Abbey Wood.[68] Hampstead Heath was the favoured retreat of Sir Joshua Waddilove, 'credit agency proprietor'; and the lower slopes of Hampstead were home also to Henry Tetley, a bulldog rayon tycoon from Yorkshire.[69] William Lever, 1st Viscount Leverhulme – that Leviathan of soap – chose as his residence not Lancaster House or Grosvenor House (both of which he bought) but The Hill [plate 83], overlooking Hampstead Heath (1895; 1904–25): a grandiloquent Classical confection complete with underground ballroom, surrounded by pergolas without end and a belvedere fit for the Younger Pliny.[70] All these men left a million pounds in the decade 1915–25; some of them several million. All were English, all were self-made, and all ended their careers in Edwardian London. But they lived in the suburbs, a place – to echo Carlyle – where retired wholesalers look down on retired retailers, and retired manufacturers look down on both.

In the last year of the War, Mr Lackersteen, who had managed to avoid service, made a great deal of money, and just after the Armistice . . . moved into a huge, new rather bleak house in Highgate, with quantities of greenhouses, shrubberies, stables and tennis courts. Mr Lackersteen had engaged a horde of servants, even, so great was his optimism, a butler . . .[71]

George Orwell's Lackersteen went bankrupt in 1919. Others were more resilient.

Men like Samuel Palmer of Huntley and Palmer (Hampstead) and Thomas Blackwell of Crosse and Blackwell (Harrow Weald);[72] Sir Henry Tate of the future Tate and Lyle (Streatham Common);[73] or Peter Robinson of Peter Robinson (Hornsey)[74] – all these preferred the anonymity of suburbia to the gilded salons of the West End. So did several other household names worth slightly less than a million: William Edgar of Swan and Edgar, who lived in Clapham;[75] J. Lawson Johnston – 'Mr Bovril' – who settled in Dulwich at Bovril Castle;[76] James Marshall of Marshall and Snelgrove, who lived at Mill Hill;[77] and Sir Sydney Waterlow of Waterlows, who lived for a while in Highgate.[78] Sir Henry Bessemer, that self-made genius of steel, built himself a classic millionaire's mansion, Bessemer House on Denmark Hill, designed by Charles Barry Jnr in 1863. French within and Italian without, all gilded stucco and potted palms – not to mention the world's second-largest telescope – Bessemer's retreat was certainly plutocratic; but it was, equally certainly, suburban.[79] And even Sir Thomas Lipton, very much a millionaire, when not travelling the world or yachting with royalty preferred a retreat near Palmers Green.[80] In each case, though in different degrees, the temperament and background of these men kept them on the social periphery. The inner suburbs – Regent's Park, Kensington, Brompton, Hammersmith – had once been much favoured by merchants in the mid nineteenth century. Now such men – becoming richer and more demanding – were moving further out. After all, they were tycoons – northern, mostly – not sophisticates. Their natural habitat was the counting house, not the drawing room. Their wives played little part in Society. Not one of them set up a traditional town house in Mayfair or Belgravia. The West End had become the preserve of a very different class of millionaire: the cosmopolitan plutocracy.

\*

Hints of the plutocratic style can be seen in the evolution of Kensington Palace Gardens between the 1840s and the 1920s.[81] This colony of new money consisted of more than two dozen stone and stucco mansions strung out along the periphery of Kensington Palace. All – apart from one Gothic house and two with Islamic touches by Owen Jones – were Classical: Italianate, Neo-Classical or French Renaissance. Their architects – advisory or executant – belonged to the Victorian finale of the English Classical tradition: James Pennethorne, Charles Barry, Sydney Smirke, Philip Hardwick, Banks and Barry, Wyatt and Brandon, Decimus Burton, J.T. Knowles Jnr, M.D. Wyatt and Thomas Cubitt. The fact that only one house was Gothic – and the fact that this was built to his own specifications by the only aristocrat in the row, the 5th Earl of Harrington[82] – neatly establishes the issue of style. When Peto commissioned R.R. Banks to design him an Italianate palazzo at number 12 in 1846 [plate 82], he was making a statement of status: by 1861 there were sixteen living-in servants. When Alexander Collier – a City financier who followed Peto into bankruptcy in 1869 – added a Moorish billiards room to the same house in 1866, he was merely toying with fashion, not overstepping the stylistic mark. New money, as we have seen so often, played safe. But the nature of that wealth was changing. The social composition of Kensington Palace Gardens became increasingly cosmopolitan as English capitalism galloped ahead from domestic production to international finance.

The earlier residents were mostly native entrepreneurs: Thomas Grissell (building), Sir Morton Peto (railways), John Leech ('general merchant'), James Meadows Rendel (docks and harbours),[83] Alexander Collie (cotton),[84] Bevis E. Green (bookselling),[85] George Moore (lace-making),[86] Edward Antrobus (tea).[87] Their path to riches was not always easy. Peto began as a bricklayer's labourer; he and Grissell were several times on the verge of bankruptcy. Collie went spectacularly bankrupt in 1875, and avoided gaol only by hiding abroad. And Moore, a self-made industrialist whom we have already encountered in the Lake District, suffered agonies of conscience over the extent of his own extravagance. After building his Kensington palazzo, he took care to explain to Samuel Smiles that he only did it to please his wife. 'Although I had built the house at the solicitation of Mrs Moore, I was mortified at my extravagance, and thought it both wicked and aggrandizing – mere ostentation and vain show – to build such a house.'[88] The personal traumas, the hopes and hypocrisies involved in the pursuit of wealth and status, were seldom so openly expressed.

This vein of new money, English money, in Kensington Palace Gardens continued to the turn of the century with Sir Alfred Hickman, 1st Bt (iron and steel),[89] Sir Joseph Whitwell Pease, 1st Bt (railways),[90] J.E. Taylor (newspapers),[91] Sir Frederick Wills, 1st Bt (tobacco),[92] and J.M. Rendel's son Stuart, 1st Baron Rendel (armaments).[93] But their later neighbours belonged mostly to a wider world, a global network based on international finance. They were part of the new cosmopolitan plutocracy. Step forward Arthur Strauss[94] and Ernest Leopold S. Benzon,[95] German tin merchant, German steel magnate; and you, Baron Julius de Reuter,[96] German founder of the international news agency; and you, Henry van den Bergh,[97] hero of many a Dutch enterprise; and you, Don Cristobal de Murietta, with your sons Mariano and José, Spanish merchants through three generations.[98] You too, grandees of the Dominions: Sir Elliott Lewis[99] from Australia (law); Sir Chester Beatty[100] from New York via South Africa (copper); Sir Lewis Richardson, 1st Bt,[101] and Sir Alfred Beit, 2nd Bt, from South Africa again (ostrich feathers and diamonds). And all you bankers, brokers and financiers: Donald Larnach,[102] Charles F. Huth,[103] William L. Winans,[104] Gustave C. Schwabe,[105] J.P. Kennard,[106] Isaac Seligman,[107] Charles Van Raalte,[108] Henry Oppenheimer.[109] Money men, all of you; all new money men. Not to mention you, Samuel Montagu – 'foul old Swaythling' – the fastest calculator in the City.[110] Or finally you, Moritz de Hirsch, financial wizard to half the courts of Europe; you, after all, are principal adviser to the nearby court of Kensington.

Now, not all these men were millionaires. Only Hickman, Wills, Swaythling, Larnach, Hirsch and Beit actually left more than £1,000,000. But they all lived like millionaires. And all belonged to the wider world of international finance. Benzon's son even wrote a book entitled *How I Lost £250,000 in Two Years* (1889), surely a classic text for the sons of *nouveaux riches*. Their origins were certainly disparate: Strauss came from Mainz; Van den Burgh came from

Rotterdam; Lewis came from Hobart via Balliol; Winans came from Baltimore by way of St Petersburg. Another resident, Harris Lebus, at one time the biggest furniture maker in the world, emerged from Breslau via Hull.[111] But they all ended up in Kensington Palace Gardens. It might not be Mayfair or Belgravia, but – as one journal noted in 1890 – it was '*facile princeps* in the estimation of our merchant princes, bankers and other leaders of the world of finance.'[112] It had become Millionaires' Row, home to the new 'Aristocracy of London'.[113] Even so, it was essentially a new housing development for new money. The peak of plutocratic ambition lay elsewhere, in that part of London where old money had long accumulated: Mayfair.[114]

For the first century of its existence, Grosvenor Square was almost entirely the preserve of the landed aristocracy. In Arthur Dasent's words, its ground was 'strewn with strawberry leaves and blue ribbons of the garter'. In 1790, for example, out of 47 householders no fewer than 31 were members of the nobility; and these included three dukes, six earls and one viscount. Not until the second quarter of the nineteenth century did the transition from aristocracy to plutocracy really begin. As late at 1876 Edward Walford could claim that 'there is not a plebeian "professional" man living here – not even a titled MD.'[115] But in 1878 one physician did move in. And in the two decades after 1896 plutocracy arrived in force: Sir William Cunliffe Brooks, Manchester banker; Sir John Kelk, building contractor; Sir Henry Meux, brewer; Edward Anthony Strauss, hop and grain merchant; Marcus Van Raalte, stockbroker; Sir Lionel Phillips, diamond merchant; Sir Charles Tennant, chemical manufacturer; Sir Walter Palmer, biscuit baron. From Germany came the legendary financier Sir Ernest Cassel, *en route* to Park Lane. From Hartlepool came the shipping magnate Christopher Furness, *en route* to the House of Lords. From Australia came Sir Samuel Wilson; from Canada Sir Edward Mackay Edgar; from America J.P. Morgan II. From America, too, came two successive Duchesses of Manchester. And as they arrived, they refurbished and rebuilt. At number 41, in the 1880s, Charles Wilson, whom we have already met as Lord Nunburnholme, first commissioned George Devey to design a new house, and then employed a series of mysterious Parisian decorators to transform Devey's staid Jacobean Classicism into a rich variety of Gallic forms.[116] These rooms were in turn transmogrified in a Franco-Dutch manner just after the First World War. At number 26 Sir George Cooper, a Scotsman who had married an American heiress – Mary Smith of Evanston, Illinois: niece of 'Chicago' Smith – engaged Anatole Beaumetz of Paris, as well as the ubiquitous brothers Duveen, to transform an interior by Eden Nesfield into a late eighteenth-century Parisian *hôtel*, just in time for Edward VII's first Season in 1902.[117] At number 45 [plates 87–8] Sir James Miller, 2nd Bt – another mercantile Scot, whom we encountered at Manderston – employed Charles Mellier of Paris to create a French *Régence* dining room worthy of the royal racing set.[118] And Jack Barnato Joel – Barney Barnato's nephew – of Spitalfields, Kimberley, Johannesburg and Mayfair – acquired number 34 [plate 86], a house which was surely an upholsterer's dream. 'Servants ... stand stately and obsequious in the hall,' noted Louis Cohen; 'lavishly finished, gorgeously upholstered, the mansion is a receptacle for everything fashion can light on, and resembles a gilded pantechnicon.'[119] By 1903 the Grosvenor Square home of Baroness von Eckhardstein – daughter of that 'prince of upholsterers, Sir J.B. Maple' – had become 'a recognised place of international resort.'[120]

Clearly French Classicism, generically speaking, was the plutocratic style. Mr Bond Sharpe, Disraeli's star of moneylenders, resided in Cleveland Row:

> They ascended a staircase perfumed with flowers, and on each landing-place was a classic tripod or pedestal crowned with a bust. And then they were ushered into a drawing room of Parisian elegance; buhl cabinets, marqueterie tables, hangings of the choicest damask suspended from burnished cornices of old carving. The chairs had been rifled from a Venetian palace; the couches were part of the spoils of the French revolution. There were glass screens in golden frames, and a clock that represented the death of Hector, the chariot wheels of Achilles conveniently telling the hour.[121]

Sometimes the Classical synthesis was still as much Italian as French. When Edward Steinkopf, the Tory mineral water tycoon, moved into

47 Berkeley Square, his house took the form of a Florentine palazzo, designed in 1891 by Ernest George and Peto.[122] But, on the whole, French was the plutocratic preference. When that mighty brewer Michael Bass, 1st Baron Burton, moved into Chesterfield House, South Audley Street [plates 89–90] – in itself a symbolic transition from aristocracy to plutocracy – he gladly took over Isaac Ware's sumptuous French *rocaille*, then over-egged the soufflé with furniture of an altogether heavier type: décor of the 1740s plus furnishings of the 1890s.[123] When Henri Bischoffsheim moved into nearby Bute House at 75 South Audley Street – again a symbolic transfer – his new *dix-huitième* interiors (1873; 1902) turned it, according to one contemporary, into 'a Versailles in miniature'.[124] When Julius Wernher moved into Bath House, Piccadilly [plate 96] – succeeding the equally plutocratic Baron de Hirsch – eighteenth-century France was again the chosen style. Beatrice Webb's puritan response was scathing: 'hugely overdone – wealth, wealth, wealth was screamed aloud wherever one turned ... there might as well have been a Goddess of Gold erected for overt worship ... [though of course, she added discreetly,] our host was superior to his wealth'.[125] At 52 Grosvenor Street, in 1902–4, William Peel (later 1st Viscount and Earl Peel) – who had married the heiress daughter of Ashton the linoleum king – employed a firm of decorators called Hoydonk and Co. to Frenchify the interior with Louis XVI Rococo panelling.[126] At number 33, in 1912, Prince Hatzfeldt – or rather his wife, Clara Huntingdon of Detroit – filled the house with imported French *boiserie*.[127] And at 66, in 1913–14 Robert Emmet – who had also married an heiress, in this case the daughter of a New York banker – employed Romaine-Walker to do much the same, incorporating genuine Louis XV and Louis XVI Rococo panelling in a sequence of elegant interior transformations.[128] Close by, at 69–71 Brook Street, Walter Burns of New York – who married J.P. Morgan's sister – employed a Franco-Dutch decorator in 1891 to supply a lavish suite of Louis XV interiors complete with a ballroom of silver and blue.[129] And they were not alone: F.W. Isaacson did much the same at 18 Upper Grosvenor Street, in 1886.[130]

Now, Isaacson's money came from coal and silk: he married Elizabeth Jäger. Peel's money came from linoleum; Wernher's came from diamonds and gold. Bass was a brewer, Emmet and Burns were bankers. But they all employed French interior decorators. 'These breathing masses of bank notes and diamonds', sniffed Escott, 'are as little diversified by originality of taste as by good breeding.'[131]

Grosvenor Place was not quite in Mayfair; but it was very much part of this architectural *entente cordiale*. As Mrs Humphry Ward put it, these houses were 'terribly smart'.[132] Here could be found – successively – Hugh and Henry McCalmont of the Irish stockbroking dynasty; and Davison Dalziel, financier and speculator, of Pullman Car fame.[133] All three were millionaires twice over. And here Joseph Joel Duveen installed a veritable shop-window of plutocratic taste. His client was Sir Arthur Wilson, shipowning brother of Lord Nunburnholme, and a close friend of the Prince of Wales. Wilson's country seat, Tranby Croft, Yorkshire, had of course been the setting for the famous baccarat scandal of 1890. Whether or not baccarat was also on the menu at 17 Grosvenor Place [plates 91–92], its interior was certainly extravagant. Gillow and Co. were supposedly the decorators, but Duveen seems to have supplied the furniture and *objets d'art*. The 'decoration and furnishing', Duveen recalled, 'was the finest advertisement I could have had . . . [Wilson's] rich friends almost fell over each other to get beautiful things too.'[134] At 6 Grosvenor Place, in a house filled with French furniture and staffed by twenty servants, lived Henry Campbell-Bannerman, a Glasgow merchant's son and future prime minister.[135] And at number 5 lived Sir Edward Guinness, eventually 1st Earl of Iveagh. His parties were legendary. In June 1879 Augustus Hare attended a ball 'on which £6000 are said to have been wasted. It was a perfect fairy land, ice pillars up to the ceiling, an avenue of palms, a veil of stephanotis from the staircase, and you pushed your way through a brake of papyrus to the cloak-room.'[136]

More restrained, perhaps, but equally French (Louis XVI, in fact) were the interiors of two typically Mayfair houses, 27 Berkeley Square [plate 95] and 38 Hill Street. The plutocrats this time were Sir Robert Mond of the chemical and metallurgical dynasty and Sir Carl Meyer – whom we last encountered as squire of Shortgrove – a leading figure in the De Beers diamond empire.[137] Less French, and certainly less restrained, were the interiors commissioned at 11 Hill Street [plate 99] by George Coats, 1st Baron Glentanar: the boudoir was Raphaelesque, the library Wrenaissance (both probably by J. Leonard Williams).[138] All these were palatial but none could equal 1 Seamore (now Curzon) Place, the Mayfair home of that most luxurious bachelor, Baron Alfred de Rothschild. Here French interiors and Dutch paintings of the highest quality set a standard old money could rarely match.[139]

Piccadilly, once a haunt of Georgian aristocracy, was similarly plutocratised during the late Victorian period. At Bath House [plate 96] (number 82, on the corner of Bolton Street, rebuilt in 1821 for Lord Ashburton) lived the legendary Baron de Hirsch who had built railways in Germany, Belgium, Holland and Russia. 'Turkish Hirsch' took the Prince of Wales shooting in Moravia, and was said to be worth an extraordinary £20 to £25 million at his death in 1896.[140] And when Hirsch moved out Wernher moved in, remodelling the house once more in 1900. Not far away at number 119 lived – and died – Sir William Pearce, 1st Bt, who made a million building ironclads on the Clyde.[141] And further up, at number 139 [plate 97], designed by R.S. Wernum in 1891, lived England's first press baron, Algernon Borthwick, 1st Baron Glenesk, proprietor of the *Morning Post*. 'He is the friend and host of his Sovereign,' noted Escott, 'not because he owns the *Daily Telegraph*, but because he lives like a lord, and with lords, [and] possesses first class shooting.'[142] The Prince of Wales actually presented him with a model pheasant of solid gold in return for one memorable day's sport.

But it was higher up Piccadilly that the plutocrats clustered most thickly. No address in late nineteenth- or early twentieth-century London was smarter than numbers 141 to 148: Piccadilly Terrace, as it was called, or (more colloquially) Rothschild Row [plates 100–101]. By the 1880s the Rothschilds were to Piccadilly what the Vanderbilts were to Fifth Avenue. Between Hamilton Place and Hyde Park Corner, next door indeed to Apsley House, an eighteenth-century terrace was gradually transformed into a sequence of palatial mansions for the very rich. These houses survived no more than a single lifetime. They were demolished partly in 1961, partly in 1971, after a memorable 'sit in' by protesting hippies whose painted slogan was 'We are the writing on your wall'. At 141 (later 1 Hamilton Place) [plate 103] lived George

Herring, bookmaker, speculator and – latterly – philanthropist. Of 'somewhat rough exterior . . . simple habits [and] uncultivated mind', Herring was a publican's son who lived to mingle with royalty. He was indeed the very model of a modern parvenu.[143] Next door, at 142, lived Alice de Rothschild, invalid niece of Baron Lionel. At 143 lived Sir William Coddington, 1st Bt, a cotton-spinner from Lancashire.[144] When he moved in – or rather, up – from Grosvenor Square, he replaced Baron Ferdinand de Rothschild. At 144 lived Wentworth Blackett Beaumont, 1st Viscount Allendale, a Northumbrian landowner hugely enriched by mineral royalties.[145] And at 145 [plate 98] lived Hamar Bass, of the Burton brewing dynasty.[146] Each of these houses boasted an interior bedizened with some form of French Classicism. At 146 [plates 105–6] lived Sir Sigmund Neumann, 1st Bt, an Anglo-Bavarian banker who did well in South Africa and hustled himself into the Prince of Wales's set. He even rented Invercauld Castle to be near Balmoral, and Raynham Hall to be convenient for Sandringham.[147] Predictably, his 'lounge' was vaguely Louis XVI.[148] Finally, at 147–148 stood Rothschild House itself [plate 100], designed by Nelson and Innes in 1861–62.[149] This was the very flagship of new money, home in turn to Barons Lionel and Nathan de Rothschild, right next to No. 1 London, the residence of the Duke of Wellington. Here the interiors were as much Italian as French, and the contents were gorgeously eclectic. The furniture even included a set of chairs, elaborately inlaid with ivory, once part of the treasure of the Nawab of Arcot.

International finance, cotton-spinning, coal-mining, banking: Piccadilly Terrace was itself an epitome of the new plutocracy. And just around the corner, Hamilton Place was scarcely less typical. Here in those palmy Edwardian years – cheek by jowl with older examples of newish money, Lady Londonderry and Lord Northbrook: mining and banking, respectively – lived two of the newest *nouveaux riches*: Sir Richard Garton, a millionaire three times over from the profits of brewing sugar;[150] and Marcus Samuel, later 1st Viscount Bearsted, co-founder of the mighty Shell petroleum company.[151] Here also lived Meyer Elias Sassoon, grandson of David Sassoon of Bombay, and two men whose houses summed up the millionaire style to perfection. At number 4 [plate 102] lived Leopold Albu, a German-South African mining financier whose rooms were extravagantly done up in the French Grand Manner by A.N. Prentice.[152] And at number 5 [plates 94, 104] lived Leopold de Rothschild, a leading member of the Prince of Wales's racing set, whose palazzo, designed by W.R. Rogers in 1879–81, has somehow survived the general holocaust of Park Lane to become – most appropriately – a gambling club. Rothschild's Louis XV interiors were said by contemporaries to rival their supposed originals in the palace of Chantilly.[153]

Of course old money was still building occasional new London houses on the grand scale. Lord Windsor chose Fairfax B. Wade to design 54 Mount Street (1896–9) [plate 117]; Lord Ribblesdale chose Sidney R.J. Smith to design 32 Green Street (1887–9): both palatial mansions in mixed Classical style; both built by aristocrats, even if they were aristocrats newly enriched by industrial and mineral wealth.[154] There was certainly a good deal of new money still in old hands. In 1908 Lord Howard de Walden even decorated Seaford House, Belgrave Square, with a staircase faced entirely with slabs of onyx. Marriages were still plotted at Devonshire House or London-derry House. And of course aristocratic hostesses continued in nominal control of the Season. But, as often as not, the marriages arranged turned out to be alliances between old titles and new money. At Sunderland House, designed by Achille Duchêne in the 1890s,[155] for instance, the Duchess of Marlborough was actually rather better known as Consuelo Vanderbilt. It was she – the 'Yankee billionaire's heiress' – who paid the bill for that overblown mansion, one of London's last Beaux-Arts palazzi: her dowry was reputed to be £2,000,000. New money was making the running now. The Tories still had the Duchess of Buccleuch and Lady Ellesmere; the Liberals – neatly absorbing newer forms of wealth – still had Lady Wimborne and Lady Tweedmouth. But Society itself had been diluted. Invitations to receptions at Lady Glenesk's or musical soirées at Lady Speyer's were highly prized. Dining *chez* Hirsch was a memorable experience. And who could afford to turn down a Rothschild or a Sassoon?

The guest lists on such occasions were now as international as the menu. The dinner famously consumed by Charles Dickens in the Champs-Élysées in 1856, at the home of Émile de Girardin, might just as easily have been eaten in Piccadilly.

> ... Truffles ... for eight people [costing] at least five pounds ... the finest growth of champagne and the coolest ice ... Port wine ... which would fetch two guineas a bottle at any sale ... Brandy, buried for 100 years ... Coffee brought ... from the remotest East, in exchange for an equal quantity of Californian gold dust ... Cigarettes from the Hareem of the Sultan, and ... cool drinks in which the flavour of the Lemon arrived yesterday from Algeria struggles voluptuously with the delicate Orange arrived this morning from Lisbon ... [All this; not to mention] Tea direct from China ... [and] a ... plum pudding ... served with a celestial sauce in colour like the orange blossom and in substance like the blossom powdered and bathed in dew ... [156]

As in food, so in fashion: Paris and London competed for the same moneyed clientèle. By the 1880s, Escott noted, 'Mrs Bischoffsheim [plate XIII] and Mrs Oppenheim [had] more influence upon fashion in feminine costume than any two other ladies in London'.[157] By the turn of the century, Lady Dorothy Nevill concluded, the City had indeed 'conquered the West End'.[158] And this process of change, from the old order to the new, was most conspicuous in Park Lane.

During the 1820s Park Lane had been virtually rebuilt as the most fashionable address in London. Apsley House, Londonderry House, Dudley House, Grosvenor House: a new generation of private palaces established the tone of the area. Bows, balconies and verandas blossomed, enjoying for the first time a view westwards across Hyde Park. Dudley House was refurbished – and Dorchester House rebuilt – in the 1850s; Brook House was transmogrified in the 1860s. New money was beginning to make an entry. But it was not until the closing decades of the century that the plutocrats really made their presence felt. Park Lane was reconstructed once more: R.W. Hudson (soap) at Stanhope House [plate 108]; Sir Ernest Cassel (international finance) at Brook House [plates 110–111]; Sir Joseph Robinson (diamonds and gold) at Dudley House [plates 112–114]; Alfred Beit (more diamonds and gold) at Aldford House [plate 115]. New money was in the ascendant now: Leopold Albu (gold and diamonds), Barney Barnato (diamonds and gold); Tom Brassey (railways), Whitaker Wright (company flotation), James Hall Renton (railway speculation), Stephen Ralli (grain), and Friedrich Eckstein (still more diamonds and gold).[159] Just across the road, at Speakers' Corner, anarchists and socialists hurled abuse. But Edwardian Park Lane remained the very mecca of plutocracy. Strategically, one of the Duveen brothers took up residence at number 38 in a house designed by Romaine-Walker with interiors by White Allom and Co.[160] Park Lane was beginning to look more like Fifth Avenue than Grosvenor Square. And this cosmopolitan, increasingly American, trend was reinforced after the First World War: the building of the Grosvenor House Hotel marked an irreversible shift from private palaces to luxury apartments. Hotel and restaurant had replaced drawing room and club as key points on the map of London Society. The Dorchester replaced Dorchester House. At dances these days, complained Sir Philip Burne-Jones in 1913, people no longer knew each other.[161] Society had outgrown its aristocratic boundaries.

This progressive expansion of Edwardian Society – 'a swift and systematic conversion to gentility ... throughout the whole commercial upper-middle class' – was keenly recalled by H.G. Wells in *Tono-Bungay* (1909).

> We became part of ... that multitude of economically ascendant people who are learning how to spend money ... financial people, the owners of ... businesses, inventors of new sources of wealth ... [It includes] nearly all America [at least] as one sees it on the European stage ... [And they all have one thing] in common: they are all moving, and particularly their womankind ... towards a limitless expenditure ... Bond Street, Fifth Avenue, and Paris ... With an immense astonished zest they begin *shopping* ... jewels, maids, butlers, coachmen, electric broughams, hired town and country houses ... as a class, they talk, think, and dream possessions ... Acquisition becomes the substance of their lives ... [At first] they join in the plunder of the 18th century ... [but they end with] a jackdaw dream of ... costly discrepant old things.[162]

At the highest level, much of this social expansion came from the pressure of wealth accumulated in southern Africa. The Randlords numbered little more than two dozen, but their influence was out of all proportion to their numbers. Together they founded their own fortunes, and – incidentally – the fortunes of a new nation. They were trained in a hard school: Johannesburg was once described as 'Monte Carlo superimposed on Sodom and Gomorrah'. From England came both gentlemen and players: Cecil Rhodes, George Farrar, C.D. Rudd, F. Baring-Gould and George, 4th Baron Harris (a minor Randlord and a major cricketer), as well as the Jewish tribes of Isaacs, Phillips, Barnato and Joel. From Germany came a remarkable generation of Jewish dealers and entrepreneurs: Anton Dunkelsbuhler, Carl Meyer, Ludwig Breitmeyer, Max ('Mikki') Michaelis, Sigmund Neumann, Louis Reyersbach, 'little Alfred' Beit, George and Leopold Albu, Adolph Goertz, Ernest Oppenheimer. And then there were the non-Jewish emigrants, notably Julius Wernher and Hermann and Friedrich Eckstein. Out on the Vaal, already digging, they encountered their principal rival: J.B. Robinson, the Cape-born Buccaneer, a man with eyes which pierced you like a diamond drill and a tombstone for a soul.

The collective impact of these men on the financial markets of the West has yet to be assessed. Socially, however, their place in late Victorian London was never in doubt: it had to be Mayfair, that network of streets bounded by Piccadilly and Park Lane. Here, in the 1890s, young Beatrice Webb (née Potter) – herself the daughter of a minor railway magnate – noticed their influence on Society's 'coarsening scale of values'.

> Some of [them] had neither manners nor morals; and all of [them] were immeasurably inferior in charm and refinement, if not to the Rothschilds, most assuredly to the Barings and Glyns, the Lubbocks, Hoares and Buxtons, who represented money power in the London Society of the seventies and eighties.[163]

Still, the upward mobility of these new men was remarkable. At least ten of the Randlords achieved baronetcies; Wernher became at length the great-grandfather of two duchesses. And most of them lived at least part of their time in the most fashionable parts of London. Cecil Rhodes was an exception. He never aspired to a London house. As we have seen, he did buy a country retreat, Dalham Hall, near Newmarket; but he seldom visited it. In fact, houses of any kind meant little to him: his visions were rather more grand. Much of his life was spent in a corrugated iron shack in Kimberley. And when it came to rebuilding Groote Schuur, as home for the Prime Minister of the Cape, he insisted on simplicity. 'Make it big and simple,' he told Herbert Baker; 'barbaric if you like, I like teak and whitewash.'[164] Not so his rivals.

Only part of Sir Ernest Cassel's vast fortune stemmed from South Africa. But his nexus of finance was very much part of the Johannesburg–New York–London triangle. Beginning as a protégé of Bischoffsheim and Hirsch, progressing as an ally of Jacob Schiff, Cassel lived to surpass them all, becoming in effect the most powerful individual financier in Europe.[165] And his influence with Edward VII – he succeeded Hirsch as royal financial adviser – gave him an impregnable social base. In the end, his granddaughter married Lord Louis Mountbatten. When Cassel took over Brook House from Lady Tweedmouth in 1899, he turned a political salon into a focus of worldwide finance. He even died at his desk in Park Lane.

Brook House [plate 110], rebuilt in 1870 by T.H. Wyatt for the brewing banker Sir Dudley Coutts Marjoribanks, was already opulent. The dining room panelling had been brought from Drapers' Hall, and the staircase was a medley of mahogany and marble.[166] When Marjoribanks became Lord Tweedmouth in 1881, the entertainments at this palace became more dazzling still. 'There is no need for dwellers in Brook House to dream that they dwell in marble halls,' wrote one columnist in 1902; 'they do dwell in them.'[167] But there was not enough marble here for Cassel. In 1905–8, and again in 1912–13, he summoned Arnold B. Mitchell and Sir Charles Allom (decorator of Buckingham Palace and Marlborough House) to reconstruct the interior; the entrance lobby, the hall, the stairway, even all six kitchens were lined with marble. There were panels of lapis lazuli, and blue marble from Ontario, and white marble – 800 tons of it – from Michelangelo's quarry at Sarravezza in Tuscany. 'The historians of art', it was noted in 1913, 'have garnered for us the treasures of twenty generations of artistic effort. They have opened a Pandora's box from which may be taken elements of aesthetic expression meet for every phase of modern life.' Such eclecticism, explained the American architect Thomas Hastings, must surely be regarded as perennial: after all, aesthetically speaking, 'we are still working in the 18th century'.[168] Joseph Duveen, who filled Brook House with treasures, no doubt agreed. The apsed dining room (Tweedmouth's old billiards room) had seating for one hundred guests, as well as 'four superb Van Dycks'. 'It is the great merit of [this] Jew of taste', noted Sir Almeric Fitzroy, 'that he never overloads his walls with pictures.'[169] Other critics were less impressed. Christopher Hussey remembered the general effect – before demolition in 1933 – as 'sumptuous but ugly'.[170] Younger visitors gasped at the marble imperial staircase [plate 111] and christened it 'the Giants' Lavatory'.[171]

   J.B. Robinson, the 'Buccaneer', had made one fortune from diamonds in Kimberley and another from gold in Johannesburg before he took over Dudley House as a first step in his conquest of London Society. Litigious, tight-fisted, cantankerous, Robinson must have been one of the best-hated men of the age: his obituary in the *Cape Times*, celebrating a life of unmitigated selfishness, was headed 'Nil Nisi Malum'. Dudley House, noted *Mayfair* in 1910, 'is famous for its brilliant musical entertainments, although strange to say the owner himself suffers from deafness'.[172] Similarly, Robinson's collection of paintings was just a social gesture: nothing to do with aesthetic sensibility.[173] The interiors of Dudley House (1824–7) [plates 113–114] had been grandiosely refurbished by the 1st Earl of Dudley – vastly rich from coal royalties – in 1855–8. His architect had been S.W. Daukes; but the interior decorations – inevitably Louis Seize – were by Laurent and Haber of Paris.[174] Robinson revelled in their splendour. 'I remember a concert given by J.B. Robinson in Dudley House,' recalled Lady Glover, 'a wonderful display of orchids and fairy lights, every delicacy in and out of season and the choicest wine in profusion . . . [even] the divine Sarah [Bernhardt was there] . . . "And to think", chuckled Robinson, "that I [once] was glad to sleep on the ground under a tent." '[175] He sent his sons to Eton, he shaved off his beard, he changed his pith helmet for a top hat. All in vain. When Lloyd George suggested a peerage for the old Buccaneer, George V dismissed the idea as 'an insult to the Crown'.[176]

Robinson was not the only Park Lane magnate who made his money in South Africa. His near neighbours included Friedrich Eckstein at number 18, and Alfred Beit at Aldford House. By comparison with Robinson, Beit was a model of probity and restraint.[177] Perhaps he hoped to embody those qualities in his Park Lane mansion. If so, he surely failed. Aldford House [plate 115], designed by Eustace Balfour and Thackeray Turner in 1894–7, combined elements of mongrel Classicism from the Loire with what one contemporary journal called just 'a suggestion of the Archaic'.[178] Balfour did a good deal of work as architect to the Grosvenor Estate, but he became an alcoholic and died of drink.[179] Thackeray Turner was an Arts and Crafts man who should have known better.[180] The result seems to have pleased nobody, except perhaps Beit himself.[181] One critic remarked that Aldford House was 'remarkable [only] for looking so much like what it is – the African lodge transplanted' to Mayfair.[182] The exterior certainly lacked coherence. The interior was without consistency of style; so much so that after Beit's death G.A. Crawley was called in by Captain F.E. Guest, MP (or rather, by his American wife, the heiress Amy Phipps) to translate the principal rooms into Louis XVI.[183]

In 1896 Barney Barnato, a music-hall turn from Whitechapel who made millions in the diamond fields of Kimberley, began to build a house at 25 Park Lane [plate 116], on the corner of Great Stanhope Street. The architects – Smith and Sayer – were obscure; the design unlovely.[184] But there was no mistaking its size. 'I shall have', boasted the great Barnato, 'the finest entrance hall, stairs and dining room in London.'[185] While it was building, he needed a *pied-à-terre*, so he rented Spencer House. 'It's not a bad position,' he remarked, 'exactly half-way between the Prince of Wales in Marlborough House and the Prime Minister in Arlington Street.'[186] He hoped to finish in time for Queen Victoria's Jubilee in 1897. Alas – in a fate which curiously anticipated that of Robert Maxwell in 1992 – he was drowned at sea in mysterious circumstances. Cynics said that the statues on his unfinished mansion were petrified creditors waiting for payment. On the other side of Great Stanhope Street lived the aged Lady Llanover. As Barney's house rose higher it cut off the sunshine from her drawing room windows. As the light faded, day by day, Lady Llanover sat, flanked by her 'ladies in waiting', mute witness to the eclipse of aristocracy by plutocracy.[187] Though her mother was a Glanville, Lady Llanover herself had once married into newish money: her husband, 'Big Ben' Hall, was a grandson of William Crawshay I of Cyfarthfa. Still, her losing battle with the *arrivistes* – new money eclipsed by newer money still – will serve as a useful image of social change.

Barney's death did little to improve the view. His house was bought by Sir Edward Albert Sassoon, whose family – the Rothschilds of the East – had gravitated to London from selling cotton and opium in Baghdad, Bombay and Shanghai. It was Sir Edward's son, Sir Philip Sassoon, who turned Barney's old home into a plutocrat's dream. In 1927 Lord Crawford attended a small luncheon there, and wrote down a memorable description:

> Lunched with Sassoon; Lord Lansdowne there and Arthur Lee ... What a lunch Sassoon gives! I have always had a pardonable ambition to make the acquaintance of a *Grande Cocotte*. Sassoon's lunch is precisely the style and manner of the lunch I should expect from the G.C. Table napkins are yellow satin. Fruit for the four of us would have fed twenty people. Salad for four filled a bowl as big as a large washing basin. The waste, the robbery of it all – and yet I derive great pleasure from a combination which makes me extremely greedy; and Sassoon himself, despite an Asiatic outlook, remains quite simple and unaffected in the midst of all this opulence.

And in 1932, when royalty came to tea,

> I went to Sassoon's house to help him entertain the King and Queen who came to see the Exhibition called 'The Age of Walnut' ... After a longish peregrination we retired to the dining room and sat down to a magnificent tea. I never remember such a tea ... Some wonderful grouse sandwiches arrived – the King refused them: he could not stop eating haddock sandwiches ... Then we fell to again and a chocolate cake of unique and incomparable distinction was handed round in quarter pound slabs. I could not eat it having partaken so freely of the grouse: but Lady Desboro' was undaunted ...[188]

It was not only the food which was extravagant. Around his own person – turning himself into an icon of new money – Philip Sassoon created a tableau of almost Firbankian glitter. Harold Nicolson remembered him as 'a strange, lonely, un-English little figure . . . the most unreal creature I have ever known'.[189] But there was nothing unreal about his wealth; it was part Sassoon, part Rothschild. In one respect, however, Nicolson was right: the mundanities of life formed no part of Sassoon's existence. Eating lobster Newburg, he used to say – in soft, sibilant tones – was rather like digesting a 'purée of white kid gloves'.[190] His London house became his stage-set. Here Philip Tilden inserted a hanging corridor faced with oyster-coloured glass, 'darkening shade by shade to brilliant black. I can assure you', Tilden tells us, 'that deep red roses in porphyry vases reflected in black glass gives an effect which is not without uniqueness.' In the 1920s these rooms seemed always to be 'packed with sweet hyacinths, [while] Lady Rocksavage, hung with pearls, received the world . . . princes, prime ministers, diplomats, authors and artists, and the loveliest women . . . [even] Georges Carpentier [was there].'[191] The glass-panelled ballroom was the talk of Europe: its mirrored glass was painted in blue and silver by José Maria Sert, the Catalan artist who decorated Diaghilev's ballets.[192] Max Beerbohm protested that the room was 'too big for less than a thousand diners . . . [it was all] chatter and clatter and hustle and guzzle' – though he did admire so many crystal bowls awash with floating pink carnations.[193] Sir Philip Sassoon liked his drainpipes gilded and his visitors glamorous. 'It is Easter,' one of his friends wrote to him; 'Christ is risen. Why not invite him to lunch?' 'Though Jewish,' Chips Channon recalled, 'he hated Jews. What he really loved were jewelled elephants and contrasting colours – the bizarre and the beautiful.'[194] At his death in 1939 it was remarked that 'his baroque was worse than his bite.'[195]

From the world of Barney Barnato to the world of Philip Sassoon was not in fact a very great distance. The difference was that Barney Barnato had remained socially eccentric, that is, outside the citadel of acceptability. On one occasion, for a bet, he went three times round the Palm Court of the Savoy, on his hands. When in 1895 the Lord Mayor of London gave a banquet at the Mansion House in his honour, the Rothschilds refused to attend. Philip Sassoon, however, was a Minister of the Crown; though always an exotic, he was a confidant of statesmen, a familiar fixture in the drawing rooms of Mayfair. Even his private aeroplane was painted in Old Etonian colours. Appropriately, after his death many of his treasures went on to Houghton Hall, Norfolk: old money enriched by new.

By that time money itself had become the only realistic index of status. Instead of absorbing new money, as Lady Dorothy Nevill noted in 1910, the aristocracy itself had been absorbed by 'the forces of mammon'.[196] 'Society', concluded Lady Londonderry in 1938, 'now means nothing, and it represents nothing except wealth and advertisement ... England has become Americanised.'[197] Perhaps she was thinking of London's newer hostesses – Elsa Maxwell, Laura Corrigan, Nancy Astor, Emerald Cunard: these had replaced the hieratic chatelaines of old. But there was a more fundamental point to her remark. Wealth had indeed replaced breeding as the index of social prestige, and that wealth was no longer measured in broad acres but on the share indexes of the stock market. Society had given way to café society. There were still great houses in London, but they were no longer solely aristocratic. For aristocracy itself had been plutocratised. And when the great house came to die, it would die not of financial starvation but because its function as a focus for the ritual of the Season was fast becoming irrelevant.

81. Dorchester House, Park Lane, the great hall (1846–63):
Built to designs by Lewis Vulliamy for R.S. Holford, who inherited a fortune
derived from law and bullion speculation. Demolished 1929

82. 12 Kensington Palace Gardens (1846; 1866):
Designed by R.R. Banks for Samuel Morton Peto, contractor;
extended for Alexander Collier, a City financier

83. The Hill, Hampstead (1895; 1904–25): Terraces and pergolas designed by
T.H. Mawson for William Lever, 1st Viscount Leverhulme,
the millionaire soap magnate

84. 46 Grosvenor Street (1910–11): A Franco-Florentine palazzo designed by
Detmar Blow and Fernand Billerey for Sir Edgar Speyer, banker

85. Grosvenor Square, north side: These eighteenth-century houses were increasingly occupied by New Money from the 1880s onward

86. 34 Grosvenor Square, drawing room (1890):
'A gilded pantechnicon' – the Mayfair home of
Barney Barnato's nephew, Jack Barnato Joel

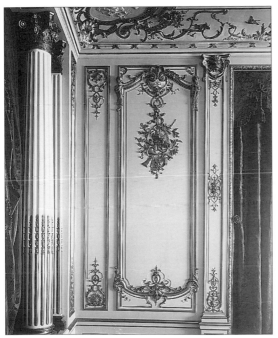

87 and 88.
45 Grosvenor Square, dining room
(1897): Refurbished by Charles
Mellier of Paris and London for Sir
James Miller, 2nd Bt,
heir to a Scottish trading fortune

89 and 90. Chesterfield House, South Audley Street, drawing room
and music room (1890s): Rococo interiors of the 1740s by Isaac Ware,
refurbished for Michael Bass, 1st Baron Burton, the millionaire brewer

91 and 92. 17 Grosvenor Place, staircase hall and ballroom (*c.* 1890):
Refurbished by Joel Joseph Duveen for Sir Arthur Wilson, a shipowner
from Hull and friend of the Prince of Wales

93. 12 Hyde Park Gardens, bedroom (*c.* 1907):
Furnished for Anton Dunkels (né Dunkelsbuhler),
a Jewish diamond dealer from South Africa

94. 5 Hamilton Place, bathroom (*c.* 1880): Fitted up
by W.R. Rogers (né Rodriguez) for Leopold de
Rothschild, banker

95. 27 Berkeley Square, drawing room (*c.* 1900): Decorated for Sir Robert Mond, of the chemical and metallurgical dynasty

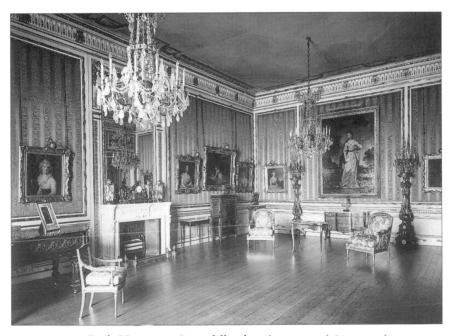

96. Bath House, 82 Piccadilly, drawing room (1821; 1900): Rebuilt for Lord Ashburton; refurbished for Baron de Hirsch; remodelled for Sir Julius Wernher. Demolished 1960

97. 139 Piccadilly, study (1891): Designed by R.S. Wornum for Algernon Borthwick, 1st Baron Glenesk, proprietor of the *Morning Post* and *Daily Telegraph*

98. 145 Piccadilly, drawing room: London home of Hamar Bass, of the Burton brewing dynasty

99. 11 Hill Street, library (*c.* 1903): Designed by J. Leonard Williams for George Coats, 1st Baron Glentanar, heir to a Paisley cotton fortune

100. 141–148 Piccadilly: No. 147–8 (*centre left*) was designed in 1861–2 by T.M. Nelson and C. Innes for Baron Lionel de Rothschild. By the 1880s the Rothschilds were to Piccadilly what the Vanderbilts were to Fifth Avenue, New York

101. 141–144 Piccadilly: These houses were demolished, for road improvements, in 1961 and 1971 after a memorable 'sit-in': the slogan reads 'We are the writing on your wall'

102.  4 Hamilton Place, drawing room (*c.* 1889): Refurbished by A.N. Prentice for Leopold Albu, a German–South African mining financier

103.  1 Hamilton Place (1906): Remodelled by Romaine-Walker and Francis Besant after the death of George Herring, bookmaker, speculator and philanthropist

104. 5 Hamilton Place (1879–81): Designed by W.R. Rogers for Leopold de
Rothschild, gambler and racegoer

105 and 106. 146 Piccadilly, study and drawing room: Fitted up for Sir Sigmund Neumann, 1st Bt, an Anglo-Bavarian banker who made a fortune in South Africa

107. 138–139 Piccadilly (1798; 1891): Both remodelled by R.S. Wornum; No. 139 was the home of Lord Glenesk, the first press baron

108. Stanhope House, 47 Park Lane (1899–1901): Designed by W.H. Romaine-Walker for Robert Hudson, a soap magnate from Birkenhead

109. Dudley House, 100 Park Lane (1824–7): Built for the 4th Viscount Dudley and Ward, coal owner; later remodelled

110. Brook House, Park Lane (1870): Rebuilt to designs by T.H. Wyatt for the brewing banker Sir Dudley Coutts Marjoribanks, later Lord Tweedmouth. Demolished 1933

III. Brook House, Park Lane, staircase hall (1905–8; 1912–13):
Reconstructed by Arnold B. Mitchell and Sir Charles Allom for Sir Ernest Cassel,
the millionaire financier and adviser to King Edward VII. Demolished 1933

112. Dudley House, Park Lane (*c.* 1890): Winter-garden, overlooking Park Lane and Hyde Park

113 and 114. Dudley House, Park Lane, picture gallery and ballroom
(1855–8): Remodelled by S.W. Daukes – with interiors by Laurent
and Haber of Paris – for the 1st Earl of Dudley. Later leased by
J.B. Robinson, the South African diamond millionaire

115. Aldford House, Park Lane (1894–7): Designed by Eustace Balfour and Thackeray Turner for Sir Alfred Beit, the South African diamond magnate. Demolished 1932

116. 25 Park Lane (1895–6): Designed by T.H. Smith and C.E. Sayer for Barney Barnato, the Jewish diamond millionaire. Remodelled in the 1920s for Sir Philip Sassoon by Philip Tilden. Demolished

117. 54 Mount Street (1896–9): Designed by Fairfax B. Wade
for Viscount Windsor, newly enriched by coal royalties

118. 5 Belgrave Square, dining room (1935–6): The 'Amalienberg' room,
designed by Stéphane Boudin of Paris for Sir Henry ('Chips') Channon,
husband of a Guinness heiress. Dismantled

## 5
# THE AGE OF MONEY
## *Images of a New Élite*

'We left Rottingdean because Rottingdean was getting too
populated . . . Then we discovered England . . . and went to
live in it [at Bateman's, Burwash, Sussex]. England is a
wonderful land. It is the most marvellous of all foreign
countries that I have ever been in. It is made up of trees and
green fields and mud and the Gentry: and at last I'm one of
the Gentry!'

Rudyard Kipling, 1902

## I. The House of Commons, 1846: Repealing the Corn Laws

Dawn at Westminster: 4.15 a.m., to be precise, on 16 May 1846. The
tellers are counting the votes at one of the great symbolic moments in
English Parliamentary history. The Ayes have it: the Corn Laws are to
be repealed. Voting has cut across party, across class and even across
family; but in the No lobby are those MPs who identify most vehe-
mently with land. These are the men who, within a few weeks, will
take their vengeance on Sir Robert Peel: 'the Manners, the Somersets,[1]
the Bentincks, the Lowthers and the Lennoxes'; Disraeli's 'men of
metal and large-acred squires . . . the Mileses and the Henleys . . . the
Duncombes, the Liddells and the Yorkes.'[2] But who is that, lurking
among the squirearchy? Can it really be George Hudson, the railway
king, Carlyle's 'great swollen gambler'?[3] Well, indeed it is; and there
are other names in the list, almost equally unexpected; men whose
lineage is certainly not antique. Like Disraeli himself, they have been
assimilated rather recently.

Joseph Bailey Snr and Jnr, for example; Welsh ironmasters from

Brecon. Father Joseph – Richard Crawshay's nephew, Chairman of the Birkenhead Docks Co. and master of the Nantyglo Ironworks – became first an MP, then a baronet, lord of an estate of nearly 30,000 acres centred on Glanusk Park, near Crickhowell, a Tudor Gothic seat designed by Robert Lugar in 1825–30.[4] His son Joseph predeceased him, but not before he too had bought an estate, at Easton Court, near Ledbury.[5] The father died in 1858 worth £600,000. His grandson – educated at Harrow and Christ Church – became the 1st Baron Glanusk.[6] Through property and title the Baileys had thus become part of the landed establishment. And there are other ironmasters in that lobby too: Richard Blakemore, owner of a tinworks in Glamorgan;[7] T.S. Forman, co-founder of a mighty fortune in Merthyr Tydfil;[8] and T.C. Whitmore, squire of Apley Park, Shropshire, whose family hailed from the very birthplace of the industrial revolution: Coalbrookdale.[9] These men are new, but they are also new recruits to landed society. So too are a number of cotton-spinners: George Arkwright of Sutton Scarsdale, great-grandson of the great Sir Richard;[10] John Hornby of Raikes Hall, Lancashire;[11] and Thomas Houldsworth, a Mancunian manufacturer with an estate in Nottinghamshire.[12] With them are two brewers: Henry Broadwood and Frederick Hodgson;[13] and several miscellaneous merchants: Henry Broadley,[14] J.S. Brownrigge,[15] Aaron Chapman[16] and Thomas Sheppard.[17] These were just the sort of men whom Peel had recruited to the new Conservative party; now he has lost them to the mythology of Disraelian Toryism.[18]

For Disraeli, in his romantic way, was really the prince of parvenus. There was always a touch of fantasy about his life at Hughenden. His initial estate of 750 acres had been bought on borrowed money. When he moved there in 1848 he owed £35,000. But by the time of his death in 1881 his landholding had nearly doubled and he was (apart from land) worth over £80,000 – perhaps four million today – considerably richer than Gladstone. 'An estate', he liked to think, 'is a little kingdom.' 'I have a passion', he admitted, 'for books and trees. When I come down to Hughenden I pass the first week in sauntering about my park and examining all the trees, and then I saunter in the library and survey the books.'[19] Lord Stanley, used to the splendours of Knowsley, was more prosaic:

Hughenden [he noted in 1851] is small but comfortable, the situation pleasant . . . It is a very fine retreat for an overworked politician, or man of letters desiring undisturbed seclusion . . . For what are usually called rural pursuits, as shooting, farming, gardening, laying out plantations or roads etc. [Disraeli] has no taste . . . But he has a good library; and in fine weather passes the whole day in walking about the neighbourhood.[20]

In other words, Hughenden was an ideal stage-set for a potential Tory prime minister. But it was some time before Dizzy could afford to dress his stage-set properly. Only in 1863 did E.B. Lamb – perhaps Mrs Disraeli's choice as architect – complete the casing of his Georgian stucco villa with red-brick Gothic trim.

We have realised a romance we have been many years in meditating [he announced]; we have restored the house to what it was before the Civil Wars, and we have made a garden of terraces in which cavaliers might roam and saunter with their lady loves.

Dizzy clearly enjoyed playing the squire. 'Nothing', he once admitted to Rosebery, 'could equal the egotism of a landed proprietor on a Sunday afternoon.' After all, this was Buckinghamshire, the county of Edmund Burke. What could be more agreeable than visiting 'the Pauncefort Duncombes of Brickhill Manor . . . Colonel Hanmer of Stockgrove Park . . . the Chesters of Chicheley . . . the Lovetts of Liscombe . . . the Dayrells of Lillingstone Dayrell . . . all of whom, by their ancestors, came in with the Conqueror.'[21]

Like many others in the NO lobby that night in 1846, Disraeli had bought his way into county society. London bankers like Praed of Tyringham and Baring of Norman Court; country bankers like Spooner of Birmingham and Plumptre of Kent; merchants turned financiers like William Thompson of Underley Hall, Westmorland and Philip Miles of Kingsweston, Bristol; traders too from further afield, like William Astell, once of Canton, later of Woodberry Hall, Cambridgeshire; and – taking a longer view – all those nabobs and planters whose wealth had originated two or three generations earlier in the gold of India and the sugar of the West Indies: Clive of Powis, Lascelles of Harewood, Lopes of Maristow, Codrington of Dodington.[22] All these men – whose wealth was new, at least within the three-

generational definition of novelty – had now clearly identified themselves with land. And it was this permeability – what Bagehot called
the ladder of removable inequalities – which constituted one of the
main planks in Disraeli's eulogy of the landed interest:

> There is nothing exclusive or restrictive in this territorial constitution ...
> From the days of Sir Robert Walpole to the present moment, with one
> solitary exception [Nathan Rothschild], all those who have now realised
> huge fortunes in our great seats of industry have deposited the results of
> their successful enterprise in the soil of their country ... Every family
> which has acquired great wealth has invested that wealth in the purchase
> of land ... [In Buckinghamshire alone], within the last twenty years ...
> one third of the land ... has changed hands ... no man need despair of
> obtaining the highest places in our free aristocracy.[23]

That was 1846, and Disraeli was more prescient than he knew. By
1883, as we saw in Chapter 1, new men were in possession of at least 10
per cent of all the greatest estates in England. And after that date the
process of change accelerated. Of the families included in the 1863
edition of Burke's *Landed Gentry*, at least half had dropped out by the
time of the 1914 edition; by 1937 one-third of gentry families had no
land at all, by 1952 the figure had risen to one-half.[24] The escalator of
mobility could move down as well as up.

## II. Scotland: New Money in the Highlands and Islands

Twenty years after the Repeal of the Corn Laws, in a different economic climate and at the opposite end of the kingdom, the housekeeper of Drummond Castle in Perthshire is writing a report to Lady
Carrington. It is summer, 1865. The castle has been let for the shooting to a Lancashire banker, William Cunliffe Brooks, and the housekeeper is not at all pleased. 'It appears to me', she writes, 'that this is a
Manchester Party [which has] merely taken it on speculation of
making it pay and giving Sport to others of their clique, all common
people.'[25]

There are several layers of snobbery here. Drummond is Lady Carrington's family home: the Drummonds have been there for centuries.

Her husband, the eccentric 2nd Baron Carrington, is however marginally parvenu: he is the third son of William Pitt's banker, though wealth and temperament have long since distanced him from the counting house. 'Mr Brooks or Mr Snooks', as the housekeeper calls him – mimicking his Lancashire accent – is undoubtedly *nouveau riche*. Although he has Rugby and the Inner Temple, and St John's College, Cambridge behind him – he is even a stalwart of the Ecclesiological Society – his money (cotton-based banking in Manchester and Blackburn) is not only new, it is provincial. It has yet to be assimilated into the metropolitan establishment. His family home, Barlow Hall at Chorlton-cum-Hardy, is worlds away from a banker's seat in Hampshire or Sussex. Still, he is only forty-six, and recently widowed: in less than thirty years he will emerge as a baronet and Tory MP, a member of the Carlton Club, with a house in Grosvenor Square and a castle and shooting box in Aberdeenshire; his daughter will be the next Marchioness of Huntly; and he will die with a million pounds in the bank.

The daily life of Sir William Cunliffe Brooks, 1st Bt, MP, in the Forest of Glen Tanar, Aberdeenshire, was engagingly recorded about the turn of the century by his landscape gardener, T.H. Mawson.

> Promptly at seven o'clock in the morning the piper's wail began, first indistinctly as he left his cottage, and then by degrees gathering power as he approached. At five minutes past he was going the rounds of the house, piping as if to wake the dead. At ten minutes past a footman came with a cup of tea, informing you that your bath was ready; then breakfast at 7.45; prayers at 8.20; next the carriage and pair with the piper (who was general factotum) at 8.30, and away to the minute. Every day there was a big programme of work ... [Mawson and Cunliffe Brooks would survey the estate, supervising the laying of roads, building of farmsteads etc., stopping only for sandwiches and more tea, while most of the guests went fishing and shooting]. If we were lucky we would [return to] Glen Tanar by 6.45 ... [Then came dinner] ... each evening the ghillies deposited in the dining room the kill of the day, whether of rod or gun, and the company rose ceremoniously, inspecting the kill, paid compliments, and heard comparisons from Bailey, the head ghillie. One evening something went wrong, and Bailey was in disgrace. 'Do you know you are a fool, Bailey?' said Sir William. 'Yes, Sir William', replied Bailey, touching his hat, or rather his hatless head.

217

This 'tyrannical' banker had 'an absolute passion for building and road-making, and kept a regular staff of 250 workmen'. While his guests slept, he conducted his business correspondence by candlelight. One morning Lord Swansea got up early, at six o'clock, and found his host already dictating letters. 'I tell you what, Brooks; I wouldn't have your job for ten thousand a year.' 'Neither would I,' grunted Sir William.[26]

Cunliffe Brooks brought Aboyne Castle in 1888, and the Glen Tanar estate in 1891, having previously leased them for more than twenty years from the spendthrift Marquess of Huntly. He employed George Truefitt, better known as an ecclesiastical Rogue architect, to extend Glen Tanar as a shooting box in 1869 [plates 30, 31]. Together architect and patron turned the old manorial kitchen into a High Church or at least Episcopal chapel, its roof thatched with heather, its interior festooned with stags' heads, its lancet windows stained with the legend of 'The Saint of the Forest'.

> It was divided into nave and choir; the floor was lined to a pattern in granite and red porphyry, and the roof timbers were of locally grown peeled pine, overlaid with home-grown pine boards, and covered with rough stone flags. A strange but Gothic effect was produced by rows of stags' skulls, their antlers making a perfect forest overhead, many of them 'royals'. Inscribed upon each skull was the name of, or initials of, the sportsman who had brought the stag down. The seats were constructed in semi-rustic fashion, out of home-grown timbers, and upholstered with home-grown wool and covered with deerskins. In one of the window slits, was a beautiful stained glass window depicting the Saint of the Forest. The effect upon the mind was that you were in a baronial hall, or in the comfortable private chapel of an old baron.[27]

Truefitt, that High Victorian Rogue, had already designed Brooks's Bank, Manchester (1867–70) in a style defiantly eclectic. Here, at St Lesmo (1872), deep in the Forest of Glen Tanar, he could toy a little with the ecclesiology of the chase. It was a long way from Grosvenor Square, and further still – socially speaking – from Chorlton-cum-Hardy.

Of course the English had been shooting and fishing in Scotland increasingly since the eighteenth century. When Colonel Thomas Thornton went on a sporting tour of the Highlands in 1786, he found many a loch and stream still splendidly unfished. By the 1840s that was certainly no longer true. But it took active royal patronage to turn random visits into a fashionable cult; and it was the arrival of the railway which turned the sporting holiday into a pastime fit even for the busiest of *nouveaux riches*. In one and the same year, 1852, Queen Victoria settled her purchase of Balmoral, and Lady Willoughby d'Eresby – Lady Carrington's mother – set about building the gargantuan Trossachs Hotel. By 1857 Lady Meux was stalking at Ceannacroc. A new invasion of the Highlands had begun. Increasingly, sheep gave way to deer, and pasture to forest, as the market for sporting territory developed. On 25 August 1866, at Achnashellach in Ross-shire, the Hon. Geoffrey Hill shot no fewer than 122 ptarmigan, a record bag of the world's most expensive game bird. By 1872 over 10 per cent of Inverness-shire had been converted to deer forest. By 1883 Sir Edward Guinness was paying £2,900 a year to rent the forest of Strathconon. 'Scotland is overrun during the shooting season,' noted Charles Milnes Gaskell in 1882, 'not by English squires, for they have not the means, but by wealthy stockbrokers, by the heads of large establishments in London, by the owners of funded property.'[28] To a lesser degree, something similar had been happening in Ireland, especially after the passing of the Encumbered Estates Act of 1848–49. J.G. Adair – 'Black Adair', the notorious land speculator – built up an estate of 28,000 acres at Glenveagh Castle, Co. Donegal (1867; 1900). The fence surrounding his deer park was reputed to be twenty-eight miles long. But Adair was at least Irish, though of Scottish descent. Most of his competitors were English. William Orme Foster (iron) in Wexford; Nathaniel Buckley (cotton) in Tipperary and Limerick; Mitchell Henry (cotton goods) in Connemara – all these bought land, and a great deal of it, too.[29] New money from industrial England certainly made itself felt in the remoter counties of Ireland. But Irish land never carried quite the same status; communications were more difficult, sporting facilities more spartan. Besides, the political climate made land-purchase rather more of a gamble. The situation in Scotland was very different. There all indicators were set fair: climate, economics, transportation and fashion conspired to favour the expansion of recreational estates. A 'pernicious alliance between the *nouveaux riches* of England and the impecuniosity of the Highlands' was quickly established, clearly measurable in the development of the railway network. From the 1880s until 1914, for instance, the London and North Western Railway provided a special service throughout the shooting season: a horse and carriage special, overnight, from Euston to Inverness. The shooting box and the fishing lodge were now potential items in every plutocrat's portfolio.

Brewers like Bass, Meux, Guinness and Gretton; ironmasters like Crawshay and Hickman; contractors like Pearson, financiers like Faringdon, chemical magnates like Allhusen, to say nothing of international industrialists like Carnegie and Vanderbilt: all these acquired sporting estates in Scotland. Sir John Fowler, engineer of the Forth Bridge, bought Braemore in 1865 and Inverbroom in 1867. Braemore Castle, set high above Loch Broom, seemed almost to defy the laws of gravity; it certainly defied the laws of economics. In that respect it was not alone. Sir Alfred Hickman rented Dunbeath Castle, Caithness, for the fishing. Lord Burton leased Glenquoich, Inverness-shire, for the stalking: soon he was reported to have bagged a twenty-point stag. In 1885 the shipowner Donald Currie – son of a Belfast hairdresser – bought up 10,000 acres in the Perthshire paradise of Glenlyon. And so the process continued. In 1904 Lord Faringdon bought an estate at Glenalmond, Perthshire; in 1906 Viscount Cowdray purchased Dunecht, Aberdeenshire, the ancient stronghold of the Lindsays. Viscount Devonport, better known as the grocer Hudson Kearley, acquired the Kinloch estate, Perthshire. There was even a Watney (beer) in the Forest of Fannich and a Shoolbred (furniture) by the shore of Loch Glass. W.K. Vanderbilt took over Glenstrathfarrar, and – to the horror of the natives – W.L. Winans, a Yankee railway tycoon whom we last met in Kensington Palace Gardens, leased no less than 200,000 acres of forest and moorland between Beauly and Kintail. That cost him £8,000 per year in rent alone. His son, Walter Winans, was not just a millionaire – he was also a celebrated marksman: during Bisley week the Star-spangled Banner flew from his competition headquarters. In 1883 he shot 196 stags in twenty-eight days. These were

not of course the only transatlantic lairds. But incomers to the Highlands were less likely to be American than English. Sir Charles Cayzer,
shipowning son of an East End school teacher, bought up estates at
Gartmore, Perthshire; Kinpurnie, Forfarshire; and Lanfine, Ayrshire.
The future Sir James Roberts, 1st Bt, chairman of Titus Salt and Sons,
acquired Strathallan Castle, Perthshire, once the seat of Viscount
Strathallan, a 'diehard' peer of 1832. Charles Flower, a brewer from
Stratford-upon-Avon, bought Glencassley Castle at Rosehall, Sutherland, in 1875 and decorated it with murals telling the story of
Macbeth. Such men made a deliberate choice to move north, at least
for the sporting season.

Every August and September, the migration northwards followed a
familiar pattern: Barings to Lochluichart, Ramsdens to Ardverikie,
Morrisons to the Isle of Islay [plate 46]. Some were satisfied with
short-term leases, renting properties from the local nobility. Baron
Hambro, for example, once a Dane but latterly more English than the
English, rented the Old Place at Mochrum from the Marquess of
Bute. Edward Wagg, a stockbroking bachelor, regularly rented shooting at Glenlochay, on Loch Tay. And Invercauld Castle, Aberdeenshire, designed by J.T. Wimperis in 1870–5 – romantically baronial
and enticingly close to Balmoral – was taken in turn by a newspaper
tycoon, Lord Glenesk, and a diamond magnate, Sir Sigmund
Neumann. But those with the longest purses preferred, in the end, to
buy: by the end of the century the Barings and the Guests, the Morrisons and the Schröders, had all become Scottish territorial magnates.
Sir Ivor Guest, later Lord Wimborne, spent £75,000 buying up the
estates of Coolin and Achnashellach. By 1883 his shooting box at
Glenarron, Ross-shire, was centred on an estate of 60,000 acres. And
all for show: the value of this vast tract of property was only £1,180 a
year. Such extravagance seems to have been contagious. Lord Abinger
spent £40,000 rebuilding Inverlochy Castle in 1861; Lord Ashburton
refurbished Lochluichart in 1874 to the very height of fashion, with
the assistance of W.E. Nesfield. But few of these newly-fabricated
lodges had any architectural merit. Wyvis Lodge, Evanton [plate 34],
for example, built by Walter Shoolbred in 1886 on the edge of Loch
Glass, was little more than a half-timbered suburban villa tossed into a

sublime setting. Still, they served their purpose, and that purpose was social rather than aesthetic. Blair Airon, Caithness, was

> a great Scotch estate of moor, sea-shore, and morass, in the extreme north-west of Scotland ... All new men have a mania for buying Scotch shootings, and if there was little or nothing to shoot at Blair Airon the fact served for a laugh at the clubs when the purchaser was not present. The purchaser, however, knew well that there were no deer, and that there was scarce a feather on the barren soil ... [but he also knew that those who sold it to him] held that magic key to the entrance of good society which he so ardently coveted, He was prepared to pay very liberally to obtain that key ... [In fact] William Massarene, millionaire ten times over ... had the power of the purse in his pocket and meant to buy Great Britain and Ireland with it ... [After all] his financial value was recognised by Conservative leaders ... [and] Lady Kenilworth, the high priestess of smartness, held out her hand to him.[30]

Ouida's diagnosis was correct. It was out on the moors – as much as in the drawing rooms of Mayfair – that the alliance between old and new money was forged. For Neumanns, Rothschilds or Sassoons, a shooting box in the Highlands was primarily a stepping-stone on the road to Balmoral. When Sir Edward Hamilton stayed at Tulchan Lodge, Advie (*c.* 1848) in September 1899 – between visits to the Duke of Fife at Mar Lodge and Lord Tweedmouth at Guisachan – he noted that 'the Neumanns have taken [Invercauld] for a few years. (They want, it is said, to be called *New*manns in future).' Predictably, when Neumann organised a shooting party that same month, he made sure that the Devonshires were on the list. 'The Duke', noticed Hamilton, 'did not seem quite to understand why he should be dragged off there.' The Duchess, however, was more astute: 'the Duchess seems to delight in giving helping hands to *nouveaux riches*; partly (it may be) with a view to promoting Charlie Montagu's interests in the City.'[31] Ultimately, money was thicker than blood.

Stories of 'Siggy' Neumann – 'MacNeumann' of the Highlands – must have lightened many a drizzly shoot. Glenmuick, Aberdeenshire – built by Sir Morton Peto in 1872 – eventually became his estate, but Balmoral remained his dream. His house parties at Invercauld were almost a parody of *nouveau-riche* style. On one occasion he arranged a particularly lavish luncheon, only to infuriate his royal guests by failing to find its location on the map. Louis Cohen, a fellow South African Jew, was not the only one to scoff at Neumann's enthusiasm for tartan: 'though he does not wear a kilt for fear of the wind'. The cost of such junketing was certainly considerable. Even less ostentatious incomers 'rained gold' on the Highlands in the form of estate improvements. In one period of eighteen years Sir John Fowler spent £105,000; Lord Tweedmouth £50,000; and Sir John Ramsden £180,000. Most of the businessmen who rented property in Scotland, however, were rather less extravagant. When Henry Ashworth left behind his cotton mills for Glenfearnach Lodge, Perthshire, in 1859 it cost him only £400 annually for 10,000 acres; when he rented Rottall Lodge, Forfarshire, the price was £500 a year for 14,500 acres. John Bright often stayed with him for the fishing. Yes, even John Bright, defender of the Radical faith, could enjoy a little sport: 'Keep in mind', Ashworth once remarked to Cobden, 'that this is the veritable John Bright.'[32]

As the native Highland aristocracy crumbled, they were replaced by the new plutocracy. Out went the Mackenzie of Seaforth; Lewis, Kintail and Glenshiel were all largely sold by 1844. Out went Walter Campbell of Islay – old family, new money – bankrupt by 1848, sold up by 1853. And out went The Macneil of Barra, The Macleod of Harris, The McDonald of Bornish and The MacDonald of Boisdale. Sales even began to deplete the territories of Aberdeen and Gordon. In came men like James Morrison the draper: he bought Islay House [plate 46] from Campbell in 1849; men like Lord Nunburnholme, the shipowner: he bought thousands of acres in Aberdeenshire from the Marquess of Huntly and the Earl of Aberdeen; and men like John Ramsay the Glasgow industrialist: he set himself up at Kidalton House, Islay, a plain, stone-built retreat designed by John Burnet in 1866–8, all set in 54,000 acres of Hebridean scrub. By 1884 the traditional landlords of Scottish deer forests – Lovat and Lochiel, Breadalbane and Sutherland – were feeling the challenge of new money. 'Do you know Lord Iveagh?' the 4th Duke of Sutherland asked Henry Chaplin in 1892; 'if so would you ask him if he would take Dunrobin and Stafford House for a year.' The social landscape of the Highlands was clearly in a state of flux. Alongside The Chisholm and The Mackintosh there were landlords of rather different vintage: Wimborne and Abinger, Ramsden and Ellice, Loder, Hermon and Meux. Men like Robert Stewart, the Glasgow distiller: he bought Kinlochmoidart from The Macdonald of the Isles. And men like James Baird, the Glasgow ironmaster, at one time the richest commoner in the three kingdoms: he bought the Knoydart estate in Inverness-shire from The Macdonell of Glengarry. Even men like Sir Ernest Cassel, though in fact there was nobody quite like Sir Ernest Cassel: predictably he too bought an estate, at Guisachan, Inverness-shire. By the last quarter of the nineteenth century, new landowners were in control of 70 per cent of the mainland and insular parishes of western Argyll, Inverness and Ross.[33] At the same time, new money had bitten deep into the heartlands of Perthshire, Aberdeenshire and the Northern Isles.

W.H. Mallock's cotton-spinning parvenu, Sir George Ambrose, was very much a man of this type: an 'advanced Liberal' manufacturer, with a seat in Gloucestershire and a moor in Scotland; 'a modern M.P. with more than a million of money'. One morning, over breakfast, Mr Herbert – Mallock's parody of Ruskin – intones the substance of a letter he has just received from 'the greatest of modern thinkers' (Thomas Carlyle):

> 'Yes, here they come, with coats of the newest fashion, with pedigrees of the newest forging, with their moors in Scotland, with their rivers in Norway, with their game preserves in England, with some thousands of human beings calling them masters, somewhere – they probably forget where – Here they come, our cotton-spinning plutocrats, bringing in luxury, and vulgarity, and damnation.'
>
> Those last words came like a thunderclap ... [But] Lady Ambrose did not cry. She did something better – she laughed.
>
> 'What would poor Sir George say?' she whispered ... 'He is fishing in Norway at this very moment.'[34]

Yet what is really striking about nineteenth-century rural Scotland is the resilience of the territorial aristocracy. Cameron and Macleod, Home and Fraser: they had been there for generations, and they would not be moved. Newcomers, however rich, cut but a puny figure beside the Dukes of Argyll and Sutherland. Many an old landowner – Lord Lovat of Beaufort Castle, for example – profited from the Sassenach. And where new money did make major inroads – notably in the Western Isles – the new men were, as often as not, Scots rather than English. When the Modern Doomsday for Scotland – as surveyed in 1873 – revealed the distribution of landholdings, its findings underscored the dominance of the old landed families. Of the twenty-one landowners who were shown to control no less than one-third of Scotland, only four could possibly be described as *nouveau-riche*: Sir James Matheson, the China merchant (400,000 acres); Evan Baillie, whose family made a fortune in the West Indies (300,000 acres); Charles Morrison, son of the haberdashery king (67,000 acres); and James Baird, the Glaswegian ironmaster (60,000 acres). Of these only Morrison was not a Scot. The Victorian Highlands were not overrun by the English alone; they were bought up by other Scotsmen.

> Loughlinter was all of cut stone, but the stones had been cut only yesterday. It stood on a gentle slope, with a greensward falling from the front entrance down to a mountain lake. And on the other side of the Lough, there rose a mighty mountain to the skies, Ben Linter. At the foot of it ... there ran the woods of Linter, stretching for miles through crags and bogs, and mountain lands. No better ground for deer than the side of Ben Linter was there in all those Highlands ... Behind the house the expanse of drained park land seemed to be interminable; and then, again, came the mountains. There were Ben Linn and Ben Lody – and the whole territory belonging to Mr Kennedy. He was laird of Linn and laird of Linter ['here in summer, gone in winter'] ... And yet his father had walked into Glasgow as a little boy – no doubt with the normal half-crown in his breeches pocket.
>    'Magnificent – is it not?' said Phineas to the Treasury Secretary, as they were being driven up to the door.
>    'Very grand – but the young trees show the new man. A new man may buy a forest; but he can't get park trees.'[35]

The Baird family will stand as a prime example of Trollope's fiction.[36] Their progress – from Lanarkshire to Rutland, from ironmaster to Master of Foxhounds, via baronetcy and barony – follows the classic *nouveau riche* trajectory. By the 1860s, Baird's ironworks at

Gartsherrie was reputed to be the largest in the world, producing 300,000 tons of iron per annum. Thirty or forty thousand souls were dependant on the firm's prosperity. In good years profits topped £1 million. Murray's *Handbook for Scotland* is seldom eloquent, but Gartsherrie clearly astonished:

> [This is] the heart of the *Black Country* . . . the centre of a group of blazing *Iron Furnaces*, surrounded by a network of railways, on the *Monkland Canal*. It is a desolate, black district – of smoke, coal and ashes – treeless, sunless, the verdure of nature's surface scarified and loaded with rubbish heaps. Yet it deserves to be seen as a busy and crowded hive of human industry.[37]

Quite so. Here, amid noise and squalor, fortunes were made. Houldsworth, Colt and Belhaven became rich men. And the Bairds became very rich men.

Alexander Baird (d. 1833), a farmer turned coalmaster, was the founder of the firm; he spent his days at Lochwood House, not far from the black hole of Coatbridge. There he grew prosperous, and his sons emerged as millionaires. William, the eldest, left £2 million in 1864; another son, James, left £1,190,000 in 1876 – both sums, of course, excluding property – after settling half a million on the Church of Scotland. Both men became Tory MP for Falkirk, and both accumulated land on a grand scale. William bought the Elie estate in Fife for £145,000 and extended Elie House in 1854–55. James's purchases were more lavish still. First came Cambusdoon House, Alloway, Ayrshire, a 20,000-acre estate on the river Doon which he secured for £22,000 in 1853; then in 1857, for £90,000, came 60,000 acres at Inverie House, Knoydart, a picturesque retreat in Inverness-shire; then in 1862–63 came further purchases at Auchendrane and Muirkirk in Ayrshire: this time the cost was £135,000. Not to be outdone, another brother, Douglas, bought up a fine Neo-Classical house, Closeburn Hall, Dumfriesshire. Another brother, David, in 1853 acquired the Stitchell estate for hunting; another brother, George, bought up an estate at Strichen in 1855. Another, Robert, bought the Auchmedden estate in Aberdeenshire in 1854 for £60,000. And another, Alexander, secured an 11,000-acre estate at

Urie near Stonehaven, Kincardineshire, also in 1854. This he promptly rebuilt in Tudor style as Urie House (J. Baird, 1855; extended 1883–5). Yet another brother, John, inherited Urie in 1862, leaving his sons in turn to expand the property to 10,000 acres by adding neighbouring land at Rickarton in 1875, plus a further 1,400 acres at Drumkilbo, Perthshire, and 2,000 more at Inshes, Inverness-shire. In less than a quarter of a century the Baird family had built up a formidable stake. By 1876 their total landholding was rumoured to be worth £2.5 million. Two of the founder's granddaughters eventually married into the peerage; one of his grandsons achieved a baronetcy; one great-grandson achieved two further titles, the barony and viscountcy of Stonehaven; and another became High Sheriff of Rutland and Master of the Cottesmore.

And what of the ironworks? By the turn of the century, even the chairman of the firm, a mining engineer named Robert Angus – 'the busiest man in Ayrshire' – had set himself up as a country gentleman at Ladykirk House, near Monckton, designed by J. and R.S. Ingram in 1902–5. There, in eclectic comfort – an Elizabethan hall, a French drawing room, a Georgian dining room and a Jacobean library – Angus carried on the Baird family's patrician dream until well into the twentieth century. His son, an enthusiastic Master of the Eglinton Hunt, even entertained the future King Edward VIII. And the Angus family were not alone. With the Eglinton Hunt – the Quorn of the Lowlands – rode several of Scotland's richest *nouveaux riches*. The hunt had been founded in 1861 by the 14th Earl of Eglinton. Within a generation Matthew Arthur, 1st Baron Glenarthur – Glasgow's leading exporter of cotton goods – was scouring the Carrick Hills with the Borwicks of Blair and the Galbraiths of Barskimming. He even joined the ranks of the Royal Company of Archers.

This commitment to land – and with it to permanence, order and hierarchy – could be paralleled in the life-style of many a Scottish *nouveau riche*. James Reid, the Glasgow locomotive builder, might stand as another example. Starting life as a blacksmith's boy, he lived to be laird of Auchterarder House, Perthshire, and a well known patron of art. When he died in 1894 – playing golf at St Andrew's – he was worth £677,624. But Reid established no long-term dynasty. The

Coats family, sewing-thread magnates, certainly did.[38] Their houses near Paisley – Ferguslie (bought 1845; rebuilt 1892), Maxwelton (bought 1868) – were essentially villas. But at Auchendrane House, on the river Doon – bought 1869; enlarged 1880–1 – they began to approach the authentic way of life of the established landowner. And seven members of the family left more than £1 million, a quite extraordinary tally. Even so, they never matched the scale of the Baird family's acquisitions. Nor, for that matter, did William Weir. A millionaire twice over and James Baird's nephew too, Weir bought up as many as a dozen estates in Ayrshire on the back of huge profits in iron and coal. But he never equalled his uncle's dynastic network.[39] Nor did the Baxters of Dundee. That remarkable family might well have been a closer parallel, but their pre-eminence was never more than local. While it lasted, however, their fortune was as striking as any.

Dundee, the saying goes, was built on jam, journalism and jute. Marmalade certainly brought John Keiller (d. 1899) half a million, plus an estate in Aberdeenshire and a shooting box, Craigandarroch Lodge, near Balmoral. Newspapers, equally certainly, brought long-term wealth to the Thomson family. But it was the Baxters' jute mills which produced the most spectacular profits of all. The firm first came into prominence during the Napoleonic wars: the canvas on Nelson's *Victory* was woven in Dundee. With the Crimean War and the American Civil War demand grew mightily. Canvas sheeting, tarpaulins, gun covers, biscuit bags; tents, hammocks, horses' nosebags – the uses of jute and flax were legion. During the 1860s Sir David Baxter, 1st Bt – son of William Baxter, founder of the firm – received nearly £600,000 in salary, profits and interest. When he died in 1872 he left £1,200,000. And it was not only family members who made vast profits. When Peter Carmichael, manager of the Lower Dens Mill for half a century, died in 1891 he left £516,000. His workers earned an average of sixteen shillings per week.[40] An *average*: in 1846 several girls had been sentenced to ten days' hard labour for staying away from work and asking for an extra halfpenny per day.[41] Such extraordinary disparities did not last long. The demand for jute peaked in the Edwardian period; thereafter came decline, and change. Sir David Baxter's statue looks out today over a rather different social landscape.

And nothing remains of Kilmaron Castle, Fife [plate 37], designed by Gillespie Graham *c*. 1820 and extended in 1860. Bought with 1,200 acres in 1856 as a symbol of economic and social triumph, the Baxters' house was gutted in 1970 and demolished in 1984.[42]

Besides rich Scots, there were of course rich Englishmen who settled permanently in Scotland on newly-bought land. Thomas Valentine Smith, a millionaire distiller, retreated from Grosvenor Road, London, to 12,000 acres at Ardtornish, Lochaber. His transfer brought wealth (six to eight thousand a year) to a poor area; but architecturally speaking his move was not a success. Ardtornish, designed by Alexander Ross in 1885, has been described – despite its beautiful setting – as 'a suburban villa afflicted with elephantiasis'; it was certainly rebuilt and extended, largely in cast iron and concrete, in a variety of styles: Lombardo-Jacobean outside, French Grand Hotel within.[43] Thomas Middleton – a Birmingham leather merchant who made a fortune out of army saddles – did manage to display a little more restraint. He employed W.R. Lethaby in 1898 to build him the perfect Arts and Crafts hideaway, Melsetter House on the Isle of Orkney.[44] But John Bullough – the Lancashire industrialist who gave the world the ring-spindle – carried this searching for tranquillity almost to the level of megalomania. Not content with 32,000 acres at Meggernie Castle, Perthshire [plate 33] – bought at a cost of £103,000 – he also purchased Kinloch Castle on the Isle of Rum [plate 45]. This his son, the future Sir George Bullough, 1st Bt, dramatically rebuilt employing the Halifax firm of Leeming and Leeming in 1897–1901 and 1906. In doing so he came near to creating the ultimate millionaire's refuge: Tudor outside, Jacobean and Adamesque within. Inside its great hall souvenirs of the chase mingled with the latest mechanical gadgetry. On festive occasions the tranquil air of the island was riven by the sound of an electric organ. Today the family rests nearby in the Bullough Mausoleum, a Doric temple between hill and water in a setting worthy of Arcadia.[45]

All these men – Smith, Middleton, Bullough – left a substantial memorial. They were all incomers and unmistakably new. But such English *nouveaux riches* were by no means the rule. Most of the incoming magnates were themselves Scots, albeit Scotsmen who had often made their fortunes elsewhere. Edward Mackenzie, the railway baron, made his money in England and bought an estate in the Thames Valley; but he could not resist the lure of Auchenskeoch in Kirkudbright, the ruined fortress of the Mackenzies. Others turned sentiment to more practical use; they not only re-purchased ancestral estates, they took on at least some of the responsibilities of the clan: witness, for example, the names of Fletcher, Jardine and Matheson.

No Scot returned home with greater éclat than James Fletcher (né Jack). Born in 1807 at Elgin in Morayshire – his mother (Fletcher) was petty gentry, his father (Jack) was a blacksmith – he took the road south and joined his elder brother John in Liverpool. John Jack was already building up a fortune, trading in alpaca wool between Liverpool and Peru; he came back to England in 1835, retired in 1848, and in 1852 bought from the Marquess of Abercorn a 2,000-acre estate at Dale Park, Sussex, complete with pillared Classical house by Joseph Bonomi (1784–5).[46] Ten years later he was High Sheriff, with a son at Harrow and a house in Eaton Place; his grandson – Eton by now – married a sister of the 7th Earl Fitzwilliam. Meanwhile, back in Liverpool, James Jack had prospered mightily on his own account. After a spell in Peru, trading wool with the Indians of Lake Titicaca, he returned to England in 1849, a rich man. First he bought an eighteenth-century Classical house, Woolton Hall, Liverpool, and added a *porte-cochère*.[47] Then he married fashionably and in 1856 – following his brother's example – adopted his mother's name and sent his son and heir to Eton. In 1864 he spent £145,000 buying up the 'big house' at Avoch plus 11,000 acres, close to his mother's place of birth. The house in question was Rosehaugh, on the Black Isle, seat of the 'Bluidy Mackenzie'; and in 1872 Fletcher commissioned Alexander Ross to Italianise its existing Neo-Classical form. At the same time great agricultural improvements were set in train; and a second estate – Letham Grange, Arbroath – was brought in 1876 for £121,800 as a social springboard for a younger son. At his death in 1885 James Fletcher left nearly £1.5 million, an impressive sum by any standards (say £60 million today), but in the context of a nineteenth-century fishing community like Avoch a legacy almost beyond belief. His younger son James Douglas Fletcher – Eton and Balliol – was the lucky heir. He became Chairman of the Highland Railway and set up the Rosehaugh Tea and Rubber Company. But building was his passion; so much so that he ran through much of the family fortune. According to legend, he once had hopes of marrying Nellie Bass, heiress to the brewing dynasty, She, however, took one look at Rosehaugh and refused: 'my father provides better accommodation for his horses'. So Rosehaugh was reconstructed yet again, to designs by William Flockhart, in 1898–1908 [plate 29]. And this time the cost, including marble swimming pool, Turkish bath and electric turbine, was an extraordinary quarter of a million pounds. There was a Baronial hall, a Rococo drawing room and a Florentine dining room. There was an Elizabethan bedroom and a Jacobean bedroom, a William and Mary bedroom, a Dutch bedroom and a Georgian bedroom, to say nothing of two more bedrooms in the styles of Louis XIV and Louis XVI. The *boiseries* were specially imported from Paris by Duveen. 'Mr Fletcher', it was said, 'could not stand anything plain.' The result was a monument to new money, one of the biggest houses in the Highlands, a vast mixed Scottish Renaissance pile towering high above the Moray Firth. Its stylistic ingredients were eclectic: English, French, Italian and Scottish. And the results were undeniably grand.[48] J.D. Fletcher's tombstone was designed by no less an architect than Lutyens. But the days of such extravagance were numbered. Only the outbuildings, in Arts and Crafts vernacular, survive. The Fletchers' hard-won symbol of status was demolished in 1959.

The names of Jardine and Matheson have turned out to be rather more durable. Their story is one of the sagas of British imperial commerce. Founded in 1832 by William Jardine and James Matheson – a Lowlander and a Highlander – the firm grew to dominate British trading in the Far East. Whatever the rights and wrongs of the opium trade – and the Opium War of 1840–42 suggests more wrongs than rights the profits accruing to the participants were enormous. Neither Jardine nor Matheson was exactly self-made; both came from old families of petty gentry status. But the scale and speedy acquisition of their riches made them essentially parvenu. William Jardine, MP (d. 1843), a hard-faced bachelor known in Canton as 'the iron-headed rat', might have been content – when not sailing the seas – with a house in Belgravia and membership of the Oriental Club.[49] In fact, at Callander, Perthshire, he constructed Lanrich Castle (1791; 1815), a battlemented seat set in impressive grounds. And his partner Andrew Jardine extended the family's investment in land still further: nearly 3,000 acres in Perthshire and nearly 10,000 in Dumfriesshire. At his death in 1881 he left over a million and a quarter, mostly to his kinsman Robert Jardine, MP, of Castlemilk in the latter county.[50] Sir Robert, 1st Bt, as he became in 1885, had already rebuilt Castlemilk in the Scots Baronial style to designs by David Bryce in 1864–70 [plate 38]. Turreted, crow-stepped, gabled, asymmetrical – totally replacing a Neo-Classical house of 1786 – Castlemilk had become, if nothing else, a statement of status: a prime example of plutocrat's eclecticism.[51] When Sir Robert died in 1905, his fortune – diversified by that date into Rio Tinto Copper – was still more than £1 million. But the family's involvement in trade was already dwindling. His heir, the second baronet – Eton and Cambridge, now – had other interests: one of his addresses was The Kremlin, Newmarket; his son became MFH Dumfriesshire. Even so, the second baronet left more than £1.5 million in 1927.

Meanwhile the Matheson side of the partnership had followed a very similar route. James Matheson built up both the mercantile and banking aspects of the business to a formidable degree.[52] But he never forgot that he was the eldest son of the chief of the clan Matheson of Sutherland. Retiring from active trade in 1842, aged only forty-six, he began to pump his considerable fortune into the Highlands. First came the laird's house at Achany in Sutherland, a token of local loyalty. Then in 1844 he bought from The Mackenzie of Seaforth – for £190,000 – the entire island of Lewis in the Hebrides. At a stroke he became the second-largest landed proprietor in the United Kingdom, with nearly 425,000 acres to his credit. Over the years £380,000 were spent on improvements. And at Stornoway, the capital of his new fiefdom, on the site of Seaforth House, he constructed Lews Castle to designs by Charles Wilson in 1848–60 [plate 36]; a Tudoresque fortalice – towered, battlemented, machicolated – it was the grandest mansion in the Western Isles.[53] Thanks to the fondness of the Chinese for narcotics, the crofters of Lewis were fed during years of famine, and James Matheson, MP, became a baronet and Lord-Lieutenant of Ross.

Such a career aroused ambivalent emotions.

> The late Sir James Matheson was a great man [recalled a Stornoway solicitor in 1884]; a public benefactor, a resolute pioneer of progress, the architect of his own colossal fortunes, most hospitable, and sometimes profusely benevolent ... Alas, there was another side to this picture. The policy of the estate was a tortuous, subtle, aggressive one in pursuit of territorial aggrandisement and despotic power, so absolute and arbitrary as to be universally complained of.[54]

His nephew, Alexander Matheson, was more despotic still. After the obligatory period of money-making on the Calcutta–Canton circuit, he returned to become a prominent London merchant and Director of the Bank of England. He also married into the nobility, choosing a sister of the 8th Baron Beaumont. But his roots were in the north: his family had been in Ross for six centuries. What could be more natural than to buy up the estate of Lochalsh, forfeited by his ancestors in 1427? In the end £150,000 were spent on improvements. First he employed David Rhind in 1846 to enlarge the old house of Ardross; then he called in Alexander Ross to redesign Duncraig Castle – that cost another £70,000 – gloriously poised above Loch Carron; and then in 1880–1 he summoned Ross once more to create a truly symbolic seat: a new Ardross Castle [plates 41, 42]. Set in woodlands, and looking out over the Black Isle, Ardross was very much a monument to commercial wealth and territorial pride: a fusion of new money and old land. Its exterior was Scots Baronial. Its interiors, just as predictably, were Franco-Jacobethan. At his death in 1886 Sir Alexander Matheson, 1st Bt, lord of nearly a quarter of a million acres, left £644,000. Within a year his crofting tenants were in rebellion. The new châtelaine of Lewis fled to France, and her shooting lessee – W.H. Brancker, a Liverpool sugar *rentier* – narrowly escaped stoning.[55]

The Mathesons' island empire had been sustained by external funding. When the family eventually sold Lewis to Lord Leverhulme in 1918 – 700 square miles, 30,000 people – the price was only £143,000. Next year the benevolent soap king added two more islands

– Harris and St Kilda – to his territory, paying £36,000 to the Earl of Dunmore and £20,000 to Sir Samuel Scott. He was now the biggest private landowner in the United Kingdom, outstripping even the Duke of Sutherland and the Duke of Buccleuch. He even established a new town – Leverborough – and in 1918 built himself an Arts and Crafts retreat nearby called Borve Lodge. His fortune seemed limitless; not so his patience. Exasperated by both government and crofters, Leverhulme abandoned his island experiment almost as soon as he began it – apart, that is, from Macfisheries – writing off £2 million in the process. For once, his infallible business sense had deserted him: the magic of the Western Isles had perhaps been just too potent.[56]

By the end of the nineteenth century, the wealth of the Jardines and the Mathesons – even in a Scottish context – was less rare than it had been at the start of the Victorian period. The number of Scots leaving over £100,000 rose from eight in 1876 to thirty-two in 1913. Many of these were Glaswegians. Of the thirteen £2-million fortunes left in Britain between 1900 and 1914, four originated on the Clyde.[57] Much of this commercial wealth was channelled into country estates strung out along that river's northern bank. Renfrewshire certainly had its *arrivistes*: William Todd Lithgow, for example, a shipbuilding tycoon who left over a million in 1908 and bought an agreeable Georgian house called Drums (1770), overlooking the Clyde at Landbank.[58] But it was Dumbartonshire – strategically close to Glasgow and enviably near Loch Lomond – which proved to be the more powerful magnet. This was a territory long ruled by one ancient family in particular, the Colquhouns of Luss. Their Neo-Classical villa at Rossdhu (1773–4), looking out across Loch Lomond, set a standard few parvenus could match.[59] Classical too was Strathleven House, seat of the Crum-Ewings, a more recent East India family with whom the Colquhouns shared the Lord-Lieutenancy.[60] Predictably, a good deal of new money followed where these older families led. William Dunn, a self-made spinning-machine maker, built Mount Blow (*c.* 1840) in Italianate style;[61] John Mathieson – a calico-printer who dropped dead in Sauchiehall Street in 1878 worth £385,135 – was content with a modest Georgian villa, Cordale House (*c.* 1760);[62] but at Methlan Park, built to designs by J. McLeod in 1880, the shipbuilding Macmillans could not resist erecting a campanile to overlook their steamships on the Clyde;[63] and at Helenslee, designed by J.T. Rochead in 1866–8, Peter Denny, another shipbuilder, built himself one of the proudest *nouveau-riche* houses in florid French Renaissance.[64] The Dennys were not in fact super-rich, but their wealth is unusually well documented. Peter Denny left nearly £200,000 (perhaps £8 million today); Helenslee cost him nearly £10,000 to build, plus about £3,000 a year to run; his furnishings alone were worth another £6,000. And in the world of Glasgow shipbuilding, he was a great man:

> All hail to thee, fair mansion, Helenslee!
> We greet a new hope for the world in thee.
> How royally thou sittest on thy throne
> Of greenest verdure, with thy belted zone
> Of neatly ordered woodland . . .[65]

But the imagery of the Scottish country house was seldom wholly Classical. For centuries it was the castle which had been the Scotsman's icon of hierarchy. This was transmuted, through the Renaissance and the 'auld alliance' – and thence through the imagination of Sir Walter Scott – into a more sophisticated image of status: the Franco-Scottish château. Most of Glasgow's richest *nouveaux riches* plumped therefore for some form of Scots Baronial.

> The peculiar features of the style [explained Robert Kerr in 1871] are chiefly these: small turrets on the angles of the building, sometimes carried up from the ground, and sometimes built out on corbelling; crow-stepped gables; battlemented parapets; small windows generally; the introduction almost always of a main tower; and over the whole, in one form or another, a severe, heavy, crude, castellated character . . . [in] style . . . primarily French of the Tudor period, and Scotch only by modification . . . In a word . . . [it is] an uncivilised style, [which] ought never to be brought into juxtaposition with anything more highly cultivated than the beautiful heather-braes of Loch Lomond, or the fir-woods and birch-covered banks of the Dee.[66]

In short, like the Franco-Italianate mode beloved by Sassenach millionaires, Scots Baronial was a style born of emulation. When William

Leiper designed a carpet factory for John Templeton of Glasgow in 1880, he could afford to mimic the Doge's Palace, Venice; but when he designed Knockderry Castle, Cove, for the same patron in 1896, it had to be Baronial.

So for Glaswegian *nouveaux riches* the imagery of Scots Baronial was the imagery of aspiration. Sir John Lumsden, for example, a successful stationer and publisher, employed it at Arden House, Alexandria (J. Burnet; 1866–8) [plate 39];[67] so did George Martin, an East India merchant, at Auchendennan (A.N. Patterson; 1885) [plate 32];[68] and so did J.W. Burns, heir to part of the mighty empire of Cunard, at Kilmahew, Cardross (J. Burnet; 1871).[69] All these houses combined several distinct elements of the Scots Baronial mode. Another – West Shandon (J.T. Rochead; 1850) [plate 44], built at Gareloch for Robert Napier, 'the father of steam shipbuilding' – was even more eclectic. Gothic, Elizabethan, and Castellated too, Napier's retreat was coyly described in Murray's *Handbook* as 'a somewhat fantastic building'.[70] Here was a style, for sure, which hovered on the brink of fantasy. But when the component elements of Scots Baronial were disentangled the result could certainly be impressive. Tullichewan, Alexandria, for instance, the castellated seat of Sir James Campbell, draper and father of the future Liberal prime minister, designed by Robert Lugar in 1822;[71] or Dalmoak – castellated again – built in 1866 for John Aiken on a striking site above the Vale of Leven;[72] or Auchentorlie, near Bowling (*c.* 1880), a gabled Tudoresque house set in 2,000 acres and home to yet another shipbuilder, Andrew Buchanan.[73] All these were powerful images of recent wealth.

Whatever their stylistic preference – Renaissance, Gothic, Tudor, Castellated, or even a mixture of all four – the *haute bourgeoisie* of Glasgow shared a similar taste in location: what they liked best was the northern hinterland of the Clyde. Here new money from shipyard and factory encroached remorselessly on the ancestral territories of Montrose. But it would be wrong to think that these Glaswegian *nouveaux riches* set out to compete with the old aristocracy as landowners. It was the image they coveted, not the substance of territorial possession. Tullichewan's 2,000 acres, for instance, were acknowledged to be 'totally inadequate to support the dignity of a castle'; that dignity clearly depended on the profits of 'manufacture and commerce'.[74] Yet houses like Arden, Auchendennan and West Shandon – and Auchenheglish, seat of yet another shipbuilder, Walter Brock[75] – all embody a peculiarly Scottish parvenu dream, redolent of forests, ethnicity and wealth. Arden especially, 'cosily embosomed in its well-known woods', seemed 'the very *beau idéal* of a place wherein to enjoy one's *otium cum dignitate*'.[76]

None seems to have enjoyed it more than John White III, 1st Baron Overtoun. The Whites were a dynasty of Glasgow chemists who built a colossal fortune out of bichromate of potash (a key ingredient in the dyeing process). John White I lived close to his chemical works at Rutherglen. John White II owned an enviable hideaway called Ardarroch: a villa at Row on the shores of Loch Long.[77] His brother, James White, decided on something larger. In 1859–62 be built Overtoun House [plate 40], a Scots Baronial mansion designed by Prince Albert's own architect, Smith of Aberdeen, all set in spacious policies. It was from this seat that John White III eventually took the title of Lord Overtoun. Four members of the family left over half a million each: John White £886,496 in 1881, James White £904,113 in 1884, and Overtoun himself £689,023 in 1908; Overtoun's nephew, W.J. Crystal, left over £1 million in 1921. These are formidable figures: in 1899 their labourers were earning four pence per hour. Predictably profits were translated into all three normative symbols of status: land, castle and title.

[Overtoun House] rears its proud head high up on the breast of the spur of the Kilpatrick Hills, which has for its crest the barren trappean Lang Craigs ... [Fortunately] the residence is completely sheltered from the keen, biting, northern and eastern winds [and heated with electricity]. To the south of the mansion a view is obtained of one of the fairest scenes in bonnie Scotland. The panorama embraces the Castle and town of Dumbarton, a goodly portion of the Leven and Clyde Valleys, and all the Firth of Clyde as far seaward as Dunoon, and pervading these varied scenes there are evidence of bustle and lusty life in abundance. But change your position and climb the near-at-hand Lang Craigs, and you enter a savage highland solitude, the abode of winged and other game, a perfect paradise for sportsmen, where you might easily fancy yourself to be in the heart of the Highlands ...'[78]

In other words, Lord Overtoun's dividends might derive from the commercial application of potash, but with 2,000 acres he could play the laird convincingly; after all, his hobbies were shooting and fishing.

But was he invited to Ptarmigan Lodge? Ptarmigan Lodge on Ptarmigan Hill, near the shadow of Rob Roy's Rock: here was the shooting box of the 5th Duke of Montrose, hereditary Sheriff of Dumbartonshire.[79] Not far away from Overtoun, geographically speaking; but rather too far in terms of Society. Overtoun in any case was a Presbyterian Liberal, and rich but not hugely rich. A more likely guest would have been a genuine millionaire, who happened to be Tory MP for Dumbartonshire: Sir Archibald Orr-Ewing, 1st Bt, the king of turkey-red dyers. Orr-Ewing's empire stretched from Glasgow to Stirling, and his castle at Ballikinrain, near Killearn [plate 28], designed by David Bryce in 1862–4, was Baronial enough to make a marquess blush. Turreted, crow-stepped, castellated, bartizaned, it outdid the seat of every other Glasgow magnate.[80] With an estate in the Highlands and a mansion in London, to say nothing of a son at Cambridge and membership of the Carlton Club, Orr-Ewing had clearly arrived. He may not have been exactly self-made – his family were petty gentry – but he rose quite extraordinarily fast. In 1893 he left £1,077,234; forty years previously his father had left just £316.[81] Among Glasgow parvenus he had only one serious rival, Sir Charles Tennant. But then Tennant's social talents – still more, the talents of his dazzling daughters – took him into rather a different world.

## III. High Society: The Smart Set and the Souls

Friday at Royal Ascot, 1883. Young Margot Tennant catches the eye of the Prince of Wales; Lady Dalhousie effects an introduction. Margot is not exactly unknown: in 1880 her father, Sir Charles Tennant, had become a Liberal MP and owner of a house in Grosvenor Square; in 1882 she had been presented at Court; at her coming-out ball she had even danced the quadrille with Mr Gladstone.[82] But this is the moment, make or break. The Prince asks if she will bet with him on the result of the next race: not for the last time, Margot backs the winner. 'I felt my spirits rise', she remembered years later, 'as walking slowly across the crowded lawn in grilling sunshine, I observed every-one making way for us with lifted hats and low curtsies.'[83] Next day the Prince sends her a gold and sharkskin cigarette case with a diamond and sapphire clasp. After that there is no looking back. But then – as her sister Laura noted in her diary – 'who could not help being conquered by her: she carries victory in her eyes'.[84]

Laura Tennant is soon to marry Alfred Lyttelton, the golden boy of Edwardian Society. Her sister Charlotte – most beautiful of the three – is already wedded to handsome Lord Ribblesdale. And Margot herself will eventually marry H.H. Asquith: her marriage certificate will carry the names of four prime ministers. Sir Charles Tennant can take such things in his stride. After all, he is Glasgow's paramount chemical king; one of the richest men in Europe, with a 5,000-acre estate and a castle – Glen, Peeblesshire (D. Bryce; 1858, 1874; R. Lorimer, 1906) [plate 27] – which Lord Rosebery once described to Gladstone as 'the most perfect of all modern houses, architecturally speaking'.[85] Perfect in other ways, too: by 1897 there were 105 indoor and outdoor staff.

> Pepper-pot turrets, high pitched roofs like a French château ... All was spick and span, superbly groomed and appointed. The gravel was ... meticulously combed ... the lawns as smoothly ironed ... Only the hills were rugged and unkempt ... Everything else was new ... 'Each pine[apple] we eat costs us five pounds' ... Sir Charles [would] say whilst the dessert was being handed round.[86]

Tennant's industrial empire stretches from the ironworks of Lanark-shire to the gold fields of Mysore. His factory at St Rollocks pollutes the air of Glasgow with clouds of hydrochloric acid; its giant chimney (Tennant's Stalk) rises higher than St Paul's Cathedral, higher even than the campanile at Cremona. But his sons are at Eton; his friends include half the Liberal Cabinet; and his temperament is as buoyant as his bank balance. Things are more difficult for Lady Tennant: although she is a granddaughter of the founder of *The Times*, she seems scarcely to know who is dining at her own table. But then the kaleidoscope of guests in Grosvenor Square is calculated to bewilder. 'Our standard of success was so high', Margot recalled, 'that nothing short of Sir W. Harcourt dancing or Ld Acton being spontaneous satisfied us.' Life seemed one perpetual waltz. It was all, noted Mary Gladstone, 'the maddest, merriest whirl from morn to night'.[87]

It was around this time – the early 1880s – that 'good society', according to Lady Frances Balfour, began to disintegrate. Before that, 'certain things were not done, certain people not received'. Chaperonage was almost a state of mind. But the mores of the next generation – the more open manners of the parvenue – were impatient of convention: 'the first moment of change undoubtedly came with a family highly gifted of totally unconventional manners, with no code of behaviour, except their own good hearts, the young women of the Tennant family.'[88] Clearly the Tennant sisters' explosive high spirits, and their father's unlimited largesse, had some destabilising effect. But Society was already fragmenting: it was changing from monolithic matriarchy into a mosaic of competing coteries.

> When I first knew London Society [recalled Lady Dorothy Nevill in 1910], it was more like a large family than anything else. Everyone knew exactly who everybody else was … Mere wealth was no passport … In the [eighteen] forties none of the millionaires had yet appeared. There were rumours of Hudson, the railway king, and his wife ['dress me for ten; dress me for twenty'], but they were never in Society … [But] very soon the old social privileges of birth and breeding were swept aside by the mob of plebeian wealth which surged into the drawing rooms, the portals of which had up till then been so jealously guarded. Since that time not a few of that mob have themselves obtained titles, and now quite honestly believe they are the old aristocracy of England.[89]

It was in this way, losing the cohesiveness of inherited codes, that Society disintegrated into 'sets'.

Eight years after that great day at Ascot, Edward Hamilton – bachelor, gossip and Treasury mandarin – retreated to Waddesdon [plate 66], exhausted by the Season, and inserted in his diary for 10 August 1891 a vignette of Society's current state of play. There were, he explained, two principal sets, the Smart Set and the Souls.[90]

[First] the *smart set* ... Louise Duchess of Manchester, Gosfords, Eddie Stanleys, the reigning Duchess of Manchester, Lady Dudley, all the Rothschilds, Arthur Sassoons, Lister Kayes, Miss Emily Yznaga, Hindlips, Lady Bulkeley and her daughter, Lord Arlington and his daughters, Owen and Hwfa Williamses, Falkiners, Leinsters, Muriettas, Gerards, Oppenheims, Francis Knollys's, Randolph Churchills, Horners, Wellingtons, Londonderrys, de Greys, Brooks, Carringtons, Suffields, W. Caringtons, Algy Lennoxes, and a certain number of single men such as Hartington, Oliver Montagu, J.C. Sykes, Horace Farquhar, Henry Chaplin, Bully Oliphant, Soveral, J. Baring, Fr. Mildmay, M. Guest, C. Hill, Bertie Tempest, Rotton, R. Winn, Clifden etc. A man like Rosebery is of course of the set, but as a matter of fact is not much in it.

This is a strikingly parvenu list: four American heiresses; several heirs to industrial fortunes (beer, coal, iron, railways, spinning); and a whole clutch of international bankers and financiers. There are courtiers there, of course, and a sprinkling of ancient families: Stanley, Fitzroy, Cavendish, Tempest. But these are more than matched by a galaxy of *nouveaux riches*.

The next most distinctive set [Hamilton continues] consists of the '*Souls*', which includes such people as the Harry Whites, Cowpers, Brownlows, Pembrokes, Tennants, Ribblesdales, Brodricks, Wenlocks, Granbys, Percy Wyndhams, Ldy Grosvenor and G. Wyndham, Arthur Balfour, W. Grenfell, George Curzon, Harry Cust, and others to whom the last addition has been Haldane by virtue of his being the translator of Schopenhauer.

This second list is much more traditional. Their critics may think of them as a self-absorbed intelligentsia, always looking into the state of their own souls. But at least their membership crosses political boundaries: the Balfours are Tory and the Tennants Liberal. And it is homegrown. Henry White, an American diplomat in London, is the only transatlantic figure there; though Curzon is soon to marry an heiress from Chicago. Haldane, of course, is rather a new man, though of petty gentry stock; so in a way is Asquith, but then he will soon be plutocratized by marriage. Otherwise, it is mostly old money. The Cowpers, for example, lived at Wrest Park, Bedfordshire (1833–9), a Louis Quinze mansion elegant beyond the aspirations of even the richest *nouveau riche*. Maurice Baring was an occasional visitor:

A constellation of beauty moved in muslin and straw hats and yellow roses on the lawns of the gardens designed [in the fashion of] Lenôtre, delicious with ripe peaches on old brick walls, with the smell of verbena and sweet geraniums . . . and we bicycled in the warm night past ghostly cornfields by the light of the large full moon.[91]

Wrest Park was French but not flashy; it had been designed by an aristocratic amateur, Earl de Grey, first President of the RIBA. Its understatement is very much part of the Souls' own image of themselves. And the contrast between the country houses of the Smart Set and the country houses of the Souls is striking. Compare Witley with Whittinghame; compare Waddesdon with Wilton; compare Mentmore with Belton; compare, above all, Halton and Hindlip with Stanway and Clouds. Old money takes its wealth for granted. The eclecticism of new money is defiantly opulent; almost – as Pamela Wyndham noted at Glen – as if William Morris had never lived.[92] For the Smart Set it is all chandeliers and French furniture; for the Souls it is understated Classicism or else the rustic vernacular of the Arts and Crafts. Scots Baronial – and Glen [plate 27] is more Baronial than most – somehow manages to combine the two: it has all the hybridity of the vernacularised château.

Hamilton's listing of the Smart Set and the Souls did, however, make one point conclusively: Society had indeed expanded. In the 1820s Society numbered about four hundred adults; by the end of the century the figure probably approached six thousand. That, at least, was the opinion of the *Saturday Review* in 1900. 'The 30,000 families listed in the Court Guide', it was noted, 'couldn't possibly take part in Society.' Even so, the inner circle now numbered thousands rather than hundreds. This did not mean, however, that Society was now open to 'mere wealth'. It was open to great wealth.

When people say that money, in the social world, will do anything, they forget that the money in question must be money in very great quantities. A man with fifty thousand a year, or even with twenty thousand, may, if he knows his business, make his way in Society, no matter how obscure his origin; but five or six thousand a year will socially do nothing for anybody, who is not socially eligible for reasons quite other than his income . . . [Besides] new fortunes of twenty thousand a year and upwards are even in

these days rare . . . [and] even the possession of a great fortune is not sufficient by itself to secure social position.[93]

That point is worth remembering. But there had been a change, and it
involved a change of style. Looking back on the heyday of aristocracy,
the Marquis of Aberdeen recalled that 'you had to be seen at Holland
House, Sion House, Argyll Lodge and Osterley Park to be anyone . . .
the appearance of captains of industry and local magnates at a Society
function would still excite comment'. By the 1890s that sense of exclusivity had clearly gone. The rituals of Society – the receptions and
dinners between November and April, the balls in May and June, the
garden parties in July, the shooting and dancing between August and
October – all these still counted. But not quite as before. The *drama-
tis personae* were more numerous now, and their invitations carried an
unwritten price-tag. In Escott's sonorous phrase, the nineteenth
century had become 'the Age of Money . . . in all its glory, ostentation, power and vulgarity'. 'Disguise it as we may,' he concluded in
1879, 'wealth is the governing force in our social system.'[94]

One night in January 1896, soon after the Jameson Raid, the
Asquiths went to dine at Lord Reay's. Margot was introduced to
Joseph Robinson, the Buccaneer, famously deaf and infamously rich.

> I was introduced to the great South African millionaire, Robinson of
> Robinson's gold mines, who had taken Dudley House for the London
> season. He was tall and deaf, and, as he offered me his arm to take me to
> dinner, he paused on the stair, looked at me and said in a voice of
> thunder:
> 'What's your name!'
> To which I replied, almost as loud: 'Asquith!'
> Still standing in the middle of the staircase and blocking the way to the
> dining room, he said:
> 'Any relation to the famous Asquith?'
> At which I shouted 'Wife!' . . .
>
> [Over dinner, the conversation gets down to basics]
>
> Mr Robinson: 'Are you rich?' to which I answer no, but that my father
> was . . .
> Mr Robinson: 'Oh, well, I'll tell you how I made my money, if you'll
> tell me afterwards how he made his.'[95]

## IV. Pall Mall and St James's: The *Nouveaux Riches* in Clubland

Now pause a moment at 1890. Forty members of the Reform Club are assembling in their Morning Room for a composite portrait. The clubhouse, designed as a Renaissance palazzo by Sir Charles Barry in 1839–41, has recently been redecorated by E.M. Barry in sombre shades of brown, crimson and gold.[96] The members crowd together, a little self-consciously. The artist, T. Walter Wilson of the *Illustrated London News*, has no doubt been asked to exercise some imagination. But here, in all its diversity, is the Victorian Liberal élite. The grandees are there, of course: Spencer, Ripon, Harcourt, Rosebery, Granville and Hartington. But their presence is partly for show: they must have been far happier in Brooks's. There are a few top doctors and lawyers.[97] Even a couple of writers.[98] But it is the business element which is strongest – men like Sir Edward Watkin, 'the Railway Machiavelli',[99] and his Radical ally, H.D. Pochin, the grocer's son who became a major force in china clay, chemicals, iron, steel and shipping.[100] There are three London merchants: R.K. Causton, later 1st Baron Southwark, stationer;[101] Sir Andrew Lusk, 1st Bt, grocer;[102] and Sir Sydney Waterlow, 1st Bt, printer.[103] And there are a clutch of traders from the Liberal heartlands of the midlands and the north: George, later 1st Baron Armitstead, a Russia merchant educated in Weisbaden and Heidelberg;[104] Joseph Cowen, a Jingo-Radical, Home-Ruling coal-owner, heir to a fire-clay factory in Newcastle;[105] and William Agnew – a future baronet – a Swedenborgian art dealer and principal proprietor of *Punch*: his fortune comes from marketing art in Liverpool and Manchester.[106]

The Reform Club is grand but not exactly exclusive. There among the Liberal tycoons is Henry Broadhurst: his autobiography, *From the Stone Mason's Bench to the Treasury Bench*, will one day be regarded as a classic text of Victorian self-improvement; he has even been at Christ Church, Oxford – fixing chimney-pots.[107] And there is A.J. Mundella, a self-made hosiery magnate whose father was an Italian refugee and whose mother was a framework knitter.[108] Typical of Liberalism in quite another way are three representatives of the party's Nonconformist roots: W.S. Caine, a Liverpool metal merchant and

Baptist temperance reformer; [109] and two Quaker industrialists: Sir Joseph Pease, 1st Bt,[110] and Jacob Bright.[111] There is another temperance reformer here too, though this time from a landed background: Sir Wilfrid Lawson, 2nd Bt, MFH, the man who emptied Castle Howard's wine cellar into the lake.[112] Not for nothing is the Reform the only place in Pall Mall with a barley-water pump in the entrance lobby.

The Whig–Liberal tradition was patrician in origin but progressive by instinct, and in the late nineteenth century it faced in two directions: backwards to the Utilitarians and forwards to Collectivism. One day that division would turn out to be its Achilles heel. In the meantime, one man who will eventually straddle both wings of the party is visible here: a rich Glasgow draper's son, the future prime minister, Sir Henry Campbell-Bannerman.[113] His fame lies in the future. But another whose career certainly spans the gamut of Victorian Liberalism is prominent already: Sir John Pender, textile merchant and submarine telegraph magnate; he is an entrepreneur with feet in several political camps, as well as a house in Arlington Street – Horace Walpole's old home – and seats in Scotland and Kent.[114]

The Reform Club's 'back-benchers' contain a striking proportion of parvenu business men. Mr Japhet Snapper would have felt quite at home.

> Mr Japhet Snapper was an opulent member of Parliament ... struggling to be recognised as a leader of the Radical party ...
>
> 'That man!' exclaimed Miss Mildred. 'One can hardly bear to think of him.'
>
> Mrs Harley [disagreed] ... 'Mr Snapper, Mildred, is the future Prime Minister of England.'
>
> 'Never!' said Miss Elfrida ... 'Fancy a man who, in public, lives by demeaning gentlemen, and in private does nothing but vainly struggle to imitate them!'[115]

W.H. Mallock's caricature – half-way between John Bright and Joseph Chamberlain – contains more than a grain of malicious truth. The club membership list for 1890 includes five Brights, five Tennants, three Courtaulds, three Morrisons, two Sassoons, three Willses, three Rathbones, five Peases, four Petos, five Gregs, three Muntzes and six Potters. And quite a number of these families are closely related to each other. Hugh Mason, himself almost a caricature of the hard-faced Victorian industrialist, is linked to three other spinning dynasties: his mother was a Holden, his first two wives were Buckleys, his third wife is an Ashworth.[116] And as for the Barclays and Gurneys, they are the very embodiment of the Quaker – and Quaker-allied – business fraternity; Robert Barclay (d. 1921), for instance: his grandmother is a Gurney, his mother is a Leatham, his wife is a Buxton, and one of his sons will eventually marry a Birkbeck.[117]

Among the selected forty, that morning in 1890 – once more setting aside the great Whig landowners – there is only one millionaire: William Agnew. Among the 'back-benchers', however – again, setting aside magnates like Bedford, Westminster and Lansdowne – there are more than two dozen. Quite a number we have already met, shooting in Scotland, refurbishing houses in London, building villas in the Lake District, or enlarging mansions in the Home Counties. But here they are *en masse*, and they make a formidable list. J.P. Thomasson (cotton);[118] Sir Donald Currie,[119] T.H. Ismay[120] and William Pirrie (shipping);[121] Nathaniel Clayton (engineering);[122] Sir Charles Tennant, Ludwig Mond, John Brunner and Christian Allhusen (chemicals); Charles Morrison and 'Chicago' Smith (finance and property); John Nixon, Wentworth Beaumont and James Joicey (coal);[123] Sir Robert Jardine (China trade); Sir James Kitson (railways); Thomas Birkin (lace); William McEwen (beer); Sir Frederick and W.H. Wills (tobacco); Samuel Montagu, Sydney and Herbert de Stern, Sir Julian Goldsmid, Edward and Louis Raphael and Baron Ferdinand de Rothschild (all finance, and very high finance, too) – all these men, members of the Reform Club in 1890, left over a million pounds, several of them much more than that. And a roster of comparable length could easily be made up of members of exactly the same vintage whose fortunes were very nearly as great. Just look at the list of names; it reads like a roll-call of Victorian capital: Samuel Courtauld (silk), Hamar Bass (beer), Baron Brassey (railways), Sir John Jaffray (banking),[124] John Walter (newspapers), Sir Morton Peto (contracting), Sir Joseph Pulley (finance),[125] Charles Wilson (shipping),

L.J. Baker (stockbroking),[126] Sir Frederick Mappin (cutlery), Sir Lowthian Bell[127] and Charles Bölckow (steel),[128] Jeremiah Colman (mustard)[129] and John Corbett (salt), besides a whole covey of spinners and clothiers with names like Brocklehurst,[130] Pilkington,[131] Bright,[132] Cheetham,[133] Hollins,[134] Holden, Feilden, Illingworth,[135] Armitage,[136] Greg, Barran,[137] Buckley and Hoyle.[138] The Reform Club on a crowded night must have seemed a veritable pantheon of capitalism. Still, there were limits: W.H. Smith was blackballed in 1862, and Andrew Carnegie in 1885;[139] but then, they were surely Tories at heart.

Quite a number in this long list – all Reformers, vintage 1890 – had used some of their huge entrepreneurial profits to invest heavily in land: Morrison, Jardine and Tennant in Scotland; Buckley in Ireland;[140] Walter in Berkshire;[141] Wilson and Bell in Yorkshire; Goldsmid in Kent; Rothschild in Buckinghamshire. By this date they were numbered among the greatest of landed proprietors. And many more could boast, if not a great estate, then at least a sizeable country house.

> Carew ... descried emerging from the ... lodge ... a man who seemed, from a distance, to be dressed for Piccadilly or Bond Street ... Was he the undertaker's man? Was he a doctor? ... few doctors but those of the lowest class could invest the quiet of their dress with such a loud ostentation of quiet ... he could hardly be the undertaker or the mourning man, for his trousers had a purple stripe on them, and in his little finger there was embedded a diamond ring ...
> 'Snapper, sir – that's his name,' ... [said the bailiff; 'he has] his eye upon this property ...'[142]

Many a Reformer must have felt the goading of Mallock's satire. Others, no doubt, rose above it – Joseph Whitworth, for example. A self-made industrial engineer, inventor of the Whitworth rifle-screw, he began life as a working mechanic. He ended as one of Manchester's greatest philanthropists. When Jane Carlyle visited his factory in 1846, she noted that 'Whitworth, the inventor of the besom [street-cleaning] cart, and many other wonderful machines, has a face not unlike a baboon; speaks the broadest Lancashire; could not invent an epigram to save his life; but has nevertheless a talent that might drive the Genii to despair.'[143] By 1869 he was an MP and FRS, a baronet, and a member of both the Reform Club and the Athenaeum. At his death in Monte Carlo in 1887 he had over half a million in the bank, a villa in Manchester – The Firs, designed in 1851 by Edward Walters – and a sizeable seat at Stancliffe in Darley Dale, near Matlock, complete with winter-garden and cast-iron billiards table.

Here then, in their Pall Mall headquarters, are the Liberal *nouveaux riches*. And they are not just individuals. We are talking of dynasties: the Pease family, for instance. By the last decade of the nineteenth century, the Pease dynasty – makers of Darlington, co-creators of Middlesborough – had climbed from wool and coal, through iron and steel, via railways and banking, to commanding positions in the social hierarchy of the North East. One became the first Quaker MP; another the first Quaker baronet. Five left between a quarter and a half a million pounds each. Between them they owned more than a dozen seats; two of these – Hutton Hall, Guisborough (1864–71) and Mowden Hall, Darlington (1881) – were designed by Alfred Waterhouse.[144] Their collective land holding must have amounted to 20,000 acres or more. They might have been Quakers; they were certainly conscientious masters; but their worldly goods were not inconsiderable. And in the twentieth century, with two baronies and two baronetcies, they ended up voting Tory. In some ways the Colmans were a comparable tribe. Jeremiah Colman, the first mustard king, spurned Gladstone's offer of a baronetcy. But in 1888 he could not resist adding an estate at Gatton Park, Surrey to the Colman home near Norwich; and then, having purchased this sizeable mansion, the family felt impelled to stamp it with the insignia of their new-found county status: a marble hall modelled on the Corsini Chapel, Rome, and fronted by a grandiloquent Corinthian portico [plate 10].[145] Likewise the Holdens. Sir Isaac Holden, 1st Bt – son of a Scottish coal-face worker – had made himself master of the largest wool-combing and worsted-manufacturing business in the world. He ended his days at Oakworth House, Keighley.[146] His son Angus, the second baronet and later 1st Baron Holden, progressed still further. While still a comparative youth he was given an estate of his own, Nun Appleton, Yorkshire, a house furiously enlarged by E.B. Lamb in 1864. By early middle age he was thus already a fully paid-up member of the gentry.[147]

Industry and commerce growing into landownership and finance: the classic *nouveau riche* pattern is clearly visible in the Reform. And religious background seems to have made little difference: the Peases were Quakers, the Crossleys were Congregationalists, the Feildens were Anglicans, the Holdens were Wesleyans, the Ashtons were Unitarians; but they all bought land and built houses. Thomas Bazley of Manchester – an Anglican who accepted a baronetcy from Gladstone – retired to Gloucestershire with one estate for himself (Eyford Park) and another for his son (Hatherop Park); perhaps 13,000 acres in all.[148] Thomas Ashton, a second-generation spinner from Didsbury – a Unitarian who declined a baronetcy – had saved up £526,451 by the time of his death in 1898. His son was less inhibited: he accepted a barony (Ashton of Hyde) and retreated to Sussex, leaving only half as much as his father in 1933.[149] The Gregs of Styal – one of the founding families of the textile industry – lasted a little longer, but faded away in the third generation. For many years they remained in the North West, staying within their Nonconformist tribe; but by the end of the century things were very different: they owned half a dozen seats and several steam yachts, and their world-famous mills at Quarry Bank were sinking towards oblivion.[150]

But among Liberal examples of gentrification – and entrepreneurial decline – one family surely takes the prize: the Crossleys of Halifax.[151] The Crossleys of Dean Clough Mills were proprietors of the world's biggest carpet factory. Steam-powered from 1852, their looms produced carpets for an international market. John Crossley (d. 1837), who founded the firm, was too busy to bother with country seats; still less with London clubs. But his three sons – all at one time near-millionaires – began the predictable process of ascent: from merchants to gentry; from *haute bourgeoisie* to post-industrial aristocracy. The first two sons, John (d. 1879) and Joseph (d. 1868), were at first content with sizeable Gothic villas called Manor Heath and Bromfield, both in suburban Halifax. When John Crossley II's son Louis built himself a more substantial residence, Moorside – designed by H.J. Paull in 1870–2 – he made sure that there was still 'complete telegraphic communication' between home and factory. But the founder's third son, Francis Crossley (d. 1872), had married into a grander Reform Club textile family, the Brintons of Kidderminster, and his horizons were wider. First he built an ambitious mansion in Louis XIV style, to designs by G.H. Stokes in 1856–67, and christened it Belle Vue [plate 7]; next he secured a baronetcy, in 1863; and then, within a year, he purchased Somerleyton Hall, Suffolk [plate 51] – complete with 3,224 acres – from a failing contractor (and fellow Reformer), Sir Morton Peto.[152] Somerleyton's excess – 'a design characterised by a good deal of pretentiousness, and that of an unsuccessful kind'[153] – struck exactly the plutocratic note. Stone had been brought from Caen and Aubigny. There were glasshouses designed by Paxton. There were grottoes and aviaries; there were palm houses and orangeries. There was a clock – made by Vulliamy in 1847 – which had been judged too expensive for the House of Commons. There were thousands of gas jets which illuminated the East Anglian sky like some vision of Kubla Khan. Nothing was too expensive for Somerleyton. Its owner could even afford to indulge in considerable philanthropy, erecting a model village and setting up a profit-sharing scheme. He still left £800,000, perhaps £40 million today. Francis's son, the second baronet, was educated at Eton and Balliol, and eventually emerged as Baron Somerleyton: no longer 'in trade', but a *rentier*; no longer a Congregationalist but an Anglican; no longer a Liberal but a Unionist; no longer a Reformer but a member of Brooks's. And in the church at Somerleyton, a stained-glass window proclaims the memory of the first baronet, heir to a carpet fortune and founder of a county dynasty: 'HE IS RISEN'. No wonder the Secretary of the Anti-Corn Law League once tugged at John Bright's sleeve as they walked into Barry's palazzo: 'John, John, how can we keep honest if we live in such palaces as this?'[154]

Such uncertainties were never part of the Carlton Club's *mentalité*. When in 1890 the *Illustrated London News*[155] followed its piece on the Reform with a composite portrait of the Carlton, it chose a set of representative types, aristocratic, professional or plutocratic, generally capitalist and imperialist, but above all establishmentarian: the archetypal Carlton men, blue in tooth and claw. Many were landed figures, as one would expect in 'the aristocratic party': Henry Chaplin, for instance, doyen of sporting squires, son-in-law of a duke and future father-in-law of a marquess.[156] But there were others with little provenance and less pedigree. In fact, looking at the Carlton in the 1890s we see, for every old-style magnate – men like Sir Walter Long[157] or Sir Michael Hicks-Beach[158] – new men of talent and sometimes of comparable wealth: W.H. Smith (newsagent), C.T. Ritchie[159] and Aretas Akers-Douglas[160] (career politicians), James Bailey (hotelier),[161] Henry Bemrose (printer), James Bigwood (vinegar brewer), and John Penn (marine engineer).[162] The *nouveaux riches* are here in force.

Sir Algernon Borthwick, for example: MP, 1st Bt and eventually 1st Baron Glenesk. We have met him before, of course, in London and in the Highlands; but here he wears a political hat. Grandson of a Scottish shepherd; son of an MP; married to a niece of the 4th Earl of Clarendon – she was a famous hostess and friend of Queen Victoria – Borthwick became editor and proprietor of the Tory *Morning Post*. He entertained the Prince of Wales in Piccadilly, holidayed at the Château St-Michel in Cannes, shot and fished in Scotland on the 2,000-acre estate which he bought in 1883, and yet he still managed to leave £400,000. John Derby Allcroft is an even better example. An evangelical Birmingham glove-maker – without, it was said, an aitch to his name – he eventually retired to a 6,000-acre estate at Stokesay Castle, Shropshire, bought from the Earl of Craven at the top of the market in 1869 for £215,000. In London he lived in an Italianate stucco palazzo in Lancaster Gate, filled with Louis XIV furniture and contemporary English paintings. In Shropshire he spent £150,000 developing his estate and building a brutish Jacobethan mansion, Stokesay Court (1889–91), to designs by 'Victorian' Harris. Despite notable philanthropy – he spent £30,000, for instance, on E.B. Lamb's St Martin's, Gospel Oak (1865) – Allcroft still left nearly half a million. Clearly the Carlton had no prejudice against parvenus.[163] In fact, by the 1880s old-style county members like Sir William Bartelott of Sussex and Sir Rainald Knightley of Northamptonshire had become the exception rather than the rule.

There were fewer Jewish members at the Carlton than at the Reform, but they were certainly not excluded – the Stern family, for example; or, more strikingly, Henri Bischoffsheim. 'Bish' and his wife Clarissa [plate XIII] – a famous beauty from Vienna – were never anglicised; but invitations to their parties were widely prized. One daughter married the 4th Earl of Desart, another – as we have seen – married the 20th Knight of Kerry. Racing at his Newmarket house, The Severals; weekending at Warren House, Stanmore; or throwing glittering soirées at Bute House – Bischoffsheim was the epitome of a city magnate absorbed into the political establishment. Related to Goldsmid, to Hirsch, to the Sterns – located at the very heart of the Jewish international banking network – he nevertheless became something of a star in London Society, a favourite at Court and an indispensable fixture in the Season. In the 1880s he was said to give the best dinners in London. He left over £1.5 million in 1908, and rests today beneath an enormous Classical monument in the Jewish Cemetery at Hoop Lane, North London.[164] But he never became a landowner, and in that respect he was never quite the authentic Carlton man.

When John Bateman tabulated the final edition of his *Great Landowners of Great Britain and Ireland* in 1883 – that is, landowners with more than 2,000 acres – he found that 642 of them belonged to the Carlton Club.[165] That was three times the number in Brooks's; nearly four times the number in White's; more than six times the number in the Reform; and more than twice the total in White's and Boodle's combined. Admittedly the Carlton was a very big club; but it was scarcely bigger than the Reform. This huge preponderance of territorial magnates – 642 out of a club membership of twice that number – tells us a great deal about the ethos of later Victorian Conservatism. In 1879 it was calculated that 856 great landowners belonged to Tory clubs, as against 348 for the Liberals. Bateman himself, the lexicographer of land, was inevitably a Carlton man. For land lay at the heart of Tory loyalties, and the Carlton was first and foremost a political organisation: unlike the Reform, its constitution gave Parliamentarians priority at ballots; and unlike every other major club, it rigorously excluded guests.

In 1836 Disraeli crossed its new-built threshold for the first time and wrote excitedly to his sister: 'the Carlton is a great lounge, and I have found a kind friend in Francis Baring, Lord Ashburton's eldest son'. There were in fact four Barings in the Carlton at that date, and four Peels too, to say nothing of three Gladstones; so the parvenu element was by no means negligible. But the membership list of 1836 was still dominated by the landed aristocracy and gentry; four dukes, five marquesses, seven earls, and half the squirearchy of England: Dugdale Dugdale was there, and Cresswell Cresswell; so were Wyndham and Yorke, Villiers and Vyvyan, Shirley, Mount, Mordaunt and Manners. No wonder the favourite club drink was very dry champagne: 'Young England's nectar'. Those were the days when James Morrison, the parvenu MP, could ask the Chief Whip for a pair and receive the cutting reply: 'Gloves or stockings?'[166]

Half a century or so later, when Coningsby Disraeli is elected to the Carlton in 1892, the picture looks rather different. Many of the historic names are still there; land is still the key cultural determinant. But the infusion of new money is striking. Just look at the membership lists for the later 1890s. There are four Guinnesses, two Allsopps, two Grettons, a Meux, a Bonsor, a Garton, a Greenall, a Bullard, a Combe, a Walker and a Morrell – and those are only the brewers. Spinning – not only cotton, but silk and wool – is well to the fore: Coats, Coddington, Hornby, Houldsworth, Brocklehurst, Foster, Cunliffe-Lister, Cheylesmore, Whiteley, Isaacson, Fison, Hermon-Hodge and Ecroyd as well as the now historic names of Strutt, Arkwright and Peel. Then there are the ironmasters: Hardy, Whitelaw, Torbock, Vaughan, Noble, Forbes-Leith, Hickman, Cruddas and Guest. And of course there are the shipbuilders and shipowners: Donkin and Houston, Rollit, Wilson and Bibby, Cayzer and MacIver, Harland and Wolff. There are chemical magnates like Allhusen, and a whole clutch of contractors: Aird, Brassey, Cubitt, Mackenzie and Mount Stephen. And of course there are the newer entrepreneurs: Maple (furniture), D'Arcy (oil), de la Rue (printing), Jackson (leather), Peek (biscuits), Orr-Ewing (dyeing), Horlick (malted milk) and Steinkopf (mineral water). The Carlton Club of the 1890s yielded nothing to the Reform in its roll-call of tycoons. Its list of new-money millionaires is positively Homeric.

But it was in the City – the financial engine-room of the late Victorian economy – that the Carlton outpaced its Liberal rival. City magnates had long been – at least until the 1870s – just as likely to support Gladstone as Disraeli. With the rise of 'Radical Joe' Chamberlain, however, and the prospect of interventionist legislation, the City began to move to the right. By 1893 not a single director of the Bank of England was a Liberal. Not surprisingly, membership lists for the 1890s show more than seventy bankers or bank directors at the Carlton: more than twice the number at the Reform.[167] By the end of the century bankers, and crucially the new breed of international financiers, made up a formidable Tory lobby. Several of these we have encountered already; but here they are in their tribal headquarters, a veritable alphabet of City money: Abel Smith, Ashburton, Astor, Bischoffsheim, Cassel, Cazalet, Denison, Farquhar, Gibbs, Gilliat, Goschen, Hambro, Hillingdon, Loder, McCalmont, Morrison, Neeld, Quilter, Ralli, Robinson, Samuel, Sassoon, Schuster, Stern and Wernher – heavyweight names, all of them; a formidable roll-call of international finance. There are certainly as many millionaires at the Carlton as there are at the Reform. But the emphasis is different. If anything, the new money is slightly less new: second- and third-generation rather than first; and further away from the source of production: banking, broking and insurance rather than manufacturing industry. Finally, and to a greater extent than at the Reform, a significant portion of all this accumulated capital has been ploughed back into a type of asset which is symbolic rather than productive: land.

As it grew in architectural grandeur – first Robert Smirke's Neo-Classicism (1833–6), then Sydney Smirke's Renaissance (1846–8; 1854–6), then Reginald Blomfield's Beaux-Arts (1923–4) – the Carlton Club developed a membership best described as Establishment plutocrat. After its refurbishment in 1878 and 1896 it could claim to be the most luxurious club in London.[168] As an institution it was certainly a powerful engine of assimilation. Sir Robert Fowler, 1st Bt, and Sir Cuthbert Quilter, 1st Bt, will stand as examples. Fowler was born into a modest family of Tottenham Quakers. By his death in 1891 he was not only an Anglican Freemason, but a prominent financier with an Italianate banking house in Cornhill; he became MP for the City of London and then Lord Mayor, with a mansion in Cavendish Square and an estate in Wiltshire. Indeed, he ended almost as a parody tycoon, an anti-Boer John Bull, hunting with the Beaufort from his mansarded seat, Gastard House near Corsham, and caricatured in *Vanity Fair* as the classic City Tory: 'he drives in a gilt coach to the club and gives dinners'.[169] Fowler's fortune was not huge: £114,000 (perhaps £5 million today), and he clearly spent freely. But twenty years later Quilter left more than twelve times as much. Born in Park Lane – his father was first President of the Institute of Accountants – Quilter was not exactly self-made. But his career as stockbroker, art collector and landowner took him rapidly to the heart of the new moneyed Establishment. In 1881 he founded the National Telephone Company; in 1883 he bought a barren 9,000-acre coastal estate at Bawdsey, near Felixstowe; and in 1886 he began building Bawdsey Manor, blowing up a Martello tower in the process. Quilter's seat was an unlovely, red brick Jacobean pile with green copper cupolas soaring high above the sea. There he bred Suffolk sheep and large black pigs, collected old and new masters, sailed yachts, brewed 'pure beer', and set up a celebrated stud of Suffolk Punches. His sons and grandsons went to Eton and Harrow – one married a daughter of the 2nd Baron Penrhyn – and settled into a gentry way of life at Methersgate Hall, near Woodbridge.[170]

Land and finance, finance and land: these, by the end of the nineteenth century, had become the twin bases of Carlton Club membership. Like the Reform, the Carlton supplied fast-track advancement for ascending *nouveaux riches*. But unlike the Reform, which remained pluralist at heart, the Carlton aspired to Establishment monopoly. Its church, after all, was the Church of England. And in the 1880s Escott spotted another difference. The Carlton was socially comprehensive in a way that Brooks's, the Reform and the National Liberal could never be.[171] The Carlton was home to all Tories and Conservatives: the official leaders, the patrician chiefs and the rank-and-file. In other words, one nation, one club. During the 1850s and 1860s there was even room for a relic of the Railway Boom: George Hudson. By comparison the Liberals were fragmented: Whig grandees at Brooks's, leading party figures at the Reform, provincial radicals at the National Liberal, and eventually Liberal Unionists at the Devonshire. Of course, the

255

existence of the Junior Carlton and Conservative Clubs – the latter known as the 'Ultratorium' – caused some duplication in the Tory ranks. And of course there were individual anomalies: the 14th Earl of Derby lived and died a member of Brooks's; Gladstone had been happier in the Carlton than he was ever to be at the Reform or even at the National Liberal; Palmerston was apparently unaware that both he and Bright were simultaneously members of the Reform. And as for Disraeli, his peculiar genius was indefinable in terms of conventional clubbability. Spotting him once on the steps of the Carlton, dressed in exotic colours, Abergavenny sent him packing: 'Dizzy, this will never do.' Even so, the Liberal and the Tory tribe each had its accepted system of assimilation.

Through the doors of the Carlton came landowning farmers, lawyers, churchmen, ironmasters, shipowners and brewers, as well as bankers, brokers, speculators and diamond magnates. There they met the landed aristocracy and gentry. Through the portals of the Reform came manufacturing tycoons, wholesalers and retailers, traders and financiers, and professional dissenters of all kinds. There they met not a few of the great Whig landowners. Each club acted as an avenue of ambition, a mechanism for the socialising of new money. When Cecil Rhodes settled his final deal with Barney Barnato, the clinching throw is said to have been an offer to put him up for the Rand Club: 'Barney, I'm going to make you a gentlemen.' The great Barnato never lived long enough to became a member of the Carlton, but several of his rivals – Robinson, Wernher, Cassel – certainly did. Like the newly founded (or refounded) public schools, the Victorian club developed into an ingenious apparatus for the manufacture of gentlemen. Those long years of Victoria's reign established and consolidated a social revolution: the remaking of the upper middle class.

> Sixty-four years that favoured property, and . . . made the upper middle
> class; buttressed, chiselled, polished it; till it was almost indistinguishable in
> manners, morals, speech, appearance, habit, and soul from the nobility.[172]

Soames Forsyte – himself a synthetic gentleman – presumably had in mind the evolution of the public school ethos; but clubland had its part to play, too. Rugby and Uppingham, Clifton, Shrewsbury and

Oundle: these could transform the children of businessmen into scions of gentility. But it took the alchemy of Pall Mall to turn new money into old within the time-span of a single generation.

It is worth pondering, for a moment, just how this came about. A generation earlier, Almack's (established 1765) had symbolised the exclusivity of the *ancien régime*. Tickets for Wednesday-night balls were coveted by the dandies of White's and the gamblers of Brooks's; they were, in fact, as difficult to procure as a summons for presentation at Court. Even the Duke of Wellington was turned away, twice. In 1814 the doors of Almack's – in effect, the entrance to Society – were guarded by just six *grandes dames*: Lady Castlereagh and Princess Esterházy, Lady Cowper and Lady Jersey, Lady Sefton and the Countess (later Princess) Lieven. 'This is selection with a vengeance,' noted the *New Monthly Magazine* in 1824; 'the very quintessence of aristocracy. Three-fourths of the nobility knock in vain for admission. Into this *sanctum sanctorum*, of course, the sons of commerce never think of entering.'[173] Then came the age of reform. In Escott's phrase, 'the prestige of achievement' replaced 'the prestige of position'. By 1840 even Almack's had been breached: new money was actually seen dancing the quadrille. 'Clear proof', observed the *Quarterly Review*, 'that the palmy days of exclusiveness are gone by in England.'[174] Of course Society – even at Almack's – had never really been impermeable. Lady Jersey herself was the granddaughter of Mr Child the banker. But the era of reform coincided with the dissolution of Society as an exclusive coterie. When Almack's became Willis's Rooms, the quadrille and the waltz gave way to concerts and lectures, readings and recitals. For Brummel and d'Orsay read Thackeray and Dickens. And into this fast-expanding social world came a new species of organisation: professional, political, entrepreneurial, male. The Victorian clubs of Pall Mall emerged as potent rivals to the eighteenth-century venues of St James's.

Even White's, supposedly the ultimate citadel of privilege, was not immune to change.[175] 'Cotton' Peel – the first baronet, a self-made millionaire, father of the future prime minister – was elected in 1813. By 1892 no fewer than fourteen Peels had become members. Henry Baring was elected in 1822. Seventy years later, thirteen Barings had joined the roll. Pascoe Grenfell, Jnr was the first of his family to be elected; by 1892 as many as fifteen Grenfells had been admitted. By the time Disraeli's nephew Coningsby was elected in 1888 he would have found, alongside many of his uncle's 'men of metal', a financier (Oppenheim), an ironmaster (Guest), two brewers (Hindlip and Guinness), half a dozen spinners (assorted Peels and Arkwrights), to say nothing of at least one celebrated speculator (Moreton Frewen). And in the following year young Coningsby would have seen a truly extraordinary infusion of commercial wealth: two Gurneys, two Thelussons, two Rallis, two Oppenheims, one Rothschild, one Morrison, three Peels, three Barings, three Hambros, three Loders and five Grenfells – all of them elected in a single year, 1889.

This cascade of new money reflected a real crisis at White's. In 1871 the freehold of the club had been put up for auction. A consortium of members entered the ring; to their consternation they were outbid by an outsider. White's was knocked down for £46,000 to H.W. Eaton, MP, later 1st Baron Cheylesmore, a haberdasher turned silk-broker – he is said to have begun as a bus-conductor. He seems to have had his eye on White's for some time: his candidature had already been blocked, and now he was threatened with blackballing.[176] Eaton promptly took pre-emptive action; having bought the club, he proceeded to put up the rent. In 1887 the club tried to heal the breach by electing Cheylesmore's son, the future 2nd Baron (he was, after all, an Etonian and a collector of mezzotints); alas, he in turn declined to attend, and again increased the rent. Meanwhile membership had been falling fast. Declining agricultural incomes, plus competition from Pall Mall, had even obliterated the waiting list. By 1882 there were only about two hundred subscribing members. And the symbol of this decline was appropriately club-like: a dispute over permission to smoke. When older members refused more than a partial lifting of the ban, the Prince of Wales took his custom – and his cronies – to the Marlborough.

But the root cause of the trouble was much more fundamental. The basis of Society was shifting fast. England, as Escott pointed out in 1879, had entered the Age of Money. In Pall Mall the newer clubs had been reflecting this change since the 1830s. At White's, things took a little longer. But in the end new money had to be absorbed, and the club building had to be expanded.[177] By the 1890s the list of members included a string of brewers (Whitbread, Combe, Meux, Hanbury and Allsopp), several manufacturers (Kemp, flannel; de la Rue, printing; Houldsworth, cotton), as well as a clutch of City financiers (Hillingdon, Schuster, Goldsmid and Levita). There were American fortunes, too: Walter Burns of New York and A.J. Forbes-Leith of Illinois. And so the process continued. By 1935 the Earl of Inchcape was there, along with a Coats and a Pease, a Quilter and a Sassoon. By that date the committee of management included a Guinness, a Guest, a Samuel, an Oppenheim and a Ralli. Colonel C.W. Sofer Whitburn – son of the millionaire bill-broker – was by then one of four Trustees (the others, representing an older world altogether, were the Earl of Ellesmere, Earl Fitzwilliam and Lord Leconfield). And finally Eaton's grandson, the 4th Baron Cheylesmore – grandchild of the bus-conductor – had actually been made an Honorary Member, joining at that dizzy height eight representatives of the royal families of Europe. White's Club – once the very symbol of landed supremacy – had been well and truly permeated by the *nouveaux riches.*

Interestingly, Brooks's – White's traditional rival – managed to delay the onrush of plutocracy a little longer. Boodle's of course remained the refuge of the gentry. But Brooks's – with the Reform as its middle-class annexe – was still a bastion of the great Whig grand-motherhood. There might be the occasional Bass, the occasional Tennant, even the occasional Crossley. But that was only a sprinkling of new money. Several of the richest men in Britain – Alfred de Rothschild, H.W. Schneider, Mitchell Henry, Samuel Morton Peto – knocked in vain for admission. Several others – 'Natty' Rothschild, W.O. Foster, George Moore, Tom Brassey, Pandeli Ralli – were admitted only at the second attempt. In 1864 two Rothschilds were blackballed in a single night.[178] Clubland could still keep a few of its secrets.

# V. The Royal Yacht Squadron: New Money at Cowes

September 1904; Frederick Harrison, the ageing *enfant terrible* of Radicalism, is staying with Andrew Carnegie at Skibo Castle, Sutherland (1899–1903) [plate 43]. Sir Thomas Lipton – 'Tom Tea' – arrives in his luxurious steam yacht *Erin*, and invites the house party aboard for lunch. It is 'a noble ship of 1400 tons', Harrison reports to Lady Dorothy Nevill; truly 'a floating palace'.

> Sir T. gave us a royal luncheon served by Congolese waiters in white frocks and long black hair like a woman's. Then we landed at [the Duke of Sutherland's seat] Dunrobin and enjoyed the magnificent gardens and terraces, like a villa round Florence – only intensely green and luxurious … Both at Dunrobin and at Skibo the ancient gardens are in perfection of bloom … This is a royal palace. I believe [Edward VII] would like to swop Balmoral for it. We have a large party [at Skibo] of Principals, Provosts, and Professors from St Andrew's University of which our host is to serve this year as Lord Rector! He is a real genius, full of knowledge, keenness, and sympathy with all good things and good men and women. They are making me learn golf in my old age. [Joseph H.] Choate [the US Ambassador] and John Morley have just left – not to speak of H.M., who was charming when here … we have all been in the new swimming bath, a sort of Winter garden with a marble bath of warm sea water – men and woman all tumbling about like seals in the American fashion.[179]

Carnegie – 'the star-spangled Scotsman' – doubtless coveted Dunrobin. Lipton, a self-made grocery tycoon, would have settled for membership of the Royal Yacht Squadron. Despite the favour of Edward VII, however, 'Tom T' was not elected to 'the Club' – as it was universally known at Cowes – until 1931, just before his death.[180]

Even more than White's, the RYS was a bastion of exclusivity which enjoyed a love–hate relationship with new money. During the Commodoreship of the Prince of Wales, 1882–92, Cowes Week came almost to rival Ascot as the zenith of the social season. And the steam yachts which thronged the Solent every August were turned into floating house parties for acolytes of the *nouveaux riches*.

From coffee and from supper room,
From Poplar and Pall Mall,
The girls on seeing me exclaim:
'Oh what a champagne swell'.[181]

The Brasseys on *Sunbeam*, the Guinnesses on *Cetonia*, the Jameses on *Lancashire Witch*, the Revelstokes on *Waterwitch*: 'Cowes is no longer a half-civilised resórt of the sailorman,' noted one commentator in 1881, 'it is now a Court.' The crush of spectators was occasionally overwhelming: one year W.H. Smith – Disraeli's (and Gilbert and Sullivan's) First Lord of the Admiralty – fell in at the Castle Landings, and a boat from Lord Bute's yacht capsized, tipping Lady Howard of Glossop into the water. Neighbouring houses on the mainland and on the Isle of Wight were rented out at a premium. Tom Brassey was paying £100 per week for Egypt House in 1882; Mrs Baring's garden party at Nubia House in 1884 was said to rival those at Holland House, Kensington. Mrs Markham's party at Solent Lodge, Mrs Cust's at Hippesley House, Lady Harrington's at Stanhope Lodge: with flowers and Chinese lanterns, and catering by Gunters, Cowes was *en fête* throughout those languid weeks between Goodwood and the Glorious Twelfth. There were so many fair visitors on the Castle Lawn that it became known as the Dear Park. 'The Prince appears, and a flutter ensues as the pretty ladies edge insensibly towards him ... He disappears, and the flutter ends in a comparison of frocks.' By the 1900s quite a number of these ladies were American or Continental, and a great many of them represented new money. Lady Randolph Churchill and her sister Mrs J. Leslie; the Marchioness of Ormonde; Miss Polk (later Mme de Charette), Miss Stevens (later Mrs Arthur Paget); Princess Lynar and her sisters ... 'It is no longer a small family party who come down to live seafaringly with their lovers and brethren, but a large crowd, mostly new people, who flit in and out of the little town with the one object of showing dresses, seeing the latest beauties, and keeping clear of the hated sea.'[182] In 1884 the King of Sweden was a visitor as well as the Crown Prince of Germany; in 1889 it was the German Emperor himself. In 1900 Lionel de Rothschild installed his family at Inchmery House on the Beaulieu

River; ten years later he bought the Exbury estate nearby. No longer simply aristocratic, Cowes had become plutocratic, royal, imperial.

In the twelve years 1888 to 1900 only 112 members of the Royal Yacht Squadron were elected out of 207 proposals. Blackballing, or 'pilling', was fierce: one inveterate blackballer was known as 'the Piller of Society'. Even so, the march of the *nouveaux riches* proved irresistible. Tom Brassey arrived in 1859, Albert Brassey followed in 1879; Samuel Morton Peto was there as early as 1853. By the turn of the century seven Barings had been elected, four Guests, four Guinnesses, three Rothschilds, three Orr-Ewings, two McCalmonts, two Houldsworths and two Grettons. Thereafter the trend becomes still more pronounced: Wythes, Fairhaven, Portal, Lister Kaye, Runciman, Sopwith . . . No wonder that when F.E. Smith was elected – thanks to the support of King George V – one member was heard to remark: 'We do not want any more of his sort in the squadron.'[183]

Terah Hooley made no bones about his ambition: 'most newly made millionaires buy a yacht at some time or other' – often enough, it seemed, the very same yacht. One of Hooley's vessels, *Venetia*, had previously been owned by Lord Ashburton; it passed to his partner Martin Rucker, and then to Whitaker Wright (who renamed it, appropriately, *Sybarite*); its eventual owner was Cornelius Vanderbilt. At different times Hooley also owned Lord Lonsdale's *Varena* and Lillie Langtry's *White Way*; he even tried in vain to buy the Royal Yacht *Britannia*.[184] Henry McCalmont's yacht *Giralda* – capable of 22 knots – became eventually the Spanish Royal Yacht.

Even the most high-minded politician was not averse to accepting a little marine hospitality. 'The Great Man [W.E. Gladstone]', noted Edward Hamilton in 1880, 'has gone off with Donald Currie on board one of his steamships, *Grantully Castle* . . . I presume . . . Currie aspires at least to a baronetcy.'[185] Sure enough, having been (as he put it) thoroughly 'curried', Gladstone felt obliged to present his host with a knighthood the following year. *Vanity Fair* nominated the new KCMG a 'Knight of the Cruise of Mr Gladstone'. And Gladstone was not alone: 1898 saw Rosebery taking Lord Rendel's yacht to Naples and Ferdinand de Rothschild's yacht to Amsterdam.[186] The musings of one Treasury socialite – the invaluable Hamilton – make the political function of yachting only too clear:

*Sunday 6 Aug. 1882:* (Yacht *Palatine*. Off Swanage.) Lord W[olverton] was pilled last week for 'the Club' – RYS – a really monstrous shame. He has taken the pilling very good naturedly. We came on here last night from Bournemouth where we had spent the day to enable Ld W. to run over to Iwerne [Minster] for a few hours. Lady W. unfortunately cannot stand yachting. We are having most lovely weather, and I am enjoying the change enormously . . . The life of yachting is so demoralising and lazy-like that it is next to impossible to get through anything in the shape of reading beyond the newspapers . . . Nobody could have been kinder than Lord Wolverton. It was too bad his being blackballed for 'the Club' [in fact he was elected the following year]. I am sorry [however] that he thinks he has been passed over [for political office]. He virtually considers himself much aggrieved – that he ought to have at least had such an office as the Chancellorship of the Duchy of Lancaster, with a seat in the Cabinet! It is certainly strange how badly some people gauge their own métier . . .

*23 Nov. 1882:* Sir Stafford Northcote [Tory leader in the Commons] is unwell and has to take himself off for a complete rest. W.H. Smith places his splendid yacht at his disposal.[187]

Three years later, Smith became Secretary of State for War to Northcote's First Lord of the Treasury.

So a yacht gave a new man status; it gave him mobility. Albert Salisbury Wood, a Liverpudlian chain-and-anchor manufacturer, was said to own a collection of thirty-five. It was all part of the acceleration, the diversification of social life noted by Lady Dorothy Nevill in 1906:

Half a century ago . . . life . . . was slow, rather solemn, inexpensive, not undignified, but according to modern ideas, dull. What is the life of the rich man today? A sort of firework! Paris, Monte Carlo, big-game shooting in Africa, fishing in Norway, dashes to Egypt, trips to Japan . . . houses, hotels, motors, pictures . . . and very likely, in addition to all of these, most costly of all – a yacht.[188]

## VI. Parliament, 1911: Commons, Lords and Plutocrats

August 9th, 1911: one of the hottest days on record – the thermometer touches 100° Fahrenheit. That night, August 10th–11th, in a packed and stifling House of Lords, the 'last-ditch' Unionists fight out their battle against the encroaching power of the Commons. Peers fill every seat and doorway; peeresses crowd the galleries. Only the throne is vacant. At 10.40 p.m. the tellers announce their verdict on the Parliament Bill: the Liberals are home and dry by seventeen votes, and the Lords' veto is sacrosanct no more. 'We were beaten', growls George Wyndham, 'by the Bishops and the Rats.'[189]

In reality, they were beaten by George V's reluctant agreement to create, if necessary, an avalanche of new Liberal peers. Asquith had prepared a list of 245; that list survives,[190] and it makes interesting reading, so interesting that it deserves to be better known. Apart from the sons of existing peers – and scientists, writers and musicians, from Thomas Hardy to Gilbert Murray, via J.M. Barrie, Bertrand Russell and Baden-Powell – it consists very largely of *nouveaux riches*. Sir Edgar Vincent, speculator and socialite, is there; so are Sir Abe Bailey and Sir Sigmund Neumann (Randlords); so is Sir Edgar Speyer, the pro-German banker; so are Sir George Riddell of the *News of the World* and Sir Frank Newnes of *Tit-Bits*; and so are Sir William Lever (soap), Henry Oppenheim (finance), Sir Thomas Borthwick (colonial trade), Sir Hubert Longman (publishing), Sir Walter Runciman (shipping), Frank Debenham (haberdashery), David Davies (coal), Sir Jeremiah Colman (mustard), Sir Thomas Lipton (tea), Joseph Rowntree (chocolate), Sir Edward Holden (banking), F.J. Horniman (tea), Sir Frank Hollins (spinning), Sir Alexander Kleinwort (banking), Sir John Dewar (distilling), Isaac Seligman (banking), T.R. Ferens (bleaching), Lawrence Currie (banking), Sir Walter Gilbey (wine), F. Thomasson (cotton), Sir Joseph Lees (coal) and Sir Archibald Williamson (South American trade). New men, all of them, and very, very rich. H.J. Tennant is there too, son of the chemical magnate and brother-in-law to the Prime Minister, plus a number of others – Wilson Marriage, J. Weston Stevens – whose names are now forgotten. No doubt quite a few were not exactly welcome to the King, though he seems to have rejected only one: the mysterious Baron de Forest (né Bischoffsheim; adopted heir of Baron de Hirsch). Forest was a Radical millionaire who appears to have been universally distrusted; he eventually transferred his nationality to Liechtenstein and died in Biarritz.[191] Many of those on the list never did attain the status of a peerage; but Asquith's secret memorandum gives us more than a glimpse of at least half the Edwardian plutocracy, the Liberal half.

As it happened, Parliament's plutocratic credentials needed little bolstering from counterfactual peers. Both the House of Commons and the House of Lords had long since gone over to new money. Look first at the Commons.

In 1846 there were only seven MPs who would leave more than half a million: four free-traders – Beckett (banking), Brocklehurst (silk), Guest (iron) and Muntz (metal); plus three protectionists – Bailey (iron), Kemble (insurance) and Thompson (finance). Fifty years later the tally of millionaires and half-millionaires had soared to 93: 20 Liberals, 17 Liberal Unionists and no fewer than 56 Conservatives. By 1884 nine out of ten MPs were identifiably rich.[192] Liberal new money was strongest among manufacturing industries, especially in the provinces: Thomas Owen and Albert Spicer (paper), Sir Thomas Lea (sauce), F.J. Horniman (tea), Sir W.H. Wills (tobacco), J.A. Jacoby (lace), Sir Frederick Mappin (cutlery) and Lewis Fry (chocolate). Liberal Unionist money tended to be a little less new and, as often as not, City-based: Sir Julian Goldsmid, for instance, or Walter Morrison; or magnates like W.C. Quilter, Ferdinand de Rothschild and Sir Samuel Montagu. As for the Conservatives, by the end of the century their *nouveau riche* MPs had clearly swamped the Government back benches: from Sir Blundell Maple and H.C. ('Inky') Stephens to Francis Tress Barry (copper) and Robert Cox (gelatine); from James Bigwood (vinegar) to James Bailey (hotels); from F.W. Isaacson (silk) to Victor Milward (needles). Plutocrats, all of them, not to mention Sir Edward Harland and Gustav Wolff, shipbuilders both, regularly returned 'unopposed' for East and North Belfast. Shipping is also represented by C.W. Cayzer, J.M. Denny, R.S. Donkin, Sir Arthur Forword and Sir Charles Palmer. All new men; all Tory new men. And to speak for iron, steel, railways and heavy engineering there are names like Aird,

Baird, Baldwin, Brassey and Hickman. As for the City, it has by now become thoroughly Conservative: Beckett, Farquhar, Gibbs, Gilliat, Goschen, Loder and Samuel are all Tory MPs. And the brewing industry (apart from Bass and McEwan) is of course overwhelmingly Tory: Allsopp, Bonsor, Bullard, Charrington, Combe and Gretton are all predictably there. On the social side, there is T.G. Bowles of *Vanity Fair*; and on the philanthropic front that doyen of hypergamous mobility, the American spouse of England's greatest heiress:

> For fortune hunting to eternal fame stands
> William Pole Tylney-Long-Wellesley-Tylney-Long's name.
> But he was scarcely fit to lick thy boots
> William Lehman Ashmead Burdett-Coutts-Bartlett-Coutts.

During the same period – the later nineteenth and early twentieth century – the number of landowners in the House of Commons had been falling steadily: from three-quarters of the total in the 1840s, to one-half by 1886, and one-tenth by 1910.[193] New money was clearly moving into the ascendant. Even if we include the hundred or so Irish MPs, very few of whom were rich, we find that something like one-seventh of the entire House of Commons at the end of the nineteenth century would – in modern terms at least – be counted multi-millionaires. More remarkable still are the statistics in contemporary national terms: of the two hundred or so full-blown millionaires alive in Britain at the turn of the century, nearly one-third – that is, sixty or so – were sitting together in the House of Commons.

And as for the House of Lords . . . The reciprocal process by which plutocracy infiltrated aristocracy – and aristocracy accommodated itself to the ways of plutocracy – must by now be so familiar to readers of this book that it hardly needs repeating. The image of land, despite its falling value, did not lose its appeal. After all, as J.A. Froude pointed out in 1877, 'land is sought after for . . . social consequence . . . for political influence [and] for an ambition to leave our names behind us, rooted in the soil.'[194] That impulse remained; only the personnel changed. 'The days', noted Shaw-Lefevre in 1881, 'when great lawyers like the Howards, the Cokes or the Bridgemans, or great generals like the Marlboroughs and the Wellingtons, could acquire great properties of land, and could found families in the first rank of landowners seem to be past ... [Instead we see] successful merchants, manufacturers, brewers, coalowners, ironmasters, or tradesmen.'[195] And as new money acquired an increasing stake in Society, so Society learnt to play according to new rules. 'There are now', concluded Lady Dorothy Nevill in 1906, 'many scions of noble houses who exhibit nearly as much shrewdness in striking bargains in the City, as a South African millionaire himself; whilst, on the other hand, the sons of the millionaires in several instances do not conceal their dislike for business, and lead an existence of leisurely and extravagant ease ... So matters adjust themselves, [and thus is] Society ... transformed.'[196]

Quite so: the fusion of old and new. Taken together – when Commons joined Lords on the occasion of the Queen's Speech, for example – the Houses of Parliament must have presented, to outside eyes at least, an almost monolithic image of capital. 'It is likely', Rubinstein concludes, 'that any state opening of Parliament ... [at the turn of the century] saw a greater concentration of Britain's economic wealth at one time in one place than ever in British history, and possibly among any legislature anywhere.'[197] Landed wealth was still represented, of course; its social prestige was still magnetic; but its days of political influence were numbered. From a position of hegemony, landowners had slipped during the course of the nineteenth century into just one of several interconnected élites, part of a new multifaceted Establishment. In any case, land itself had by then been absorbed into the world of City finance; it had become only one of several options in an international investment portfolio. In the period between 1918 and 1925 land sales would follow the imperatives of the financial market, transforming the English countryside through the fragmentation and multiplication of estates.[198] But here, at Westminster, on the eve of the First World War, we can visualise Britain's new ruling class in all its opulence: 'an amalgam of rentier money, service employments and the remnants of landed society'.[199] Fit representatives indeed for an Age of Money, and an extraordinarily tempting target for some anti-capitalist Guy Fawkes.

# VII. Sporting Rituals: Shooting, Hunting, Racing

For property, 1912 is a 'Strenuous Year'. Liberal taxation is beginning to bite; one after another the old landed estates are being broken up; and Thomas de Grey, 6th Baron Walsingham – the finest shot in England – decides to sell: he is going to live abroad and devote the rest of his days to collecting butterflies. 'It is generally recognised', notes *The Times*, 'that the present is a time of change.'[200] Well, yes: when even Walsingham – the man who shot 1,070 grouse in a single day at Blubberhouse Moor in 1888 – cannot afford to maintain his Yorkshire shoot, then the future for landed society must indeed be bleak. But wait: not far from Walsingham's other property, in Norfolk, is a rather different sort of estate. The shooting at Elveden is reputed to be the finest in England. By 1900 its game bag totals 100,000 birds; by 1921, 145,000. The head keeper commands a force of 76 men, with 16 gamekeepers, 9 underkeepers, and 28 warreners to cull the rabbits. Each beat is connected to its neighbours by telephone. There are even fifteen miles of private roads. But then, the Elveden estate does not have to be self-supporting; it is a property of Edward Guinness, the future 1st Earl of Iveagh. It costs him £30,000 a year to maintain – perfectly affordable, given the fact that he has an annual income of half a million (perhaps £20 million today).[201] The de Greys cannot match that sort of money. Shoots like Elveden – or West Dean, or Trent Park, for that matter – are now the prerogative of the *nouveaux riches*.

'What monstrous extravagance this shooting is; it surely cannot last long.' That was John Bright in 1856, and he was wrong. Eight years later he went to stay with his old Anti-Corn Law ally, Thomas Bazley – Matthew Arnold's 'arch Philistine' – at Hatherop Park, Gloucestershire. 'What our host will do with us for several days, I know not – as he has no game, and if he had, we don't shoot – and we cannot spend all the time fighting our old battles over again.'[202] This time he may have been right; but Bazley was by no means typical. The Victorian and Edwardian *nouveaux riches* proved to be among the greatest champions of country sports. Robert Peel, the future Prime Minister, was renting Cluny Castle on the Spey as early as 1818. Even Bright enjoyed salmon-fishing. And it was the richest of the new men who pursued game most ferociously, or at least most conspicuously. Hall Barn, Buckinghamshire – seat of Lord Burnham, owner of the *Daily Telegraph* – still holds the record for the number of pheasants shot in a single day: 3,937 on 18 December 1913.

> Gaydene, [home of Mr Sidney Wilton, was] the most beautiful and the most celebrated villa in England; only twenty miles from town, seated on the wooded crest of the swan-crowned Thames, with gardens of delight, and woods full of pheasants, and a terrace that would have become a court, glancing over a wide expanse of bower and glade, studded with bright halls and delicate steeples, and the smoke of rural homes ... Towards the end of [December] the premier came down, and the Blue Ribbon covert [was] reserved, though he really cared little for sport.[203]

By Endymion's day, the ritual of country sport was already an end in itself. By the time Augustus Hare came to visit Elveden, ritual was fast becoming holy writ. As at Sandringham, the clocks were kept half an hour fast to guarantee maximum shooting time. When the moment came to change for dinner, a gong reverberated through the marble hall [plate 57].

> This place is the most wonderful shooting in England. The soil is so bad that it is not worth cultivating and agriculture has been abandoned as a bad business. Game is found to be far more profitable. Each day I have gone out with the [ladies to the] luncheon party, and we have met the shooters at tents pitched at different parts of the wilderness, where boarded floors are laid down, and a luxurious banquet is prepared with plate and flowers. The quantity of game killed is almost incredible, and the Royal Duke [the future George V] shot more than anyone.[204]

No doubt when the party at last returned home, Augustus did not decline the offer of tea in the Durbar Hall.

These sporting rituals came almost to exist independently of the mundanities of business which actually maintained them. Lady Dorothy Nevill was amazed that Sir Henry Meux's brewing fortune continued to increase – £200,000 in 1841, £600,000 in 1858 – 'in spite of a career of fifteen years' neglect of business, of hunting and racing, of French cooks, collecting china, and every kind of extravagance; of battues, moors and deer-forests; of Epsom, Newmarket, and Ascot; and an entire lack of attention to the brewing business.'[205] She underestimated, of course, the juggernaut of capital formation; and she preferred not to grasp the assimilative function of sporting ritual. Once a preserve of the landed gentry, country sports had become too expensive for the mere countryman; they were now the *lingua franca* of *rentier* society. They were also part of the process by which the new rich, and their epigoni, were grafted on to the hierarchical structure of class. When Rudyard Kipling was offered a fishing holiday in 1890 as guest of Andrew Carnegie, he accepted with all the eagerness of an *arriviste*.

> We go this afternoon [from Sussex] to London – then all night in the [railway] cars which, in England, is an enormous journey – and arrive at Creich Manse, Bonar Bridge [Sutherland], at 11 tomorrow. The Manse is the Presbyterian minister's house almost six miles from Carnegie's [Skibo] Castle and half a mile from a trout-loch. I've got my rods and tackle into working order as well as a choice collection of rainbow coloured salmon flies ... and I hope the fish will take half as much trouble for me as I've taken for them.[206]

Such rituals had come to represent much more than conspicuous consumption. They were now built into the new hierarchy of wealth, negotiable items in the endless interchange of patronage and profit.

Sir Edward Hamilton witnessed at close quarters this blending of City and County; the interaction of politics, sport and money. A few extracts from his diary suggest the flavour of the day.

> *22 Nov. 1881:* two days at Charlie Tudway's [Stoberry Park, near Wells] – an excellent 'well appointed' house, good shooting, good cooking, good company, where we had the Normantons, Walronds, etc ...

> *3 Dec. 1881:* Old Bass [plate IX], who declines to have a baronetcy himself, is very anxious that one should be conferred on his eldest son with remainder to the younger and his issue. Mr G[ladstone] is rather averse to such an arrangement, which amounts (he says) to giving *two* baronetcies. However, I have found a precedent (Salomons in 1869) ...

> *11 Dec. 1881:* F. Milbank, MP, wants a baronetage. No exception can probably be taken to this. Mr G. is thinking of offering a like honour to

Darwin, which would probably give great and general satisfaction in scientific circles. He is said to be a wealthy man . . .

*4/7 Oct. 1882:* [Escrick, Yorkshire] is very comfortable and roomy. One or two of the rooms have recently been done up by Lady Wenlock in truly aesthetic style . . . Beilby Lawley makes the most delightful of hosts . . . [he] is, I think, the best and most sportsmanlike shot I have ever seen. I fancy he is very little behind [Lord Walsingham's half-brother] de Grey . . .

*14 Oct. 1882:* [Lord] Aberdeen is said to have spent £100,000 on [Haddo House] in [Adamesque] alterations and decorations . . . it makes a fine pile.

*18 Oct. 1882:* [Taymouth Castle, Perthshire] is a truly glorious place . . . [and here, amid the nobility of Scotland are] the Edward Guinnesses, he of porter repute and she of London ballroom fame . . .

*2 Nov. 1882:* In deference to the Prince of Wales, Oscar Clayton has been submitted for a Knighthood. It is to be hoped that no disagreeable stories will come out about him . . .

*9 Nov. 1882:* Childers wants a baronetcy for Sir J. Adye. But there seems to be insufficiency of means [i.e., wealth]. One would have thought a GCB would have been sufficient . . . Mr G. suggested a Privy Councillorship [later the Queen objected] . . .[207]

And so it continues. By 1903, Hamilton is ready for his first visit to Sir Ernest Cassel at Newmarket: no doubt his host is anxious to talk about the impending Budget.

*22 March 1903:* [Moulton Paddocks, Newmarket] now belongs to Cassel – Bully Gerard spent a large sum on it some years ago . . . [it is quite] the nicest place here. The party [includes] the Duke of Devonshire . . . I regard Cassel as the ablest man in the City . . . His has been a marvellous rise.[208]

Morton Frewen surely envied Cassel's financial genius. But his own rake's progress in the 1880s was rather more typical of the *nouveaux riches*.

From November to April Melton, then a month's fishing in Ireland . . . in May, June, July, London; then Goodwood and Cowes; then 'grouse' some-where and Doncaster; next a broken week or two at Newmarket . . .[209]

Newmarket had in fact been a focus of new money since at least the 1870s. Cassel's predecessor at Moulton Paddocks had been George Baird, the racing-mad millionaire from Gartsherrie. And it was, after all, at Newmarket that Mrs Disraeli introduced the young Lord Rosebery to Hannah de Rothschild.[210] But the golden age came a little later, towards the end of the century. Within riding distance was W.H. Smith's Great Thurlow Hall, Suffolk and Henry McCalmont's Cheveley Park, Cambridgeshire.[211] McCalmont, appropriately, was the local Tory MP. Closer to Newmarket Heath – just a canter away, in fact – was Leopold de Rothschild's Palace House [plate 55] and Henri Bischoffsheim's mansion, The Severals. There was American money at Avenue House, where C.F. Garland held court; and South African money at Cecil Lodge, where Siggy Neumann – 'Neumann of Newmarket' – dispensed hospitality. From South Africa too came Sir William Dunn, 1st Bt, of The Retreat, Lakenheath, Suffolk and Solly Barnato Joel [plate III] of Sefton Lodge (designed respectively by A.N. Prentice and by Lord Iveagh's architect William Young).[212] Then there was Sir Herbert Mackworth-Praed, 1st Bt (banking), at Owsden Hall, Suffolk; Sir Robert Jardine, 2nd Bt (China trade) at The Kremlin; the 1st Viscount St Davids (finance) at Landwade Hall; W.J. Tatem, 1st Baron Glaneley (shipping) at Exning House; H.L. Raphael (finance again) at The Cottage, Falmouth Avenue; and James Buchanan, 1st Baron Woolavington, a Lloyd George whisky peer, at Grove House – all these within close range of the very mecca of the turf.[213] Within a few years Washington Singer will replace Raphael, and E.W. Baird will replace Tatem; Eustace Loder will appear at Severals Lodge and Frank Bibby at The Avenue. Even Cecil Rhodes seems to have been tempted to join the racing fraternity: he bought Dalham Hall, as we have seen, from Sir Robert Affleck, though he never really lived there. But it was Cassel who trumped them all, at Moulton Paddocks: there, or so it was said, the Prince of Wales's kippers were grilled to order by the Jockey Club's own housekeeper.

The prominence of Moulton Paddocks among the racing set, the pre-eminence of Elveden in the world of shooting – these were but symbols of a revolution which was much more generally diffused. In this Age of Money only the richest could take the lead. Collectively

calculated, the scale of extravagance had become alarming: it was estimated, for example, that by 1900 Royal Ascot cost £175,000, or
£2,900 per minute of racing (say, £120,000 per minute today).[214] Old
money was beginning to take fright. During the 1880s, the gentry's
political influence had been seriously weakened by the Third Reform
Act; its economic basis had at the same time been fatally undermined
by the import of foreign foodstuffs, a belated result of repealing the
Corn Laws. All that remained – and it amounted to a great deal, of
course – was the social importance of land, and the sport. With prices
falling, and estates fragmenting, land was there for the buying; and
during the Edwardian period its purchase was increasingly dictated
not by financial but by social and recreational factors. More than ever,
land was simply the icing on a plutocrat's portfolio.

Escott's words of 1879 proved to be only too accurate:

> Disguise it as we may, wealth is the governing force in our social system
> ... What barrier opposes it? It surmounts its newly-found escutcheon with
> a coronet, and takes its seat amongst the Howards and the Talbots ... It is
> sworn in the Privy Council and is enrolled in the Cabinet ... It buys up
> lands, castles, halls and manor-houses, it is put into the commission of the
> peace, wears the scarlet and silver of the deputy-lieutenant and the gor-
> geous uniform of the yeomanry, and constitutes itself an important section
> of the landed gentry. It contracts brilliant marriages; it enters, and some-
> times leads, society; its sons officer the crack regiments; its daughters
> command the matrimonial market ... Instead of the pedigree chart we
> have substituted the banker's book ... [For] what is the income of a
> leading barrister, or a renowned physician, of a bishop, or an ambassador,
> or a statesman, when compared to the colossal profits of a great tea-broker,
> corn-merchant, brewer, distiller, warehouseman, stockbroker, or ...
> general merchant? No wonder that the sons of peers gladly accept partner-
> ships ... that dandies go on Change, and that the voice of Fashion
> declares that 'there is nothing like trade nowadays'. Privilege ... is dead
> and buried, and over its newly-raised mausoleum Capital and Competi-
> tion dance in jubilant triumph.[215]

In an Age of Money, land was no longer the cement of the rural
community; it was simply a negotiable asset. The years 1918 to 1925
proved to be a watershed. By 1924 Edward Wood – the future Lord

Halifax, then Minister of Agriculture – could point to a 'silent revolution', a seismic shift which had visibly transformed the English countryside, 'the gradual disappearance of the old landowning class'. 'Within the last five years', he concluded, 'the number of occupying owners has almost exactly doubled.' Records indicate that between 1917 and 1921 as much as a quarter of all the land in England changed hands.[216] No doubt the bulk of these transactions represented transfers from landowner to farmer; but many undoubtedly involved the injection of new money. More and more, the country estate – divided and subdivided – was becoming a weekend adjunct of the metropolis. The motor car was already blurring county identities. And land ownership was becoming increasingly internationalised. When in 1909 the Scudamore-Stanhope family put Holme Lacy, Herefordshire on the market – the first sale of these estates since the Norman Conquest – the eventual buyer was a brewer from Sydney, Australia, Sir Robert Lucas-Tooth. The new men – and the new women – had arrived.

None newer, and none more shiny, than the Cunards of Nevill Holt. Sir Bache Cunard, 3rd Bt – MFH, 1878 to 1888 – was a grandson of the founder of the great shipping line. He bought his estate, on the borders of Leicestershire and Rutland, in 1881, specifically for hunting.

> Being by birth a Cunarder [noted *Vanity Fair* in that year], he resolved to become a sportsman. He bought a Polo pony. He bought Holt. He bought a yacht ... he bought the Billesden hounds, and conquered the Quorn. He has not yet bought a seat in Parliament, or a wife.

The last of these, at least, was not wanting for long.

Those in any case were the golden years of hunting in the Shires: the Quorn, the Cottesmore, the Belvoir and the Pytchley. The railway had made the whole thing so much easier. From Melton Mowbray one could hunt six days a week without missing breakfast or dinner. No wonder Ambrose Clark – the Singer sewing-machine heir – leased Warwick Lodge for several seasons. Soon, as Lord Stalbridge remembered, the very word 'Fernie' would send 'a thrill down the spine, not only of every fox-hunter but of any sportsman the length and breadth of the land'.[217] C.W.B. Fernie himself was in the field between 1888 and 1919; and with him rode Sir Harold Wernher, and Marshall Field III, and many of the *nouveaux riches* of England. Not far away Sir Harold Nutting, whose fortune came from bottling Guinness, was a keen follower of the Quorn; 'Tommy' Bouch (construction engineering) and George Colman (mustard) followed the Belvoir. And the Belvoir itself was led by a brewer, Sir Gilbert Greenall, 2nd Bt, 'the first un-Ducal Master of a great pack'. Running a hunt – at, say, four to six thousand a year – was becoming too much for Surtees' Duke of Tergiversation. Ever since Thomas Assheton-Smith turned the profits of his slate quarries into hunting with the Quorn and the Belvoir, even famous packs had depended to some degree on new money. And there was never a shortage of aspirant Masters. Charlie Morrell took the Tetbury, Worcestershire and South Oxfordshire fox hounds in turn. Surtees knew such men only too well, Mr Puffington of Hornby House for example: 'Above all Puff felt that he was a new man in the country, and that taking the hounds would give him weight.' With Brassey at the Heythrop, Baird at the Cottesmore, and Rothschild money at the Whaddon Chase, the old order was increasingly on the defensive. The South Herefordshire pack was successively subsidised by an ironmaster (Foster) and a chocolate maker (Fry). During the summer months Brassey would even arrange the next season's meets from his yacht on the Mediterranean. The sense of displacement must often have been acute. The traditional gentry were still there; but many more of the hunting fraternity were cast in the mould of Mr Joseph Large, Surtees' 'rich, very rich' teapot manufacturer. There can have been few tears when Lowenstein – the hunting financier of Thorpe Satchville – disappeared in mysterious circumstances. And yet some sort of assimilation was possible. When Joseph Watson the soap-boiler bought Compton Verney and its 20,000 acres from the 19th Baron Willoughby de Broke in 1921, he soon settled down to serious hunting: so serious that he died in the hunting field a year later.[218]

So while Sir Bache pursued the fox, far from the shipyards of Liverpool, Glasgow and New York, Lady Cunard entertained. Maud Cunard – Emerald, as she preferred to be known – would glitter and sparkle her way through a thousand dinner parties between the 1890s and the 1940s; in Leicestershire, in Grosvenor Square, and latterly at the Ritz and the Dorchester. Cynthia Asquith once compared her to 'an inebriate canary'. That was too harsh. Chips Channon was kinder, recalling the 'rococo atmosphere – the conversation in the candlelight, the bibelots and the books'. From an opulent childhood in New York and San Francisco, she emerged in 1895 as mistress of Nevill Holt, a romantic manor house of the fifteenth century. Thereafter the weekends never ceased. That was how her daughter Nancy remembered it:

> . . . grey and yellow stone and old stucco . . . a church . . . ancient stables . . . loggia . . . porch . . . oriel window . . . A great lawn between two avenues of very tall beech-trees, a terrace looking towards sunset, walled gardens . . . oaks and elms . . . [and] the chestnut avenue with its iron gate standing ever open between the stone piers that bear the arms of the Nevills.[219]

In the shadow of those ancient walls – over-restored, of course, and filled with ritzy furniture – a topiary garden had been laid, decorated with horseshoes spelling out a cliché: 'Come into the garden, Maud'.

> My picture of Holt is one of constant arrivals and departures during half the year, of elaborately long teas on the lawn with tennis and croquet going on, of great winter logs blazing all day in the Hall and Morning Room, with people playing bridge there for hours on end. Beautiful and exciting ladies move about in smart tailor-mades; they arrive in sables or long fox stoles, a bunch of Parma violets pinned into the fur on the shoulder. Summer-long, in shot silk and striped taffeta they stroll laughing and chatting across the lawns . . . All . . . veils . . . [and] feather boas . . . [and] trailing teagowns of beige lace, of lilac, wisteria and cream-coloured chiffon.[220]

It would last a little longer, but not much. After the Great War, the Cunards moved on to Marble Hill, Middlesex: Sir Bache was rather old for hunting now, and Emerald preferred Grosvenor Square. As we take our leave of Nevill Holt – hatbox in the luggage rack; gravel crunching on the drive – the world of the Victorian and Edwardian *nouveaux riches* begins to fade into the pages of a diary. But just a minute: their story has an epilogue, the 'long weekend' between the First World War and the Second.

# VIII. Postscript: From Belgrave Square to Port Lympne

June 11th, 1936: Chips Channon – grandson of a Chicago ship's chandler, married recently to a Guinness heiress – is giving a dinner party for the King. Wallis Simpson will be there, of course (her second husband has discreetly declined); and Philip Sassoon, and Emerald Cunard; Duff Cooper, too, and the divine Diana; no room, alas, for Laura Corrigan. For nearly a year workmen have been in and out of 5 Belgrave Square [plate 118], creating a Rococo dining room to rival the Mirror Room at the Amalienberg near Munich. Boudin of Paris – 'the greatest decorator in the world' – has done his best (this room alone has cost £6,000), and the walls are 'a symphony of blue and silver'. Frankly, it is a stage set, a fabrication of crystal and mirrored glass – 'baroque and rococo and what-ho and oh-no-no' – designed, at the very least, to 'shock and outrage'. Even the parquet floor has been imported from Vienna. Not for nothing is Channon the author of *The Ludgwigs of Bavaria*. 'Will it', he wonders nervously, be hailed as 'London's loveliest room?' The Duke of Kent arrives punctually at 9.05. Lady Cunard is late. Then the doors are 'flung open, and ... everyone's breath [is] quite taken away by the beauty of the dining room'. The guests advance from an ante room of darkest green, through a passage of apricot and silver, to emerge in a shimmering cavern of silver and blue. There are blinis on the menu, filled with caviare; then sole Muscat, and *boeuf Provençal*. The gossip is French, the accents American. Amid all the 'glamour and candlelight', the King seems to be 'in ecstasies' over the décor. Lady Colefax arrives with the coffee. Upstairs in the drawing room, two pianists from the Ritz play 'Austrian music and eventually jazz'. The King asks Mrs Simpson to dance, but she politely declines. The King leaves at 1.45; the others by 2.10. In the bedroom of 'Schloss Chips', Channon writes up his diary in triumph. 'It was the very peak, the summit, I suppose. The King of England dining with me! But I wish I too had only drunk Vichy water.'[221]

That August, Channon re-visited Port Lympne [plate 80]. By the late 1930s, Sir Philip Sassoon was in sumptuous decline. Between 1912 and 1921, on a spectacular site overlooking Romney Marsh, he had employed Sir Herbert Baker and Philip Tilden to create a dramatically un-English nirvana. Baker's work at Port Lympne had been Kentish Cape Dutch. Tilden's additions were more eclectic still: Moorish, Renaissance and Roman. In fact, the terraces and fountains, the balustrades and marbles might almost be described in racing parlance: 'by Alma-Tadema out of Cecil B. De Mille'. Here Sassoon loved to stroll with friends, exchanging epigrams in clipped, sibilant whispers. 'It is so quiet at Lympne', he used to say, 'one can hear the dogs bark at Beauvais.'[222] Chips Channon first went there in the early 1920s. Then it had seemed 'a triumph of beautiful bad taste and Babylonian luxury, with terraces and flowering gardens, and jade green pools and swimming baths and rooms done up in silver, blue and orange. A strange hydro for this strangest of sinister men.'[223] By August 1936 – weekending with the Aberconways, Max Aitken, Duff Cooper and Norah Lindsay – he found its luxury was beginning to cloy:

> We were received at [Sassoon's] fantastic villa by armies of obsequious white-coated servants who seemed willing enough, but second-rate ... The house is large and luxurious, and frankly ugly. Honor [Channon, née Guinness] said it was like a Spanish brothel. The drawing room is a mixture of fashionable whites, distressed white, off-white, cream, and even the famous frescoes [by Sert] have been whitewashed ... [Still, it is] lovely weather, and the scent of magnolias [is] overpowering. Honor and I have the so-called Alhambra suite [by Tilden] ... [But] the whole affair is second-rate, even the lavish lapis dining room [with its frieze by Glyn Philpot], and especially the white-coated footmen, who will wait on one at tea, always a bad sign.[224]

Was Channon at last beginning to tire of the *beau monde*? No, not at all. Though now the squire of Kelveden, Essex, he was still impatient of mere gentility.

> *18 November 1938* ... went to dinner locally with the 'county' in a ghastly house smelling of gentry – china in cabinets higgledy-piggledy, watercolours in gilt frames on the walls. Horror.[225]

What had changed was his perception of the *nouveaux riches*. Instead of seeing them as an outside, energising force – rather as Escott had –

he was beginning to find them *outré*, incapable of assimilation into the mainstream of English life. Strange, indeed, for a Chicago parvenu with his eye on a peerage. And yet, not so strange. As Channon became increasingly Anglicised – 'I have put my whole life's work into my Anglicisation' – his involvement with 'old England' came more and more to inhibit his understanding of the world beyond the Home Counties. The alchemy of assimilation was working only too well. As late as 1937 he was still trying hard to believe that 'the territorial aristocracy ... still rules England', preferring to forget that it was now a rather different sort of aristocracy.[226] Like so many *nouveaux riches* before him, Chips Channon had in the end gone native.

Not so Philip Sassoon. At Trent Park, Hertfordshire [plates 76, 77], from 1926 onwards, he created a gilded simulacrum of English country living. Years later, Bob Boothby remembered the strange unreality of those summer days between the wars.

> The white-coated footmen serving endless courses of rich but delicious food, the Duke of York coming in from golf ... Winston Churchill arguing over the teacups with Bernard Shaw ... Balfour dozing in an armchair, Rex Whistler absorbed in his painting, Osbert Sitwell ... laughing in a corner ... The beautifully proportioned red brick house, the blue bathing pool surrounded by such a profusion of lilies that the scent at night became almost overpowering, the flamingoes and ducks, the banks of exquisite flowers in the drawing room, the red carnation and the cocktails on one's dressing-table before dinner ...[227]

Such artifice merely emphasised its creator's own exoticism: the very bricks had been transported from Devonshire House, Piccadilly. Harold Nicolson sensed something of this in 1931.

> Motor down to Trent. Philip alone in the house, a slim Baghdadian figure, slightly long in the tooth, dressed in a double-breasted silk-fronted blue smoking-jacket with slippers of zebra hide. He has now finished the decoration of Trent and is a strange, lonely, un-English little figure, flitting about these vast apartments, removed from the ordinary passions, difficulties and necessities of life. He always seems to me the most unreal creature I have known. People who care over much for the works of men end by losing all sense of the work of God, and even their friends become for them mere pieces of decoration to be put about the room.[228]

This then was the house of Croesus: Henry James's 'gilded bondage'; new money embalmed in aspic. But Nicolson spoke for an older England. Not 'the old Edwardian world of bath-salts and ortolans' – that he felt sure was 'doomed to disappearance'[229] – but a still older ideal, an England of inherited identity, of civility and restraint; architecture as order; religion as good manners. 'We are humane, charitable, just and not vulgar,' he wrote. 'By God, we are not vulgar!'[230] But those new Victorians were vulgar, and the Edwardians still more so: all baccarat and onyx, all ptarmigan and champagne. And to Nicolson's generation, 'rich vulgarity [was always] worse than poor vulgarity'.[231]

> Cliveden, I admit, is looking superb [he wrote to Vita in June 1936]. Great groups of delphiniums and tuberoses, great bowers of oleander. The party also is lavish and enormous ... [But], how glad I am that we are not so rich. I simply do not want a house like this where nothing is really yours, but belongs to servants and gardeners. There is a ghastly unreality about it all. Its beauty is purely scenic. I enjoy seeing it. But to own it, to live here, would be like living on the stage of the Scala Theatre in Milan.[232]

Well, perhaps. But the view from the terrace at Cliveden – or the view from the *scala regia* at Port Lympne [plate 80] – was rather more prophetic than Nicolson's snobbish disdain for capitalism. The future would indeed be *nouveau-riche*: Escott's age of money, but in diluted, democratic form. In that sense, we are all *nouveaux riches* now.

March, 1935; Chips Channon's turn to visit Trent Park [plates 76, 77]. This time he plays a little golf in Sassoon's re-creation of an eighteenth-century landscape. His partner is Lady Diana Cooper: 'Who else has ever lent a Greek goddess his niblick or putted with Helen of Troy?' Both seem to have fallen completely under the spell of Sassoon's aesthetic fiction: 'Trent is a dream house, perfect.' But then he begins to notice those white-coated waiters again: 'the servants are casual, indeed almost rude; ... this often happens in a rich Jewish establishment'.[233] We can almost hear the voice of the 27th Earl of Crawford: Sassoon may be a Trustee of the National Gallery, but he does talk too much at meetings, and in that confounded foreign accent.[234]

And now it is Spring 1939; a lone aeroplane casts a slim shadow above the gardens of Trent Park. The ashes of Sir Philip Sassoon are scattered over the landscape he created. There will be other *nouveaux riches*, of course, and others with even greater wealth and influence. But none will embody quite so well the dreams of the Victorian and Edwardian parvenu: 'Take down the Union Flag, it clashes with the sunset.'[235]

# NOTES AND BIBLIOGRAPHICAL REFERENCES

## Abbreviations

| | |
|---|---|
| B of E/S/W/I | *Buildings of England/Scotland/Wales/Ireland* (1951– ) |
| Bateman | J. Bateman, *The Great Landowners of Great Britain and Ireland* (1883) |
| Boase | F. Boase, *Modern English Biography* (1892–1921) |
| *DBB* | *Dictionary of Business Biography* (1984–6) |
| *DNB* | *Dictionary of National Biography* (1885– ) |
| NMRE/S/W | National Monuments Record, England, Scotland, Wales (RCHME/S/W) |
| Walford | E.W. Walford, *County Families: Titled and Untitled Aristocracy* (1860– ) |
| *WWW* | *Who Was Who* (1896– ) |

(Place of publication: London unless otherwise stated).

## Introduction

Epigraph: *The Correspondence of H.G. Wells*, ed. D.C. Smith (1998), iii, 406: 5 January 1932.

1. B. Disraeli, *Sybil* (1845; Bradenham edn 1927), 87 *et seq.*
2. Quoted in J.R. de S. Honey, *Tom Brown's Universe: the Development of the Victorian Public School* (1977), 326. James was in fact a clergyman's son, educated at a Welsh Grammar School and at Jesus College, Oxford. He later became President of St John's College, Oxford (*WWW*, iii).
3. *Punch*, 1843, 40, 59.
4. A. Trollope, *The Way We Live Now* (1875; World's Classics, 1957), 116.
5. 'The Fascination of Money', *The Spectator*, 23 Nov. 1872, pp. 1454–6, 1486–7. This list was reprinted, with additions for the years 1873–83, in F.A. Binney, *Millionaires, the cause of poverty: with proposals for taxing them* (1884), 5–8.
6. L.G. Chiozza Money, *Riches and Poverty* (1905; 3rd edn 1906), 42, 52.
7. L. Stone, *The Crisis of the Aristocracy* (Oxford, 1965), intro.
8. *Spectator, loc.cit.*
9. For an analysis of Victorian middle class collectors, see D.S. Macleod, *Art and the Victorian Middle Class* (Cambridge, 1996). This lists 146 'major Victorian collectors', less than a dozen of whom left over £1 million.

## Chapter 1:
## Crossing the Line

Epigraph: Alan Bennett, 'Diary', in *London Review of Books*, 4 January 1996.

1. *Oxford English Dictionary*, ix (1989), 785–6 and x (1989), 562. 'Millionist' and 'millionary' never became popular as an alternative to 'millionaire'.
2. B. Disraeli, *Vivian Grey* (1826; Bradenham edn 1928), vol. 1, chapters xii, xiv.

3. W.L. Burn, *The Age of Equipoise: a Study of the Mid Victorian Generation* (1964).

4. W.D. Rubinstein, *Men of Property: the very wealthy in Britain since the Industrial Revolution* (1981), 61.

5. W.H. Mallock, *Memories of Life and Literature* (1920), 69–70.

6. H. L. Malchow, *Gentlemen Capitalists* (1991), 367; H. Berghoff and R. Möller, 'Tired pioneers and dynamic newcomers? . . . English and German entrepreneurial history, 1870–1914', in *Economic History Review*, xlvii (1994), 276.

7. Quoted in P. Magnus, *Gladstone* (1954), 163.

8. E. Walford, *County Families* (1860), preface.

9. J.V. Beckett, *The Aristocracy in England* (1986), 74; R. Trainer, 'The Gentrification of Victorian and Edwardian Industrialists', in A.L. Beier, D. Cannadine and J.M. Rosenheim, eds, *The First Modern Society* (1989), 120.

10. R.O. Knapp, 'The making of a landed élite: social mobility in Lancashire' (Ph.D., Lancaster, 1970); H. Perkin, in *Journal of British Studies*, xxiv (1985), 498–500.

11. J.M. Lee, *Social Leaders and Public Persons: a study of county government in Cheshire since 1888* (Oxford, 1963); C.H.E. Zingeri, 'The Social Composition of the County Magistracy in England and Wales, 1831–87', in *Journal of British Studies*, xi (1971), 113–25.

12. Quoted in D. Kynaston, *The City of London*, ii (1995), 331–2. For Shortgrove, see B of E, *Essex* (1965), 306. The family appear in Sylvia Thompson's *The Hounds of Spring* (1926).

13. *Punch*, 1843, 99–100.

14. H.G. Wells, *Tono-Bungay* (1909; 1912), 313. 'Distancing' is one of the themes of L. Stone and J.C.F. Stone, *An Open Elite? England 1540–1880* (Oxford, 1984).

15. W.H. Mallock, *The Old Order Changes*, ii (1886), 28. For peers listed as directors of companies – 167 in 1896; 232 in 1920 – see *Complete Peerage*, v, 780, Appendix C.

16. W. Morris, *Hopes and Fears for Art* (1880), 170.

17. Countess of Cardigan, *My Recollections* (1911), 174.

18. E. Gaskell, *North and South* (1855), ed. A. Easson (1973), 111.

19. Bateman (1883) records 4,341 acres worth £2,523 p.a. Rebuilt in Neo-Georgian style by Wimperis and Best (*Academy Architecture* (1906), ii, 49: ill. and plans).

20. Sale particulars, B.L. Maps, 137c1 (7); *Country Life*, x (1901), 464–70 and lxxxvii (1940), 252–6, 276–80; C. Hussey, *English Country Houses: late Georgian, 1800–1840* (1955). The Fieldens sold Grimston *c.* 1960.

21. B.R. Law, *Fieldens of Todmorden* (Littleborough, Lancashire, 1995), 221–2; sale particulars, 1868, B.L. Maps 137b7 (16); *The Builder*, xxxii (1874), 50–53, and xxxv (1878), 1146; B of E, *Surrey* (1963), 62. For Joshua Fielden, MP, at Nutfield, see L. Fielden, *The Natural Bent* (1963).

22. For Condover, see Law, *Fieldens*, 134, 261, ills; B of E, *Shropshire* (1958), 112; *Country Life*, iii (1898), 368–400 and xliii (1918), 508–13, 530–36; *Catalogue of . . . Pictures by Old Masters . . . removed from Condover Hall* (Christie's, 1897). For Holmewood, see Law, 253, ill., and *Victoria County History: Huntingdon* iii (1936). Joshua Fielden was Joint Master of the Warwickshire Hounds, with the 19th Lord Willoughby de Broke, from 1911 to 1924 (*Country Life*, lxvi, 1929, 673–6).

23. R. Kee, *The Laurel and the Ivy: the Story of Charles Stewart Parnell and Irish Nationalism* (1993), 37.

24. Law, *Fieldens*, 141. The weaving shop was 'a room measuring 100 yards by 60 yards . . . lighted from above by skylights, filled with 900 or 1000 pair of looms placed as close together as is possible to allow passage for the 400 or 500 men, women and children who attend to them. It is scarcely possible to see to the other end through the interminable lines of shafts, straps, warps and beams' (Murray's *Handbook for Yorkshire* (1882), 446).

25. Todmorden town hall (J. Gibson, 1870–75) cost £54,000, rather less than Dobroyd Castle (J. Gibson, 1865–69); the Unitarian Church (J. Gibson, 1865) cost £35,835. See Law, *Fieldens*, 175–9.

26. H.S. Taylor, *The Crawshays of Cyfarthfa Castle* (1967), 46–7. Bought in 1826 for £17,500; sold in 1838 for a profit. See also *Gentleman's Magazine*, Sept. 1867, 933–5.

27. Taylor, *Crawshays*, 22, 52. For William Crawshay's £2 million will, see *Illustrated London News*, 7 Sept. 1867, 274. Lady Charlotte Guest described him as 'beyond

all rule and description . . . quite one of
those meteoric beings whom it is quite
impossible to account for' (R. Guest and
A.V. John, *Lady Charlotte* (1989), 27). For
the Crawshay family see also *DNB* and J.P.
Addis, *The Crawshay Dynasty* (Cardiff,
1957).

28. Henry Crawshay (d. 1879), second son of
the third Iron King, built Italianate
Oaklands Park, Gloucestershire in the 1840s,
and Jacobean Blaisdon Hall,
Gloucestershire, in 1870 (*Victoria County
History: Gloucestershire*, x (1972), 8).

29. Taylor, *Crawshays*, 156. George Crawshay
(1822–96), nephew of W. Crawshay II, died
penniless, having had to sell Haughton
Castle, Northumberland (*DBB*, i, 816–8).

30. E.M. Sigsworth, *Black Dyke Mills*
(Liverpool, 1958); *DBB*; *Fortunes Made in
Business*, ii (1884), 3–107; Boase, i, 1089 and
v, 834–5; Burke's *Landed Gentry* (1965).

31. F.M.L. Thompson, 'Business and Landed
Elites in the 19th century', in *Landowners,
Capitalists and Entrepreneurs: essays for Sir
John Habakkuk* (Oxford, 1994), 165.

32. B. Disraeli, *Henrietta Temple* (1837;
Bradenham edn 1927), 294–5.

33. For what follows, see R.A. Pumphrey, 'The
Introduction of Industrialists into the
British Peerage', in *American Historical
Review*, lxv (1959–60), no. i, 1–16; W.D.
Rubinstein, 'The Evolution of the British
Honours System since the mid 19th
century', in *Elites and the Wealthy in Modern
British Society* (1987) 222–61; and F.M.L.
Thompson, 'Britain', in D. Spring, ed.,
*European Elites in the 19th century*
(Baltimore, 1979), 30.

34. C. Erickson, *British Industrialists: Steel and
Hosiery, 1850–1950* (Cambridge, 1959), 48.

35. D. Nevill, *Reminiscences*, ed. R. Nevill
(1906), 99.

36. B. Webb, *Our Partnership*, ed. B. Drake and
M.I. Cole (1948), 412–13: 27 July 1908.

37. Boase, iii, 356; *The Times*, 12 June 1897,
p. 10d. *Catalogue of the . . . Ancient and
Modern Pictures of Joseph Ruston Esq.*
(Christie's, 1893). He lived at Monk's
Manor, Lincoln, and 5 St George's Place,
Hyde Park. He left each of his five daughters
£30,000 on condition they did not give
more than half to their husbands.

38. For this debate see W.D. Rubinstein,

'Cutting Up Rich', in *Economic History
Review*, xlv (1992), 354–9 *versus* F.M.L.
Thompson, *The Rise of Respectable Society*
(1988), 155–163; 'The Landed Aristocracy and
Business Elites in Victorian Britain', in *Les
Noblesses Européennes au XIXe Siècle*
(Collection de l'Ecole Française de Rome,
Milan, 1983), 267–79; and 'Stitching it
together again', in *Economic History Review*
(1992), 362–75; plus the extensive literature
cited below, esp. p. 287, n.1. For London bankers
see Y. Cassis, *City Bankers, 1890–1914*
(Cambridge, 1994) and P. Thane and
J. Harris, 'British and European Bankers,
1880–1914: an Aristocratic Bourgeoisie?' in
P. Thane, G. Crossick and R. Floud, eds,
*The Power of the Past* (Cambridge, 1984).
For house-building figures see J. Franklin,
*The Gentleman's Country House and its Plan,
1835–1914* (1982), 25; M. Girouard, *The
Victorian Country House* (1979), 8–9;
J. Franklin, 'The Victorian Country House',
in G. Mingay, ed., *The Victorian
Countryside*, ii (1981), 410.

39. H.G. Wells, *Tono-Bungay* (1909; 1912),
11–13, 77.

40. B of E, *S. Lancashire* (1969), 320 (now
Shirley Institute); J. Franklin, 'Troops of
Servants: Labour and Planning in the
Country House, 1840–1910', in *Victorian
Studies*, xix (1975–6), 229; *Building News*,
xxv (1873), 222, 722; *British Architect*, i
(1874), 9: ill.

41. *Building News*, xliii (1882), 10 (Buchan Hill)
and xc (1906), 98 (Pickenham Hall).

42. *Cornhill Magazine*, N.S., ii (1897), 474–86.

43. W.H. Mallock, *Memoirs of Life and
Literature* (1920), 113. *British Architect*, xxxiii
(1890), *passim* (Avery Hill); Franklin,
*Gentleman's House*, 124–5. For Bearwood see
*Country Life*, xi (1902), 336–43; for
Westonbirt, see *ibid.*, cli (1972), 1226–9,
1310–13.

44. Walford (1860; 1872; 1885); Bateman (1883);
D. Brown, 'From "cotton lord" to Landed
Aristocrat: the rise of Sir George Philips Bt',
in *Historical Research*, lxix (1996), 62–82;
P. Reid, *Burke's and Savile's Guide to
Country Houses*, ii (1980), 183–4.

45. A. Badeau, *Aristocracy in England* (1886),
239.

46. Walford (1872; 1885); Bateman (1883) records
21,062 acres worth £28,426 p.a. Apley was

demolished in 1955. See also *The Times*, 2
Oct. 1899, p. 4; *Illustrated London News*,
11 Nov. 1899, p. 698; N. Mutton, 'The
Foster Family: a . . . Midland Industrial
Dynasty' (Ph.D., London, 1974); and Reid,
*Country Houses, op.cit.*, 76.

47. B of E, *N.E. and E. Kent* (1969), 261–2 and
*W. Kent* (1969), 147; *Academy Architecture*,
xlix (1916), 82–3; Murray's *Handbook for
Yorkshire* (1882), 434; Walford (1885); Boase,
i, p. 1332; *Fortunes Made in Business*, i (1884),
89–128; Burke's *Landed Gentry* and *Peerage*.
For Davis see p. 165.

48. See note 38 above; also *The Spectator*, 23
Nov. 1872, p. 1487 and 26 Aug. 1876,
pp. 1076–7.

49. F.M.L. Thompson, in *Times Literary
Supplement*, 7 Sept. 1984, p. 990. That was
certainly the case among cotton
manufacturers: about 10 per cent bought
estates of more than 1,000 acres (A. Howe,
*The Cotton Masters* (Oxford, 1984), 29–30).
After much debate, Rubinstein agrees with
Thompson that 'the wealthiest – by and
large – [were] purchasing the most land'
(*Business History*, xxxiv (1992), no. ii, 71).

50. H.G. Wells, *Tono-Bungay* (1909; 1912), 75.

51. Quoted in H. Perkin, *The Origins of Modern
English Society, 1780–1880* (1969), 32 (Holles),
59 (Defoe) and 87 (Cobbett).

52. N. Harte, *A History of George Brettle and Co.
Ltd., 1801–1964* (1973), 49, 63–7.

53. H. Evans, *Our Old Nobility*, ii (1879), 226.

54. W.D. Rubinstein, 'New Men of Wealth and
the Purchase of Land in 19th century
Britain', in *Past and Present*, no. 92 (1981),
135.

55. A. Carnegie, *The Gospel of Wealth* (New
York, 1900), 77.

56. See G.M. Attwood, *The Wilsons of Tranby
Croft* (Beverley, Yorkshire, 1988). For Warter
Priory (demolished 1972) and Tranby Croft,
see *British Architect*, i (1874), 300–301 and B
of E, *E. Yorkshire* (1995); for the Villa
Maryland, see *Country Life*, xxviii (1910),
816–25, 862–70. Gordon Cumming owned
40,000 acres at Altyre and Gordonstoun.
After selling the Wilson Line to Ellerman in
1916, Arthur's son Kenneth Wilson retired
to Cannizaro Park, Wimbledon Common
(B of E, *London: South* (1983), 457).

57. G. Brodrick, *English Land and English
Landlords* (1881), 153.

58. [Escott,] *Society in the New Reign* (1904). For
the concept of 'pseudo-gentry', see F.M.L.
Thompson, 'English Landed Society in the
19th century', in P. Thane, G. Crossick and
R. Floud, eds, *The Power of the Past: essays
for Eric Hobsbawm* (1984), 211.

59. When G.C. Raphael bought Castle Hill,
Englefield Green, Surrey (originally Elvills),
the estate consisted of only 33 acres. See
*Country Life*, 25 July 1991.

60. *The Spectator*, 4 March 1876, pp. 305–10,
reviewing *The Return of Owners of Land*
(1875).

61. *The Economist*, 16 July 1870, pp. 880–81.

62. Escott, *Society in the Country House* (1907),
483; B of E, *Warwickshire* (1966), 187.
Chamberlain left £125,495 in 1914; he and
his brothers had sold their screw-
manufacturing business to Nettlefolds in
1874 for £600,000 (*DBB*, i, 643–8). His
previous home was Southbourne, Augustus
Road, Birmingham.

63. Quoted by Escott, *Society in the Country
House* (1907), 484–5.

64. Brodrick, *op.cit.*, 412–3, 458–9. For the
broadening recruitment of High Sheriffs
and Deputy-Lieutenants, see Howe, *Cotton
Masters*, 258, 261; C.H. Zingeri, 'The Social
Composition of County Magistrates in
England and Wales, 1831–87', in *Journal of
British Studies*, xi (1971), 113–25.

65. *WWW*, iii; B. Webb, *Our Partnership*, ed.
B. Drake and M.I. Cole (1948), 294: 20 June
1904.

66. B of E, *W. Kent* (1969), 229–30.

67. B of E, *Buckinghamshire* (1994), 703–6;
D. Ottewill, *The Edwardian Garden* (1989),
196.

68. *WWW*, iii; *DBB*, iii, 153–6; *The Times*, 21
March 1934; D. Wainwright, *Henderson . . .
Alexander Henderson, 1st Lord Faringdon*
(1985).

69. Ottewill, *Edwardian Garden*, 153.

70. 'Gavin Faringdon [has] . . . all the
aristocratic delicacy of feature and figure
that you often find in the third-generation
parvenu' (K.B. McFarlane, *Letters to Friends,
1940–1966* (1977), 48: 26 Aug. 1945).

71. J. Lees-Milne, *Midway on the Waves* (1987
edn), 32: 11 April 1948. The same author
notes that visitors were sometimes
bewildered by so much 'socialism-cum-
plutocracy' (*Caves of Ice* (1984 edn), 116: 20

December 1946). Lees-Milne himself was of *nouveau-riche* stock: a compound of cotton, iron and coal.

## Chapter 2:
## The Style of Millionaires

Epigraph: Margot Asquith, *Autobiography*, ii (1922), 103–4.

1. W.D. Rubinstein, 'British Millionaires, 1809–1949', in *Bulletin of the Institute of Historical Research*, xlvii (1974), 202–23. The debate on this subject continues to grow. A select bibliography would begin with the following: R.E. Pumphrey, 'The Introduction of Industrialists into the British Peerage', in *American Historical Review*, lxv, no. 1 (Oct. 1959), 1–16; F.M.L. Thompson, *English Landed Society in the 19th Century* (1963) and *The Rise of Respectable Society* (1988); W.D. Rubinstein, ed., *Wealth and the Wealthy in the Modern World* (1980), 'The Victorian Middle Classes: Wealth, Occupation and Geography', in *Economic History Review*, 2nd series, xxx (1977), 602–23, *Men of Property: the Very Wealthy in Britain since the Industrial Revolution* (1981), *Capitalism, Culture and Decline in Britain, 1750–1990* (1993), 'New Men of Wealth and the Purchase of Land in 19th Century Britain', in *Past and Present*, no. 92 (1981), 125–47 and 'The Structure of Wealth-Holding in Britain, 1809–39', in *Historical Research*, lxv (1992), 74–89; M. Weiner, *English Culture and the Decline of the Industrial Spirit, 1850–1980* (1981); W.H. Chaloner, 'Was there a Decline of the Industrial Spirit in Britain, 1850–1934?', in *Transactions of the Newcomen Society*, lv (1984), 211–8 and bibliography; B. English, 'Probate Valuations and the Death Duty Registers', in *Bulletin of the Institute of Historical Research*, lvii (1984), 80–91; R. Britton, 'Wealthy Scots, 1876–1913', *ibid.*, lviii (1985), 78–94; N.J. Morgan and M.S. Moss, 'Listing the Wealthy in Scotland', *ibid.*, lxix (1986), 189–95; F.M.L. Thompson, The Land Market in the 19th Century', in *Oxford Economic Papers*, ix (1957), 'English Landed Society in the 19th century', in *The Power of the Past: Essays for Eric Hobsbawn*, ed.

P. Thane *et al.* (1984), 195–214, 'Britain' in *European Landed Estates in the 19th century*, ed. D. Spring (1977), 22–44, and 'Life After Death: how successful 19th century businessmen disposed of their fortunes', in *Economic History Review*, 2nd series, xliii (1990), i, 40–65; C. Dellheim, 'Notes on Industrialisation and Culture in 19th century Britain', in *Notebooks in Cultural Analysis*, ii, eds N.F. Cantor and N. King (Duke UP, 1985); D. Cannadine, *The Decline and Fall of the British Aristocracy* (1990); D. Spring, 'English Landowners and 19th century Industrialism', in J.T. Ward and R.G. Wilson, eds, *Land and Industry: the Landed Estate and the Industrial Revolution* (Newton Abbot, 1971); E. Spring, 'Businessmen and Landowners Re-engaged', *Historical Research*, lxxii (1999), no. 177, 77–91; T. Nicholas, 'Businessmen and Land Ownership in the Late Nineteenth Century, *Economic History Review*, lii, 1 (1999), 27–44.

2. B of E, *Lincolnshire* (1989), 133–9; B of E, *Wiltshire* (1975), 121–3.

3. In 1870–9, 14 per cent of all recorded British, non-landed millionaires were Jewish (W.D. Rubinstein, 'Jews among Top British Wealth Holders, 1837–1969', in *Jewish Social Studies*, xxxiv (1972), 78–84).

4. B of E, *W. Yorkshire* (1967), 380–82.

5. B of E, *Durham* (1983), 382–9. For lists of landowners who benefited from coal, see D. Spring, 'English Landowners and 19th century Industrialism', in J.T. Ward and R.G. Wilson, eds, *Land and Industry* (1971), 32.

6. B of E, *Oxfordshire* (1974), 726–30. An earlier form of duties at death, known as stamp duty, had been imposed in 1694; legacy duty was added in 1796; and succession duty in 1853.

7. P. Deare and W.A. Cole, *British Economic Growth, 1678–1959* (Cambridge, 1967); N. Ferguson, *The Worlds Banker* (1998), 1034–6.

8. B of E, *Dorset* (1972), 126–7.

9. *The Builder*, xxv (1869), 883 and xxxiii (1875), 953; B of E, *W. Yorkshire* (1967), 522. Built 'to immortalise the name of Fielden', Dobroyd Castle cost £71,589. He left £551,000 personalty and £280,000 realty. For the Fielden family, see Boase, i, 1043; *DNB*; and B.R. Law, *Fieldens of Todmorden* (Littleborough, Lancashire, 1995).

10. J. Mordaunt Crook, 'Mr Holloway's Architect and Mr Holloway's Château', in *Centenary Essays*, ed. M. Moore (Egham, 1987), 26–40; *DBB*, iii, 323–5. Holloway spent over one million – £900,000 on college and asylum, plus £300,000 endowment – and still left over half a million.

11. For Holford's art collection see C. Sebag-Montefiore, 'Three Lost Collections of London', in *National Art Collections Fund Magazine*, Christmas 1988, no. 38, 50–56.

12. *Building News*, xxvi (1874), 694–8: ills and plan; *The Architect*, xi (1874), 254: ills; B of E, *Devon* (1992), 704–6. The house cost £78,500, including fittings.

13. M. Girouard, *The Victorian Country House* (1979), 243–51; *Country Life*, xi (1902), 624–9.

14. B of E, *Devon* (1992), 245–7.

15. B of E, *Cheshire* (1972), 300–2; Girouard, *Victorian Country House*, 154–63.

16. *DNB*.

17. B of S, *Highland and Islands* (1992), 570–77; *DNB*.

18. *DBB*, ii, 436–40; *DNB*.

19. Salting inherited from his father, a Danish immigrant to Australia; the bulk of his collection of decorative art went to the Victoria and Albert Museum, his paintings to the National Gallery (*The Times*, 1909: 14 Dec., p. 10b; 15 Dec., p. 10c; 17 Dec., p. 8a; 23 Dec., p. 9f; 25 Dec., p. 6a).

20. Clanricarde died in 1916 worth £2,500,000. In 1906 he was described by an Irish Nationalist in the House of Commons as 'the curse of his class . . . a standing menace to the peace [who] . . . had cursed [his estate of 56,000 acres with] . . . misery and bloodshed' (*The Times*, 29 Nov. 1906, p. 6e). His fortune descended to the Lascelles family of Harewood, Yorkshire. He is buried in Highgate Cemetery.

21. Designed by W. Thomas and T. Gardner, 1789–90 and 1791–5. See B of E, *Derbyshire* (1978), 159–60; *DNB*.

22. Designed by G.G. Scott, 1856–58. 'Very ugly: the ugliness of carelessness and insensitivity, not of protest. Harsh Gothic with a big Geometrical billiard room at the back' (B of E, *Surrey* (1971), 168). Forman – also of Penydarryn House, Merthyr Tydfil, Glamorgan – left £250 p.a. for the upkeep of

his shrubbery (*The Times*, 16 Oct. 1869, p. 10f). The bulk of his collection – Anglo-Saxon, Greek, Roman and Egyptian antiquities – was bequeathed to Major A.H. Browne of Callaly Castle, Northumberland (see *Catalogue* by W. Chaffers, 1892); Browne's son inherited most of Forman's £1-million fortune.

23. Hornby Castle (Paley and Austin, *c.* 1849–52 and 1889) was bought by John Foster I in 1860 for £205,000 (*DBB*, ii, 406–8; Boase, v, 334; *Fortunes Made in Business*, ii (1884), 3–56, 59–107; B of E, *N. Lancashire* (1969), 147). His son, William Foster I, left £1,180,000 in 1884 (*Illustrated London News*, 23 Feb. and 24 May 1884). W.O. Foster (no relation) bought Apley Park (1812) in 1868 for £550,000 and then enlarged it (*DBB*; B of E, *Shropshire* (1958), 60).

24. J. Mordaunt Crook, 'Strawberry Hill Revisited', in *Country Life*, cliii (1973), 1598–1602, 1726–30, 1794–7, 1886 (reprinted 1974). For the Stern family, see *DBB*, v, 329–32.

25. J. Mordaunt Crook, 'Thomas Harrison: a reluctant Goth', in *Country Life*, cxlix (1972), 876–9. For Bibby, see Boase, iv, 394 and J. Plight, *History of the Bibby Line* (Liverpool, 1949).

26. Boase, iii, 869.

27. B of E, *Sussex* (1965), 404–7; Boase, iv, 688; *History of Battle Abbey by the Duchess of Cleveland* (1877).

28. J. Mordaunt Crook, *William Burges and the High Victorian Dream* (1981).

29. B of E, *Cheshire* (1972), 207–13; Girouard, *Victorian Country House*, 4. The first Gothic rebuilding of Eaton Hall (W. Porden; 1802–12, 1820–25) was financed by the lead mines at Halkin in North Wales; the second, designed by Waterhouse, stemmed from the profits of the Grosvenor Estate in London.

30. Demolished 1947. See J. Mordaunt Crook, 'Sir Robert Peel: Patron of the Arts', in *History Today*, xvi (1966), 3–11.

31. Designed by H.J. Stevens; demolished 1966. See B of E, *Derbyshire* (1978), 295; R. Strong, J. Harris and M. Binney, *The Destruction of the Country House* (1974), pls 182, 293. Wright left £700,000. See *The Times*, 12 May 1873, p. 9f. His son became 'John Osmaston'.

32. John Hodgson's fortune stemmed from Thomas Hodgson of Bowness, Cumberland and Wanstead, Essex; it passed to his brother William (1803–86) and thence to William's nephew E.S. Bowlby, Master of the Essex Hounds (*The Times*, 8 Nov. 1902, p. 7f). Bateman (1883) records 2,091 acres worth £3,248 p.a.

33. B of E, *Cheshire* (1972), 238, 364; Boase, v, 492.

34. Now Preston College (B of E, *Sussex*, 1965, 563: misprinted as 'Park Hill Park'). Sturdy, of Baker and Sturdy, stockjobbers, left over £1 million; of which £100,000 went in tax. His London house was 3 Cadogan Square (*The Times*, 6 Sept. 1906, p. 11f).

35. *WWW*, i; photographs, NMRE. For Quilter's collection at 74 South Audley Street, see *Sir Cuthbert Quilter's Pictures: London Collection* [1908]. The Bawdsey Manor collection was sold at Christie's, 26 June 1936. His father, William Quilter, an accountant and collector, lived at Lower Norwood.

36. B of E, *Staffordshire* (1976), 224; *Building News*, liii (1887), 576: ill. and plan. Bateman (1883) gives Michael Bass of Rangemore 2,283 acres worth £17,317 p.a.

37. Bedford Lemere archive, no. 5331 (exterior). 'The house is simply gigantic,' noted Lady Monkswell in 1883; even so, in 1884 a new wing was added, 90 yards from the living room (*Journals*, i, 1873–95, ed. E.C.F. Collier (1944), 43–4, 110, 111–17). Goldsmid's house at Cannes was the Villa Fiarenta; see Boase, v, 434–5.

38. Not too far away stands another seat of similar stamp, Witherslack Hall, Westmorland (1874–76), built for the equally aristocratic brother of Prime Minster Derby. See B of E, *N. Lancashire* (1969), 144–5; B of E, *Cumberland and Westmorland* (1967), 299.

39. B of E, *Dorset* (1972), 239 (now Claysmore School); *DNB*.

40. B. Disraeli, *Coningsby* (1844; Bradenham edn 1927), 147 *et seq*. Agatha Christie seems to have subscribed to the popular misconception that *nouveau-riche* houses were typically Gothic: Rutherford Hall – the scene of the crime in *4.50 From Paddington* (1957) – is portrayed as a miniature version of Windsor Castle, built in 1884 by Joshua Crackenthorpe, a Berkshire biscuit baron

(modelled no doubt on Palmer of Huntley and Palmer's biscuits). See p. 189.

41. Like Mr Ardenne in Disraeli's *Lothair*, Shirley was 'a man of ancient pedigree . . . who knew everybody else's'. For Ettington see *Building News*, xvi (1869), pt. i, 158: ill.

42. For Walton see *The Builder*, xviii (1860), 560–61: ill. and plan.

43. W.H. Mallock, *The New Republic* (1878), 4: Lytton, *Pelham* (1828), vol. 1, xxiii, 193. Lytton – scion of an old family – built himself a conspicuously Gothic house at Knebworth, Hertfordshire (H.E. Kendall; 1843).

44. B of E, *Derbyshire* (1978), 126–39.

45. B of E, *W. Yorkshire* (1967), 539–45.

46. B of E, *Northamptonshire* (1973), 78–83.

47. B of E, *Sussex* (1965), 301–7.

48. B of E, *Nottinghamshire* (1979), 365–72.

49. J. Cornforth, in *Country Life*, clvii (1975), 1678–81.

50. A Trollope, *Doctor Thorne* (1925 edn), ch. 19, 209–10.

51. B. Disraeli, *Coningsby* (1844; Bradenham edn 1927), 168–8, 172, 174, 178, 380–82. For Henry Ashworth see R. Boyson, *The Ashworth Cotton Enterprise, 1818–80* (Oxford, 1970), 257–9.

52. B. Disraeli, *Endymion* (1880; Bradenham edn 1928), 126, 128.

53. B. of E, *Middlesex* (1951), 141 (later called Grovelands). 'Great as a batsman, great as a bowler, great as a fieldsman, and greatest perhaps of all as a captain.' See *The Times*, 1906: 4 Jan., p. 5e; 8 Jan., pp. 7d, 15c.

54. Demolished *c.* 1960. See M. Bence-Jones, *Burke's Guide to Country Houses: Ireland* (1978), 6; Boase, iii, p. 1450. He also owned Rochestown, Cahir, Co. Tipperary (Sir T.N. Deane; 1867).

55. *Victoria County History: Oxfordshire*, xi, 134; *Country Life*, xviii (1905), 270; B of E, *Oxfordshire* (1974), 647–9; B of E, *Cheshire* (1971), 119; Boase, ii, 384. Brassey's sons and grandsons built or rebuilt Normanhurst, Catsfield, Sussex; Preston Hall, nr Maidstone, Kent; Copse Hill, Lower Slaughter, Gloucestershire; Heythrop, Oxfordshire; Apthorpe, Northamptonshire; Dauntsey Park, Wiltshire; and Weston Little Court, nr Devizes, Wiltshire. See also C. Walker, *Thomas Brassey: Railway Builder* (1969).

56. J. Mordaunt Crook, 'The New Square Style: Sir Robert Smirke's Scottish Country Houses', in *Scottish Country Houses*, ed. I. Gow and A. Rowan (1995), 206–16.

57. B of E, *Berkshire* (1966), 76–8; Rubinstein, *Economic History Review* (1977), 610; *DNB*; *DBB*, iv, 341–5. Carr's dining room at Basildon was elaborately redecorated in 1990 by Alex Cobbe. In London Morrison first owned Balham Hill, near Clapham, and then 57 Harley Street. For his sons he bought Fonthill Pavilion, Wiltshire; Hole Park, Kent; Malham Tarn, Leeds; and Hamptworth Lodge, Wilts. – each with large estates. Much of his art collection was inherited by Alfred Morrison, see *Catalogue of the Pictures at Basildon Park, the property of Capt. Archibald Morrison* (typescript, colln C. Sebag-Montefiore) and C. Wainwright, 'Alfred Morrison: a forgotten collector', in *Grosvenor House Art and Antiques Fair* (1995).

58. *DBB*, iii, 598–601.

59. B of E, *Hampshire* (1967), 581–3 (South Stoneham House); H.M. Colvin, *Biographical Dictionary of British Architects, 1660–1840* (1978), 393 (Norman Court); J.C. Levenson *et al*, eds, *The Letters of Henry Adams*, i (1982), 465; L.M. Montagu, *Montagu, Baron Swaythling* (1910). For Townhill Park, near Southampton, a Neo-Georgian house designed later for Swaythling by L. Rome Guthrie, see *Academy Architecture*, xxxvi (1909), ii, 47 and xl (1917), 37.

60. B of E, *Hertfordshire* (1977), 287; *The Times*, 11 Aug. 1900, p. 12b. Smith left over £1.5 million.

61. B of E, *London*, ii (1983), 692; *The Times*, 21 April 1891, p. 9f. He retired from Overend, Gurney and Co. six years before the collapse of 1866.

62. B of E, *Buckinghamshire* (1960), 134–5; B of E, *Essex* (1965), 174; Boase, iii, p. 1549. Wythes left £1,524,787 in 1883. The history of Copped (Copt) Hall – extended 1895, gutted 1917 – involves several architects, see Colvin, *Dictionary* (1978), 495, 588, 666, 716, 787, 946. Wythes' granddaughter married Frederick Hervey, later 4th Marquess of Bristol and thus financed the reconstruction of Ickworth, Suffolk, in 1907–10. The Copt Hall estate amounted to

5,857 acres worth £20,098 p.a. (Bateman, 1883); besides Fawley Court, Mackenzie and his son owned estates in Norfolk, Suffolk and Inverness amounting to 27,750 acres worth £12,850 p.a. (*ibid.*).

63. B of E, *Hertfordshire* (1977), 360; B of E, *Bedfordshire* (1968), 120; B of E, *Surrey* (1971), 399. James Wyatt's Ottershaw Park was rebuilt by D.B. Niven and H. Wigglesworth.

64. B of E, *Herefordshire* (1963), 73. For Cawley see *WWW*, iii and *The Times*, 31 March 1937, p. 12b. He left £901,138.

65. For Peckover, see Boase ii, p. 1429; for Grimthorpe, see P. Ferriday, *Lord Grimthorpe* (1957).

66. Quoted in B. Bramson and K. Wain, *The Hambros, 1779–1979* (1979), 261: 1862. Carl Joachim Hambro left £500,000 in 1877; his son Sir Everard Hambro left £2,323,710 in 1925.

67. B. Disraeli, *Endymion* (1880; Bradenham edn 1927), 84–6, 98, 354–7, 372.

68. B of E, *Surrey* (1971), 158; Boase, i, 3.

69. *Country Life*, xx (1906), 162–72; *Building News*, iv (1858), 399–401; *Academy Architecture*, 1902 (I), 39; 1874 sale catalogue: B.M. Maps 136a; *DBB*, iii, 343–4; *The Times*, 10 May 1921, p. 10d. His London house was 2 Carlton House Terrace.

70. For Maple Hayes, see B of E, *Staffordshire* (1974), 201; *WWW*, ii. For Pengreep, see B of E, *Cornwall* (1970), 135; Boase, vi, 892; *The Times*, 17 Feb. 1880, p. 8b. As head of Williams, Foster and Co., copper-smelters of Redruth, he also inherited Caerhayes Castle.

71. B of E, *Warwickshire* (1966), 437–8; Boase, ii, 1031–2; Dod's *Parliamentary Companion* (1846). Muntz bought the 2,486-acre estate in 1874.

72. Designed by J.T. Knowles Snr. See P. Metcalf, *James Knowles* (1980), 144–5; M. Brockwell, *Catalogue of the Pictures at Doughty House, Richmond, Surrey, in the collection of Sir Herbert Cook, Bt* (1932); C. Sebag-Montefiore, 'Three Lost London Collections', in *N.A.C.F. Magazine*, Christmas 1988, 50–56.

73. *DNB*; *Illustrated London News*, 11 June 1859; *Jewish Chronicle*, 6 May and 9 June 1859; J. Mordaunt Crook, 'The Villas in Regent's Park', in *Country Life*, cxliii (1968), ii, 84–87

(reprinted 1980). He also owned Wick House (Furze Hill), near Brighton, a villa by Decimus Burton.

74. B of E, *Nottinghamshire* (1979), 106. Knowles progressed in other ways too: not only from Lancashire to Nottinghamshire, but from the Reform Club to Brooks's (Walford, 1885; *WWW*, ii).

75. B of E, *Berkshire* (1966), 105–6; *Architectural Review*, xxv (1909), 288–91; *Country Life*, xxxviii (1915), 662–9, 698–705.

76. *Illustrated London News*, 29 Dec. 1883, 779: ill.; Boase, vi, 202. For life at Theobalds, see V. Surtees, *The Actress and the Brewer's Wife* (1997). The contents of Theobalds Park – including Lady Meux's collection of Egyptian antiquities – were dispersed in 1911. George Fenwick, a millionaire banker, shared some of these acquisitive instincts: he filled his retreat at Crag Head, Bournemouth with furniture made from the oak fittings of Sir John Soane's old Law Courts at Westminster. See *The Times*, 10 Oct. 1913, p. 9e.

77. C. Dickens, *Great Expectations* (1861), ch. 22.

78. J. Fenwick Allen, *Some Founders of the Chemical Industry* (1906), 233, 248, photo; B of E, *Buckinghamshire* (1960), 248; *DBB*, i, 40–42; *DNB Missing Persons* (1993); Boase, iv, 97.

79. B of E, *Oxfordshire* (1974), 692.

80. B of E, *London*, ii (1983), 448–9; *The Times*, 5 March 1906, p. 9f. The Hatfields married into the Taddy family, tobacco, tea and snuff merchants since the eighteenth century; they were the first to introduce cigarette cards, and purchased Morden Hall in 1882.

81. R. Gatty, *Portrait of a Merchant Prince: James Morrison, 1789–1857* (Pepper Arden, 1977), 108, 121, 133–7; *Disraeli's Reminiscences*, ed. H.M. Swartz and M. Swartz (1975), 113. The bulk of Fonthill Splendens had been demolished in 1807 (B of E, *Wiltshire* (1975), 247). Basildon was designed by Carr of York in 1776–84, and extended first by Papworth in 1839–44, then by Brandon. After quarrelling with Papworth, Morrison variously employed C.R. Cockerell, David Brandon, W.A. Nesfield and Edward Kemp. In London James Morrison lived first at Balham Hill,

then at 95 Upper Harley Street. For Basildon, see J. Cornforth in *Country Life*, clxi (2), (1977), 1158–61, 1227–30, 1298–1301.

82. [Escott], *Society in the New Reign* (1904), 270; B of E, *Hertfordshire* (1977), 127–8; Christie's sale catalogue (1978). In 1907 it was bought by another (near) millionaire, Jack Barnato Joel (1862–1940).

83. A. Trollope, *The Prime Minister*, i (1876), ch. xix, 310–13. For Tidworth, see J.E. Eardley-Wilmot, *Reminiscences of Thomas Assheton-Smith* (1860), ills.

84. B of E, *W. Kent* (1969), 532–3. See also J.M. Cohen, *The Life of Ludwig Mond* (1936).

85. *DBB*, iv, 287–95. In collecting early Italian paintings, he was advised by the art historian J.P. Richter. See Richter, *The Mond Collection*, 2 vols (1910).

86. B. of E, *W. Yorkshire* (1967), 224; *DBB*, ii, 443–9; *DNB*. Dining Room ill.: N. Cooper, *The Opulent Eye* (1967), 41, pl. 139.

87. *DBB*, i, 17–20; B of E, *Buckinghamshire* (1960), 294. Wilton Park was demolished in 1967. Aird also bought Highcliffe Castle, Hampshire (W.J. Donthorne; 1830–34); his London house in Hyde Park Terrace contained a private theatre (*WWW*, iii; R.K. Middlemas, *The Master Builders*, 1963).

88. B of E, *Leicestershire and Rutland* (1984), 387–9.

89. R.W. Liscombe, *William Wilkins* (1980), pl. 48; *DNB*.

90. B. Disraeli, *Falconet* (Bradenham edn 1927), 493–5; *DNB*; J. Mordaunt Crook, 'Sydney Smirke: the Architecture of Compromise', in *Seven Victorian Architects*, ed. J. Fawcett and N. Pevsner (1976), 60–5, 141–4, 152.

91. B of E, *W. Kent* (1969), 182–3, pl. 79. Samuel Scott died, worth £1,400,000, in 1869 at the Villa Oscar, Nice.

92. Demolished 1992. See B of E, *S. Lancashire* (1969), 405; *DBB*, iv, 999–1004; *DNB*; *The Times*, 20 July 1992, p. 14. See also D.A. Farnie, *John Rylands of Manchester* (Manchester, 1993).

93. M. Bence-Jones, *Burke's Guide to Country Houses: Ireland* (1978), 1, 28–9 and 93; A. Rowan in *Country Life*, cxli (1967), 456–60, 516–20. For McCalmont see Boase, ii, 568. He also bought the Bishop's Wood estate in the Wye valley in the 1880s. For Craig see *The Times*, 24 July 1900, p. 4d; he left over £1 million, of which £600,000 was

registered in England. Mulholland's son John, 1st Baron Dunleath, left £971,747 in 1895; see *Truth*, 19 Dec. 1895.

94. B of E, *Wiltshire* (1969), 261–2. Rundell's will was printed in full in *The Times*, 5 March 1827. Neeld in turn left the bulk of his fortune to Queen Victoria.

95. B of E, *Herefordshire* (1963), 318–9; *Country Life*, clvii (1975), 702–5, 774–7. The cost was £21,500.

96. B. Lytton, *A Strange Story* (1862; 1884 edn), ch. xliv, 267.

97. Walford (1872; 1885); *Building News*, xcv (1908), 689: ill. and xcvii (1909), 754: ill. John Lancaster II (1816–84) left £194,446. The family's London home was Frankfort House, Fitzjohns Avenue, Hampstead.

98. B of E, *Sussex* (1965), 642–3; *The Architect*, xxix (1883), 113, 339; *Building News*, lxxiii (1897), 365; *The Builder*, lxxiii (1897), 204 and lxxv (1898), 433; *Architectural Review*, ii (1897), 39. For Pearson, see *DNB*; J.A. Spender, *Weetman Pearson, 1st Viscount Cowdray* (1930); D. Young, *Member for Mexico*. In 1909 he bought Cowdray Park, Sussex, from the eccentric Lord Egmont.

99. For Redcourt see B of E, *Surrey* (1971), 304; *The Times*, 3 Nov. 1908, p. 11c. Schillizzi left over £2 million. His London house was 31 Cromwell Road. For Moundsmere see *Country Life*, xxvii (1910), 378–85.

100. Boase, ii, 885; *Country Life*, clxv (1979), 390–3, 466–9, 542–5; C. Aslet, *The Last Country Houses* (1982), 121–7. Miller's sister, Mrs Hunter, had already aggrandised a nearby Palladian villa – Thurston Hall, Berwickshire (J. Kinross; *c.* 1895) – turning it into a sizeable Neo-Baroque mansion (Aslet, *op.cit.*, 329).

101. Later Springwell House; now St Leonard's School. For Love's story – from pit-boy to plutocrat – see G.E. Milburn, 'Piety, profit and paternalism: Methodists in the North East of England, *c.* 1760–1920', in *Wesley History Society*, 1983, 35–6. He became notorious during the 'Rocking Strike' of 1863; see R. Fynes, *History of the Northumberland and Durham Miners* (1873), 225–30. *Ex inf.* Dr N. Emery. His son, J.H. Love, left half a million in 1935.

102. Victoria Buildings (1874), Newcastle was designed for Scott in Italianate style by Matthew Thompson (B of E, *Northumberland* (1992), 491).

103. *Ibid.*, 206–7. Allendale's estates were reputed to extend for 30 miles from Northumberland to Durham.

104. B of E, *Hertfordshire* (1977), 259 and *Norfolk, N.W.* (1962), 245–6; Boase, ii, 891.

105. M. Bence-Jones, *Burke's Guide to Country Houses: Ireland* (1978), 123. Bought 1873.

106. R. Rhodes James, ed., *Chips. The Diaries of Sir Henry Channon* (1967), 21: 8 Jan. 1935; A. Hare, *The Story of My Life* (1896–1900), vi, 400; M. Alexander and S. Anand, *Queen Victoria's Maharaja* (1980), 100–11, 341. See also *The Builder*, xxviii (1871), 906–7: ill. and plan; B of E, *Suffolk* (1974), 199–200 (incorrectly attributed) and C. Aslet in *Country Life*, clxxv (1984), 607–10, 672–5. The 1st Earl of Iveagh also tried to buy Tottenham Park and its estate in Savernake Forest from the Marquess of Ailesbury in 1892. When the 2nd Earl built Pyrford Court, Surrey (Clyde Young, 1910; J.A. Hale, following Iveagh's own designs, 1920–29), it is conservatively Wrenaissance. See *Country Life*, cxxxv (2) (1964), 1118–19.

107. *DBB*, v, 438–43; *DNB*; *Country Life*, 22 May 1997. At Allerton, near Liverpool, he also owned Allerton Beeches (A. Waterhouse; 1884).

108. P. Metcalf, *James Knowles* (1980), 143–50, pl. 80.

109. *DNB*; Boase, iii, p. 1159; D. Mallet, *The Greatest Collector* (1979). For Sudbourne Hall, see *Academy Architecture*, 1907 (I), 65–8; B of E, *Suffolk* (1974), 451 and K. Clark, *Another Part of the Wood* (1974). Clark's grandfather invented the cotton spool.

110. For the gardens at Somerleyton, see *The Builder*, ix (1851), 355, 363; *Country Life*, clxxi (1982), 1668–72. For Preston Hall, see B of E, *W. Kent* (1969), 136–7 and *The Builder*, xxxv (1878), 1131. For H.A. Brassey, see Boase, iv, 487; *The Times*, 13 Aug. 1891, p. 6b. At one time his London residence was Bath House, Piccadilly.

111. *Correspondence of Lord Overstone*, ed. D.P. O'Brien, ii (1971), pp. 893, 1007, 1072. Overstone also rebuilt Sywell Hall.

112. *The Builder*, xx (1862), 149–51; B of E, *Northamptonshire* (1973), 368–9. *Descriptive Catalogue of the Pictures at 2, Carlton*

Gardens . . . *Lockinge House . . . [and]*
*Overstone Park . . . belonging to Lord*
*Overstone* (3 vols, 1875). Loyd left over £2m.
in securities and over £3m. in land (*DBB*, iii,
868–72; *DNB*).

113. *The Builder*, xxiii (1865), 412–13, ill. and
plan; B of E, *Gloucestershire, Cotswolds*
(1970), 378–80 (now Rendcomb College);
*DNB*. The cost was £40,000. Goldsmid
died on Waterloo Station in 1878.

114. Designed by Habershon, Brock and Webb
after a scheme by Hector Horeau (*The
Builder*, xxv (1867), 410–11: ill. and plan;
*Destruction of the Country House*, pl. 188;
*Country Life*, clxv (1979), 1284). See also
A. Maskell, *Catalogue of Works of Art and
Curiosities at Normanhurst Court . . . and 24
Park Place* (1878). Each of Thomas Brassey's
three sons – Thomas at Normanhurst,
Henry at Preston Hall and Albert at
Heythrop – chose some form of enriched
Classicism. Two other Brassey houses,
however, adapt vernacular styles: Copse
Hill, Upper Slaughter, Gloucestershire (by
C.F. Hayward for Henry Brassey, 1871–5:
*The Architect*, xvi (1876), 386) and Chelwood
Manor, Nutley, Surrey (by A.N. Prentice for
Earl Brassey's widow, 1904: *Building News*,
lxxxvi (1904), 675).

115. N. Nicolson, *Lord of the Isles* (1960), 10. For
Thornton Manor, Neston, Cheshire, see
Bedford Lemere archive, no. 8941; M.H.
Shippobotham, 'Viscount Leverhulme: a
study of the architectural patron and his
work' (MA, Manchester, 1977); and Aslet,
*Last Country Houses*, 329.

116. *The Crawford Papers: the journals of David
Lindsay, 27th Earl of Crawford and 10th Earl
of Balcarres . . . 1892–1940*, ed. J. Vincent
(Manchester, 1984), 527: 5 Oct. 1928. See
also T.H. Mawson, *Life and Work of an
English Landscape Architect* (1927), 127–8 and
J.M. Robinson, *A Guide to Country Houses
of the North West* (1988), 230. For Port
Sunlight see B of E, *Cheshire* (1971), 303–13.

117. B of E, *Durham* (1983), 87–8. His seat,
Streatlam Castle, near Gateshead (1718; 1841;
demolished 1933: 43,200 acres in 1883), was
more conventionally Baroque (*Destruction of
the Country House*, pl. 51).

118. Designed by George Bridgeman (*The
Architect*, 27 June 1874; B of E, *Devon* (1989),
839–40; now Oldway House, council

offices). For Singer's scandalous career in
New York and Paris, see R. Brandon, *Singer
and the Sewing Machine* (1977).

119. For Minley (extended 1885–8 and 1898 by
Devey and Castings) see Eastlake, *Gothic
Revival*, ed. J. Mordaunt Crook, Appendix
no. 163; [L. Currie], *Catalogue of the . . .
Works of Art at Minley Manor, printed for
private circulation by A.L. Humphreys* (1908);
for Bedgebury see *RIBA Transactions*, xiv,
103–15 and S.A. Clark, *A History of
Bedgebury* (1949); for Ashford (extended,
1870s onwards, in Baronial style by J.F.
Fuller and G. Ashlin for Guinness's son the
1st Baron Ardilaun), see M. Bence-Jones,
*Burke's Guide to Country Houses: Ireland*
(1978), 12–13; for Danesfort, see *ibid.*, 99.

120. M. Girouard, in *Country Life*, cxlvi (1969),
542–5, 614–17. Hughes left £356,300 gross in
1911 (*The Times*, 22 Sept. 1911, p. 7e).

121. *A series of picturesque views of castles and
country houses in Yorkshire* (Bradford, 1885),
45 *et seq.*, quoted in D. Linstrum, *West
Yorkshire: architects and architecture* (1978),
85–7; P. Thornton, *Authentic Décor: the
domestic interior, 1620–1920* (1984), pl. 450.
The decorators were Harland and Son, and
Greenwood of Paris.

122. *Country Life*, cvii (1950), 1282–5;
R. Trevelyan, *Grand Dukes and Diamonds:
the Wernhers of Luton Hoo* (1991), 148–9; *The
Wernher Collection*, intro. Sir H. Wernher
(Luton Hoo, 1950). For Jagger of Bradford
and Monte Carlo, see Brewer's *Dictionary of
Phrase and Fable* (rev. I.H. Evans, 1970),
680. Smith's *Cabinet Maker's and
Upholsterer's Guide* was published in 1826.

123. [Escott], *Society in London* (1885), 86–7;
Escott, *Society in the Country House* (1907),
472–3.

124. R.V. Surtees, *Ask Mamma* (1858), 282.

125. *Crawford Papers, op.cit.*, 599: 22 July 1939;
*DNB*; *DBB*, iv, 946–53; B of E, *Hertfordshire*
(1977), 369–70; C. Gere, *19th-century
Decoration* (1989), pl. 39. Bateman (1883)
records 15,378 acres worth £28,091 p.a.

126. L. Masterman, ed., *Mary Gladstone: Her
Diaries and Letters* (1930), 361. For more
sympathetic appraisals, see H. Tait, *The
Waddesdon Request: the Legacy of Baron
Ferdinand de Rothschild to the Nation* (1981)
and M. Hall, 'The Rothschilds as
Collectors', in G. Heuburger, ed., *The*

*Rothschilds: Essays on the History of a European Family* (Frankfurt am Main, 1994). For fittings at Waddesdon imported from France, see *Country Life*, 1 October 1992, 74, and B. Pons, *Architecture and Panelling: the James A. de Rothschild Bequest at Waddesdon Manor* (1998). For the Rothschilds worldwide, see N. Ferguson, *The World's Banker* (1998).

127. *Crawford Papers, op.cit.*, 49: 18–20 June 1898 and 599: 23 July 1939; *DNB*; *Country Life*, iv (1898), 208–11, xii (1902), 808–14, cxxvi (1959), 66–9; B of E, *Buckinghamshire* (1994), 708–12; Mrs J. de Rothschild, *The Rothschilds at Waddesdon Manor* (1979); S. Eriksen, *Waddesdon Manor* (1982); Girouard, *Victorian Country House* (1979), 300; *Country Life*, 4 Sept. 1997, 62–5 (gardens) and 4 June 1998, 62–7 (bachelor's wing); H. Tait, *Catalogue of the Waddesdon Bequest in the British Museum*, 3 vols. (1986, 1988, 1991).

128. H. James, *Letters*, ed. L. Edel, iii (1981), 98: 22 August [1885], to Grace Norton.

129. H.G. Hutchinson, ed., *Private Diaries of the Rt Hon. Sir Algernon West, GCB* (1922), 84, 305. For Halton, see Bedford Lemere archive, no. 11743 (saloon; decoration by George Jackson and Sons); B of E, *Buckinghamshire* (1994), 145–6, 321–2, 364–5; A.E. Adam, *Beechwoods and Bayonets, The Book of Halton* (1983); N. Cooper, *The Opulent Eye* (1976), pls 8–10; J. Franklin, 'The Victorian Country House', in G.E. Mingay, ed., *The Victorian Countryside* (1981), pl. 115; C. Davis, *Description of the Works of Art . . . of Alfred de Rothschild* [at 1 Seamore Place, Piccadilly, and Halton], 2 vols (1884): ills. of interiors. For Sir Anthony de Rothschild, see *DNB*. For Baron Alfred de Rothschild, see *DBB*, iv, 946–53. Leopold de Rothschild's half-timbered seat at Ascott, near Wing, Buckinghamshire (G. Devey, 1874–88) – a cottage, but 'a palace-like cottage', as Mary Gladstone called it – follows a very different pattern. But a later Rothschild seat – Exbury, near Beaulieu, Hampshire – was once again Classical, if rather more restrained (*The Field*, April 1994, ills). See also N. Davis, *The English Rothschilds* (1983) and J. Allibone in *Country Life*, 16 Feb. 1989.

130. F. Balfour, *Ne Obliviscaris*, i (1930), 221;

C. Gere, *19th-century Decoration* (1989), pl. 37. For recollections of E. Field, gardener, see *Country Life*, cliv (1973), 1062–4. For Eythrope, see B of E, *Buckinghamshire* (1994), 321–2.

131. Bedford Lemere archive, no. 11826 (drawing room); *Country Life*, ix (1901), 592–7; B of E, *Worcestershire* (1968), 137–8. Site architect, R. Phené Spiers.

132. B of E, *Surrey* (1971), 164; for Combe, see *WWW*, ii.

133. *Building News*, xxii (1872), 359, ills; for Goschen see *WWW*, i: he left £141,568 in 1907.

134. For Noble see Girouard, *Victorian County House*, 297.

135. R. Meinertzhagen, *Diary of a Black Sheep* (1964), quoted in J. Franklin, *The Gentleman's Country House and its Plan, 1835–1914* (1982), 30. For Shabden see *The Builder*, xxxi (1873), 626–7: ill. and plan. For Wykehurst, see *The Builder*, xxx (1872), 565–7: ill. and plan; *Building News*, xxviii (1875), 206, 262; 288: ills and plans. The cost was £35,000. Cattley died in 1863 worth £250,000; Frederick Huth, of Harley Street, left *c.* £500,000 personalty in 1867.

136. *Building News*, xxix (1875), 418: ill. and plan; *Country Life*, ix (1901), 368–71 and xlii (1917), supp. 1–3; *Destruction of the Country House*, pl. 195; Girouard, *Victorian Country House*, 298–9. Francis Tress Barry, with his brother-in-law James Mason, developed the San Domingo copper mines, and became a Portuguese baron in 1876 and an English baronet in 1899. He also owned Keiss Castle, Caithness [plate 47]. He left £648,367 in 1907. See *The Times*, 1 March 1907, p. 8b.

137. H.G. Wells, *Tono-Bungay* (1909; 1912), 301–2.

138. Quoted in C. Aslet, *The Last Country Houses* (1982), 265. See also I. Gow in *Country Life*, 7 Aug. 1997. Floors Castle was decorated by Lenygon and Morant. Esher Place, Surrey (1895–98) was designed in French Renaissance style by G.T. Robinson and A. Duchêne for Sir Edgar Vincent, 1st Baron d'Abernon (*Country Life*, vii (1900), 16–21).

139. *DBB*, v, 649–54; *Country Life*, xcvii (1945), 992–5, 1036–9. The architect, from 1855 onwards, was Samuel Daukes. For the formal gardens and fountains see *Gardener's*

*Magazine*, 8 June 1872, 766. The elaborate 'Golden Gates', sold in 1938, are now at Lake Havasu, Arizona.

140. H.G. Wells, *Tono-Bungay* (1909; 1912), 76. King's Walden Bury was designed in 1893 by Beeston and Burmester (*The Builder*, 10 Feb. 1894) and rebuilt in 1972 by Quinlan Terry (*Country Life*, 27 Sept. and 4 Oct. 1973). For Redleaf, now demolished, see NMRE and *The Times*, 29 July 1892, p. 6d. Redleaf was previously the home of William Wells, shipbuilder and collector.

141. Lady Eastlake, *Memoirs*, ii, 224.

142. Quoted in Moneypenny and Buckle, *Disraeli*, iv, 77: 29 April 1857.

143. R. Rhodes James, ed., *Chips: The Diaries of Sir Henry Channon* (1986), 21: 8 Jan. 1935 and 435: 11 Feb. 1951.

144. Margaret Drabble suggests Mentmore as the original of James's Poynton (*A Writer's Britain* (1979), 136); Bernard Richards more plausibly proposes Montacute (*The Spoils of Poynton*, World's Classics edn (1982), xxii). James suggested a photograph of part of the Wallace Collection as a frontispiece for the New York edition (1908). See also H. James, *Letters*, ed. P. Lubbock, i (1920), 76: 28 November 1880, to mother. For Mentmore, see B of E, *Buckinghamshire* (1994), 472–6. The sale became a *cause célèbre*. Kenneth Clark secretly advised the government that – unlike Waddesdon – the collection was not worth saving as a whole. Peter Conrad noted in *The Times*: 'it is difficult not to be exhilarated at the dispersal of [so many] geegaws and hideous rarities . . . [such] coarse and unlovely embodiments of wealth' (quoted in J. Herbert, *Inside Christie's* (1990), 25–6).

145. Channon, *Diaries, op.cit.*, 206–7: 4 Aug. 1939. Mrs Greville was the daughter of a brewer, John McEwen – 'the Bass of Scotland' – who left £1.5 million in 1913. See also *Country Life*, clxix (I) (1981), 378–81, 442–5 and *ibid.*, 1 October 1992, 74.

146. P. Tilden, *True Remembrances* (1954), 51–9.

147. *The Spectator*, 16 Nov. 1872, p. 1456.

148. B of W, *Powys* (1979), 123. He later bought Gregynog Hall nearby, briefly owned by the millionaire colliery-owner, James, 1st Baron Joicey; and formely a seat of the bankrupt 4th Baron Sudeley. For Davies, see H. Williams, *Davies the Ocean* (1991) and

I. Bulmer-Thomas, *Top Sawyer: a biography of David Davies of Llandinam* (1938); for Joicey see *DNB* and *DBB*, iii, 521–3.

149. *DNB*; *DBB*, i, 68–73; B of E, *Northumberland* (1992), 244–6; *Country Life*, cxlvi (1969), pp. 1446–50, 1640–3, 1694–7; Girouard, *Victorian Country House*, 304–17; O. Garnett, 'The Art Collection of Lord Armstrong at Cragside', in *Apollo*, cxxxvii (1993), 253–8.

150. In 1951 Pevsner – not then Chairman of the Victorian Society – simply noted: 'large and clumsy, brick with a tower, 1872' (B of E, *Nottinghamshire* (1951), 34); in the 1979 edition this appears as 'romantic . . . North French rather than "Old English" . . . a step towards . . . the Domestic Revival' (*ibid.*, 67–8).

151. For Ismay – of *Titanic* fame – and Dawpool, see *DBB*, iii, 455–61; Boase, v, 754; *Country Life*, xxix (1911), 234–41; Girouard, *Victorian Country House*, 329–35; Bedford Lemere archive, no. 13481 (exterior).

152. For Heywood and Cloverley, see *DNB*; Boase, v, 649; H.-R. Hitchcock, 'Cloverley Hall', in *The Country Seat*, ed. H.M. Colvin and J. Harris (1970), 252–61.

153. B of E, *London*, ii (1983), 430; *Academy Architecture*, xlv (1914), 130–31 and xlvi (1914), 102–3. For Sutton's life and social housing, see H. Butcher, *The Sutton Housing Trust* (Tring, 1982) and P.L. Garside, *Building a Legacy* (Tring, 1994).

154. B of E, *Surrey* (1971), 250; *Academy Architecture*, xlix (1916), 28–9; R.S. Lambert, *The Universal Provider: a Study of William Whiteley and the Rise of the London Department Store* (1938); *DNB*; *The Times*, 25 Jan. 1907 *et seq.*

155. B of E, *Surrey* (1971), 421 (demolished 1954); H. Hobhouse, *Thomas Cubitt* (1971), ill.; *Destruction of the Country House*, pl. 141. For Cubitt and Denison see *DNB*.

156. Benjamin Bacon Williams left £600,000 in 1870. Robert Campbell returned from Sydney, became an MP, joined the Reform Club, bought Buscot, and sent his son to Eton (Walford, 1860; 1875).

157. B of E, *London*, iii (1991), 294. Knox D'Arcy's partner in Australian gold rush days, Thomas Skarratt Hall, similarly set himself up at Weering, nr Brandon, Norfolk, and sent his son to Eton.

158. Extended in classical style, 1900; later Needwood School. M.T. Bass (1799–1884) and his son M.A. Bass, 1st Baron Burton (1837–1908), joined with Richard Ratcliff (1830–98) and John Gretton (1833–99) – all millionaires – to form the firm of Bass, Ratcliff and Gretton.

159. *DNB*. He left over £2¾ million in 1893.

160. B of E, *Buckinghamshire* (1960), 204–5. Hudson also owned Bidston Court, Birkenhead, reincarnated as Hill Bark, Frankby in Wirrall, a half-timbered house of 1891–2 by G.E. Gregson and E. Ould (Bedford Lemere archive nos 12841, 12844; moved 1929–31). See J. Lees-Milne, *People and Places* (1992), 22. He sold out to Lever Bros for £1 million in 1908, and retired to the Villa Paloma, Monte Carlo, where he died in 1937 aged 81, leaving £215,214 in England. See also C. Wilson, *A History of Unilever* (1954), 120.

161. B of E, *Buckinghamshire* (1960), 134–5; Boase, ii, 626; *The Times*, Sept. 1880, p. 9f; M.M. Chrimes *et al.*, *Mackenzie: Giant of the Railways* (1994).

162. B of E, *Buckinghamshire* (1960), 205; *Academy Architecture*, xxxvi (1909), ii, 50: ill.; *The Builder*, lxxxvi (1904), 198 and xcvi (1909), 524: ill. When the Devonports moved to Sussex they commissioned an equally Classical house (Peasmarsh Place, designed by Sir Edwin Cooper in 1937).

163. *Country Life*, clxxxviii (1994), no. 28, 70–3. W.J. Green (1856–99) exhibited a design for Greenlands at the Royal Academy in 1872. There were minor alterations by Norman Shaw in 1884–5, 1894 and 1905; Henley Management Centre since 1946. Marjoribanks, senior partner in Coutts and Co., left £600,000 in 1868; Smith bought the estate in 1871. When the 2nd Viscount Hambledon built North Bovey Manor, Moretonhampstead, Devon (W.E. Mills and D. Blow; 1907) it was Jacobean in style but equally old-fashioned. W.H. Smith had purchased the 500-acre estate in 1890 from the Earl of Devon. Between 1877 and 1891 he spent *c.* £450,000 on nearly 7,000 acres in Devon and Suffolk (H. Maxwell, *Life and Times of W.H. Smith*, ii (1893), 138). See also *DNB* and C. Wilson, *First With the News: the history of W.H. Smith* (1985).

164. Escott, *Society in the Country House* (1904), 419; *Country Life*, xxxii (1912), 808–18, 854–9; lxx (1931), 38–44, 68–74. See also N. Crathorne, *Cliveden: the Place and the People* (1995). Astor bought Cliveden for $1.25 million; from 1903 onwards he spent $10 million restoring Hever Castle, Kent; in 1894–5 he bought the lease of 18 Carlton House Terrace and the site of 2 Temple Place (D. Wilson, *The Astors* (1993), 141).

165. Quoted in D. Kynaston, *The City of London*, i (1994), 184. He had been worth £750,000 in 1855 (*ibid.*, 183). He is today remembered as the benefactor of Boston Public Library (*DNB*).

166. Girouard, *Victorian Country House*, 236–42, 450; *Country Life*, cxxxiv (1963), 804–7, 876–9; 29 June 1995, 60–4: ills. Peter Thelusson, an Anglo-Swiss banker and jewel merchant, left *c.* £800,000 in 1797, an extraordinary sum for that date (*Economist*, viii (1850), 705). His disputed will is said to have given Dickens the plot for *Bleak House*. Brodsworth cost about £50,000.

167. For the planning of Somerleyton, see R. Kerr, *The Gentleman's House*, (1871). Thomas also worked for Glasgow new money (*Furniture History*, 1998).

168. Ednaston Manor, Brailsford, Derbyshire: *Country Life*, liii (1923), 398–405; Great Maytham, Rolvenden, Kent: *ibid.*, xxxii (1912), 446–53; Heathcote, Ilkley, Yorkshire: *ibid.*, xxviii (1910), 54–65.

169. T.H. Mawson, *The Life and Work of a Landscape Artist* (1927), 83; *Country Life*, liii (1923), 280–3. Mallows' plans were exhibited at the Royal Academy in 1901.

170. M. Asquith, *Autobiography* (1922), 103–4.

## Chapter 3:
## Privilege and the Picturesque

Epigraph: *Letters of Alfred Lord Tennyson*, ed. C.Y. Lang and E.F. Shannon, i (1982), 333–4: *c.* 1 Aug. 1850.

1. J. Ruskin, 'The Poetry of Architecture', *Complete Works*, ed. Cook and Wedderburn i, 74.

2. *Ibid.*, 81.

3. *Ibid.*

4. *Ibid.*

5. *Ibid.*, 134.

6. *Ibid.*

7. *Ibid.*, 118. 'There never was, and never can be, a universal *beau idéal* in architecture' (*ibid.*, 116).

8. *Ibid.*, 118.

9. *Ibid.*, 119.

10. *Ibid.*, 103.

11. *Ibid.*, 82–4, figs. 12–13. Similarly the Villa Sommariva (Villa Carlotta, Cadenabbia), 'one of the most delicious habitations that luxury ever projected, or wealth procured . . . in one of the loveliest situations that hill, and wave, and heaven ever combined to adorn' (*ibid.*, 159).

12. *Ibid.*, 87.

13. *Ibid.*, 95.

14. *Ibid.*, 102.

15. *Ibid.*, 127.

16. *Ibid.*, 167 and note.

17. *Ibid.*, 187.

18. *Ibid.*, 167–8, note.

19. *Ibid.*, 163.

20. *Ibid.*

21. The architect considers himself licensed to try all sorts of experiments', like 'a bad chemist mixing elements . . . The chemist, however, is more innocent than the architect, for the one throws his trash out of the window if the compound fail; while the other always thinks his conceit too good to be lost' (*ibid.*, 167).

22. *Ibid.*, 181.

23. *Ibid.*, 185–6.

24. *Ibid.*

25. J.M. Robinson, *A Guide to Country Houses of the North West* (1991), 289; C. Jones, *John Bolton of Storrs, 1756–1837* (Kendal, 1959). The Storrs estate was bought in 1807 from Sir John Legard.

26. Robinson, 166.

27. Walford (1882). Redmayne bought Brathay in 1834.

28. Robinson, 267. Hartley Coleridge described it as 'in a style which neither Vitruvius, Palladio, Inigo Jones, Piranesi nor Sir Jeffrey Wyatville ever dreamed of even in a nightmare or under the influence of opium'.

29. Perhaps the brother of Sir Thomas Brancker, sugar refiner and Mayor of Liverpool, who died in 1853 worth £14,000.

30. Robinson, 266. Set 'in a marshy bottom . . . a site so unhappily selected, as to exclude any interesting view of the enchanting scenery that surrounds it' (*Gentleman's Magazine*, 1805, ii, 919).

31. Watson was a shameless Whig pluralist, who at one time held sixteen posts worth £5,000 p.a. He became Professor of Chemistry at Cambridge, though he knew nothing of the subject; and Regius Professor of Divinity, though he never lectured (*DNB*).

32. Robinson, 285.

33. P. Bicknell and R. Woof, eds, *The Discovery of the Lake District, 1750–1810* (Dove Cottage (1982), 25); *Country Life*, lxxxvii (1940), 98–101, 120–23.

34. See W. Wordsworth, *Guide to the Lakes* (1782).

35. 'Poetry of Architecture', *Complete Works*, i, 77.

36. Robinson, 255.

37. 'Poetry of Architecture', *Complete Works*, i, 143, note.

38. W.G. Collingwood, *The Lake Counties* (1932), 355. Perhaps a misprint for £6,000. The *Westmoreland Gazette*, 24 April 1847, suggested £20,000 (G. Beard, *The Greater House in Cumbria*, Lancaster (1978), 42).

39. 'Poetry of architecture', *Complete Works*, i, 140–3, 145. 'There are few objects that harmonise more agreeably with the feeling of ordinary English landscape, than the large, old, solitary, brick manor house, with its group of dark cedars on the lawn in front, and the tall wrought-iron gates opening down the avenue of approach.'

40. *Ibid.*, 140, 151, 153.

41. 'This is the residence of the Duke of Norfolk's gamekeeper, and here his Grace usually reposes for a fortnight in the autumn . . . The apartments are furnished in the simplicity of cottage neatness, the ceilings low and the floors of tile. The windows command the whole course of this imperial lake' (*Gentleman's Magazine*, 1806, i, 223).

42. P.Bicknell and R. Woof, eds, *The Lake District Discovered, 1810–50* (1983), 34–5. His terrifying experience at Lyulph's Tower – haunted by a shrieking ghost – forms the plot of Wordsworth's *Somnambulist*. In 1831 he emigrated to Tasmania.

43. Quoted in F. Welsh, *The Lake District* (1987), 212. For the origins of the cult of the Lake District, see also W. Roberts, *A Dawn of Imaginative Feeling: the contribution of*

*John Brown (1715–66) to 18th-century thought and literature* (Carlisle, 1997).

44. Robinson, 182. Later the home of Francis Brett Young, novelist of Lakeland.

45. Robinson, 198.

46. A. Howe, *The Cotton Masters, 1830–1860* (Oxford 1984), 29, citing R.D. Knapp, 'The Making of a Landed Elite' (Ph.D., Lancaster, 1970). For Langworthy, see Boase, ii, 303.

47. Howe, *op.cit.*, 253; Bateman (1883), 359.

48. See B of E, *S. Lancashire* (1969), 89, 306, 325; J. Murray, *Handbook for Lancashire* (1880), 85–6; T.R. Slater, 'Family, society and the ornamental villa on the fringes of English country towns', in *Journal of Historical Geography*, 4 (1978), 129–44. Thomas Agnew left £80,000 (Boase, i, 29); so did Edward Tootal; Armitage was knighted for his steadiness in face of the Chartists (Boase, i, 83).

49. *British Architect*, i (1874), 9; *The Architect*, xii (1874), 157 ('vulgarian' houses outside Liverpool, Glasgow and Manchester, and in Wimbledon, Sydenham and Chistlehurst). See also two villas outside Batley, Yorkshire, in *Building News*, xxviii (1875), 344: ills and plans.

50. Sir T. Brocklebank (Springwood, 1839); John Bibby (Hart Hill); J. Grant Morris (Allerton Priory; A. Waterhouse, 1867–70); Henry Tate (Allerton Beeches; R.N. Shaw, 1884); Joseph Leather (Cleveley; Sir G. Scott, 1865). For all these see B of E, *S. Lancashire* (1969), 209–11.

51. See p. 162.

52. Wrigley was a patron of Manchester Grammar School and Owens College (Boase, iii, p. 1524). His art collection was given by his children to Bury City Art Gallery in 1897. For Ashton Hall, see Robinson, 153. For Williamson, see P.J. Gooderson, *Lord Linoleum: Lord Ashton, Lancaster and the rise of the British Oilcloth and Linoleum Industry* (Keele, 1996). He left £10.5 million in 1930, four times the combined estates of his two closest linoleum rivals, Michael (d. 1915) and John (d. 1928) Nairn of Kirkaldy. He lived also at Ryelands, Lytham St Anne's, and Alford House, Princes Gate, London.

53. R. Gatty, *Portrait of a Merchant Prince: James Morrison, 1789–1859* (Pepper Arden,

1977), 291; W.R. Mitchell, *Walter Morrison* (Settle, 1990), 13: ill. Charles Kingsley wrote *The Water Babies* (1863) there.

54. W.G. Rimmer, *Marshalls of Leeds, Flax-Spinners, 1788–1886* (Cambridge, 1960), 94–8, 247, appendix table 13. Much of what follows derives from this pioneering study.

55. Quoted, *ibid.*, 91.

56. H. Heaton, 'Benjamin Gott and the Industrial Revolution', in *Economic History Review*, iii (1931); J.P. Neale, *Views of Seats*, 1st series, v (1822), pl. The gardens were by Repton, 1809. His son, John Gott, left £350,000 in 1867.

57. Speaking in fact of Kirkby Lonsdale.

58. Quoted in Rimmer, 99, 113.

59. J.V. Beckett, *The Aristocracy in England, 1660–1914* (1986), 76.

60. *Gentleman's Magazine*, 1806, i, 227.

61. Rimmer, 114. In 1846 William Marshall bought the 1,000-acre Enholmes estate at Pattrington, Yorkshire (B of E, *E. Yorkshire* (1995), 645). His London house was 85 Eaton Square.

62. Robinson, 284, ills.

63. *Ibid.*, 95. Bateman (1883) lists 4,129 acres worth £3,549 p.a.

64. Quoted in Rimmer, 117.

65. *Ibid.*, 221; Robinson, 104.

66. Robinson, 222, ill.

67. Rimmer, 224.

68. *Ibid.*, 204–6, ills; B of E, *W. Yorkshire* (1967), 334–5, 641; J.S. Curl, *The Egyptian Revival* (1982), pl. 121; J. Combe, in *Journal of the Institution of Civil Engineers*, 10 May 1842 and *Surveyor, Engineer and Architect*, xxiv (1842), 152. The total cost was £27,443.

69. Quoted, Rimmer, 206. James Fergusson suggested Temple Mill as a model for the British Museum (Fergusson, *Observations on the British Museum, National Gallery and National Record Office*, 1849).

70. B. Disraeli, *Sybil* (1845; Bradenham edn 1927), 210–12.

71. Rimmer, 268. For a comparison between the poverty of workers and the luxury of owners, see *Leeds Express*, 18 August 1871 (cited in Rimmer, 284n.).

72. J. Murray, *Handbook to the English Lakes* (1889), xxxii.

73. *Oxford Magazine*, 9 Mar. 1887, 129.

74. Robinson, 105: Neo-Classical.

75. Robinson, 180–81: Italianate. Ellel had been

built – on land his family had owned for three hundred years – by William Preston, a Liverpool wines and spirits importer who left nearly a quarter-million in 1871; the Sandeman family – also wine merchants – eventually inherited Ellel, and received a Portuguese peerage in 1883. See *Country Life*, clxvi (ii) (1979), 2084–5.

76. He left £1,900,000, but declined a baronetcy and peerage. His collection of prints was sold 10 June 1893 (Roberts, *Memorials of Christie's* (1897), ii, 217–18). See *The Times*, 11 May 1877, p. 10; Boase, v, 648–9.

77. Robinson, 269. William Heywood demolished the previous house, famous as the home of Professor John Wilson (alias 'Christopher North') (1785–1854) of Edinburgh University. 'I cannot recollect any spectacle . . . which so much delights with a sense of power and aerial sublimity as the terrace view from [old] Elleray' (Thomas De Quincey, quoted in Murray's *Handbook*, 1889). Heywood left £160,544. His father, Sir Benjamin Heywood, 1st Bt, of Claremont and Avesfield, Salford, left *c.* £400,000. See also *WWW*, i. For Wilson, see H.A.L. Rice, *Lake Country Portraits* (1967), 54–5.

78. Robinson, 264. Schneider (1817–1887) was a chemist and ironmaster of Swiss extraction, one of the makers of modern Barrow; he lived in style at Belsfield, which had been built by the Countess de Sternberg (d. 1869). He left £204,937. See A.G. Banks, *H.W. Schneider of Barrow and Bowness* (Kendal, 1984).

79. B of E, *N. Lancashire* (1969), 147; Robinson, 202; W.O. Roper, 'Hornby Castle', in *Transactions of the Historical Society of Lancashire and Cheshire*, xli (1890), 123.

80. George Borwick (1806–89), a London drysalter, invented German baking powder for making bread without yeast and puddings without eggs; he left £267,684. His son, the 1st Baron Borwick (1845–1936), bought Eden Lacy, Great Salkeld, Cumberland, and extended it in Tudor style; he left £377,030. Sir William Bowring, 1st Bt, a Liverpool shipowner, of Beechwood, near Aigburth, left £364,535 in 1916; his son, of Bowring's Insurance Brokers, bought Whelprigg, near Kirkby Lonsdale, in 1924. Alexander Brogden,

engineer of the Furness Railway, built himself a house on Holme Island, Grange-over-Sands (*Victoria County History: Lancashire*, viii (1914), 278). The Cropper family moved from an Italianate house, Ellergreen near Kendal, to seventeenth-century Tolson Hall (Robinson, 290; Walford, 1885). Joseph Harris, who left £301,609 in 1946, rebuilt Brackenborough Tower, Plumpton Wall, Cumberland (R. Lorimer; 1902–3); see Robinson, 90. Samuel Heginbottom IV built Croft House, Ashton-under-Lyne, Lancashire (1810–12); *ibid.*, 175. Peter Dixon II built Holme Eden Hall (J. Dobson; 1837); *ibid.*, 114; Walford (1860). J.D. Carr bought Newbiggin Hall, near Carlisle; see Robinson, 130. George Howarth built Langdale Chase, Windermere at a cost of £32,000 (J.T. Lee, 1890–91); *ibid.*, 275. Jonas Burns-Lindow, a Cumbrian barrister, built Irton Hall, Cumberland (G.E. Grayson; 1874); *ibid.*, 119. Sir Francis Ley, 1st Bt, a Derbyshire ironmaster, bought Lazonby Hall, Cumberland, and left upwards of half a million in 1916; *ibid.*, 122. Sir James Ramsden, one of the makers of Barrow-in-Furness – whose family had owned much of Huddersfield since the Middle Ages – lived at Abbot's Wood, Furness Abbey, and left nearly £70,000 in 1896; *ibid.*, 30–31. Francis Ainsworth, who left over £55,000 in 1888, lived at The Flosh, Cleator, Cumberland; *ibid.*, 108. Charles McIver, one of the founders of the Cunard Line, lived at Wanloss How, Ambleside, overlooking Windermere; *ibid.*, 291. John Mercer built Alston Hall, Longrigg, Lancashire (A. Darbyshire; 1876); *ibid.*, 153, Walford (1885). Hamlet Riley enlarged Ennim Bank, Glencowe, Cumberland (*c.* 1880); see Robinson, 106. John Robinson of the Elterwater Gunpowder Co. built Elterwater Hall (1841); *ibid.*, 270. William Tipping, a Wigan cotton-spinner, eccentric and uneducated, bought Bold Hall, St Helens, a Palladian seat by G. Leoni, in 1858; *ibid.*, 164. Joseph Torbock, a Middlesborough ironmaster, married the heiress to the Sandringham estate and bought Crossrigg, near Penrith, in 1912; see *Burke's Landed Gentry* (1952). Thomas Horrocks built Eden Brows (D. Birkett; 1874) high up above the Eden Valley, but conveniently accessible by rail; see *British Architect*, i (1874), 136: ill.

81. Quoted in O.F. Christie, *The Transition to Democracy, 1867–1914* (1934), 147.

82. For Leck Hall and Barbon Manor see Robinson in *Country Life*, 4 August 1988. For Flass, Underscar and Pull Woods see Robinson, 140, 270. Crossley left £591,636 in 1911. For the garden at Underscar, by Edward Kemp, see R. Kerr, *The Gentleman's House* (1864).

83. Quoted in J.V. Beckett, *The Aristocracy in England, 1660–1914* (1986), 77.

84. Tennyson, 'Edwin Morris or, The Lake'.

85. O.M. Westall, ed., *Windermere in the Nineteenth Century* (Lancaster, 1976), 42.

86. John Bibby (1810–83), a Liverpool shipowner, built Hart Hill, Allerton, in Classical style, and left £447,232. His youngest brother James Bibby (1813–97) bought Hardwicke Grange, Shropshire, from Viscount Hill in 1868, and left £1,778,717; his London house was 25 Hill Street. He also bought Sansaw, Clive, Shropshire.

87. Bateman (1883), 214; Dod's *Parliamentary Companion*; *Complete Peerage*, s.v. 'Headfort'; Robinson, 290–91. The 3rd Marquess of Headfort left £775,659 in 1894; eight years later his son and heir married a Gaiety Girl from Tipperary called Rosie Boote. Thompson also owned Penydarryn House, Glamorgan; his London house was 12 Whitehall Place. Lady Charlotte Guest did not approve of him: 'Mr Thompson is the Alderman in every sense, and has not the uprightness which I should be inclined to give most City Merchants credit for' (R. Guest, and A.V. John, *Lady Charlotte* (1989), 27).

88. The Priory was built by the local firm of Pattinson; the architect of the adjacent Congregational Chapel (1880) was Robert Walker. See *Building News*, lvi (1889), 588; C. Stell, *Nonconformist Chapels . . . in the North of England* (1994), 184; G. Beard, *The Greater House in Cumbria* (Lancaster, 1978), 49; Robinson, 284.

89. Walford (1872). The architect may have been James Henderson of Wigton (B of E, *Cumberland and Westmorland* (1967), 208).

90. Overlooking the Rothay, 'in a beautiful

nook among the Westmoreland hills' (*DNB*). He left £16,000.

91. Boase, ii, p. 1086.

92. The house was built for her at Wordsworth's suggestion (*DNB*; Boase, ii, 776). She wrote *A Complete Guide to the English Lakes* (1855), and left *c.* £10,000.

93. Robinson, 269.

94. *Millionaires and How They Became So* (1884), 101; *Illustrated London News*, 1876, 530, 533; Boase, ii, 846–7; Walford (1872); Robinson, 142. After buying Whitehall in 1858, Moore employed Salvin to extend it in 1862 in plain Tudorbethan style. See *Whitehall in Cumberland* (1865).

95. T.H. Mawson, *Bolton as it is and as it might be, Six Lectures on Town Planning* (1916), 9 and *Life and Work of an English Landscape Architect* (1927), 22–3, 97.

96. Walford (1885); Burke's *Landed Gentry* (1927), 22–3; Robinson, 168, 349. Another northerner who removed to Torquay was Crampton the paper-maker; he spent £20,000 completing Watcombe, a mansion begun by Brunel (*British Architect*, i (1874), 271).

97. For recent descriptions see B. Hanson, *Brantwood: John Ruskin's Home, 1872–1900* (Brantwood, n.d.) and C. Wainwright, in *Country Life*, clxxvi (1984), 234–8, 316–20.

98. Ruskin may have been inspired to build himself a house by the Turcophile diplomatist David Urquhart: he built a chalet at St-Gervais, near Chamonix (*Complete Works*, xxxvi, p. cxv).

99. 'Poetry of Architecture', *Complete Works*, i, 177. Or 'hill villa' (*ibid.*, 182).

100. *Ibid.*, 60, note.

101. 'Poetry of Architecture', *Complete Works*, i, 187.

102. *WWW*, ii. Toulmin (1857–1923) left £73,828.

103. Rickards' father left £511,188 in 1886 (Boase, vi, 468–9); the projected house was to be called Broome Cottage, Windermere.

104. Henry Currer Briggs (1829–81), a Liberal paternalist, owned the Whitwood Colliery near Wakefield in the West Riding of Yorkshire, where Voysey also designed buildings. He left £47,537. His sons were E.E. Briggs (1866–1913), a mining engineer turned artist, and Arthur Currer Briggs, Lord Mayor of Leeds. See *WWW*, i and vii and *DBB*, i, 445–7.

105. Robinson, 222; J. Symons, ed., *Catalogue RIBA Drawings Collection: Voysey* (1976), 45–6.

106. Robinson, 166–7; Symons, 45; *The Architect*, lxxix (1908), 208: ills. The contractor was G.H. Pattinson, the landscape gardener T.H. Mawson.

107. Robinson, 273.

108. *Architectural Review*, vii (1900), 202. Robinson, 264; *WWW*, i. Holt (1849–1928) left £1,290,200. He also had houses at Holmacre, Alderley, Cheshire and Woodthorpe, Prestwich, Lancashire.

109. 'A pretty cottage orné washed by a bay of the lake', and overlooking 'the empurpled majesty of Skiddaw' (*Gentleman's Magazine*, lxxv, ii (1805), p. 1123); Robinson, 103.

110. Scott – who left £207,726 in 1913 – bought the Storrs estate in 1896, and rebuilt a farmhouse in vernacular style; in 1906 he and his son F.C. Scott employed W.T. Dobson and T.H. Mawson to make Classical additions; in 1961 his grandson Peter Scott employed Basil Ward to build Matson Ground nearby in International Modern style (Robinson, 281, 294).

111. Robinson, 277; G. Christie, *Storeys of Lancaster, 1848–1964* (1964).

## Chapter 4:
## The New Plutocracy

Epigraph: *Letters of Thomas Babington Macaulay*, i (1974), 262, 311: 1831.

1. T. Veblen, *The Theory of the Leisure Class* (1899).

2. O. Sitwell, *Left Hand, Right Hand* (1945), 242.

3. W.E.H. Lecky, *The Map of Life* (1901 edn), 294.

4. I. Balla, *The Romance of the Rothschilds* (1913), 7, 34.

5. *Country Life*, xxix (1911), 2: leader; *Landed Gentry of Ireland* (1912), preface.

6. 'The *ne plus ultra* of the exotic vulgarian' (*Survey of London*, xxxix, 155–6). The woodwork was co-ordinated by L. Buscaylet of Paris; the metalwork was by W. Bainbridge Reynolds. 'This noble mansion . . . is . . . in the Florentine style, and is a stately work of art of beautiful proportions. The interior presents a series of splendid apartments in various styles ranging from the Florentine and Venetian to the Queen Anne and Lousi XVI . . . [all] executed regardless of expense . . . probably the most unique modern Residence of any city . . .' (sale advertisement and comment, *Country Life*, lii (1922), 796). For Speyer see *The Times*, 18 Feb. 1932, p. 17b. From the tower of his country house (Sea Marge, Overstrand, Norfolk, 1908–12) he was suspected of signalling to the enemy.

7. [Escott], *Society in London* (1885 edn), 47. Junius Morgan, father of J.P. Morgan, had lived at 13 Prince's Gate and Dover House, Roehampton. For Astor see D. Wilson, *The Astors* (1993) and P. Sinclair, *The Astors and their Times* (1983). In 1905 he bought the Villa Labonia, in Sorrento, and spent *c.* $500,000 turning it into the Villa Serena.

8. T.H.S. Escott, *King Edward and his Court* (1903), 224–5; 'The New Reign and the New Society', in *Fortnightly Review*, lxx (1901); *Society in the New Reign* (1904), 191–2, 198–9.

9. *The Crawford Papers: the journals of David Lindsay, 27th Earl of Crawford and 10th Earl of Balcarres . . . 1892–1948*, ed. J. Vincent (Manchester, 1984), 62: 22 June 1902.

10. W.D. Rubinstein, *Men of Property* (1981), 156. See also *Society in London* (1887 edn), 86–7.

11. H.G. Wells, *Tono-Bungay* (1909; 1912), 308–9.

12. R. Jenkins, *Mr Balfour's Poodle* (1954; 1968), 125; G.R. Searle, *Corruption in British Politics* (Oxford, 1987), 26; *Spectator*, 22 May 1897, p. 732.

13. C.F.G. Masterman, *England After War* (1922), 32.

14. E.g., from 864 members to 2,000 between 1850 and 1877, of whom 5 per cent were Jewish (D. Feldman, *Englishmen and Jews, 1840–1914* (1994), 80).

15. Henry Lowenfield, quoted in D. Kynaston, *The City of London*, ii, 469. See also W.D. Rubinstein, *Capitalism, Culture and Decline in Britain* (1993), 27–9.

16. Demolished 1882. See Boase, v, 467–9; *Diaries of E.H. Stanley, 15th Earl of Derby, 1868–78* (Camden Society, 5th ser., iv, 328: 20 Sept. 1876). Grant lived at Cooper's Hill, Englefield Green (F. and H. Francis, 1865) before building Kensington House,

Kensington Gore (1872). His barony was Portuguese. See P. Metcalf, *James Knowles, Victorian Editor and Architect* (1980), pl. 13, p. 250. His pictures were sold at Christie's, often at a loss, 27–8 April 1877; many had come from the sale (15 March 1875) of the collection built up by Samuel Mendel, a Mancunian cotton magnate, of Manley Hall, nr Manchester. Some of Grant's pictures were in turn bought by Armstrong of Cragside (G. Agnew, *History of Agnew's* (1967), 21–2). Grant eventually retired to Bognor, Sussex.

17. *DNB*; *DBB*, v, 901–4. For Lea (later Whitley) Park, nr Brook, Surrey, see *Country Life*, cliv (1973), 2190; *Destruction of the Country House* (1974), pl. 200; R. Pearsall, *Edwardian Life and Leisure* (1973), 260–62.

18. *DBB*, i, 129–34; Walford (1885).

19. *WWW*, ii.

20. *The Times*, 1, 2, 5 July and 4 August 1927.

21. *DBB*, iii, 110–14; bankruptcy: *The Times*, 25 January 1930, p. 14f.

22. *DNB Missing Persons* (1993); G.R. Searle, *Corruption in British Politics, 1895–1930* (Oxford, 1987), 88. St Paul's Cathedral had to return the gold plate which Hooley had presented.

23. *DNB Missing Persons* (1993). J.T. North was an Hon. Colonel of the Tower Hamlets Volunteers. See Kynaston, *City of London*, i (1994), 400.

24. Derby, *Diaries*, op.cit., 160, 227.

25. G. Du Maurier, *English Society* (1897) and *Social and Political Satire* (1892), 74–6.

26. A. Trollope, *The Way We Live Now* (1875), intro. N. Annan (1992), 27. See also B. Cheyette, *Constructions of the 'Jew' in English Literature and Society: Racial Representations, 1875–1945* (Cambridge, 1993), and J. Sutherland, 'Is Melmotte Jewish?', in *Times Literary Supplement*, 4 Aug. 1995, p. 13.

27. Escott, *King Edward and his Court*, 1; [Escott], *Society in the New Reign* (1904), 11; K. Middlemas, *The Pursuit of Pleasure: High Society in the 1900s* (1977), 15.

28. Sir P. Magnus, *Edward VII* (1964), 246.

29. H.G. Hutchinson, ed., *Private diaries of the Rt Hon. Sir Algernon West, GCB* (1922), 314.

30. [Escott], *Society in the New Reign* (1904), 65–9, 226–7. Alfred Morrison, collector, took over 16 Carlton House Terrace from S.M. Peto in 1866, and stayed until 1893, in rooms elaborately decorated by Owen Jones.

31. D. Nevill, *Note Books*, ed. R. Nevill (1907), 32 and *My Own Times* (1912), 164; H.E.M. Stutfield, *The Sovranty of Society* (1909), 93, 180–81.

32. D. Read, *Edwardian England* (1972), 72; H.J. Hanham, 'The Sale of Honours in Late Victorian England', in *Victorian Studies*, 1960, 279; D. Cannadine, *The Decline and Fall of the British Aristocracy* (1990), *passim*.

33. *Truth*, xxxviii (1895), 137.

34. Hanham, *op.cit.*, 281.

35. W. Bagehot, *The English Constitution* (ed. R.H. Crossman, 1963), 121–3; *The Times*, 16 April 1998, p. 21.

36. Ouida [M.L. de la Ramée], *The Massarenes* (1897), 132.

37. F.M.L. Thompson, 'Britain', in D. Spring, ed., *European Landed Elites in the 19th century* (Baltimore, 1977), 31–2; Cannadine, *Aristocracy*, 335.

38. W. Towner, *The Elegant Auctioneers* (New York, 1971), 187–242. Yerkes died on 29 December 1905 at the Waldorf Astoria, New York. His mansion at 864 Fifth Avenue – where he slept in Ludwig of Bavaria's bed – was said to have cost $5 million.

39. Marriages were recorded annually in [C.P. Depew], *Titled Americans: a list of American ladies who have married foreigners of rank* (New York, 1890–1915). For analysis see M.E. Montgomery, *Gilded Prostitution: Status, Money and Transatlantic Marriages, 1870–1914* (1989) and R.W. Davis, 'Anglo-American Marriages in the later 19th century', in *Proceedings of the American Philosophical Society*, cxxxv (1991), 140–99.

40. [Escott], *Society in the New Reign*, 118, citing *New York World*. 'Between 1874 and 1909 approximately 500 American girls wedded titled Europeans, and $220 million changed hands as a result of these vows. Whitneys, Vanderbilts and Goulds from New York, Leiters from Chicago and Washington, DC, Thaws from Pittsburgh, Wards from Detroit and Longworths from Cincinnati were among the prize catches in the transatlantic matrimonial market' (F.C. Jaher, in W.D. Rubinstein, ed., *Wealth and the Wealthy in the Modern World* (1980), 200).

41. Quoted in R. Brandon, *The Dollar Princesses* (1980), 71.
42. Cannadine, *Aristocracy*, 407; *idem.*, *Historical Journal*, xxi (1978), 463; G.D. Phillips, *The Diehards: Aristocratic Society and Politics in Edwardian England* (1979), 36. The involvement of aristocracy in the City had been growing for years: in 1866 the *Saturday Review* noted 'the City is rapidly becoming another branch of that system of relief for the aristocracy which Mr Bright denounces' (W.D. Rubinstein, 'Wealth, Elites and the Class Structure of Modern Britain', in *Past and Present* (1977), 114–15).
43. Cannadine, *Aristocracy*, 316; J.V. Beckett, *The Aristocracy in England* (1986), 471; G.R. Searle, *Corruption in British Politics, 1895–1930* (Oxford, 1987), 353.
44. Bedford Lemere archive no. 20034; *The Times*, 7 Feb. 1911, p. 11d. With his agent Ernest Oppenheimer, he became one of the founders of the giant Anglo-American Corporation (B. Roberts, *The Diamond Magnates* (1972), 69–70; W.D. Rubinstein, *Capitalism, Culture and Decline in Britain, 1750–1990* (1993), 132).
45. Stable by J.T. Wimperis (Bedford Lemere archive, no. 1016). See *The Times*, 14 January 1901, p. 4e, 18 January 1901, p. 6b and 26 January 1901, p. 13f. He was the founder of the charitable Lewis Housing Trust. For his life and philanthropy, see G. Black, *Lender to the Lords, Giver to the Poor* (1992).
46. L. Weinthal, ed., *The Anglo-African Who's Who* (1910), 62; *DBB*, ii, 24–8; *The Times*, 21 Feb. 1939, p. 16d; A.S. Gray, *Edwardian Architecture* (1985), 182; *WWW*, iii. He left £394,518. His wife, Mary Bensusan Harford, was a celebrated artist in painted fans and embroidered shawls.
47. *Complete Peerage*. His portrait is now in the Tate Gallery.
48. Cannadine, *Aristocracy*, 335.
49. P. Tilden, *True Remembrances* (1954), 58. For Beck, a beer baron and society *flâneur*, see S. Blow, *Broken Blood: the rise and fall of the Tennant family* (1987), 160–63. Selfridge reputedly spent £2 million on the Dolly sisters between 1924 and 1931.
50. Bedford Lemere archive no. 17237 (1902).
51. A. Quiney, *J.L. Pearson* (1979), 281.
52. B of E, *London*, i (1973), 511–12, 607–8.
53. M. Whinney, *Home House* (1969).
54. C. Hussey in *Country Life*, lxiii (1928), 646–53, 684–90.
55. For Rylands see *DNB*; for Dunbar see *Gentleman's Magazine*, 1862, 520.
56. Boase, v, 504. McEwen left his collection of Dutch pictures to his daughter, Mrs Ronald Greville of Polesden Lacey, Surrey.
57. For Sofer Whitburn, see *The Times*, 3 November 1891, p. 19d. His country house was Addington Manor, near Maidstone. For Brunner see *DBB*, i, 484–8 and S. Koss, *Sir John Brunner* (1970). He also owned Winnington Hall, Northwhich, Cheshire and Silverlands, Chertsey (remodelled in Renaissance style by R.P. Jones in 1909, with interiors by Aumonier; see *The Builder*, xcvii (1909), 496: ills, and *Architectural Review*, xxvi (1909), 136–41: ills and plan).
58. *DNB*; *DBB*, ii, 248–61. He also had a seaside home at Eastbourne and a Scottish retreat at Slains Castle, nr Cruden, Aberdeenshire.
59. *The Times*, 8 September, 1910, p. 10c. As a picture collector, Butler was advised by Fairfax Murray. His fine collection of Italian paintings was sold at Christie's, 25–6 May 1911.
60. *WWW*, i. For his collection of Turner water-colours, see G. Agnew, *History of Agnew's* (1967).
61. *DNB*, 229; *DBB*.
62. *The Times*, 23 October 1898, p. 7d. Beddington purchased The Limes, Carshalton, Surrey.
63. *WWW*, i. For Sebag-Montefiore's house at East Cliff, Ramsgate, see photographs, NMRE. His son-in-law was Sir Isadore Spielmann, co-founder of the National Art Collections Fund.
64. Hermann Stern (1815–87), Baron de Stern, of Hyde Park Gate; Herbert Stern, 1st Baron Michelham (1851–1919), of 26 Prince's Gate and Imber Court, Thames Ditton; H.L. Raphael (1832–99) of 31 Portland Place; E.L. Raphael (1831–1903) of 4 Connaught Place and Iden Manor, Staplehurst, Kent; G.C. Raphael (d. 1906) of Portland Place and Castle Hill, Englefield Green; J.T. Stern (1845–1912), 1st Baron Wandsworth, of 10 Great Stanhope Street and Hengrave Hall, Suffolk; and L.E. Raphael (1853–1914) of 4 Connaught Place – all left over £1,000,000.
65. Brown, an Irish-American who progressed from linen to merchant banking, founded

the Brown Library, and died at Richmond
Hill, Liverpool worth £900,000 (Boase, i,
440–41). Sir Frederich Mappin, cutler, died
at Thornbury, Sheffield, worth £946,263
(*DBB*, iv, 115–20).

66. Woodhall, Dulwich. See *DBB*, ii, 293–4.
Curiously, on 12 May 1942, at All Souls
College, Oxford, Sir Charles Grant
Robertson bet Sir Llewellyn Woodward
'that there never was an Eno connected with
Eno's Salt' (B. Harrison, ed., *The History of
the University of Oxford*, vii (1994), 87).

67. West Brow, 9 Arkwright Row (1874;
extended 1913). See *The Times*, 24 October
1916, p. 11d; *DBB*, i, 243–6. For his paintings
(sold Christie's May 1917), see C.R. Grundy,
'Sir Joseph Beecham's Collection at
Hampstead', in *Connoisseur*, xxxv (1913), and
xxxviii–ix (1914). His northern home was
Ewansville, Huyton, Liverpool (extended
1885).

68. Reckitt moved to Highgate in 1888; before
that he was at Crag View, Hessle, near Hull.
Taylor lived at Granard, Putney Park Lane;
Beasley at The Cottage, Abbey Wood,
Middlesex.

69. Waddilove lived at The Elms, Spaniards
Row (*WWW*, ii). Tetley lived at 17 Avenue
Road, Regent's Park; he died at
Alderbrook, Cranleigh, Surrey (Norman
Shaw, 1881, demolished; B of E, *Surrey*
(1971), 175).

70. B of E, *London* iv (1988), 217–18. Later called
Inverforth House, The Hill is situated in
North End Road (*Country Life*, xliii (1918),
186–93). Many of its contents were sold in
New York in 1926 for $1,248,508 (W.
Towner, *The Elegant Auctioneers* (1971), 412).
Besides Thornton Manor, Cheshire (various
architects, 1891 onwards: J.M. Robinson, *A
Guide to Country Houses, North West* (1991),
70–1), he also owned Borve Lodge at
Leverborough on the Isle of Harris, and The
Bungalow, Rivington, near Bolton,
Lancashire (see p. 59). For his activities as a
collector, see R.R. Tatlock, R. Fry etc., *A
Record of the Collection in the Lady Lever
Art Gallery, Port Sunlight, Cheshire*, 3 vols
(1928).

71. G. Orwell [E.A. Blair], *Burmese Days* (1933;
1986), 126.

72. Palmer lived at Northcourt, Hampstead. See
*The Times*, 10 April 1903, p. 8b and 2 May

1903, p. 8e; Blackwell at The Cedars,
Uxbridge Road, Harrow Weald, Middlesex
(*WWW*, i).

73. Park Hill, Streatham Common (J.B.
Papworth, 1830–41; extended 1880 onwards).
See B of E, *London*, ii (1983), 393.

74. Springcroft, Hornsey Lane, Middlesex and
Bookleigh, Esher. See Boase, iii, 228; *The
Times*, 2 November 1895, p. 6 and 30 March
1896, p. 13.

75. Eagle House, Clapham Common.

76. Kingswood, Seeley Drive, Dulwich (1812;
1892), later owned by Lord Vestey. See
B. Green, *Victorian and Edwardian Dulwich*
(Dulwich, 1995), 96; *The Times*, 24 February
1943, p. 7d. His son, Lord Luke, owned
Pavenham Bury and Odell Castle,
Bedfordshire (bought 1934).

77. Goldbeater Farm, Mill Hill.

78. At Fairseat, next to Lauderdale House; he
presented both, and the adjacent Waterlow
Park, to the London County Council. See
*DNB* and *The Times*, 4 August 1906, p. 5f.

79. By 1879 he had made about £1.5 million, but
unwise government contracts, and
generosity to his family, left him only
£92,956 at his death in 1893. He built The
Grange, next door, for his daughter. See
Green, *Victorian and Edwardian Dulwich*,
87–91; *DNB*; *DBB*, i, 309–14.

80. An 'old-fashioned house' in which he lived
alone: Osidge, Southgate, Middlesex. See
*DNB*; *DBB*, iii, 799–802; *The Times*, 3
October 1931, p. 15a. A world-famous
yachtsman, 'his physical energy in old age
was almost incredible . . . [He] made the
recital of anecdotes almost a career in
itself.'

81. For architectural details, see the
comprehensive account in the *Survey of
London*, xxxvii (1973), 151 *et seq.*; also
M. Girouard in *Country Life*, cl (1971),
1360–3. Addresses of residents are listed
annually in Boyle's *Court Guide*.

82. Executant architect, C.J. Richardson. One
critic at least was contemptuous: 'instead of
"repose" we have actual torture – the very
thumbscrews of design' (*The Builder*, x
(1852), 360, 374).

83. Hydraulic engineer; grandfather of H.S.
Goodhart-Rendel. See *DNB*.

84. Collie bought one of Sir Morton Peto's
houses for £30,000; then rebuilt it, spending

the same amount on his picture gallery alone (*The Builder*, xxxiii (1875), 452).

85. Of Longmans, Green Ltd; he left £200,000 personalty in 1869. See Boase, i, p. 1222.

86. *DNB*; Boase, ii, 947. He left £400,000 personalty in 1876. See pp. 93–6.

87. Boase, iv; author of *Anarchy and Order* (1848), *The Prison and the School* (1853) and *The Rise and Progress of Painting*, 2 vols (1862).

88. S. Smiles, *George Moore, Merchant and Philanthropist* (2nd edn 1878).

89. *DBB*, iii, 209–15. He also owned a house at Wightwick, near Wolverhampton, and leased Dunbeath Castle, Caithness.

90. Also of Hutton Hall, near Guisborough (1865–68), Woodlands, Darlington (1860) and Kerris Vean, Falmouth.

91. Of Didsbury Towers, Manchester. He left £406,615 in 1905; his water-colours went to the Whitworth Gallery, Manchester.

92. *WWW*, i. From a Congregationalist family. He also owned Manor Heath, Bournemouth, and 1,500 acres at Northmoor, Dulverton, Somerset.

93. Both J.M. Rendel's sons, George and Stuart, were prominent in Armstrong and Co., armaments manufacturers; the former ended his days at Posilippo, near Naples, the latter at Hatchlands, Surrey, and Château de Thorenc, Cannes (*WWW*, i; Boase, iii, 108; *Men and Women of our Time*, 1899).

94. For Strauss, see *WWW*, ii.

95. For Benzon, see *Times Literary Supplement*, 2 August 1972, p. 784.

96. *WWW*, i. His widow married Gordon Bennett, the aviator.

97. *WWW*, iii.

98. Boase, ii, p. 1057. Cristobal left £600,000 personalty in 1868, but his company failed in 1892.

99. *WWW*, iii.

100. *WWW*, vi. He later remodelled 19 Eldon Road.

101. *The Times*, 3 April 1934, p. 12c. 'He owned 20,000 acres ... and was probably the largest South African importer of wool, mohair, skins and ostrich feathers.'

102. Later of Brambletye, Sussex. His son, Eton and Trinity, Cambridge, won the Derby in 1898 (*WWW*, ii).

103. Boase, v, 737. Later of Oakhurst, 77 Mount Ephraim, Tunbridge Wells. A director of the Bank of England, his collection of modern pictures and drawings was sold at Christie's 6/8/9 July 1895 for £27,547, his engravings on 10/11 July for £6,850.

104. Of Ferry Bar Estate, Baltimore, Maryland; financier and railway tycoon (*WWW*, ii).

105. Of New York (*WWW*, ii).

106. *WWW*, i; Boase, ii, 194; later of Hordle Cliff, Hampshire.

107. Of Seligman Bros, described in 1910 as 'a German Jew branch of an American Bank and British in name only' (D. Kynaston, *The City of London*, ii (1995), 511).

108. Later of 46 Grosvenor Square and Brownsea Castle, Dorset; son of Marcus Van Raalte of 40 Brook Street, stockbroker (*WWW*, i). See C. Van Raalte, *Brownsea Castle* (1906).

109. *The Times*, 24 March 1932, p. 17. Born in Washington, trained in Frankfurt, he retired early from Speyer Bros to devote himself to collecting. See [K.T. Parker], *Catalogue of . . . Old Master Drawings [of] Henry Oppenheimer Esq. FSA*, intro. C.J. Holmes (Christie's, 1936).

110. *DBB*, iv, 298–301; *Champion Redoubtable: The Diaries and Letters of Violet Bonham-Carter, 1914–45*, ed. M. Pottle (1998), 50: 1915.

111. *DBB*. An associate of Maple, Lebus died in 1907 worth £510,436.

112. *The Metropolitan*, 22 November 1890, quoted in *Survey of London*, xxxvii (1973), 370.

113. See *The Aristocracy of London*, part i, *Kensington* (1863). By arranging the names of residents street by street, this publication emphasised the conjunction of old and new money. In Prince's Gate, for example, the 9th Viscount Falkland and Earl Grosvenor could be found at nos 4 and 28; H.W. Eaton ('silk broker') and Samuel Gurney ('banker and money-lender') at nos 16 and 25.

114. 'Queen's Gate and the quarters around were . . . devoted to opulent tradesmen. Even Belgrave Square, though its aristocratic properties must be admitted, still smelt of the mortar' (A. Trollope, *The Way We Live Now* (1875; 1957), 119.

115. *Survey of London*, xxxix, 87.

116. *Survey of London*, xxxix, pl. 41a and xl, p. 152. The later work may be by Keeble Bros of Grosvenor Street, who also redecorated 22 South Audley Street (1902–3) and 15 Curzon Street (1909–11).

117. *Survey of London*, xxxix, pl. 40b and p. 144;
A. Service, *London 1900* (1979), pl. 55,
p. 65. Nesfield's work of 1878 had been for
A.P. Heywood Lonsdale of the Liverpool
banking family (*Architectural Association
Notes*, xvi (1901), 110). In 1905 Sir Charles
Allom made the dining room 'English';
White Allom and A. Marshall Mackenzie
made further changes in 1909. Cooper's
country house was Hursley Park, near
Winchester (N. Cooper, *The Opulent Eye*,
pls 151–4), where J.J. Duveen fitted up the
ballroom with eighteenth-century *boiseries*
and Beauvais tapestries. For 'Chicago'
Smith, see *The Times*, 8 November 1899,
p. 9; Boase, vi, 579–80. His estate in
England was only £59,435. The bulk of his
fortune – $56 million – went initially to
his nephew, J.H. ('Silent') Smith, who
died in 1906 after a honeymoon on A.J.
Drexel's yacht. See also F. Bennett-
Goldney, *Some Works of Art in the
possession of George A. Cooper at 26
Grosvenor Square* (1903).

118. Bedford Lemere archive, nos 14086 and
14091 (dining room, 1897); *Survey of London*,
xl, p. 159 and pl. 41c (boudoir). Architect:
John Kinross.

119. Quoted in B. Roberts, *The Diamond
Magnates* (1972), 151. See *Survey of London*,
xl, p. 148, pl. 38a (during residence of C.T.
Kettlewell; architect 'Powell'; Bedford
Lemere archive nos 10163 and 10165:
drawing room).

120. [Escott], *Society in the New Reign* (1904), 62.

121. B. Disraeli, *Henrietta Temple* (1837;
Bradenham edn 1927), 350. Perhaps Henry
Padwick, moneylender and horse-breeder;
the son of a butcher, he lived for many years
off Berkeley Square, and ended as Deputy-
Lieutenant for Sussex and Deputy Keeper of
Holyrood Palace (Boase, ii, p. 1301).

122. Steinkopf died in 1906 worth £1,273,383.
Born in Frankfurt, he founded Apollinaris
in 1874, selling out to Frederick Gordon for
£2 million in 1897. He owned the *St James's
Gazette* and bought an estate at Lyndhurst,
Hayward's Heath (*The Times*, 2 March
1906, p. 10e and 18 May 1906, p. 7e).

123. Chesterfield House had been sold by the
Stanhope family in 1869 to Charles
Magniac, who reduced it in size then re-sold
it to Bass. See Cooper, *Opulent Eye*, pls 66:

Bedford Lemere archive no. 12794 (drawing
room); and 68: Bedford Lemere archive
no. 12793 (music room); *Country Life*, li
(1922), 235, 257, 308.

124. C.S. Sykes, *Private Palaces* (1985), 303
quoting *The King*, 31 May 1902; *Survey of
London*, xxxix, 153, 157. The Classical façade
by Cyrille J. Corblet dates from 1906 (B of
E, *London*, i, 656). Bischoffsheim – a
collector of Old Masters – also owned The
Severals, Newmarket and Warren House,
Stanmore, once the home of Sir Robert
Smirke (*WWW*, i). See p. 272. The firm of
Bischoffsheim and Goldsmid was satirised in
*The Way We Live Now* (1875) as Todd,
Broghert and Goldsheimer.

125. B. Webb, *Our Partnership*, ed. M. Drake
and M.I. Cole (1948), 346–7: 2 July 1906.
See also B of E, *London*, i, 627n.; Sykes,
*Private Palaces*, 317; ill. drawing room
(NMRE); Cooper, *Opulent Eye*, pl. 181:
Bedford Lemere archive no. 21163 (yellow
drawing room).

126. *Survey of London*, xl, p. 49, pl. 13c: drawing
room; Cooper, *Opulent Eye*, p. 42, pl. 144:
Bedford Lemere archive no. 18492 (mistitled
52 Grosvenor Square). His Classical country
house was Ley Dene, near Petersfield,
Hampshire, completed 1928; its flying
staircase was doubly imperial in plan
(*Country Life*, 13 November 1997, 84: ill.);
its formal knot garden was laid out in
the pattern of the firm's best-selling
linoleum.

127. Decorators led by W. Ernest Lord of Turner
Lord and Company, Mount Street (*Survey
of London*, xl, 34, 41–2 and xxxix, 153, 154).
See also S. Wingfield, *Real People* (1953).

128. *Survey of London*, xxxix, 153 and xl, p. 53,
pl. 15a: drawing room (panelling from the
Hôtel Prunelle); boudoir (panelling from
the Hôtel Cambacères). His country house
was Moreton Paddox, Warwickshire
(Romaine-Walker and E. White; c. 1910).

129. *Survey of London*, xl, 31–2. The Parisian
decorator William Oscar Bouwens van der
Boijen was born in Holland but trained
under Labrouste and Vaudoyer. The house
is now the Savile Club.

130. *Survey of London*, xxxix, 153.

131. [Escott], *Society in the New Reign* (1904),
70–71.

132. J. Sutherland, *Mrs Humphry Ward* (1990).

See *Illustrated London News*, 25 July 1868, 91–2: ill.

133. For the McCalmonts see Boase, ii, 568; for Dalziel see *DBB*, ii, 5–11.

134. J.H. Duveen, *The Rise of the House of Duveen* (1957), 64–5; Bedford Lemere archive nos 10281 (staircase hall), 10291 (boudoir), 10294 (ballroom). For Wilson see *DNB*; *DBB* v, 846–9; *The Times*, 23 October 1909, p. 11e.

135. J. Wilson, *C.B.: A Life of Sir Henry Campbell-Bannerman* (1973), 22–3, 123, 128–30. For Campbell-Bannerman's dining room, designed in opulent Jacobean by George and Peto, see *Building News*, xxxiv (1878), 402: ill. As a younger son, he bought an estate at Belmont near Meigle, Perthshire, but left only £55,000.

136. A. Hare, *The Story of My Life*, v (1900), 204: 18 June 1879.

137. For Mond see *DBB*; Bedford Lemere archive nos 19730–7 (dining room, 27 Berkeley Square). For the Mond family's important collections, see J.P. Richter, *The Mond Collection*, 2 vols (1910); T. Borenius and R. Wittkower, *Catalogue of the Collection of Drawings by the Old Masters formed by Sir Robert Mond* (1937). For 38 Hill Street, refurbished by Mewes and Davis, see NMRE Bedford Lemere photos (1891). For Meyer, see *WWW*, ii. pp. 9–10.

138. Bedford Lemere archive (1903) nos 1795 (boudoir), 17938 (library), 1793–5 (dining room); *WWW*, ii.

139. C. Davis, *Description of Works of Art from the Collection of Alfred de Rothschild*, 2 vols (1884): ills of interiors. See also *DBB*, iv (1985), 946–53 and *WWW*, ii.

140. Boase, v, 63–3 and 668–9 (double entry); *Illustrated London News*, 10th October 1891, 464: ill.; 17 October 1891, 514 and 25 April 1896, 513: ill.; *Jewish Encyclopaedia* (1904), vi, 415–17; J. Camplin, *The Rise of the Plutocrats*, 198–9; S. Adler-Rudel, 'Moritz Baron Hirsch', in *Yearbook of the Leo Baeck Institute* (1971); K. Grunwald, *Turkenhirsch: Baron Maurice de Hirsch* (Jerusalem, 1966). The shooting of 2,870 partridges in a single day in 1892 on his estate at St Johann in Hungary remains a record (J. G. Ruffer, *The Big Shots* (1984), 134).

141. *DNB*; *The Times*, 18, 19, 24 Dec. 1888.

142. [Escott], *Society in the New Reign* (1904),

82–3. Photographs (1951), NMRE. The adjoining house – Old Q's no. 138 – had been rebuilt in 1888 (*British Almanac and Companion* (1889), 295). For Glenesk see *DNB*; *WWW*, i; R. Lucas, *Lord Glenesk and the Morning Post* (1910). He also owned the Château St-Michel, Cannes.

143. *DNB*; *WWW*, i; *The Times*, 3 November 1906, p. 6a. He began 'in a boiled beef shop in Ludgate Hill'. He also owned Putteridge Park, Luton and Bridge House, Maidenhead.

144. His northern seat was Wycoller, Blackburn, Lancashire.

145. *WWW*, i. Seated at Bywell Hall, Northumberland, and Bretton Hall, Yorkshire.

146. Bedford Lemere archive nos 21921–30 (1927).

147. *WWW*, i; *The Times*, 14 September 1916, p. 9e. He also owned Cecil Lodge, Newmarket and Glenmuick, Scotland. See p. 272.

148. Bedford Lemere archive, nos 15503 (sitting room) and 15506 ('the Lounge').

149. *Builder*, xx (1862), 787: ill. and plan; Sykes, *Private Palaces*, 300, 304: staircase and ballroom (photo colln J. Rothschild); Sotheby's sale catalogue, 19–22 April 1937: ills interior and staircase. For a chimney-piece in the style of William Kent, see *Country Life*, 16 October 1980, supp. p. 50. For chairs from Vizagapatam, see Christie's sale catalogue 9 July 1998, lots 50–53.

150. *WWW*, iii. He also owned Lythe Hill, Haslemere, and Loch Buy, Isle of Mull.

151. *DNB*; *DBB* v, 43–6; *The Times*, 18 January 1927, p. 16b. In 1895 he bought The Mote, nr Maidstone, Kent, plus 600 acres. His father sold shells in Houndsditch: hence the name of the company.

152. Bedford Lemere archive nos 9386 (1889); 20663–80 (1909); Cooper, *Opulent Eye*, pl. 178, p. 46.

153. Sykes, *Private Palaces*, 305, quoting *The King*, April 1902 and 31 May 1902. See also B of E, *London*, i, 629: interiors by Jackson, Mellier, Forsyth and Barbetti; Bedford Lemere archive nos 9380–90 (1889); ills and plans in *Building News*, xlii (1882), 572.

154. *Survey of London*, xxxix, pls 36a, 37, fig. 23d and xl, pp. 324–6, fig. 78 (Mount Street); xxxix, pl. 36b and xl, p. 188 (Green Street).

155. In Curzon Street, now offices; designed in

conjunction with Romaine-Walker and E. Besant; Sykes, *op.cit.*, 319: ill. (great hall).

156. *The Letters of Charles Dickens*, viii, ed. G. Storey and K. Tillotson (Oxford, 1995), 34: 20 Jan. 1856.

157. [Escott], *Society in the New Reign* (1904), 194.

158. D. Nevill, *Note Books*, 30, 300.

159. Ralli (1829–1902) of 32 Park Lane and St Catherine's Lodge, Hove, left £1,069,000; his family came from Chios. Renton (1822–95), a railway stock jobber, of 39 (later 138) Park Lane and 11 Queen's Gardens, West Brighton, left £823,173 (Boase, iii, 115; *The Times*, 5 April 1895, 11). For Wright's house at 18 Park Lane (G. Lethbridge; 1897), see *Building News*, lxxii (1897), 919: ill.

160. Romaine-Walker designed 37A/38 (later 128) Park Lane (1905) for Henry Joseph Duveen, brother of Sir Joseph Duveen (formerly Joel Joseph Duveen) and father of Baron Duveen) who lived at The Elms, Hampstead (Cooper, *Opulent Eye*, pl. 100: ballroom; Bedford Lemere archive, nos 15451, 15455: Tudor dining room).

161. Quoted in Camplin, *Plutocrats*, 243.

162. H.G. Wells, *Tono-Bungay* (1909), 306–7.

163. B. Webb, *My Apprenticeship* (1926), 51–2. For the South African scene in general, see G. Wheatcroft, *The Randlords: the men who made South Africa* (1985), 31 etc.; for biographical details see L. Weinthal, ed., *The Anglo-African Who's Who* (1910).

164. H. Baker, *Cecil Rhodes* (1934), 21.

165. *The Times*, 23 September 1921, p. 5a–d; *DBB*, i, 604–14; *WWW*, ii; *DNB*; K. Grunwald, 'Windsor Cassel – the Last Court Jew', in *Yearbook of the Leo Baeck Institute*, xiv (1969); P. Thane, 'The Case of Sir Ernest Cassel', in *Business History*, xxviii (1986), i, 80–99. He also owned Moulton Paddocks, Newmarket; Upper Hare Park, near Cambridge; and Branksome Dene, Bournemouth; besides an apartment in Paris, a chalet in Switzerland and a villa in the south of France. In Scotland he also purchased Lord Tweedmouth's estate at Guisachan. Edward VII failed to secure him a peerage in 1902 (S. Heffer, *Power and Place: the political consequences of King Edward VII* (1998), 125).

166. *Survey of London*, xl, p. 281, pl. 72b, citing *The King*, 22 March 1902; *Builder*, xxviii

(1870), 585–7: ill. and plan. For his pictures, see Phillips sale catalogue, 5 December 1866.

167. *The King*, 22 March 1902; *Survey of London*, xl, 281; *Furniture History*, xxxii (1996), 141.

168. *Architecture*, 7 June 1913, quoting Hastings at the RIBA (ill., staircase).

169. Sir A. Fitzroy, *Memoirs*, ii (1925), 516: 18 July 1913. In fact Cassel died a Roman Catholic.

170. *Country Life*, lxxxv (1939), 682–6. For sale particulars and photos, see *The Times*, 6 Oct. 1931, 24: 'unique in the annals of notable association . . . combining the supremacy of comfort'.

171. *Grace and Favour: the memoirs of Loelia, Duchess of Westminster* (1962), 86; Camplin, *Plutocrats*, 204–5.

172. *Grace and Favour*, 169.

173. His collection of Old Masters was sold (or rather, largely left unsold, thanks to over-high reserves) at Christie's, 6 July 1923: priced catalogue, colln C. Sebag-Montefiore. Several items are now in the Metropolitan Museum, New York.

174. Bedford Lemere archive nos 10301–18 (1890), 28420 (1926); *Survey of London*, xxix, 153.

175. Lady (Elizabeth) Glover, *Memories of Four Continents* (1923).

176. Camplin, *Plutocrats*, 275. The intermediary was the husband of the Prince of Wales's mistress, Mrs Freda Dudley Ward. See also *DNB*; *The Times*, 31 October 1929, p. 19a: 'other magnates amassed wealth and retired; "J.B." amassed wealth and went on'. His obituary in the *Cape Times* ('the loathsomeness of the thing that is the memory of Sir Joseph Robinson') appeared on 7 Nov. 1929. For his country house at Lewins, Kent, see *Building News*, 6 June 1876: ill. and plan.

177. *DNB*; *DBB*, i, 253–5; *The Times*, 17 July 1906, p. 5e–f and 18 July 1906, p. 12b. He also owned a house in Hamburg, and a Regency Greek Revival house with 700 acres at Tewin Water, Hertfordshire (B of E, *Hertfordshire* (1977), 360). His artistic adviser was Dr Bode of the Berlin Museum. See W. Bode, *The Art Collection of Mr Alfred Beit at . . . 26, Park Lane* (Berlin, 1904). Much was inherited by his brother Otto Beit; see W. Bode, *Catalogue of the Collection of Pictures . . . of Mr Otto Beit* (1913).

178. *The Builders' Journal and Architectural Record*, 24 March 1897, 88: ills. and plan;

*Architecture*, April 1895, 109–16; *Building News*, lxxiii (1897), 46: ills. and plans; *The Builder*, xcvii (1909), 504; Bedford Lemere archive nos 14414–5, 28726, 28420 (1926). The exterior included sculptured panels by Henry Pegram.

179. *Letters of Arthur Balfour and Lady Elcho*, ed. J. Ridley and C. Percy (1992), 2.
180. A.S. Gray, *Edwardian Architecture* (1985), 357–8.
181. And perhaps Franz Voelklein, his secretary, the only other occupant of the house.
182. An 'architectural journalist' (1909), quoted in H. Hobhouse, *Lost London* (1971), 42. Frank Harris admired the winter-garden: 'At once a sort of rockery and palm garden . . . a room of brown rocks and green ferns and tesselated pavements – an abode of grateful dim coolness and shuttered silence . . . framed off [from] the vague hum of the outside world' (quoted in Roberts, *Diamond Magnates*, 281).
183. *Survey of London*, xv, pp. 266–8, pls 93a–c. See also G.S. Fort, *Alfred Beit* (1932), 155. Beit's entrance hall contained a fountain from the Palazzo Borghese. The taste of Beit's nephew, Sir Alfred Beit, 2nd Bt, was more strictly Neo-Georgian: he employed Lord Gerald Wellesley and Trenwith Wills to redecorate 15 Kensington Palace Gardens (*Country Life*, lxxxv (1939), 198–202: ill.).
184. For 45 Park Lane (later 25), see *The Builder*, lxxi (1896), 291: ill. and plan. The site alone cost £50,000.
185. H. Raymond, *B.J. Barnato: a memoir* (1897), 174.
186. S. Jackson, *The Great Barnato* (1970), 164.
187. Camplin, *Plutocrats*, 172, quoting the Countess of Fingal.
188. *The Crawford Papers: the journals of David Lindsay, 27th Earl of Crawford and 10th Earl of Balcarres . . . 1892–1948*, ed. J. Vincent (Manchester, 1984), 519: 17 Feb. 1927 and 544: 6 March 1932.
189. H. Nicolson (1968), 76: 1 June 1931.
190. R. Rhodes James, ed., *Chips: the Diaries of Sir Henry Channon* (1967), 203: 3 March 1939.
191. P. Tilden, *True Remembrances* (1954), 39–40.
192. S. Jackson, *The Sassoons* (1963), 186.
193. *Ibid.*, 146; J. Knox in *Country Life*, 17 November 1994.
194. Channon, *Diaries*, *loc.cit.*

195. Jackson, *Sassoons*, 220. Se also *DNB* (entry by Osbert Sitwell). For his country houses, see pp. 279–81.
196. D. Nevill, *Under Five Reigns* (1910), 140–1.
197. Quoted in Cannadine, *Aristocracy*, 355.

## Chapter 5:
## The Age of Money

Epigraph: *The Letters of Rudyard Kipling*, ed. T. Pinney, iii (1996): 30 Nov. 1902.

1. In fact the Somersets supported the final reading of the Corn Importation Bill in May 1846; but then rejoined the Protectionists in defeating Peel over the Irish Protection of Life Bill.
2. B. Disraeli, *Lord George Bentinck: a political biography* (1872 edn), 216; ed. R.W. Kamphuis (New Brunswick, 1998).
3. Hudson bought Londesborough Park from the Duke of Devonshire for nearly £500,000, but it was later re-sold; he also bought Newby Hall from Henry Vyner, but the purchase was never completed (R.S. Lambert, *The Railway King*, 1934).
4. Boase, i, 127; Burke's *Landed Gentry* (2nd edn 1848–9); Bateman (1883), 11; F.O. Morris, *Views of Seats* i (1880), 87. Demolished 1954.
5. Also Moore Green, Worcestershire (Walford, 1860).
6. He left £104,000 (£96,000 net) in 1906. Another grandson was James Lees-Milne, who recalled Lady Charlotte Guest's reference to Sir Joseph Bailey's 'low-born, purse-proud cunning' (J. Lees-Milne, *Ancient as the Hills* (1997), 11–12, 159).
7. Of Leys, Herefordshire (Burke's *Landed Gentry*, 2nd edn 1848–9).
8. W.H. Forman (d. 1869) – part of the Crawshay-Thompson dynasty – left over £1 million, see p. 40.
9. Walford (1860); F. Leach, *Seats of Shropshire* (1891), 55. Whitmore was absent in May 1846, although listed as NO (Hansard, *Parliamentary Debates*, lxxxvi, 726). Apley Park became eventually the property of W.O. Foster, of the Chillington Iron and Coal Co., Stourbridge, Staffordshire.
10. Grandson of Peter Arkwright, of Willersley Castle, Derbyshire, who left £800,000. See *Country Life*, xlv (1919), 166.

11. Walford (1860); E. Twycross, *Mansions of England and Wales*, ii (1847), 48. Hornby was absent in May 1846, but listed as NO.

12. Of Sherwood Hall, Nottinghamshire; a bachelor.

13. Hodgson, of Clarence Lodge, Roehampton, Surrey, and 3 Carlton Gardens; Broadwood, of 8 Whitehall Yard.

14. Of Welton House, near Hull, Yorkshire.

15. Brownrigge had City and Australian links.

16. Chapman was a Government contractor, Hudson's Bay and East India man, with property at Stakesby, Yorkshire and Highbury Park, Middlesex (Dod's *Parliamentary Companion*).

17. Sheppard was a cloth manufacturer from Frome, who eventually settled at Hilton Verney and Shrewton, Wiltshire and Folkington Park, near Willingdon, Sussex (Dod's *Parliamentary Companion*; Walford, 1860).

18. For a structural analysis of voting lists, see W.O. Aydelotte, 'The Country Gentlemen and the Repeal of the Corn Laws', in *English Historical Review*, Jan. 1967, 47–60. This revises statistics in J.A. Thomas, 'The Repeal of the Corn Laws', in *Economica*, April 1929, 53–60. See also N. Gash, 'The Great Disruption', in *The Conservatives*, ed. Lord Butler (1977), 83–108.

19. Moneypenny and Buckle, *Disraeli*, iii, 157–8; *Disraeli's Reminiscences*, ed. H.M. Swartz and M. Swartz (1975), 118, 130.

20. *Disraeli, Derby and the Conservative Party*, ed. J. Vincent (1978), 31: 1851; also 237 and 347. See also *Country Life*, i (1897), 433; cxiii (1953), 1604, 1698.

21. Moneypenny and Buckle, *Disraeli*, iii, 76 and 472: to Mrs Brydges Willyams.

22. Thomas Baring was the second son of Sir Thomas Baring, 2nd Bt, of Stratton Park, Hampshire. P.W.S. Miles inherited a West India trading fortune from his father P.J. Miles of Kingsweston and Leigh Court. Spooner gives his address as Brickfields, Worcestershire; Plumptre as Fredville House, near Wingham, Kent. The Clive, Codrington and Lascelles families were all old gentry enriched in the eighteenth century. The Lopes family came originally from Portugal, prospered in Jamaica and London, and ended as landowners in Devon. When Sir Manasseh Lopes, MP, died in 1831 he was reputed to be worth £800,000 (*DNB*).

23. Hansard, *Parliamentary Debates*, 3rd series, lxxxvi (1846), 86–7; W. Bagehot, *Literary Studies*, ii (1911), 125–6.

24. A.C. Fox-Davies, intro., Burke's *Landed Gentry* (1914); H. Montgomery-Massingberd, intro., Burke's *Landed Gentry*, 18th edn, iii (1972), ix; F.M.L. Thompson, 'English Landed Society in the 20th Century', in *Transactions of the Royal Historical Society*, xl (1990), 12.

25. Buckinghamshire Record Office, D/CN. C12:n.d. [1865].

26. T.H. Mawson, *The Life and Work of a Landscape Architect* (1927), 47–8, 51 and 45 pl. 12 (photo of house party). Henry Vivian, 1st Baron Swansea, a gentleman-copper-smelter who made Swansea 'the metallurgical centre of the world', left £215,033 in 1894.

27. *Ibid.*; Murray's *Handbook for Scotland* (1900), 276; Boase, iv, 507; *Illustrated London News*, 16 Jan. 1900, 802 (portrait). E.A. Waterlow exhibited *Passing Showers – Forest of Glentanar, Aberdeenshire* at the Royal Academy in 1873 (*Illustrated London News*, 22 Nov. 1873, 485).

28. W. Orr, *Deer Forests, Landlords and Crofters* (Edinburgh, 1982), 29, 31, 33, 38 and 191 (Appendix VII); C.L. Mowat, in *Journal of Transport History* NS.i (1971); C. Milnes Gaskell, in *The Nineteenth Century*, Sept. 1882; J. Holloway and L. Errington, *The Discovery of Scotland* (Edinburgh, 1978); R. Eden, *Going to the Moors* (1979). See also a debate on deer forests between J.A. Cameron, G. Malcolm and D. Cameron of Lochiel in *The Nineteenth Century*, xvi (1884), 379–95, xviii (1885), 197–208 and xxi (1887), 683–701. The Meux family estate at Glen Morriston, Inverness-shire, was purchased in 1856.

29. The *Return of Owners of Land . . . Ireland* (1876) lists Adair: 16,308 acres worth £583 p.a.; Foster: 9,724 acres worth £4,686 p.a.; Buckley: 13,260 acres worth £3,585 p.a. at Galtee Castle, Mitchelstown, Co. Tipperary, and 7,563 acres worth £1,207 p.a. in Co. Limerick; Henry: 9,252 acres worth £639 p.a. at Kylemore Abbey, Co. Galway. For Kylemore see *Country Life*, cviii (1950), 932. For Adair's activities, see

L. Dolam, *Land War and Eviction in Derryveagh, 1840–65* (Dundalk, 1981) and J. Cornforth in *Country Life*, clxxi (1982), 1636–40, 1734–7.

30. Ouida, *The Massarenes*, 34–41. In 1865 Sir John William Ramsden married Lady Helen St Maur, daughter of the 12th Duke of Somerset and heiress to Bulstrode Park, Buckinghamshire; besides Ardverikie he also owned Turweston, Oxfordshire and Byron Hall, Yorkshire.

31. Hamilton Diary, B.L., Add.MS.48, 675, f.60/61: 16 Sept. 1899.

32. R. Boyson, *The Ashworth Cotton Enterprise, 1818–80* (Oxford, 1970), 248 n.; for Neumann see L. Cohen, *Reminiscences of Kimberley* (1911), 112. For costs, see J.G. Bertram in *British Almanac and Companion* (1885), 70; *Quarterly Review* cxviii, 22.

33. T.M. Devine, *Clanship to Crofters' War: the Social Transformation of the Scottish Highlands* (Manchester, 1994); G.K. Whitehead, *Deer and their Management in the Deer Parks of Great Britain and Ireland* (1950). Kinlochmoidart House, nr Lochaber, was rebuilt in 1884 to a design by William Leiper (*Country Life*, 13, 20 Aug. 1998). Sutherland's plea to Chaplin is in Durham Co. Record Office D/Lo/F631(21). *Ex inf.* Dr James Yorke.

34. W.H. Mallock, *The New Republic* (2nd edn 1878), 12, 34–8.

35. Trollope, *Phineas Finn* (1869; 1989), 105–6.

36. *One Hundred Glasgow Men*, i (1886), v and vi (William and James Baird); A. Miller, *The Rise and Progress of Coatbridge* (Glasgow, 1864); A. McGeorge, *The Bairds of Gartsherrie* (Glasgow, 1875); Boase, i, 133–4; Bateman (1883); Walford (1860, 1872, 1885); Burke's *Landed Gentry* and *Peerage*; *Illustrated London News*, 8 July 1876, 47 and *The Times*, 24 June 1876, p. 14c, quoting *The Scotsman* (James Baird); *Kings of British Commerce* i (1876), 23–31; F. Crouzet, *The First Industrialists* (1985); A.H. Millar, *Castles and Mansions of Ayrshire* (1885). For Baird and Co's chairman and managing director, Robert Angus (1836–1923), see Phillips sale catalogue for Ladykirk House, Ayrshire, 1997: ills.

37. Murray, *Scotland*, 18.

38. For the Coats dynasty see W.W. Knox, *Hanging by a Thread: the Scottish Cotton Industry, c. 1850–1914* (Preston, 1995). Ferguslie (*Building News*, lxii (1892), 731: ill. and plan) cost £18,000; designs by Hippolyte J. Blanc. Sir Peter Coats rebuilt the Baird seat at Auchendrane in 1880–81. For James Reid, see E. Pinnington, *The Art Collection of the Corporation of Scotland* (Glasgow, 1898).

39. *The Times*, 23 Sept. 1913, p. 9c, 6 Oct., p. 9a, 10 Oct., p. 8c, 2 Dec., p. 11b.

40. A. Cooke, ed., *Baxters of Dundee* (University of Dundee, 1980). For the family see *DNB* and Boase i, 196–7.

41. T. Johnstone, *The History of the Working Class in Scotland* (Glasgow, 1922), 310.

42. 1,201 acres worth £3,287 p.a. (Groome, *Gazetteer of Scotland*). He also owned Kincaldrum, near Forfar: 581 acres worth £880 p.a. (*ibid.*). The castle had cost more than £12,000 to build, excluding contents and estate improvements. See A.H. Millar, *Fife, Pictorial and Historical*, i (1895), 130–1 (ill.) and Colvin, *Dictionary of British Architects*, 424.

43. B of S, *Highland and Islands* (1992), 225–7; D. Hart-Davis, *Monarchs of the Glen* (1988), 211; *Country Life*, 25 May 1989, 184–7 (gardens).

44. Murray, *Scotland*, 17–18; *Country Life*, clxx (1981), 566. Middleton bought the estate from the Heddle family.

45. B of S, *Highland and Islands* (1992), 263; *Country Life*, 19, 16 Aug. 1984. For Meggernie – seemingly 'built for eternity' – see *The Times*, 27, 28 Sept. 1883.

46. Demolished 1959; *Destruction of the Country House*, pl. 105.

47. B of E, *S. Lancashire* (1969), 261 (originally Woolton Hill House).

48. Resident architect Stanley Adshead. See *Building News*, Dec. 1903 and 1 Jan. 1904; *The Builder*, lxv (1893), 192: ill. and plan; *Academy Architecture*, 1903 (i), 70, 77 and 1904 (ii), 30–35: ill. and plans; B of S, *Highland and Islands* (1992), 448; Bateman (1883); Walford (1872); Burke's *Landed Gentry*; *Destruction of the Country House*, pl. 250 (incorrect entry); A.S. Gray, *Edwardian Architecture* (1985), 182 (incorrect entry); J. Mills *et al.*, *Rosehaugh: a House of its Time* (Avoch, 1996). The contents were sold in 1954. James Douglas Fletcher bought the Ardmulchan estate in Co. Meath, for

hunting, and began an extensive rebuilding. For shooting he bought an estate on Loch Gynack and built Pitmain Lodge, near Kingussie.

49. *DNB Missing Persons* (1993), 347–8; M. Keswick, ed., *The Thistle and the Jade* (1982); R. Blake, *Jardine Matheson* (1999).

50. *The Times*, 3 Nov. 1881, p. 5a.

51. A. Rowan in *Country Life*, clxii (1977), 350–53, 422–5; Groome, *Gazetteer of Scotland*; B of S, *Dumfries and Galloway* (1996), 173–6, pls 95–6; Walford (1872; 1885). Castlemilk cost over £44,000.

52. *DNB Missing Persons* (1993), 452–3; P.W. Foy, *The Opium War* (1975).

53. Groome, *Gazetteer of Scotland*; B of S, *Highland and Islands* (1992), 631; Bateman (1883); N. Nicolson, *Lord of the Isles* (1960), 42, 59, pl. 6.

54. *Crofters' Commission, Report and Minutes of Evidence* (1884), quoted in Nicolson, *Lord of the Isles*, 43.

55. Groome, *Gazetteer of Scotland*; Bateman (1883): B of S, *Highland and Islands* (1992), 383–4 (Ardross), 525–6 (Duncraig); Orr, *Deer Forests, Landlords and Crofters*, 97, 137–40. Sir Alexander Matheson's London house was 38 South Street, Grosvenor Square. By 1898 Sir Kenneth Matheson also owned Balmacara Lodge, a 'charming little villa' on the banks of Loch Duich, Ross-shire (Murray, *Handbook for Scotland* (1898), 385, 395). For Brancker, see Boase, iv, 484.

56. Nicolson, *Lord of the Isles*, 122, 236–7. Amhuinnsuidhe Castle (1865) on the Isle of Harris was eventually bought with 50,000 acres by Sir Thomas Sopwith, the aviation tycoon.

57. For lists of 'Wealthy Scots, 1896–1913', see the definitive register compiled by R. Britton in *Bulletin of the Institute of Historical Research*, lviii (1985), 78–94. For acreages see the *Return of Owners of Land* (1875) and Bateman (1883).

58. Rented 1883–95; purchased 1895. He also bought the Ormsary estate at Knapdale, Argyllshire, in 1902 for £92,165. He is reckoned to have made about £2,200,000 during his career. See M.S. Moss, 'W.T. Lithgow', in *Scottish Historical Review*, lxii (1983), 47–72; A.H. Millar, *Castles and Mansions of Renfrewshire and Buteshire* (Glasgow, 1889), pl. 22.

59. J. Irving, *The Book of Dumbartonshire*, iii (1879), pl. xvii.

60. *Ibid.*, pl. xix.

61. *Ibid.*, pl. xv. Dunn died in 1849, leaving his fortune to his brother Alexander.

62. 14 acres worth £200 p.a. See D. Macleod, *Dumbarton Ancient and Modern* (Dumbarton, 1893), pl. xliv; [J. Maclehose], *One Hundred Glasgow Men*, ii (1880), pl. lxiii. Between 1857 and 1866 he lived at Dalquharn Cottage.

63. Macleod, *Dumbarton*, pl. xxxvi.

64. 43 acres worth £2,014 p.a. For his son Archibald, Peter Denny bought a villa at Braehead (*c.* 1843; extended by J.M. Crawford, 1880s: Macleod, *Dumbarton*, pl. xxxviii); another son, John M. Denny, lived at Garnough, a Scottish Arts and Crafts house designed by J. Burnet overlooking the Clyde (Macleod, *Dumbarton*, pl. xxxvii). Another son, William Denny III, ended unhappily: his mansion at Bellfield (*c.* 1850) was destroyed by fire in 1882 (rebuilt by J. Burnet, *c.* 1885), and – following a financial crisis – he killed himself in Buenos Aires in 1887. Peter Denny left £190,979 in 1895; William Denny III left £114,180. See A.B. Bruce, *William Denny* (1888); D. Macleod, *Dumbarton, Vale of Leven and Loch Lomond* (Dumbarton, 1884), 58 *et seq.*; P.L. Robertson, 'William Denny', in *Business History*, xvi (1979), 36–47; Morgan and M.S. Moss, 'Peter Denny', in *ibid.*, xxxi (1989), 28–47; and *DNB Missing Persons*.

65. J. Gilkison, quoted in Macleod, *Dumbarton*, pl. xxxv. For Helenslee see Irving, *Dumbartonshire*, iii, pl. xiii.

66. R. Kerr, *The Gentleman's House* (1871), intro. J. Mordaunt Crook (1972), 376–7.

67. Irving, *Dumbartonshire*, iii, pl. ii. Lumsden bought the estate (1,447 acres worth £923 p.a. in 1885) from the Buchanans in 1866. He died in 1879 (*One Hundred Glasgow Men*, ii (1886), p. lii).

68. Irving, *Dumbartonshire*, iii, pl. iv; *Academy Architecture*, 1903 (I), 71–2. The estate (571 acres worth £596 p.a. in 1885) included the site of an earlier house called Belretiro (Macleod, *Dumbarton, Vale of Leven etc.*, 175–6). Martin previously lived at Greenhill, Gareloch.

69. Macleod, *Dumbarton Ancient and Modern*,

pl. xliv. Only 14 acres worth £200 p.a. in 1885; but he also bought the extensive Cumbernauld estate in 1875 for £160,000 (Irving, *Dumbartonshire*, iii, p. vii, pl. xiv). Principal control of Cunard was inherited by his cousin John Burns of Castle Wemyss.

70. Murray, *Scotland* (1898), 312; Macleod, *Dumbartonshire* (Dumbarton, 1886), 206; Irving, *Dumbartonshire*, iii, pl. xviii; *One Hundred Glasgow Men*, ii, pl. lxix. For Napier's collection, see J.C. Robinson, *Catalogue of the Works of Art . . . of Robert Napier* (privately printed, 1865).

71. Irving, *Dumbartonshire* iii, pl. xx; Walford (1885); *Destruction of the Country House*, pl. 223. Campbell, who owned 1,112 acres worth £1,820 15s. p.a., left £282,582 in 1877. His father, William Campbell, had bought the estate in 1841 from John Horrocks (*One Hundred Glasgow Men*, i, p. xx).

72. Macleod, *Dumbarton Ancient and Modern*, pl. xliii. Aiken bought the estate in 1857 and spent a good deal on its improvement.

73. Irving, *Dumbartonshire*, iii, pl. v; D. Macleod, *The Clyde District of Dumbartonshire* (Dumbarton, 1886), 39. Buchanan's 2,014 acres were worth £2,820 10s. p.a. in 1885. John Buchanan had left £371,259 in 1876.

74. D. Macleod, *Tourists' Guide to the Lake District of Scotland* (Dumbarton, 1879), 17.

75. Brock, an associate of the Denny family, died in 1907 worth £168,504. He also owned Levenford House, built for James Denny to designs by Rochead in 1853, and bought by Brock after Denny's death. A design for Auchenheglish by C. Douglas and Stevenson was exhibited in the 1862 International Exhibition (no. 2030).

76. Macleod, *Lake District of Scotland*, 24.

77. Bought in 1858. See Irving, *Dumbartonshire*, iii, pl. i; *One Hundred Glasgow Men*, ii, p. xcviii; Murray, *Scotland* (1895), 347. The house was set in 35 acres worth £180 p.a. He also owned 3,349 acres worth £5,781 p.a. at Grougar, Ayrshire.

78. Irving, *Dumbartonshire*, iii, pl. xvi; Walford (1895); Macleod, *Lake District of Scotland*, 5, and *Dumbarton, Ancient and Modern*, pl. xlii. White also owned the neighbouring estate of Garshake, and a house called Crossler, near Dumbarton.

79. Macleod, *Lake District of Scotland*, 35.

80. Irving, *Dumbartonshire*, iii, pl. vi. For John Orr-Ewing (d. 1878), founder of the firm, see *One Hundred Glasgow Men*, i, p. xxxiii.

81. *The Times*, 29 Nov. 1893, p. 7f; V. Fiddes and A. Rowan, *David Bryce* (1971), 114, pls 66, 68; Walford (1885); *WWW*, i. He also owned Gallonfield, Inverness-shire. His London house was 32 Ennismore Gardens.

82. M. Asquith, *Myself When Young* (1938), 27.

83. M. Asquith, *More Memories* (1933), 219–22; *Autobiography*, ed. M. Bonham Carter (1962), 47.

84. Marquess of Crewe, *Lord Rosebery*, ii, 193, 366: Rosebery to Gladstone, 6 Nov. 1890. See also N. Crathorne, *Tennant's Stalk* (1973), 172, ill.

85. Rosebery to Gladstone, 1890 (V. Fiddes and A. Rowan, eds, *David Bryce*, Edinburgh (1976), 65). Edward VII declined to make him a peer, preferring some 'more eligible Liberal' (S. Heffer, *Power and Place: the political consequences of King Edward VII* (1998), 127). He bought Glen from Colonel George Allen in 1852 for £33,140 and then spent as much again on its reconstruction (W. Chambers, *History of Peebleshire* (1884), 390–91). For a photograph of the 105 staff in 1897, see *Country Life*, 7 August 1997, 62–3. His London house was 35 (later 40) Grosvenor Square. Towards the end of his life he also built Broadoaks, West Byfleet, Surrey and Glenconner, North Berwick. See *DNB* and *The Times*, 6 June 1906, p. 4a. His father, son of the founder of the firm, left £75,723 in 1878, excluding property and plant reputed to be worth several millions.

86. B. Wilson, *Dear Youth* (1937), 155, 157. For life at Glen, see S. Blow, *Broken Blood: the rise and fall of the Tennant Family* (1987).

87. Crathorne, *Tennant's Stalk*, 173.

88. F. Balfour, *Ne Obliviscaris* (1930), 391–2.

89. *The Reminiscences of Lady Dorothy Nevill* (1906), 103; D. Nevill, *Under Five Reigns*, 151.

90. Hamilton Diary, B.L., Add.MS.48, 656, f.52 verso: 10 Aug. 1891. For social context see A. Lambert, *Unquiet Souls: the Indian Summer of the British Aristocracy, 1880–1918* (1984); J. Abdy and C. Gere, *The Souls* (1984) and N.W. Ellenberger, 'The Souls and London Society', in *Victorian Studies*, xxv (1981), 119–60.

91. M. Baring, *The Puppet Show of Memory* (1922), 167–8. For Wrest – inherited from the de Greys – see *Country Life*, cxlvii (1970), 1250–53 and cxlviii (1970), 18–21.

92. Quoted in S. Blow, *Broken Blood*, 115.

93. 'The Enlargement of London Society', in *Saturday Review*, lxxxix (1900), 553. 'The New Society and its Sets', in *Vanity Fair*, 2 Nov. 1889. See also 'On the significance of numbers for Social Life: Aristocracies', in K. Wolff, ed., *The Sociology of George Simmel* (1950).

94. Aberdeen, *More Cracks with 'We Twa'* (1929), 5–9; T.H.S. Escott, *Club Cameos: Portraits of the Day* (1879), 3.

95. M. Asquith, *Autobiography*, ii (1922), 20–21.

96. J. Mordaunt Crook, *The Reform Club* (1973); *Survey of London*, xxix, 408–15.

97. Robert Farquharson, physician, of Finzaen, Aboyne, Aberdeenshire (Walford, 1885); Sir William MacCormack, surgeon, of 13 Harley Street (*WWW*, i); Sir George Campbell, judge in Calcutta, of Edenwood, Cupar, Fife (Walford, 1885); H.H. Fowler, solicitor, later Viscount Wolverhampton, of Woodthorne, Wolverhampton (Walford, 1885; *WWW*, i); Sir John Hibbert, barrister, of Hampsfield, Grange-over-Sands (*DNB*); J.B. Balfour, Lord Advocate of Scotland (Dod's *Parliamentary Companion*); the future Lord James of Hereford, Attorney General, of 41 Cadogan Square: a bachelor (*WWW*, i); and the future Lord Russell of Killowen, Attorney General, of Tadworth Court, Surrey (*WWW*, i).

98. F.A. Channing, a Home Rule academic, of Pytchley House, Kettering, Northamptonshire; and Leonard Courtney, leader-writer for *The Times* (Dod's *Parliamentary Companion*).

99. Of Rose Hill, Northenden, Cheshire and the Chalet, Beddgelert, North Wales (*DNB*; *DBB*).

100. He built Bodnant, Denbighshire (W.J. Green; 1881) in a dreary Old English style (*Building News*, xli, 1881). For Pochin's career see *The Times*, 2 Nov. 1895, p. 6c.

101. Dod's *Parliamentary Companion*.

102. Of 15 Sussex Square, Hyde Park. He left £96,659 in 1909 (*DNB*; *WWW*, i;, *The Times*, 22, 25 Oct. 1909, 5 Aug. 1909).

103. *DNB*; *The Times*, 4 Aug., 29 Nov. 1906; J.E. Ritchie, *Famous City Men* (1884). Chairman of the Improved Industrial Dwellings Co., with 30,000 tenants. He lived in some style at 29 Chesham Place; Trosley Towers, Wrotham, Kent; and the Villa Aberlaw, Monterey, Cannes; he presented Lauderdale House and Waterlow Park to the public, and left £89,948. See also p. 304 n. 78.

104. Of Butterstone House, Dunkeld, and 4 Cleveland Square (*WWW*, i, addenda).

105. Of Stella Hall, Blaydon-on-Tyne (*WWW*, i).

106. *DNB*; *WWW*, i. In London he lived grandly at 11 Great Stanhope Street, leaving £1,339,413 in 1910 (details in *The Times*, 18 Feb. 1911, p. 11c).

107. A. Jones, *The Politics of Reform: 1884* (Cambridge, 1972), 246. He retired eventually to Cromer.

108. *DNB*; *DBB*, iv, 380–85; *WWW*, i. He married well (the daughter of a Nottingham manufacturer), and left £42,620 in 1897.

109. *DNB*; *WWW*, i; *Men of Note* (1901); *The Times*, 18 March 1903, p. 6b.

110. *DNB*. Banker and chairman, North East Railway. The first Quaker baronet.

111. *WWW*, i; he ended at The Lodge, Esher, Surrey, and left £5,449 in 1899.

112. *DNB*.

113. *DNB*; Walford (1885). Stracathro House, Forfarshire (A. Simpson; 1827) and estate – bought by his father with 3,848 acres – was worth £10,857 p.a. (Bateman, 1883). In 1880 Campbell-Bannerman bought and restored Belmont Castle, Lord Wharncliffe's estate near Meigle, Perthshire.

114. *DNB*. He bought Minard Castle, Argyll and Foots Cray Place, Bexley, Kent (Walford, 1885). He was a close friend of both Gladstone and the 16th Earl of Derby, and left £337,180 in 1896. For his art collection, see [W. Agnew], *Pictures, Drawings and Sculpture . . . of Sir John Pender* (1894).

115. W.H. Mallock, *The Old Order Changes*, i (1886), 83.

116. Liberal, Methodist, paternalistic and hugely energetic, Mason left £290,933 in 1886. His seat, Groby Hall, Ashton-under-Lyne, Lancashire, was the model for 'Granite Hall', seat of 'Henry Stonor' in the novel by W. Haslam Mills, *Grey Pastures* (1924). See also Walford (1885).

117. For Barclay, see Y. Cassis, *City Bankers* (1994), 211.

118. J.P. Thomasson, MP; of Woodside, near

Bolton, Lancashire; he left £1,161,792 in 1904 (*WWW*, i; Walford (1885), addenda).

119. Gladstone and Tennyson both sailed on his yachts (J.E. Ritchie, *Famous City Men*, 1884).

120. Of Dawpool, Birkenhead, Cheshire; he left £1,284,749 in 1899 (*The Times*, 24 Nov. 1899, p. 7).

121. Later 1st Viscount Pirrie, Chairman of Harland and Wolff; he left £707,785 gross in 1924.

122. Of East Cliff, Lincoln. See Boase, iv, 685 and *Proceedings of the Institute of Mechanical Engineers* (1890), 554 for Clayton and Shuttleworth, Ltd.

123. Later 1st Baron Joicey, of Ford Castle, Northumberland.

124. Of Park Grove, Edgbaston; left £621,715 in 1901 (*WWW*, i).

125. MP; of Lower Eaton, Hereford; left £374,798 in 1901 (*WWW*, i).

126. Of 10 Ennismore Gardens, Ottershaw Park, Surrey and Bambridge Park, Eastleigh, Hampshire; he married a daughter of Sir Morton Peto and left £381,416 in 1921 (*WWW*, ii).

127. Of Rounton Grange, Northallerton, Yorkshire (P. Webb; 1874–78, demolished); 3,000 acres; left £768,676 in 1904. In conjunction with Henry Bolckow, Ralph Ward Jackson and Thomas Vaughan, this 'entrepreneurial polymath' was one of the founders of the iron and steel industry in north-east England. See *DNB* and *DBB*, i, 256–60.

128. Nephew of Henry Bölckow, ironmaster, of Marton Hall, near Middlesborough, and 33 Princes Gate, who died in 1878 leaving some £800,000. See R. Gott, *Henry Bölckow, Founder of Teesside* (Middlesborough, 1968).

129. MP; left £687,024 in 1898; resworn as £883,380 in 1900. See also H.C. Colman, *J.J. Colman* (1905).

130. John Brocklehurst, of Herdsfield House, Macclesfield, silk manufacturer and banker, left £800,000 in 1870. His eldest son, William, lived at Butley Hall and Lytherington House, Macclesfield; his fourth son, Philip, lived at Swythamley Park, Macclesfield (Walford, 1885).

131. James Pilkington, MP, of Park Place House, Blackburn and Swinithwaite Hall, near Bedale; 'garrotted and robbed in London 15

July 1862', he survived to leave £147,925 in 1890 (Boase, vi, 399; Walford, 1860).

132. Bright Bros of Rochdale; John and Jacob Bright were both members of the Reform.

133. John Cheetham, of Eastwood, Staleybridge, Lancashire, left £226,489 in 1886; his son – moving on from spinning to banking – left £565,952 in 1916.

134. Hollins Bros of Preston joined Horrocks in 1885; Sir Frank Hollins, 1st Bt – Anglican and Liberal – of Greyfriars, near Preston, left £325,824 in 1924 (*DBB*, iii, 316).

135. Alfred Illingworth, MP, married Isaac Holden's daughter; like his brothers, Henry (Daisy Bank, Allerton) and Angus (Woodlands, Manningham), he lived close to the firm's factory, Whetley Mill, Bradford; he left £172,470 in 1907 (*DBB*, iii, 417–23).

136. Benjamin Armitage, of Chamlea, Pendleton, Salford; left £277,472 in 1899.

137. Sir John Barran, 1st Bt, MP; a Baptist; known as 'the Little Boy's Tailor', of Chapel Allerton Hall, Leeds and 24 Queen's Gate, London; left £408,048 in 1905 (*DBB*, i, 181–3).

138. Isaac Hoyle, MP, of Joshua Hoyle and Sons; Wesleyan; retired to Reedley, Branksome Park, Dorset and left £251,494 in 1911 (*Men of Note*, 1901).

139. Carnegie was later elected, in 1902; Smith went instead to the Carlton (G. Woodbridge, *The Reform Club, 1836–1978* (1978), 85).

140. Nathaniel Buckley, MP; Congregationalist; of Ryecroft Hall, Ashton-under-Lyne; 20,898 acres worth £6,826 p.a., mostly in Tipperary and Limerick (Bateman, 1883).

141. John Walter, MP; Eton; proprietor of *The Times*; of Bearwood, Berkshire; 7,054 acres worth £9,728 p.a. (Bateman, 1883).

142. W.H. Mallock, *The Old Order Changes*, iii (1886), 96–8.

143. Quoted in N. Atkinson, *Sir Joseph Whitworth, the World's Best Mechanician* (1996). See also *DNB*; *DBB*; E.H. Yates, *Celebrities at Home*, ii (1878), 335–44; Walford (1885); *The Times*, 24 Jan. 1887, pp. 8–9; B of E, *S. Lancashire* (1969), 326.

144. Other Pease country houses were Brinkburn, Pierremont, Hummersknott, Southend, Woodlands, Snow Hill and Headlam Hall, all near Darlington;

Pinchinthorpe, near Middlesborough; Hesslewood, near Hull; Pendower, near Newcastle-upon-Tyne; Cliff House, Marske-by-the-Sea; Nether Grange, Alnmouth; Kerris Vean, Falmouth; and, latterly, Wardington Manor, Banbury, Oxfordshire. See Boase, ii, 1426–7; *DBB*, iv, 594–601; C. Cunningham and P. Waterhouse, *Alfred Waterhouse* (Oxford, 1992); V. Chapman, *Darlington: Birthplace of the Railway* (Middleton-in-Teesdale, 1993) and *Rural Darlington* (Durham County Council, 1977); G. Dixon, *Two Ancient Townships: Studies of Pinchinthorpe and Hutton Lawcross* (Guisborough, 1991).

145. H.C. Colman, *J.J. Colman* (1905); *DNB*. Gatton was bought from the 7th Baron Monson, later Viscount Oxenbridge. The architect of the portico – designed in 1888 and built in 1891 – rejoiced in the name of Sextus Dyball (B of E, *Surrey* (1971), 152).

146. Wesleyan; he left £317,635 in 1897, having given away a reputed £2 million to members of his family. He also owned Wiganthorpe, near York. See *Fortunes Made in Business*, i (1884), 3–44; *DNB*; *DBB*, iii, 299–303; Boase, v, 683–4.

147. Extended by E.B. Lamb for Sir William Milner, Bt (*The Builder*, xxii (1864), 188–90: ill. and plan). Holden left £470,744 in 1912.

148. Bazley retired from business in 1862 and became a baronet in 1869 (Boase, i, 202–3).

149. Boase, iv, 184. The first baron , of Vinehall, Robertsbridge, left £208,926.

150. Houses owned by the Gregs included: Norcliffe Hall, Styal, near Chester; Coles Park, Buntingford, Hertfordshire; Oversley Lodge, Handforth, Cheshire; Eagley House, near Bolton. See M.B. Rose, *The Gregs of Quarry Bank Mill* (Cambridge, 1986) and 'Diversification of Investment by the Greg Family, 1800–1914', in *Business History*, xxi (1979), 79–96.

151. M. Girouard, *The Victorian Country House* (1971), 99–102. For Manor Heath (Parnell and Smith, 1852–53), see *The Builder*, xxi (1863), 206–7: ill.; for Moorside, see *Building News*, xxviii (1875), 178: ill. and plans; for Belle Vue, see *Building News*, iii (1857), 1200–1: ill. and plan. Bateman (1883) lists 3,294 acres at Somerleyton, worth £5,324 p.a. Sir Francis Crossley left

£800,000 in 1872; his town house was 60 Eaton Square.

152. For Somerleyton see *The Builder*, ix (1851), 355, 365, 407: ills.; *Country Life*, clxviii (1970), 756–60. Cousins and nephews stayed behind in Halifax; but even they built larger mansions, further out at Bemerside and Moorside. See *Fortunes Made in Business*, iii (1887), 255–312; E. Webster, *Dean Clough [Mills] and the Crossley Inheritance* (Halifax, 1988); *DNB*; *DBB*, v, 227–8; Boase, i, 772–4; S. Smiles, *Thrift* (1875), 205–17.

153. Kerr, *Gentleman's House*, 473.

154. William Rawson, quoted in Sir Algernon West, *Recollections, 1832–1886*, i (1899), 303.

155. *Illustrated London News*, 24 May 1890, 649–53.

156. Of 21 Berkeley Square; Hall Farm, Brixworth, Northamptonshire; and Blankney Hall, near Lincoln (burnt 1945; ill. J. Harris, *No Voice From The Hall* (1998), pl. 78). In 1864 Chaplin's fiancée, Lady Florence Paget, eloped with the Marquess of Hastings at Marshall and Snelgrove's store; Hastings thereupon ruined himself by betting £100,000 against Chaplin's horse in the Derby: it won by a neck. At his death Chaplin left only £4,866 17s. 5d., but *The Times* marked the event with a leading article (30 May 1923). See also *WWW*, ii (addenda); *Complete Peerage*, xiii; Lady Londonderry, *Henry Chaplin* (1926).

157. Walter Long owned the Rood Ashton estate, Wiltshire.

158. Sir Michael Hicks-Beach, 9th Bt, owned estates at Williamstrip Park, Gloucestershire and Netheravon House, Wiltshire.

159. C.T. (1st Baron) Ritchie, Chancellor of the Exchequer 1902–3, lived at 37 Princes Gate and Welders, Gerrards Cross, Buckinghamshire; he gave his recreation as 'reading' (*WWW*, i).

160. Akers-Douglas, Conservative Chief Whip, became 1st Viscount Chilston of Chilston Park, Kent and Craigs, Dumfries (*WWW*, ii; Dod, 1895).

161. Bailey of Bailey's Hotel owned the Shortgrove estate, Essex, future seat of Sir Carl Meyer, 1st Bt.

162. Bemrose lived at Lonsdale Hall, Derby; Bigwood at The Lawn, Twickenham; Penn at The Cedars, Lee, Kent (*DNB*).

163. For Borthwick see *WWW*, i; *DNB*; R. Lucas,

*Lord Glenesk and the Morning Post* (1910). For Allcroft see Bateman (1883), 8; Boase, iv, 87–8; *Illustrated London News*, 5 August 1893; 174 and 7 Oct. 1893, 460; *The Times*, 1 August 1893, p. 6.

164. *WWW* i; *The Times*, 12 March 1908, p. 12; R. Nevill and E.E. Jerningham, *Piccadilly to Pall Mall* (1908), 108.

165. Bateman (1883), 497–8. 'From a man's club may be pretty safely gathered his status, his politics and pursuits; for instance, in Brooks's one does not expect to find a violent radical; in White's a *nouveau riche*; in the Athenaeum a sporting man; in the St George's a hot Orangeman, in the National a henchman of Cardinal Manning; in the Raleigh one of the straightest sect of the Pharisees; in the Turf a great light of science; or, I might add, in the Travellers a Livingstone, a Speke or a Baker' (*ibid.*, 881). Cecil Rhodes was in fact blackballed at the Travellers.

166. Sir C. Petrie, *The Carlton Club* (1955), 45; T.H.S. Escott, *Club Makers and Club Members* (1914), 225.

167. Y. Cassis, *City Bankers, 1890–1914* (Cambridge, 1994), 265, 288.

168. For the architecture of the Carlton see *Architectural Review*, xxxvi (1914), 14–17; *The Architect*, cix (1923), 310; *Survey of London*, xxix, 354–9; R. Nevill, *London Clubs* (1911), 225.

169. *Vanity Fair*, 1881; J.E. Ritchie, *Famous City Men* (1884); H.L. Malchow, *Gentlemen Capitalists* (1991), pl. 14.

170. Quilter left £1,220,639 of which £195,000 went in tax (*The Times*, 20 November 1911, 11 and 15 January 1912, p. 11). His younger brother, Harry Quilter, succeeded Tom Taylor as art critic of *The Times*; his younger son, Roger Quilter, was a composer. Quilter's collection at 74 South Audley Street (F.G. Stephens, *Magazine of Art*, xx–xxi), was sold at Christie's on 9 July 1909 for £87,780 (*The Times*, 1 July 1909; *Connoisseur*, July 1909; catalogue by M.W. Brockwell and W. Roberts, 1909).

171. 'The Conservative is by nature a clubbable creature' (T.H.S. Escott, *England: its people, polity and pursuits* (1885), 344). Peel took the same view of the Carlton's function: 'we must educate them [all] into good

Conservatives' (*idem., Club Makers and Club Members*, 215).

172. Galsworthy, *Forsyte Saga*, ii, 413.

173. Quoted, E. Beresford Chancellor, *Memorials of St James's Street* (1922), 210.

174. *Quarterly Review*, lxv (1840), 269. For the impact of reform see T.H.S. Escott, *England: Her People, Polity and Pursuits* (1879), 35–7.

175. See [A. Bourke], *History of White's*, 2 vols (1892); P. Colson, *White's, 1693–1950* (1951); membership lists 1891, 1899, 1935; A. Lejeune, *White's* (1993).

176. A similar story concerns Baron de Hirsch and the Rue Royale Club, Paris. The first Baron Cheylesmore left £102,015 in 1891. In 1883 he owned 2,000 acres at Cheylesmore, Warwickshire. The second baron (d. 1902, worth £51,737) lived at 16 Prince's Gate (*WWW*, i). The third, also a member of White's and a noted antiquarian and collector, took particular pleasure in being lord of the manor of Cheylesmore, once a property of the Black Prince (*WWW*, ii). The Cheylesmore vault is in Highgate Cemetery.

177. Plans showing the club before and after improvements in 1888 (Bourke, *White's*, ii, 241 *et seq.*: 'the glitter of marble and polished wood, which forms so prominent a feature of modern decoration, has been excluded at White's as incongruous with the character of the place').

178. Brooks's archive – Membership Books and Ballot Books – records details of elections and non-elections. See also *Memorials of Brooks's* (1907) and *Brooks's: a social history* (1991), ed. P. Ziegler and D. Seward.

179. R. Nevill, *The Life and Letters of Lady Dorothy Nevill* (1919), 240–1: 17 Sept. [1904]. That swimming pool, remarked a detective policeman to Lord Morley, 'seems to me to savour of the *parvenoo*' (Sir A. Fitzroy, *Memoirs*, ii, n.d., 463). Harrison himself lived – rather improbably – at Sutton Place, near Guildford, and published its history in 1893.

180. Even so, he built himself Ross House at Lee-on-Solent, a half-timbered villa at the other end of the Royal Yacht Squadron start line (*The Times*, 30 July 1997, p. 39: ill.). His 200-ft *Shamrock*, built by William Fife of Fairlie, was famous for its elegance and speed.

181. G. Leybourne, 'Champagne Charlie' (1868).

182. M. Guest and W.B. Boulton, *The Royal Yacht Squadron . . . 1815–1900* (1903), 283, 313–20, 322.

183. *Ibid.*, 362, 370 *et seq.*; J.B. Atkins, *Further Memorials of the Royal Yacht Squadron, 1901–38* (1939), 7–8, 19, 161. John Gretton's retreat was Grantham Lodge, Cowes.

184. J. Camplin, *The Rise of the Plutocrats* (1978), 262. For steam yachts at Cowes see *The Field*, 1883. For Edwardian yachting, see *British Yachts and Yachtsmen* (Yachtsmen Publishing Co., 1907) and W. Portal, *Cowes Castle and the R.Y.S.* (1918).

185. D.W.R. Bahlman, ed., *The Diary of Sir Edward Walter Hamilton, 1880–85* (Oxford, 1972), 38–9.

186. The Marquess of Crewe, *Lord Rosebery*, ii (1931), 557.

187. *Hamilton Diaries, 1880–85*, 315–9, 363.

188. R. Nevill, *The Reminiscences of Lady Dorothy Nevill* (1906), 102.

189. Quoted, H. Nicolson, *King George the Fifth* (1952), 155. See also Lord Willoughby de Broke, *The Passing Years* (1924), 299.

190. Printed, as written, in J.A. Spender and C. Asquith, *The Life of H.H. Asquith*, i (1932), 329–31.

191. K. Rose, *King George V* (1983). Baron de Forest, later Count Maurice de Bendern, died in 1968 at the Villa d'Espoir, Biarritz.

192. W.D. Rubinstein, *Men of Property* (1981), 167, 174–5; F.A. Binney, *Millionaires the Cause of Poverty* (1884), 12.

193. F.M.L. Thompson, 'Britain' in D. Spring, ed., *European Landed Elites in the 19th century* (Baltimore, 1977), 24–5.

194. J.A. Froude, 'On the Uses of a Landed Gentry', in *Short Studies on Great Subjects*, iii (1877), 286–7, 290. The 15th Earl of Derby said much the same in *The Nineteenth Century*, Oct. 1881, 474.

195. Shaw-Lefevre, *English and Irish Land Problems* (1881), 41.

196. R. Nevill, *The Reminiscences of Lady Dorothy Nevill*, 103.

197. Rubinstein, *Men of Property*, 167, 174–5.

198. J. Habakkuk, *Marriage, Debt and the Estates System: English Landownership, 1650–1950* (Oxford, 1994), 692.

199. P.J. Cain and A.G. Hopkins, 'Gentlemanly capitalism and British expansion overseas', in *Economic History Review* 2nd Ser., xl (1987), 2.

200. *The Times*, 28 Dec. 1912, p. 93; 27 Dec. 1913, p. 10a; 4 Jan. 1913, p. 4d. For Walsingham see J.G. Ruffer, *The Big Shots: Edwardian Shooting Parties* (1984), 43–53, 135. His estates at Aldwark Manor, near Easingwold, Yorkshire and Merton Hall, near Thetford, Norfolk totalled 19,148 acres worth £16,578 p.a. (Bateman, 1883).

201. G. Martelli, *A Man of His Time: a life of the 1st Earl of Iveagh* (privately printed, 1956), 207–12. Iveagh may well have amassed £40 million over a lifetime; he left £13,486,000 gross in 1927, having spent about £200,000 p.a., apart from considerable donations to charity (*ibid.*, 302–4). See also *DBB*, ii, 680–9.

202. Quoted in A. Howe, *The Cotton Masters, 1830–60* (Oxford, 1984), 249.

203. B. Disraeli, *Endymion* (Bradenham edn 1927), 205–6; Ruffer, *Big Shots*, 24, 83, 124. Edward Levy (from 1875 Levy-Lawson), later 1st Baron Burnham, owned 4,000 acres in Buckinghamshire, and left £302,891 in 1916 (*WWW*, ii). His London address was 20 Norfolk Street, Park Lane.

204. A. Hare, *The Story of My Life*, vi (1900), 400–1: 14 Nov. 1895. For life at Elveden, see Martelli, *op.cit.*, and T.W. Turner, *Memoirs of a Gamekeeper* (1954).

205. Lady D. Nevill, *My Own Times* (1912), 156. For the spendthrift lives of Sir Henry Meux, 2nd Bt, and Sir Harry Meux, 3rd Bt, see V. Surtees, *The Actress and the Brewer's Wife* (1997).

206. T. Pinney, ed., *Letters of Rudyard Kipling*, ii, 373: 25 June 1890.

207. *Hamilton Diaries, 1880–85*, 185, 194, 197, 345–7, 355, 358, 366. De Grey once shot 28 pheasants in 60 seconds.

208. Hamilton Diary, B.L. ADD.Ms.48680, p. 99.

209. Quoted in S. Blow, *Fields Elysian* (1983), 25.

210. The Marquess of Crewe, *Lord Rosebery*, i (1930), 115. For Baird's eccentricities, see F. Siltzer, *Newmarket* (1923), 258–60.

211. B of E, *Suffolk* (1974), 239; N. Scarfe, *Cambridgeshire* (1981), 110.

212. Garland, of 26 Grosvenor Street and Moreton Hall, Warwickshire, left £307,864 in 1921. See also *WWW*, ii. For The Retreat – an aggrandised thatched farmhouse – see *The Builder*, lxxxiii (1902), 299: ill. and plan;

B of E, *Suffolk* (1974), 378. For Sefton Lodge
– a gabled brick mansion – see *Country Life*,
7 May 1998, p. 114: ill. and S. Joel, *Ace of
Diamonds* (1958).

213. Praed, of 29 St James's Place, left £83,470 in
1921; see *WWW*, ii. Tatem left £2,068,000
in 1942. Raphael left £1.5 million in 1899.

214. L. Davidoff, *The Best Circles* (1973), 108,
n. 8.

215. T.H.S. Escott, *Club Cameos: Portraits of the
Day* (1879), 3–7.

216. Wood, quoted in Habakkuk, *English
Landownership*, 692. For land sales see
F.M.L. Thompson, *English Landed Society in
the Nineteenth Century* (1963), 332 and H.A.
Clemenson, *English Country Houses and
Landed Estates* (1982).

217. T.F. Dale, *Foxhunting in the Shires* (1903);
C. Simpson, *Leicestershire and its Hunts*
(1926); R. Trevelyan, *Grand Dukes and
Diamonds* (1991), 308–9; G. Thompson,
*History of the Fernie Hunt* (Leicester, 1987);
S. Blow, *Fields Elysian* (1983).

218. Joseph Large features in R.S. Surtees, *Mr
Facey Romford's Hounds* (1867). For Watson,
see *Complete Peerage*, xiii (1940) and *DBB*, v,
690–92. Albert Brassey was Master of the
Heythrop from 1873 to 1918. For the
assimilative function of sport, see N. Elias,
'The Genesis of Sport as a Sociological
Problem', in E. Dunning, ed., *The Sociology
of Sport* (1970). Watson's soap business was
founded by his father, of Donisthorpe
House, Moor Allerton, Leeds. For Thorpe
Satchville, see J.B. Firth, *Highways and
Byways in Leicestershire* (1926), 265:
'International finance, biscuits and whisky
[secure] Thorpe Satchville's reputation for
opulence . . . [but] wealth abounding is not
necessarily . . . grace abounding.'

219. N. Cunard, *G.M.: Memoirs of George Moore*
(1956), 19–20.

220. *Ibid.*, 32–3; D. Fielding, *Emerald and Nancy*
(1958), 79. For the Cunard family see
*London Society* (1880), 33–47 and *Fortunes
Made in Business*, ii (1884), 327–71.

221. R. Rhodes James, ed., *Chips: the Diaries of
Sir Henry Channon* (1986), 37–9: 17 June
and 10 July 1935; 58: 1 Feb. 1936; 64: 11 June
1936; 349: 1 Feb. 1943; photo of the blue
dining room opp. p. 467, and of the black
room opp. p. 88. See also N. Nicolson, ed.,
*Harold Nicolson's Diaries and Letters*, i
(1966), 244 and C. Hussey in *Country Life*,
lxxxiii (1938), 222–6.

222. Channon, *Diaries*, 202: 3 March 1939.

223. *Ibid.*, 7 [*c.* 1924/5]. See also *Country Life*, liii
(1923), 678–84; lxvi (1929), 513–7; lxxix
(1936), 276–82.

224. Channon, *Diaries*, 73: 1–2 Aug. 1936.
Channon does not mention the 'tent' room
of 1933 by Rex Whistler (*Country Life*, lxxiii
(1933), 616–7). For work by Tilden and
Baker in 1912 and 1918–21, see *ibid.*, liii
(1923), 678–84, 714–22.

225. Channon, *Diaries*, 177: 18 Nov. 1938.

226. *Ibid.*, 130: 3 June 1937. Channon's son
eventually became Baron Kelvedon, in 1997.

227. R. Boothby, *I Fight to Live* (1947), 48–51.

228. H. Nicolson, *Diaries and Letters*, i (1966),
76: 1 June 1931. For Trent Park see *Country
Life*, xiii (1903), 240–46; xlix (1931), 40–9,
60–72.

229. Nicolson, *Diaries*, ii (1967), 170: 4 June 1941.

230. *Ibid.*, ii (1967), 57: 13 Jan. 1940.

231. *Ibid.*, iii (1968), 351: 10 Sept. 1958; also
Nicolson, 'The Edwardian Weekend', in
*The Age of Extravagance* (1955), ed. J. Laver
*et al.*, 248, 251–3.

232. Nicolson, *Diaries*, i (1966), 266: 28 June
1936.

233. Channon, *Diaries*, 28: 18 March 1935.
Channon, however, was known to have 'no
time for servants' (*The Times*, 9 May 1998,
23).

234. *Crawford Diaries*, 253: 11 Nov. 1930.

235. Misquoted in S. Jackson, *The Sassoons*
(1963), 188. As 1st Commissioner of Works,
Sassoon is reputed to have ordered the
removal of tulips from the flower beds in
front of Buckingham Palace because they
clashed with the scarlet tunics of the guards.

# INDEX

# Index